METHODS IN MOLECULAR BIOLOGY

Series Editor:
John M. Walker
School of Life and Medical Sciences
University of Hertfordshire
Hatfield, Hertfordshire, AL10 9AB, UK

For further volumes:
http://www.springer.com/series/7651

Bioinformatics in MicroRNA Research

Editors

Jingshan Huang

School of Computing, University of South Alabama, Mobile, AL, USA

Glen M. Borchert

Department of Pharmacology, University of South Alabama, Mobile, AL, USA;
Department of Biology, University of South Alabama, Mobile, AL, USA

Dejing Dou

Department of Computer and Information Science, University of Oregon, Eugene, OR, USA

Jun (Luke) Huan

Department of Electrical Engineering and Computer Science, University of Kansas, Lawrence, KS, USA

Wenjun Lan

School of Bio-Engineering, Qilu University of Technology, Jinan, Shandong, China

Ming Tan

Mitchel Cancer Institute, University of South Alabama, Mobile, AL, USA

Bin Wu

Department of Endocrinology, First Affiliated Hospital, Kunming Medical University, Kunming, Yunnan, China

Humana Press

Editors
Jingshan Huang
School of Computing
University of South Alabama
Mobile, AL, USA

Dejing Dou
Department of Computer
and Information Science
University of Oregon
Eugene, OR, USA

Wenjun Lan
School of Bioengineering
Qilu University of Technology
Jinan, Shandong, China

Bin Wu
Department of Endocrinology
First Affiliated Hospital
Kunming Medical University
Kunming, Yunnan, China

Glen M. Borchert
Department of Pharmacology
University of South Alabama
Mobile, AL, USA

Department of Biology
University of South Alabama
Mobile, AL, USA

Jun (Luke) Huan
Department of Electrical Engineering
and Computer Science
University of Kansas
Lawrence, KS, USA

Ming Tan
Mitchel Cancer Institute
University of South Alabama
Mobile, AL, USA

ISSN 1064-3745 ISSN 1940-6029 (electronic)
Methods in Molecular Biology
ISBN 978-1-4939-8376-6 ISBN 978-1-4939-7046-9 (eBook)
DOI 10.1007/978-1-4939-7046-9

Softcover reprint of the hardcover 1st edition 2017

Printed on acid-free paper

This Humana Press imprint is published by Springer Nature
The registered company is Springer Science+Business Media LLC
The registered company address is: 233 Spring Street, New York, NY 10013, U.S.A.

Preface

As a special class of noncoding RNAs, microRNAs (miRNAs or miRs for short) have been reported to perform important roles in various biological and pathological processes by regulating respective target genes. To completely understand and fully delineate miR functions, besides performing biological experiments and querying PubMed and TarBase for biologically validated miR targets, biologists can also query various miR target prediction databases/websites for computationally predicted targets. More often than not, biologists need to extract additional information for each and every miR target, either validated or putative, with regard to its related information such as protein functions and affiliated signaling pathways. In short, biologists are facing significant barriers in fully delineating miR functions and the following effective bio-curation. Therefore, there is an urgent need for a comprehensive book focusing on miR target genes, miR regulation mechanisms, miR functions performed in various human diseases, and miR databases/knowledge bases.

This book is intended to give an in-depth introduction to and discussion of miRs and their targets, miR functions, and computational techniques applied in miR research. The primary audience includes, but is not limited to, computational biologists, computer scientists, bioinformaticians, bench biologists, and clinical investigators. No prior knowledge of computer science, databases, semantic technologies, or molecular biology is assumed. But we do assume that readers have some biology background knowledge at the high-school level.

A brief overview of the book structure is as follows. Chapter 1 introduces the concepts of miRs and long noncoding RNAs (lncRNAs) as well as some recent advances in miR/lncRNA biology. Chapters 2, 3, and 4 discuss protein participants in miR regulation; viral microRNAs, host miRs regulating viruses, and bacterial miR-like RNAs; and biomarkers, diagnostics, and therapeutics aspects of miRs, respectively. Chapter 5 introduces basic concepts of relational databases and biomedical big data. Chapter 6 provides an overview of semantic technologies and bio-ontologies. Chapter 7 discusses genome-wide analysis of miR-regulated transcripts. Chapters 8 and 9 describe in detail computational prediction of miR target genes, regulatory interactions between miRs and their targets, as well as an introduction of various miR target prediction databases and relevant Web resources. Chapter 10 discusses some limitations of existing approaches that aim to improve miR target prediction accuracy. Chapters 11 and 12 introduce genomic regulation of miR expression in disease development and next generation sequencing for miR expression profile. Chapters 13 through 16 discuss advanced topics in computational/bioinformatics approaches in miR research, including the handling of high-dimension data, identification and removal of noisy data, logical reasoning, and machine learning techniques. Finally, Chapters 17–19 introduce some advances of miR research in three human diseases: diabetes, obesity, and thyroid carcinoma.

Mobile, AL, USA — *Jingshan Huang*
Mobile, AL, USA — *Glen M. Borchert*
Eugene, OR, USA — *Dejing Dou*
Lawrence, KS, USA — *Jun (Luke) Huan*
Jinan, Shandong, China — *Wenjun Lan*
Mobile, AL, USA — *Ming Tan*
Kunming, Yunnan, China — *Bin Wu*

Contents

Preface .... *v*
Contributors .... *ix*

1 MicroRNAs, Long Noncoding RNAs, and Their Functions in Human Disease 1
Min Xue, Ying Zhuo, and Bin Shan

2 MicroRNA Expression: Protein Participants in MicroRNA Regulation 27
Valeria M. King and Glen M. Borchert

3 Viral MicroRNAs, Host MicroRNAs Regulating Viruses, and Bacterial MicroRNA-Like RNAs 39
Sara-Elizabeth Cardin and Glen M. Borchert

4 MicroRNAs: Biomarkers, Diagnostics, and Therapeutics 57
Weili Huang

5 Relational Databases and Biomedical Big Data 69
N.H. Nisansa D. de Silva

6 Semantic Technologies and Bio-Ontologies 83
Fernando Gutierrez

7 Genome-Wide Analysis of MicroRNA-Regulated Transcripts 93
David Chevalier and Glen M. Borchert

8 Computational Prediction of MicroRNA Target Genes, Target Prediction Databases, and Web Resources 109
Justin T. Roberts and Glen M. Borchert

9 Exploring MicroRNA::Target Regulatory Interactions by Computing Technologies 123
Yue Hu, Wenjun Lan, and Daniel Miller

10 The Limitations of Existing Approaches in Improving MicroRNA Target Prediction Accuracy 133
Rasiah Loganantharaj and Thomas A. Randall

11 Genomic Regulation of MicroRNA Expression in Disease Development 159
Feng Liu

12 Next-Generation Sequencing for MicroRNA Expression Profile 169
Yue Hu, Wenjun Lan, and Daniel Miller

13 Handling High-Dimension (High-Feature) MicroRNA Data 179
Yue Hu, Wenjun Lan, and Daniel Miller

14 Effective Removal of Noisy Data Via Batch Effect Processing 187
Ryan G. Benton

15 Logical Reasoning (Inferencing) on MicroRNA Data 197
Jingsong Wang

16 Machine Learning Techniques in Exploring MicroRNA Gene Discovery, Targets, and Functions 211
Sumi Singh, Ryan G. Benton, Anurag Singh, and Anshuman Singh

17 Involvement of MicroRNAs in Diabetes and Its Complications 225
Bin Wu and Daniel Miller

18 MicroRNA Regulatory Networks as Biomarkers in Obesity: The Emerging Role 241
Lihua Zhang, Daniel Miller, Qiuping Yang, and Bin Wu

19 Expression of MicroRNAs in Thyroid Carcinoma 261
Gaohong Zhu, Lijun Xie, and Daniel Miller

Index 281

Contributors

RYAN G. BENTON • *Department of Computer Science, University of South Alabama School of Computing, Mobile, AL, USA*
GLEN M. BORCHERT • *Department of Pharmacology, University of South Alabama, Mobile, AL, USA; Department of Biology, University of South Alabama, Mobile, AL, USA*
SARA-ELIZABETH CARDIN • *Department of Biology, University of South Alabama, Mobile, AL, USA*
DAVID CHEVALIER • *Department of Biology, East Georgia State College, Swainsboro, GA, USA*
N.H. NISANSA D. DE SILVA • *Department of Computer and Information Science, University of Oregon, Eugene, OR, USA*
FERNANDO GUTIERREZ • *Department of Computer and Information Science, University of Oregon, Eugene, OR, USA*
YUE HU • *College of Bioengineering, Qilu University of Technology, Jinan, Shandong, People's Republic of China*
WEILI HUANG • *Miracle Query, Incorporated, Eugene, OR, USA*
VALERIA M. KING • *Department of Biology, University of South Alabama, Mobile, AL, USA*
WENJUN LAN • *School of Bioengineering, Qilu University of Technology, Jinan, Shandong, People's Republic of China*
FENG LIU • *National Research Center for Translational Medicine (Shanghai), Rui-Jin Hospital, Shanghai Jiao Tong University School of Medicine, Shanghai, China*
RASIAH LOGANANTHARAJ • *Bioinformatics Research Lab, The Center for Advanced Computer Studies, University of Louisiana, Lafayette, LA, USA*
DANIEL MILLER • *School of Computing, University of South Alabama, Mobile, AL, USA*
THOMAS A. RANDALL • *Integrative Bioinformatics, National Institute of Environmental Health Sciences, National Institutes of Health, Research Triangle Park, Durham, NC, USA*
JUSTIN T. ROBERTS • *Department of Biology, University of South Alabama, Mobile, AL, USA*
BIN SHAN • *Elson S. Floyd College of Medicine, Washington State University, Spokane, WA, USA*
ANSHUMAN SINGH • *School of Computer Science and Mathematics, University of Central Missouri, Warrensburg, MO, USA*
ANURAG SINGH • *Center for Advanced Computer Studies, University of Louisiana, Lafayette, LA, USA*
SUMI SINGH • *School of Computer Science and Mathematics, University of Central Missouri, Warrensburg, MO, USA*
JINGSONG WANG • *Oracle Corporation, Redwood Shores, CA, USA*
BIN WU • *Department of Endocrinology, First Affiliated Hospital, Kunming Medical University, Kunming, Yunnan, China*

LIJUN XIE • *Department of Nuclear Medicine, First Affiliated Hospital of Kunming Medical University, Kunming, Yunnan, China*
MIN XUE • *Xuzhou College of Medicine, Xuzhou, Jiangsu, China*
QIUPING YANG • *Department of Geriatrics, First Affiliated Hospital of Kunming Medical University, Kunming, Yunnan, China*
LIHUA ZHANG • *Department of Geriatrics, First Affiliated Hospital of Kunming Medical University, Kunming, Yunnan, China*
GAOHONG ZHU • *Department of Nuclear Medicine, First Affiliated Hospital of Kunming Medical University, Kunming, Yunnan, China*
YING ZHUO • *Kadlec Regional Medical Center, Richland, WA, USA*

Chapter 1

MicroRNAs, Long Noncoding RNAs, and Their Functions in Human Disease

Min Xue, Ying Zhuo, and Bin Shan

Abstract

Majority of the human genome is transcribed into RNAs with absent or limited protein-coding potential. microRNAs (miRNAs) and long noncoding RNAs (lncRNAs) are two major families of the non-protein-coding transcripts. miRNAs and lncRNAs can regulate fundamental cellular processes via diverse mechanisms. The expression and function of miRNAs and lncRNAs are tightly regulated in development and physiological homeostasis. Dysregulation of miRNAs and lncRNAs is critical to pathogenesis of human disease. Moreover, recent evidence indicates a cross talk between miRNAs and lncRNAs. Herein we review recent advances in the biology of miRNAs and lncRNAs with respect to the above aspects. We focus on their roles in cancer, respiratory disease, and neurodegenerative disease. The complexity, flexibility, and versatility of the structures and functions of miRNAs and lncRNAs demand integration of experimental and bioinformatics tools to acquire sufficient knowledge for applications of these noncoding RNAs in clinical care.

Key words MicroRNA, Long noncoding RNA

1 Introduction

Majority of the human genome is transcribed although only ~2% of the human genome encodes proteins [1]. The transcribed RNAs with absent or limited protein-coding potential are named noncoding RNAs and operationally divided into small RNAs and long noncoding RNAs (lncRNA) with a boundary set at 200 nucleotides in length. The small RNA family includes microRNAs (miRNA), small nuclear RNAs, and piwi-interacting RNAs. miRNAs and lncRNAs are critical regulators of development, physiology, and disease. Herein we review recent advances in the biology of miRNAs and lncRNAs and their functions in human disease.

Jingshan Huang et al. (eds.), *Bioinformatics in MicroRNA Research*, Methods in Molecular Biology, vol. 1617, DOI 10.1007/978-1-4939-7046-9_1, © Springer Science+Business Media LLC 2017

2 Functions of miRNAs and Human Disease

2.1 Biogenesis of miRNAs

miRNAs are ~22-nucleotide long single stranded RNAs that regulate gene expression via diverse mechanisms [2]. Since discovery of the first miRNA lin-4 in *Caenorhabditis elegans* in 1993, 35,828 mature miRNAs have been catalogued in 223 species in the latest release of miRBase (www.mirbase.org) [3, 4]. Biogenesis of miRNAs starts with transcription from a miRNA-hosting gene, which yields a long primary transcript named primary miRNA (pri-miRNA) [5]. Then the pri-miRNA is cleaved by the ribonulease III-type protein Drosha in the nucleus to produce a ~70-nucleotide long hairpin structure named precursor miRNA (pre-miRNA) [6]. The pre-miRNA is exported to the cytoplasm by exportin-5 and subsequently cleaved by another ribonulease III-type protein Dicer to generate a miRNA:miRNA* duplex of ~22 nucleodtides [7]. The miRNA:miRNA* duplex binds to an argonaute (AGO) protein to form an effector RNA-induced silencing complex (RISC) complex. A mature miRNA is produced when miRNA* is peeled off from the duplex. It is noteworthy that a miRNA* is not simply a nonfunctional byproduct of miRNA biogenesis but rather a functional miRNA on many occasions [8].

Besides their canonical destination in the cytoplasm miRNAs exist and function in the nucleus and secretary microvesicles called exosomes [9, 10]. Exosomes are small extracellular membrane vesicles with sizes of 30–100 nm in diameter and secreted by various types of cells in the body [11–14]. miRNAs packaged in exosomes can be taken up by neighboring cells or distant recipient cells via transportation in body fluids and function in their recipient cells, which serve as an important tool for proximal and distant intercellular communications [15–18].

Biogenesis of miRNAs can be regulated at every step of their production by physiological and pathological signals. For instance the miRNA-200 family is transcriptionally suppressed by ZEB1 during epithelial–mesenchymal transition (EMT) [19]. In another example type I collagen posttranscriptionally upregulates the expression of miR-21 by promoting maturation of pre-miR-21 to miR-21 without alteration in the amount of pri-miRNA-21 and pre-miR-21 [20].

2.2 Functions of miRNA

The classic mode of a miRNA's action is to inhibit gene expression via binding to its complementary sequences (6–8 nucleotides) within the 3′ untranslated region (3′ UTR) of its target mRNAs. This partial complementarity causes inhibition of expression of a miRNA's target via degradation or repression of translation of the bound mRNAs [21]. Because of the need of only a 6–8 nucleotide complementarity a miRNA can potentially targets hundreds of mRNAs and most mammalian mRNAs are conserved targets of miRNAs [22]. Bioinformatic tools such as TargetScan have been widely used to guide prediction and validation of a miRNA's target mRNAs [23].

The cytoplasmic miRNAs inhibit their target genes expression via degradation of mRNAs or inhibition of translation at initiation and post-initiation steps [21, 24–31]. miRNA-mediated decrease of their target mRNA levels is proposed as a major mechanism of miRNA-mediated repression of a target gene expression [32]. This action can be achieved through miRNA-induced rapid deadenylation of target mRNA as exemplified by the actions of miR-125b, a miRNA that is linked to chemoresistance in breast cancer [31, 33, 34]. miRNA-mediated suppression of translation initiation is exemplified in let-7-mediated repression of its target mRNAs as let-7-bound AGO2 represses the translation initiation by binding to the m7G cap of the mRNA targets and thereby prevents the recruitment of eIF4E, an essential translation initiation factor [35]. The post-initiation inhibition of translation by miRNAs is accomplished through rapid degradation of the peptide product encoded by the targeted mRNA, which is mediated by high rate of ribosome drop-off during translation elongation [36].

In addition to their canonical actions in the cytoplasm miRNAs are expressed in abundance in the nucleus and regulate various nuclear events such as transcription and RNA splicing via diverse mechanisms. For instance miR-320 recruits AGO1 and EZH2 to the POLR3D locus through complete complementary binding, which results in heterochromatinization and silencing of the POLR3D promoter [37]. miRNA-mediated silencing of the gene promoters harboring their target sites controls a variety of fundamental cellular processes, such as cellular senescence and neuroregeneration [38–40]. On the other hand, a few nuclear miRNAs have been reported to activate gene expression via epigenetic mechanisms. For instance miR-373 activates the expression of CDH1 and CSDC2 via AGO-miRNA complexes-mediated recruitment of positive epigenetic regulators to the target promoters [41]. Lastly nuclear miRNAs can regulate splicing of the complement pre-mRNA. In miR-122-mediated repression of splicing of the hepatitis C viral RNA a ternary complex formed between the target transcript, miRNA, and RISC masks splicing recognition motifs and thereby prevents binding of the splicing factors [42].

2.3 miRNAs and Human Disease

miRNAs govern fundamental biological processes, such as cell proliferation, death, differentiation, and development [43]. As a feedback tool with profound effects on gene expression miRNAs are the main tool to fine-tune gene expression and biological homeostasis. Dysregulation of miRNAs contributes to pathogenesis of a wide variety of human disease. In this section we review actions of miRNAs in cancer, respiratory disease, and neurodegenerative disease.

2.3.1 miRNAs in Cancer

The first documented association between miRNAs and cancer is frequent deletion and downregulation of miR-15 and miR-16 at 13q14 in chronic lymphocytic leukemia [44]. Since then, thousands of miRNAs have been reported to act as either oncogenes or tumor suppressors depending on a miRNA's targets in a particular biological context. miRNAs have been linked to each hallmark of cancer that is established by Hanahan and Weinberg [45]. Representative miRNAs associated with each hallmark of cancer are listed in Table 1 [46–62].

Genetic alterations are a common cause of dysregulation of miRNAs in cancer. More than 50% of miRNA genes are located in cancer associated genomic regions or in fragile sites [63]. One prime example is amplification of the oncogenic miR-17~92 cluster and its consequent overexpression in small cell lung cancer [47]. Deletion and loss of expression of miRNAs in cancer are exemplified in frequent deletion of the miR-15a and miR-16a

Table 1
Association between miRNA and hallmarks of cancer

Hallmarks of cancer	Representative miRNAs
Sustaining proliferative signaling	miR-17~92-mediated suppression of PTEN in lung cancer and B-cell lymphoma [46, 47]; Loss of let-7-mediated suppression of Ras by in lung cancer [48, 49]
Evading growth suppressors	Interference of cell cycle arrest by miR-675-mediated suppression of pRB in colorectal cancer [50]
Avoiding immune destruction	Enhancement of resistance to cytotoxic T-lymphocytes by miR-222 mediated suppression of ICAM-1 [51]
Enabling replicative immortality	Loss of miR-34a-mediated senescence in colon cancer [52]
Tumor promoting inflammation	miR-155-mediated inflammation in the tumor microenvironment [53, 54]
Activating invasion and metastasis	miR-10b-mediated migration, invasion, and metastasis in breast cancer [62]; Loss of miR-200-mediated suppression of EMT [55, 56]
Inducing angiogenesis	Enhanced angiogenesis by miR-296-mediated suppression of HGS in tumor associated endothelial cells in gliomas [57]
Genome instability and mutation	Impairment of DNA repair by miR-21-mediated suppression of H2AX, a histone variant essential to repair [58, 59]
Resisting cell death	Inhibition of caspase activation by miR-21-mediated suppression of PDCD4 in glioblastoma [60]
Deregulating cellular energetics	Loss of miR-99a/100-mediated suppression of mTOR in childhood adrenocortical tumors [61]

A summary of representative miRNAs associated with the hallmarks of cancer. *PTEN* phosphatase and tensin homolog, *pRB* retinoblastoma protein, *EMT* epithelial–mesenchymal transition, *HGS* hepatocyte growth factor-regulated tyrosine kinase substrate, *PDCD4* programmed cell death protein 4, *mTOR* mechanistic target of rapamycin hosting locus in chronic lymphocytic leukemia [44]. Single nucleotide polymorphism (SNP) is another common cause of dysregulation of miRNAs in cancer. In a common G/C polymorphism (rs2910164) within the pre-miR-146a coding region the C allele results in a decrease of mature miR-146a and less efficient inhibition of the miR-146a targets, which increases risk of papillary thyroid carcinoma [64]. Variation within the miRNA target site of a miRNA-targeted 3′UTR is another important source of genetic predisposition in cancer risk. In the oncogenic HMGA2 locus the open reading frame and the 3′UTR harboring the let-7 target sites are separated by chromosomal rearrangements in cancer, which leads to escape of HMGA2 from let-7-mediated repression [65, 66]. SNP in a miRNA target site can result in loss of miRNA-mediated repression in cancer. In the let-7 target site within the 3′UTR of the KRAS oncogene SNP causes elevated KRAS expression and increased risk of non-small cell lung cancer [67].

Transcriptional dysregulation of miRNA expression is another critical mechanism in tumorigenesis. The oncogenic miRNAs are often transcriptionally activated in cancer [68]. For instance the oncogenic miR-17~92 cluster is transcriptionally activated by the MYC oncogene via a MYC binding site in the promoter of the miR-17~92 cluster [69]. In contrast the tumor suppressive miRNAs are often transcriptionally repressed in cancer [70]. The promoter of the miR-200 cluster that encodes miR-200a, miR-200b, and miR-429 is transcriptionally repressed by ZEB1 and SIP1 during EMT, a process through which cancer cells acquire invasive and metastatic competency [19, 55]. More importantly the miR-200 cluster members repress the expression of ZEB1 and SIP1 via the miR-200 target sites in their 3′ UTR and this reciprocal repression between the miR-200 cluster and ZEB1/SIP1 establishes a double-negative feedback loop in regulation of EMT [19, 55]. miRNA expression can also be regulated by the signals from the tumor microenvironment, such as extracellular matrix, and in turn mediates cancer cell's responses to the tumor microenvironment [20, 56, 71, 72].

Because of the critical roles of miRNAs in cancer biology miRNAs have emerged as a family of promising targets in diagnosis and treatment of cancer. Because miRNAs are more stable than mRNAs and released by a solid tumor into the body fluids via exosomes miRNAs have emerged as promising biomarkers in tissue biopsies, blood, urine, etc. [73–75]. For instance a host of circulating miRNAs including miR-141, miR-21, and miR-92a have been tested as diagnostic biomarkers of colorectal cancer in whole plasma or serum [76–81]. miRNAs have also been developed as molecular signatures of subtypes of breast cancer and thus guide the treatment that is tailored for each molecular subtype. The miRNA signatures of ER+ and HER+ can guide anti-ER and anti-HER2 therapies, respectively [82–84]. miRNAs can potentially predict responses to chemotherapy and thus guide the choice of treatments as illustrated in the miRNA signatures that can predict response to tamoxifen and anti-HER2 monoclonal antibody Herceptin in breast cancer [85–87].

Current development of miRNA-based therapies mainly employs antagonist and oligonucleotide mimics of a miRNA of interest. miRNA mimics are used to restore tumor suppressive miRNAs that are deficient in cancer. On the contrary antagomiRs are single-stranded oligonucleotides that complement and inhibit the oncogenic miRNAs in cancer. To increase efficiency of a miRNA antagonist, miRNA sponge technology has been developed to synthesize a single stranded RNA containing multiple binding sites of a targeted miRNA to efficiently neutralize a miRNA [88]. miRNA sponges have been validated in xenograft mouse model of human breast cancer cell lines in that inhibition of miRNA-9 and miR-150 using a synthetic RNA containing several miR-9 or miR-150 binding sites reduced lung metastases [89, 90]. The miRNA targeting therapies have entered clinical trials as exemplified by a miR-34a mimics in phase I study (http://clinicaltrials.gov/ct2/show/NCT01829971). Preliminary results from the translational studies of miRNA-based therapies against cancer suggest that miRNA mimics or antagomiRs can be easily administered through local or parenteral injection routes with sufficient uptake of the agents to achieve sustained and desired effects in the targeted tissues and organs.

2.3.2 miRNAs in Neurodegenerative Disease

miRNAs have emerged as critical regulators in the control of nervous system-specific gene expression during development, aging, and disease. We review the role of miRNAs in two devastating neurodegenerative diseases, Parkinson's disease and Alzheimer's disease.

Parkinson's disease is a chronic and progressive movement disorder that is caused by a gradual loss of midbrain dopaminergic neurons [91]. Investigation of miRNAs has shed light on pathogenesis of Parkinson's disease. miR-133b is specifically expressed in the midbrain dopaminergic neurons and regulates maturation and function of the midbrain dopaminergic neurons as a node of a negative feedback circuit by targeting the paired-like homeodomain transcription factor Pitx3 [92]. Importantly, miR-133b is deficient in the midbrain tissues from patients with Parkinson's disease [92]. Gain-of-function mutations in leucine-rich repeat kinase-2 (LRRK2) cause familial and sporadic Parkinson's disease. The pathogenic LRRK2 associate with RISC to interfere the miRNA pathway and such interference leads to overproduction of E2F1/DP, a target of let-7 and miR-184* [93]. Moreover, antagomiR-mediated blockage of let-7 or miR-184* can recapitulate the toxic effects of the pathogenic LRRK2 and conversely forced expression of let-7 or miR-184* can attenuate the toxic effects of the pathogenic LRRK2 [93].

Alzheimer's disease is the most common cause of dementia in the aging population. The pathologic hallmarks of the disease are plaques composed of amyloid β and tangles composed of hyperphosphorylated tau [94]. Several miRNA profiling studies have identified dozens of miRNAs that are significantly differentially expressed between cortex from patients with Alzheimer's disease and the matching controls [95–97]. The differentially expressed miRNAs appear to be more robust and reproducible than the differentially expressed mRNAs [98]. Moreover, a joint profiling of miRNA and mRNA expression in brain cortex from Alzheimer's disease and age-matched control subjects reveals strong inverse correlations between the amount of miRNAs and their corresponding predicted mRNA targets, which suggests active microRNA functions in Alzheimer's disease [99]. Indeed the expression of miR-29a, miR-29b-1, and miR-9 is significantly decreased in Alzheimer's disease and their decrease causes aberrant increase of their target β-secretase-1 (BACE1), a protein accountable for accumulation of Aβ in Alzheimer's disease [100]. Besides BACE1, the expression of amyloid precursor protein is repressed by the members of the miR-20a family (miR-20a, miR-17-5p, and miR-106b) and this miRNA pathway appears to be compromised in Alzheimer's disease because miR-106b is substantially reduced in sporadic Alzheimer's disease [101].

2.3.3 miRNAs in Respiratory Disease

As in many other tissues miRNAs mediate cell differentiation and maintain homeostasis in differentiated cells in the respiratory system [102]. miRNA expression undergoes profound changes during lung development and the Dicer null mice are not viable due to impaired lung growth that is caused by deficiency in production of mature miRNAs globally due to deletion of Dicer [103, 104]. Moreover, expression of the miR-17~92 cluster progressively declines during lung development and forced expression of the cluster results in abnormal lung development that was characterized by continued proliferation and impaired differentiation of epithelial cells [105].

Profound alteration in miRNA expression profile has been observed in asthma and asthma undergoing steroid therapy [106, 107]. More importantly the altered miRNA expression profile observed in asthma appears to be largely driven by IL-13, a key pathogenic cytokine in asthma because the miRNA profile in asthma can be recapitulated by exposing lung epithelial cells to IL-13 [107]. T cells are important orchestrators of the chronic inflammatory response in asthma. In the circulating $CD4^+$ and $CD8^+$ T cells collected from the patients with severe asthma the expression of miR-146a and miR-146b are substantially downregulated and such downregulation potentially contributes to greater T-cell activation in severe asthma because these two miRNAs inhibit the immune response [108, 109].

Idiopathic pulmonary fibrosis is a deadly lung disease featuring excessive production and deposition of extracellular matrix components by fibroblasts and myofibroblasts in the lung interstitium. miRNA expression profiling of human lung samples, isolated lung cells, and mouse models of idiopathic pulmonary fibrosis have revealed profound dysregulation of miRNA that includes let-7d, miR-21, and miR-29 [110–114]. More importantly reversing the expression pattern of let-7d and miR-21 observed in pulmonary fibrosis can attenuate pulmonary fibrosis in mice, suggesting that these miRNAs mediate fibrosis in the lung [110–114]. It is noteworthy that miR-29 represses expression of a host of extracellular matrix proteins and has been implicated as a key regulator in fibrotic diseases in other organs as well [115].

Chronic obstructive pulmonary disease (COPD) is caused predominantly by long-term exposure to cigarette smoke and characteristic of destruction of the lung parenchyma (emphysema) and reduced lung function. A miRNA expression profiling of lung tissues collected from smokers with and without COPD has revealed a panel of 70 miRNAs that are differentially expressed between smokers with and without COPD [116]. This panel is enriched with the miRNAs linked to the pathways that underlie the pathogenesis of COPD, such as the TGF-β, Wnt, and focal adhesion pathways [116]. For instance upregulated expression of miR-15b is observed only in the smoker with COPD and correlated with a decrease of its validated target SMAD7, a well-established inhibitor of the TGF-β pathway [116]. In two other in-depth studies reduced miR-146a expression is linked to increased expression of PGE2 due to loss of miR-146a-mediated repression of COX-2 and reduced expression of miR-1 is linked to the muscle weakness observed in COPD [117, 118].

3 Functions of lncRNAs and Human Disease

lncRNA is a heterogenous family that is represented by long intergenic RNAs (defined by position), circular RNAs (circRNA, defined by structure), competing endogenous RNA (ceRNA, defined as functions), antisense RNAs (defined by orientation of transcription), etc. According to the Ensembl human genome annotation (GRch38, version 23) 27,817 lncRNAs are transcribed from 15,931 gene loci [119]. lncRNAs are of absent or limited protein coding potential. However, increasing number of genes can dually produce peptides/proteins and lncRNAs. For example, the RNA and proteins products of the steroid receptor RNA activator gene are simultaneously produced and the RNA product function as a scaffold for formation of several ribonucleoprotein complexes [120]. Similar to mRNA, most lncRNAs are transcribed by RNA polymerase II, 5′-capped, 3′-polyadenylated, and spliced into various isoforms although they tend to have fewer exons than mRNAs [1].

The importance of lncRNA genes are revealed by their proximity to developmental regulators in the genome, enrichment of tissue-specific and developmental stage-specific expression patterns, and frequent association with genetic traits [121]. lncRNAs regulate a myriad of molecular and cellular processes, such as chromatin remodeling and RNA splicing [122–126]. In the following sections we discuss the functions of lncRNAs and their role in human disease.

3.1 Functions of lncRNAs

3.1.1 Regulation of Epigenetic Modifications

A large number of lncRNAs can recruit chromatin remodeling complexes to a specific set of genes to activate or repress gene expression [127–133]. As many as 20% of lncRNAs expressed in a given cell associate with chromatin remodeling complexes and lncRNAs are commonly bound by multiple chromatin remodeling proteins [134]. One of the best-characterized interactions between lncRNAs and chromatin remodeling complexes is lncRNA-mediated recruitment of polycomb repressive complex 2 (PRC2) that catalyzes trimethylation of histone H3 lysine 27 (H3K27me3), a histone code for transcriptional repression [135].

lncRNAs can act *in cis* to recruit chromatin remodeling complexes to regulate gene expression, which is well-characterized in X-chromosome inactivation by the lncRNA X-inactive-specific transcript (XIST) [136, 137]. In mammalian females, the majority of genes on one of the two X-chromosomes in each cell are silenced. During female development, XIST is transcribed from the X-chromosome that is destined to become inactivated in each cell. XIST then coats the regions of the chromosome that is to be silenced, which results in formation of “XIST clouds” and recruitment of PRC2 to the XIST-coated region for gene silencing [138].

On the other hand, lncRNAs can act *in trans* to recruit PRC2 to repress gene expression. As a paradigm of such mechanism, the lncRNA HOX antisense intergenic RNA (HOTAIR) is transcribed from the locus between HOXC11 and HOXC12 on chromosome 12 and repress the HOXD gene cluster on chromosome 2 via recruitment of PRC2 [129]. As demonstrated by chromatin isolation by RNA purification HOTAIR preferentially occupies a GA-rich DNA motif to recruit PRC2 and nucleate broad domains of H3K27me3 [139].

lncRNAs can regulate another important epigenetic code, DNA methylation, a dynamic and reversible process that governs gene expression during development and disease. In general cytosine methylation in a CpG island located in a gene promoter marks a gene for repression. An antisense lncRNA named TCF21 antisense RNA inducing demethylation (TARID) activates TCF21 expression by inducing promoter demethylation [140]. TARID recruits growth arrest and DNA-damage-inducible-α (GADD45A) to the TCF21 promoter. GADD45A, a regulator of DNA demethylation, in turn recruits thymine-DNA glycosylase for base excision repair-mediated demethylation in the TCF21 promoter [140]. In summary lncRNA can regulate the epigenetic codes through physical interaction with chromatin or nucleotide modifiers.

3.1.2 Regulation of RNA Splicing

Besides regulation of epigenetic codes a large number of lncRNAs regulate RNA splicing. For instance the lncRNA metastasis-associated lung adenocarcinoma transcript 1 (MALAT1) regulates alternative splicing through its interaction with the serine/arginine-rich (SR) family of nuclear phosphoproteins, a key component of the splicing machinery [141, 142]. MALAT1 is required for appropriate splicing because depletion of MALAT1 results in increase of mislocalized and unphosphorylated SR proteins as well as increase of exon inclusion events [142]. It is proposed that MALAT1 serves as a structural docking site for accumulation and assembly of specific splicing factors, such as phosphorylated SR proteins and this process is essential for efficient splicing [141].

3.1.3 Regulation of mRNA Decay

Another step of a RNA life cycle regulated by lncRNAs is mRNA decay as illustrated in staufen-1-mediated mRNA degradation [143]. Staufen-1 binds to translationally active mRNAs via imperfect base-pairing between one Alu element in the 3′ UTR of a staufen-1 target and another Alu element in a cytoplasmic, polyadenylated long noncoding RNA (lncRNA) [143]. Formation of the mRNA-lncRNA-staufen-1 hetero triplex leads to degradation of the staufen-1-targeted mRNAs [143]. It is noteworthy that this process assigns a novel function to Alu, an ancient DNA repetitive element, which is echoed in a novel function of another repetitive element SINEB2 as discussed below.

3.1.4 Regulation of mRNA Translation

lncRNAs can regulate the final step of an mRNA life cycle, translation, through base-pairing with the targeted mRNAs and formation of this RNA-RNA duplex that in turn modulates the interaction between the translated mRNAs and ribosomes [144, 145]. The antisense lncRNAs that complement the targeted mRNAs at the 5′ end promote association of polysomes with the targeted mRNAs. A nuclear-enriched lncRNA antisense to mouse ubiquitin carboxy-terminal hydrolase L1 (Uchl1) can increase UCHL1 mRNA translation, which requires the presence of a 5′ overlapping sequence and an embedded inverted SINEB2 element [145]. On the contrary, lincRNA-p21 can associate with JUNB mRNA and selectively reduce its translation when lincRNA-p21 is released from HuR, a RNA-binding protein that binds to and limits the availability of lincRNA-p21 for targeting JUNB [144].

3.1.5 Molecular Scaffold for Structural/Functional Complexes

lncRNAs can serve as molecular scaffolds for assembly and positioning of structural or functional complexes so that the lncRNA containing complexes can function in an appropriate spatial and temporal manner [134, 146, 147]. HOTAIR provides a paradigm of how lncRNAs act as a modular scaffold. HOTAIR interacts with PRC2 and lysine-specific demethylase 1 (LSD1) corepressor complex to silence the HOXD locus *in trans* [148]. Assembly and positioning of a transcriptional corepressor complex containing PRC2 and LSD1 on a HOTAIR bound gene promoter can efficiently coordinate histone codes for gene silencing via PCR2-mediated addition of repression code H3K27me3 and LSD1-mediated removal of activation code H3K4me3. Such coordination is achieved through scaffolding by HOTAIR in that HOTAIR binds to PRC2 via its 5′ terminus and to LSD1 via its 3′ terminus [148].

3.2 lncRNAs and Human Disease

lncRNAs dictates fundamental cellular and developmental processes and thereby underlie pathogenesis of a broad range of human diseases. Aside from their well-established roles in cancer, lncRNAs are central to fragile X syndrome, neurodegenerative disease, respiratory disease, etc. [149–154]. In this section we review recent advances on the role of lncRNAs in cancer, neurodegenerative disease, and respiratory disease.

3.2.1 lncRNAs in Cancer

lncRNAs have emerged as novel master regulators of initiation, progression, and response to therapy in a wide variety of solid tumors and hematological malignancies [155]. Hundreds of lncRNAs are differentially expressed between tumor tissues and paired adjacent nontumor tissues in various types of cancer [156–164]. lncRNAs can act as oncogenes or tumor suppressors to regulate cancer biology via diverse molecular mechanisms [141, 158, 159, 165–167].

One of the classical and versatile cancer-associated lncRNAs is MALAT1. Elevated expression of MALAT1 has been reported in a broad range of cancers, including lung cancer and breast cancer [168–184]. Moreover, genetic alterations in MALAT1, such as multiple mutations and deletions within the SRSF1-binding sites are associated with poor patient outcome in breast cancer [185]. In colorectal cancer and osteosarcoma, MALAT1 promotes tumor growth and metastasis by binding to a multifunctional RNA-binding protein, PSF via a motif in its 3′region [186, 187]. Depletion of MALAT1 results in defective alternative splicing of a subset of transcripts that are involved in cancer such as tissue factor and endoglin [188]. Besides regulation of splicing of the cancer-associated genes MALAT1 regulates expression of the cancer associated genes via epigenetic mechanisms. For example, MALAT1 binds to polycomb group proteins to facilitate assembly of multiple corepressors/coactivators and thereby mediates activation of the growth-control gene program for proliferation [189]. MALAT1 also associates with PRC2 and alters the expression of N-cadherin and E-cadherin to promote EMT in bladder cancer cells [175]. Besides its potential as a biomarker, MALAT1 is an appealing therapeutic target for cancer metastasis because deletion or inhibition of MALAT1 reduces tumor growth and metastasis of human lung cancer cells in xenografted mice [187].

Another prime example of oncogenic lncRNAs is HOTAIR [190, 191]. HOTAIR is elevated in various cancers including breast cancer, lung cancer, colorectal cancer, and prostate cancer [159, 192–194]. Elevated HOTAIR expression is a powerful predictor of metastasis and poor survival [159]. The paradigm of HOTAIR's functions in cancer is that increased amount of HOTAIR reprograms global gene occupancy of PRC2, which results in de novo repression of hundreds of new target genes to promote invasion and metastasis [159]. HOTAIR mediates cancer cells' resistance to chemotherapy because elevated expression of HOTAIR is correlated with tamoxifen resistance in breast cancer and its overexpression promotes ligand-independent proliferative activities of estrogen receptor [195].

Similar to miRNAs lncRNAs can regulate the hallmarks of cancer via diverse mechanisms as illustrated in regulation of apoptosis and proliferation by the lncRNA growth arrest-specific transcript 5 (GAS5). GAS5 is induced upon growth arrest due to lack of nutrients or growth factors and overexpression of GAS5 induces growth arrest and apoptosis in cancer cells [196]. Acting as molecular decoy through its binding to the DNA-binding domain of glucocorticoid receptor GAS5 sequesters glucocorticoid receptor and thereby suppresses glucocorticoid-activated genes, particularly the inhibitors of apoptosis [196]. Another example of lncRNA-mediated control of cell cycle control is lincRNA-p21 whose expression is induced by p53 upon DNA damage [166]. Upon induction by p53 lincRNA-p21 interacts with ribonucleoprotein K and act *in trans* to recruit ribonucleoprotein K to repress a host of p53 targeted genes, particularly the genes that interfere with the apoptotic response to DNA damage. On the other hand, lincRNA-p21 can function *in cis* to activate expression of its neighboring gene, particularly p21, an essential mediator of p53-dependent growth arrest response to DNA damage [197].

Given their pivotal role in cancer biology lncRNAs have emerged as promising targets for diagnosis and therapy of cancer. Some lncRNAs are potential biomarkers of a broad range of cancer, such as HOTAIR that is upregulated in the majority of cancers investigated so far [191]. More importantly elevated expression of HOTAIR and MALAT1 is valuable in prognosis because their aberrant expression correlates significantly with metastasis and poor overall survival in breast, lung, and colorectal cancers [160, 191, 198, 199]. On the other hand, some lncRNAs are dysregulated in cancer in a tissue type-specific manner. For instance the lncRNA prostate cancer antigen 3 (PCA3) is upregulated specifically in prostate tumor tissue over normal/nonmalignant tissue [200, 201].

Similar to miRNAs altered expression of lncRNAs in various body fluids is often congruent to their dysregulated expression in the tumor tissues. Thus acquisition of lncRNA based biomarkers in body fluids is convenient, minimally invasive, and cost-effective relative to conventional tissue biopsies. Particularly the circulating lncRNAs exist in exosomes released by cancer cells because the lncRNAs packaged into exosomes appear to be tightly controlled and thus provide pivotal information of their parental cancer cells that otherwise requires conventional biopsies to obtain [202, 203].

One of the most explored methods to inhibit upregulated oncogenic lncRNAs is RNA interference. siRNAs targeting lncRNAs via base-pairing have yielded promising efficiency in reducing lncRNA expression and cancer growth/metastasis as observed in targeting HOTAIR in breast cancer cells [159, 204]. Another base-pairing approach is using longer antisense oligonucleotides to promote degradation of the targeted lncRNA by RNase H that was successfully applied to target MALAT1 in lung cancer cells [168]. On the other hand, the expression of the tumor suppressive lncRNAs may be enforced/introduced by delivery of an lncRNA transgene. Because lncRNAs function through physical interactions with protein partners in normal and cancer contexts one ideal approach to specifically interfere the lncRNAs' functions in cancer is to disrupt the cancer-specific interaction between lncRNAs and their protein partners. This approach has been attempted in a feasibility test that successfully identified the compounds that can disrupt the interaction between HOTAIR and PRC2 [205].

3.2.2 lncRNAs in Neurodegenerative Disease

lncRNAs have emerged as orchestrators of gene regulatory networks in the nervous system. Hundreds of lncRNAs exhibit temporal and spatial patterns of expression in the nervous system, which suggest that they play key roles in development and normal functions of the nervous system [206]. As validated by a profiling and functional analysis of lncRNAs in human embryonic stem cells efficient neuronal differentiation of embryonic stem cells requires several lncRNAs, such as lncRNA_N1 (AK124684) and lncRNA_N2 (AK091713) [207]. We review the role of lncRNAs in two neurodegenerative diseases, Alzheimer's disease and Parkinson's disease.

One salient example of lncRNAs linked to pathogenesis of Alzheimer's disease is the lncRNA named antisense transcript of β-secretase-1 (BACE1-AS). BACE1 is believed to be the culprit of accumulation of β-amyloid and the consequent formation of amyloid plaques that are pathological hallmarks of Alzheimer's disease. BACE1-AS can increase the mRNA levels of BACE1 by duplexing with and stabilizing the BACE1 mRNA [149]. More importantly BACE1-AS is elevated in the brains of patients with Alzheimer's disease, suggesting that BACE1-AS mediates upregulated expression of BACE1 in Alzheimer's disease [208]. The amount of BACE-1AS in the brains of patients with Alzheimer's is proportional to the severity of dementia [149]. Another lncRNA linked to Alzheimer's disease belongs to a family of the brain cytoplasmic (BC) lncRNAs. The lncRNA BC200 is transported to dendritic processes via ribonucleoprotein particles and regulate gene expression at the translational level [209]. BC200 declines in the frontal cortex of normal aging brain, but increases in Alzheimer's disease, and its increase is congruent to the severity of dementia [210].

In Parkinson's disease, aberrant expression of PTEN induced kinase 1 (PINK1) leads to abnormal mitochondrial morphology, impaired dopamine release, and motor deficits [211]. The lncRNA natural antisense RNA of PINK1 (naPINK1) is transcribed as an antisense transcript from the PINK1 locus and stabilizes the expression of a PINK1 splice variant (svPINK1) containing a domain homologous to the C-terminus regulatory domain of PINK1 [212]. Silencing of naPINK1 results in decrease of svPINK1 in neurons, which suggests that naPINK1 and svPINK1 are concordantly regulated during impairment of mitochondrial biogenesis related to Parkinson's disease [212].

3.2.3 lncRNAs in Respiratory Disease

Hundreds of lncRNAs are expressed in a developmental stage-specific and cell type-specific manner in the mouse lung [213]. Moreover, the lncRNA expressing genomic loci are enriched with the binding sites for the established master transcriptional regulators of lung development, such as serum response factor, forkhead box, and SP1. In particular, two lncRNAs, NANCI and LL34, regulate expression of the genes that govern the key steps in differentiation and development of airway epithelial cells [213]. These findings implicate a critical role of lncRNAs in lung development, function, and disease.

The importance of lncRNAs in respiratory disease is highlighted in characterization of the deletion of the locus harboring several lncRNAs in a rare lethal neonatal lung disorder alveolar capillary dysplasia with misalignment of pulmonary veins (ACD/MPV) [214]. The lung-abundant 16q24.1 lncRNAs transcribed from the deleted locus of ACD/MPV may contribute to long-range regulation of FOXF1 by GLI2 and other transcription factors via chromatin looping [214]. Loss of those lncRNAs due to deletion results in loss of FOXF1 expression as well as consequent vascular pathology observed in ACD/MPV. It is conceivable that similarly dysregulated lncRNA expression and function occur in pulmonary vascular remodeling in pulmonary arterial hypertension and asthma. Indeed in asthma and COPD inhibition of MALAT1 appears to be a promising approach to attenuate occlusive lesions in pulmonary arterial hypertension, inhibit airway epithelial cell proliferation, and reduce obstructive remodeling of the airways [215].

4 Regulation of miRNAs by lncRNAs

A new frontier in the noncoding RNA world is the cross talk between miRNAs and lncRNAs [216]. Recent studies have discovered and characterized naturally occurring microRNA sponges, termed competing endogenous RNAs (ceRNAs) [217]. These ceRNAs consist of a variety of RNA species that include protein-coding mRNAs, pseudogenes, and lncRNAs (including circRNAs). We focus on regulation of miRNAs by lncRNAs.

One of the well-charaterized ceRNAs is linc-RoR that is abundantly expressed in human embryonic stem cells [218]. linc-RoR sequesters miR-145 and thus protects OCT4, SOX2, and NANOG from miR-145-mediated repression [218]. The linc-ROR-mediated interference of miR-145 is essential to renewal of embryonic stem cells [218]. In a similar fashion HOTAIR antagonizes several tumor suppressive miRNAs. In gastric cancer cells, HOTAIR acts as a ceRNA to trap miR-331-3p through a complementary target site in its sixth exon and consequently increases the expression of the miR-331-3p-targeted oncogene HER2 [219]. In gall bladder cancer, HOTAIR's oncogenic activity requires its binding to and titration of miR-130a through a target site in its sixth exon [220]. Interestingly the interaction between HOTAIR and miR-130a is reciprocal because miR-130a represses the expression of HOTAIR in a target site-dependent manner [220]. The oncogenic lncRNA H19 acts as a ceRNA of two tumor suppressive miRNAs, miR-141 and let-7 and thus promotes the proliferative and invasive phenotypes of cancer cells [221, 222]. Besides cancer ceRNAs play a critical role in normal physiology. For instance linc-MD1 is a ceRNA that mediates skeletal muscle differentiation by titrating away miR-133 and miR-135 from their targets MAML1 and MEF2C mRNAs [223]. Decreased expression of linc-MD1 is believed to mediate pathogenesis of Duchenne muscular dystrophy, a devastating muscle degenerative disease due to uncontrolled repression of MAML1 and MEF2C by miR-133 and miR-135 [223].

circRNAs are structurally distinct in that they form a covalently closed continuous loop in which the 3′ and 5′ ends that are normally exposed in an linear RNA molecule are joined together in circRNAs. Several circRNAs containing multiple target sites of an individual microRNA have been characterized, which indicate that circRNAs can efficiently sequester microRNAs [224]. For instance, the circRNA sponge for miR-7, ciRS-7, contains dozens of miR-7 target sites and is enriched in the human and mouse brain [225]. More importantly, ciRS-7 regulates brain development by titrating miR-7 [225].

5 Conclusions

miRNAs and lncRNAs have emerged as central players in fundamental cellular processes, development, and pathogenesis of human disease. The complexity, flexibility, and versatility of the structures and functions of miRNAs and lncRNAs demand integration of experimental and bioinformatic tools to acquire sufficient knowledge for applications of these noncoding RNAs in clinical care.

References

1. Derrien T, Johnson R, Bussotti G, Tanzer A, Djebali S et al (2012) The GENCODE v7 catalog of human long noncoding RNAs: analysis of their gene structure, evolution, and expression. Genome Res 22:1775–1789
2. Bartel DP (2004) MicroRNAs: genomics, biogenesis, mechanism, and function. Cell 116:281–297
3. Lee RC, Feinbaum RL, Ambros V (1993) The *C. elegans* heterochronic gene lin-4 encodes small RNAs with antisense complementarity to lin-14. Cell 75:843–854
4. Kozomara A, Griffiths-Jones S (2014) miRBase: annotating high confidence microRNAs using deep sequencing data. Nucleic Acids Res 42:D68–D73
5. Lee Y, Kim M, Han J, Yeom KH, Lee S et al (2004) MicroRNA genes are transcribed by RNA polymerase II. EMBO J 23:4051–4060
6. Bortolin-Cavaille ML, Dance M, Weber M, Cavaille J (2009) C19MC microRNAs are processed from introns of large Pol-II, non-protein-coding transcripts. Nucleic Acids Res 37:3464–3473
7. Katahira J, Yoneda Y (2011) Nucleocytoplasmic transport of microRNAs and related small RNAs. Traffic 12:1468–1474
8. Bhayani MK, Calin GA, Lai SY (2012) Functional relevance of miRNA sequences in human disease. Mutat Res 731:14–19
9. Roberts TC (2014) The MicroRNA biology of the mammalian nucleus. Mol Ther Nucleic Acids 3:e188
10. Hu G, Drescher KM, Chen XM (2012) Exosomal miRNAs: biological properties and therapeutic potential. Front Genet 3:56
11. Valadi H, Ekstrom K, Bossios A, Sjostrand M, Lee JJ et al (2007) Exosome-mediated transfer of mRNAs and microRNAs is a novel mechanism of genetic exchange between cells. Nat Cell Biol 9:654–659
12. Laulagnier K, Motta C, Hamdi S, Roy S, Fauvelle F et al (2004) Mast cell- and dendritic cell-derived exosomes display a specific lipid composition and an unusual membrane organization. Biochem J 380:161–171
13. Hogan MC, Manganelli L, Woollard JR, Masyuk AI, Masyuk TV et al (2009) Characterization of PKD protein-positive exosome-like vesicles. J Am Soc Nephrol 20:278–288
14. Zhou R, O'Hara SP, Chen XM (2011) MicroRNA regulation of innate immune responses in epithelial cells. Cell Mol Immunol 8:371–379
15. Vlassov AV, Magdaleno S, Setterquist R, Conrad R (2012) Exosomes: current knowledge of their composition, biological functions, and diagnostic and therapeutic potentials. Biochim Biophys Acta 1820:940–948
16. Mittelbrunn M, Gutierrez-Vazquez C, Villarroya-Beltri C, Gonzalez S, Sanchez-Cabo F et al (2011) Unidirectional transfer of microRNA-loaded exosomes from T cells to antigen-presenting cells. Nat Commun 2:282
17. McDonald MK, Tian Y, Qureshi RA, Gormley M, Ertel A et al (2014) Functional significance of macrophage-derived exosomes in inflammation and pain. Pain 155:1527–1539
18. Putz U, Howitt J, Doan A, Goh CP, Low LH et al (2012) The tumor suppressor PTEN is exported in exosomes and has phosphatase activity in recipient cells. Sci Signal 5:ra70
19. Bracken CP, Gregory PA, Kolesnikoff N, Bert AG, Wang J et al (2008) A double-negative feedback loop between ZEB1-SIP1 and the microRNA-200 family regulates epithelial-mesenchymal transition. Cancer Res 68:7846–7854
20. Li C, Nguyen HT, Zhuang Y, Lin Y, Flemington EK et al (2011) Post-

transcriptional up-regulation of miR-21 by type I collagen. Mol Carcinog 50:563–570
21. Olsen PH, Ambros V (1999) The lin-4 regulatory RNA controls developmental timing in *Caenorhabditis elegans* by blocking LIN-14 protein synthesis after the initiation of translation. Dev Biol 216:671–680
22. Friedman RC, Farh KK, Burge CB, Bartel DP (2009) Most mammalian mRNAs are conserved targets of microRNAs. Genome Res 19:92–105
23. Agarwal V, Bell GW, Nam JW, Bartel DP (2015) Predicting effective microRNA target sites in mammalian mRNAs. eLife 4:e05005
24. Maroney PA, Yu Y, Fisher J, Nilsen TW (2006) Evidence that microRNAs are associated with translating messenger RNAs in human cells. Nat Struct Mol Biol 13:1102–1107
25. Nottrott S, Simard MJ, Richter JD (2006) Human let-7a miRNA blocks protein production on actively translating polyribosomes. Nat Struct Mol Biol 13:1108–1114
26. Petersen CP, Bordeleau ME, Pelletier J, Sharp PA (2006) Short RNAs repress translation after initiation in mammalian cells. Mol Cell 21:533–542
27. Pillai RS, Bhattacharyya SN, Artus CG, Zoller T, Cougot N et al (2005) Inhibition of translational initiation by Let-7 MicroRNA in human cells. Science 309:1573–1576
28. Humphreys DT, Westman BJ, Martin DI, Preiss T (2005) MicroRNAs control translation initiation by inhibiting eukaryotic initiation factor 4E/cap and poly(A) tail function. Proc Natl Acad Sci U S A 102:16961–16966
29. Rehwinkel J, Behm-Ansmant I, Gatfield D, Izaurralde E (2005) A crucial role for GW182 and the DCP1:DCP2 decapping complex in miRNA-mediated gene silencing. RNA 11:1640–1647
30. Behm-Ansmant I, Rehwinkel J, Doerks T, Stark A, Bork P et al (2006) mRNA degradation by miRNAs and GW182 requires both CCR4:NOT deadenylase and DCP1:DCP2 decapping complexes. Genes Dev 20:1885–1898
31. Wu L, Fan J, Belasco JG (2006) MicroRNAs direct rapid deadenylation of mRNA. Proc Natl Acad Sci U S A 103:4034–4039
32. Guo H, Ingolia NT, Weissman JS, Bartel DP (2010) Mammalian microRNAs predominantly act to decrease target mRNA levels. Nature 466:835–840
33. Liu Z, Liu H, Desai S, Schmitt DC, Zhou M et al (2013) miR-125b functions as a key mediator for snail-induced stem cell propagation and chemoresistance. J Biol Chem 288:4334–4345
34. Zhou M, Liu Z, Zhao Y, Ding Y, Liu H et al (2010) MicroRNA-125b confers the resistance of breast cancer cells to paclitaxel through suppression of pro-apoptotic Bcl-2 antagonist killer 1 (Bak1) expression. J Biol Chem 285:21496–21507
35. Kiriakidou M, Tan GS, Lamprinaki S, De Planell-Saguer M, Nelson PT et al (2007) An mRNA m7G cap binding-like motif within human Ago2 represses translation. Cell 129:1141–1151
36. Stefani G, Slack FJ (2008) Small non-coding RNAs in animal development. Nat Rev Mol Cell Biol 9:219–230
37. Kim DH, Saetrom P, Snove O Jr, Rossi JJ (2008) MicroRNA-directed transcriptional gene silencing in mammalian cells. Proc Natl Acad Sci U S A 105:16230–16235
38. Benhamed M, Herbig U, Ye T, Dejean A, Bischof O (2012) Senescence is an endogenous trigger for microRNA-directed transcriptional gene silencing in human cells. Nat Cell Biol 14:266–275
39. Zardo G, Ciolfi A, Vian L, Starnes LM, Billi M et al (2012) Polycombs and microRNA-223 regulate human granulopoiesis by transcriptional control of target gene expression. Blood 119:4034–4046
40. Adilakshmi T, Sudol I, Tapinos N (2012) Combinatorial action of miRNAs regulates transcriptional and post-transcriptional gene silencing following in vivo PNS injury. PLoS One 7:e39674
41. Place RF, Li LC, Pookot D, Noonan EJ, Dahiya R (2008) MicroRNA-373 induces expression of genes with complementary promoter sequences. Proc Natl Acad Sci U S A 105:1608–1613
42. Shimakami T, Yamane D, Jangra RK, Kempf BJ, Spaniel C et al (2012) Stabilization of hepatitis C virus RNA by an Ago2-miR-122 complex. Proc Natl Acad Sci U S A 109:941–946
43. Ha TY (2011) The role of MicroRNAs in regulatory T cells and in the immune response. Immune Netw 11:11–41
44. Calin GA, Dumitru CD, Shimizu M, Bichi R, Zupo S et al (2002) Frequent deletions and down-regulation of micro-RNA genes miR15 and miR16 at 13q14 in chronic lymphocytic leukemia. Proc Natl Acad Sci U S A 99:15524–15529
45. Hanahan D, Weinberg RA (2011) Hallmarks of cancer: the next generation. Cell 144:646–674

46. He L, Thomson JM, Hemann MT, Hernando-Monge E, Mu D et al (2005) A microRNA polycistron as a potential human oncogene. Nature 435:828–833
47. Hayashita Y, Osada H, Tatematsu Y, Yamada H, Yanagisawa K et al (2005) A polycistronic microRNA cluster, miR-17-92, is overexpressed in human lung cancers and enhances cell proliferation. Cancer Res 65:9628–9632
48. Takamizawa J, Konishi H, Yanagisawa K, Tomida S, Osada H et al (2004) Reduced expression of the let-7 microRNAs in human lung cancers in association with shortened postoperative survival. Cancer Res 64:3753–3756
49. Johnson SM, Grosshans H, Shingara J, Byrom M, Jarvis R et al (2005) RAS is regulated by the let-7 microRNA family. Cell 120:635–647
50. Tsang WP, Ng EK, Ng SS, Jin H, Yu J et al (2010) Oncofetal H19-derived miR-675 regulates tumor suppressor RB in human colorectal cancer. Carcinogenesis 31:350–358
51. Ueda R, Kohanbash G, Sasaki K, Fujita M, Zhu X et al (2009) Dicer-regulated microRNAs 222 and 339 promote resistance of cancer cells to cytotoxic T-lymphocytes by down-regulation of ICAM-1. Proc Natl Acad Sci U S A 106:10746–10751
52. Tazawa H, Tsuchiya N, Izumiya M, Nakagama H (2007) Tumor-suppressive miR-34a induces senescence-like growth arrest through modulation of the E2F pathway in human colon cancer cells. Proc Natl Acad Sci U S A 104:15472–15477
53. O'Connell RM, Taganov KD, Boldin MP, Cheng G, Baltimore D (2007) MicroRNA-155 is induced during the macrophage inflammatory response. Proc Natl Acad Sci U S A 104:1604–1609
54. Gironella M, Seux M, Xie MJ, Cano C, Tomasini R et al (2007) Tumor protein 53-induced nuclear protein 1 expression is repressed by miR-155, and its restoration inhibits pancreatic tumor development. Proc Natl Acad Sci U S A 104:16170–16175
55. Gregory PA, Bert AG, Paterson EL, Barry SC, Tsykin A et al (2008) The miR-200 family and miR-205 regulate epithelial to mesenchymal transition by targeting ZEB1 and SIP1. Nat Cell Biol 10:593–601
56. Nguyen HT, Li C, Lin Z, Zhuang Y, Flemington EK et al (2012) The microRNA expression associated with morphogenesis of breast cancer cells in three-dimensional organotypic culture. Oncol Rep 28:117–126
57. Wurdinger T, Tannous BA, Saydam O, Skog J, Grau S et al (2008) miR-296 regulates growth factor receptor overexpression in angiogenic endothelial cells. Cancer Cell 14:382–393
58. Lal A, Pan Y, Navarro F, Dykxhoorn DM, Moreau L et al (2009) miR-24-mediated downregulation of H2AX suppresses DNA repair in terminally differentiated blood cells. Nat Struct Mol Biol 16:492–498
59. Calin GA, Liu CG, Sevignani C, Ferracin M, Felli N et al (2004) MicroRNA profiling reveals distinct signatures in B cell chronic lymphocytic leukemias. Proc Natl Acad Sci U S A 101:11755–11760
60. Chan JA, Krichevsky AM, Kosik KS (2005) MicroRNA-21 is an antiapoptotic factor in human glioblastoma cells. Cancer Res 65:6029–6033
61. Doghman M, El Wakil A, Cardinaud B, Thomas E, Wang J et al (2010) Regulation of insulin-like growth factor-mammalian target of rapamycin signaling by microRNA in childhood adrenocortical tumors. Cancer Res 70:4666–4675
62. Ma L, Teruya-Feldstein J, Weinberg RA (2007) Tumour invasion and metastasis initiated by microRNA-10b in breast cancer. Nature 449:682–688
63. Calin GA, Sevignani C, Dumitru CD, Hyslop T, Noch E et al (2004) Human microRNA genes are frequently located at fragile sites and genomic regions involved in cancers. Proc Natl Acad Sci U S A 101:2999–3004
64. Jazdzewski K, Murray EL, Franssila K, Jarzab B, Schoenberg DR et al (2008) Common SNP in pre-miR-146a decreases mature miR expression and predisposes to papillary thyroid carcinoma. Proc Natl Acad Sci U S A 105:7269–7274
65. Lee YS, Dutta A (2007) The tumor suppressor microRNA let-7 represses the HMGA2 oncogene. Genes Dev 21:1025–1030
66. Mayr C, Hemann MT, Bartel DP (2007) Disrupting the pairing between let-7 and Hmga2 enhances oncogenic transformation. Science 315:1576–1579
67. Chin LJ, Ratner E, Leng S, Zhai R, Nallur S et al (2008) A SNP in a let-7 microRNA complementary site in the KRAS 3′ untranslated region increases non-small cell lung cancer risk. Cancer Res 68:8535–8540
68. Volinia S, Calin GA, Liu CG, Ambs S, Cimmino A et al (2006) A microRNA expression signature of human solid tumors defines cancer gene targets. Proc Natl Acad Sci U S A 103:2257–2261

69. O'Donnell KA, Wentzel EA, Zeller KI, Dang CV, Mendell JT (2005) c-Myc-regulated microRNAs modulate E2F1 expression. Nature 435:839–843
70. Peter ME (2009) Let-7 and miR-200 microRNAs: guardians against pluripotency and cancer progression. Cell Cycle 8:843–852
71. Li C, Nguyen HT, Zhuang Y, Lin Z, Flemington EK et al (2012) Comparative profiling of miRNA expression of lung adenocarcinoma cells in two-dimensional and three-dimensional cultures. Gene 511:143–150
72. Mouw JK, Yui Y, Damiano L, Bainer RO, Lakins JN et al (2014) Tissue mechanics modulate microRNA-dependent PTEN expression to regulate malignant progression. Nat Med 20:360–367
73. Weber JA, Baxter DH, Zhang S, Huang DY, Huang KH et al (2010) The microRNA spectrum in 12 body fluids. Clin Chem 56:1733–1741
74. Taylor DD, Gercel-Taylor C (2008) MicroRNA signatures of tumor-derived exosomes as diagnostic biomarkers of ovarian cancer. Gynecol Oncol 110:13–21
75. Skog J, Wurdinger T, van Rijn S, Meijer DH, Gainche L et al (2008) Glioblastoma microvesicles transport RNA and proteins that promote tumour growth and provide diagnostic biomarkers. Nat Cell Biol 10:1470–1476
76. Ng EK, Chong WW, Jin H, Lam EK, Shin VY et al (2009) Differential expression of microRNAs in plasma of patients with colorectal cancer: a potential marker for colorectal cancer screening. Gut 58:1375–1381
77. Huang Z, Huang D, Ni S, Peng Z, Sheng W et al (2010) Plasma microRNAs are promising novel biomarkers for early detection of colorectal cancer. Int J Cancer 127:118–126
78. Pu XX, Huang GL, Guo HQ, Guo CC, Li H et al (2010) Circulating miR-221 directly amplified from plasma is a potential diagnostic and prognostic marker of colorectal cancer and is correlated with p53 expression. J Gastroenterol Hepatol 25:1674–1680
79. Cheng H, Zhang L, Cogdell DE, Zheng H, Schetter AJ et al (2011) Circulating plasma MiR-141 is a novel biomarker for metastatic colon cancer and predicts poor prognosis. PLoS One 6:e17745
80. Toiyama Y, Takahashi M, Hur K, Nagasaka T, Tanaka K et al (2013) Serum miR-21 as a diagnostic and prognostic biomarker in colorectal cancer. J Natl Cancer Inst 105:849–859
81. Ogata-Kawata H, Izumiya M, Kurioka D, Honma Y, Yamada Y et al (2014) Circulating exosomal microRNAs as biomarkers of colon cancer. PLoS One 9:e92921
82. Lowery AJ, Miller N, Devaney A, McNeill RE, Davoren PA et al (2009) MicroRNA signatures predict oestrogen receptor, progesterone receptor and HER2/neu receptor status in breast cancer. Breast Cancer Res 11:R27
83. Volinia S, Galasso M, Sana ME, Wise TF, Palatini J et al (2012) Breast cancer signatures for invasiveness and prognosis defined by deep sequencing of microRNA. Proc Natl Acad Sci U S A 109:3024–3029
84. Foekens JA, Sieuwerts AM, Smid M, Look MP, de Weerd V et al (2008) Four miRNAs associated with aggressiveness of lymph node-negative, estrogen receptor-positive human breast cancer. Proc Natl Acad Sci U S A 105:13021–13026
85. Rodriguez-Gonzalez FG, Sieuwerts AM, Smid M, Look MP, Meijer-van Gelder ME et al (2011) MicroRNA-30c expression level is an independent predictor of clinical benefit of endocrine therapy in advanced estrogen receptor positive breast cancer. Breast Cancer Res Treat 127:43–51
86. Maillot G, Lacroix-Triki M, Pierredon S, Gratadou L, Schmidt S et al (2009) Widespread estrogen-dependent repression of microRNAs involved in breast tumor cell growth. Cancer Res 69:8332–8340
87. Ichikawa T, Sato F, Terasawa K, Tsuchiya S, Toi M et al (2012) Trastuzumab produces therapeutic actions by upregulating miR-26a and miR-30b in breast cancer cells. PLoS One 7:e31422
88. Ebert MS, Neilson JR, Sharp PA (2007) MicroRNA sponges: competitive inhibitors of small RNAs in mammalian cells. Nat Methods 4:721–726
89. Ma L, Young J, Prabhala H, Pan E, Mestdagh P et al (2010) miR-9, a MYC/MYCN-activated microRNA, regulates E-cadherin and cancer metastasis. Nat Cell Biol 12:247–256
90. Huang S, Chen Y, Wu W, Ouyang N, Chen J et al (2013) miR-150 promotes human breast cancer growth and malignant behavior by targeting the pro-apoptotic purinergic P2X7 receptor. PLoS One 8:e80707
91. Kuss AW, Chen W (2008) MicroRNAs in brain function and disease. Curr Neurol Neurosci Rep 8:190–197
92. Kim J, Inoue K, Ishii J, Vanti WB, Voronov SV et al (2007) A MicroRNA feedback circuit in midbrain dopamine neurons. Science 317:1220–1224
93. Gehrke S, Imai Y, Sokol N, Lu B (2010) Pathogenic LRRK2 negatively regulates microRNA-mediated translational repression. Nature 466:637–641

94. Blennow K, de Leon MJ, Zetterberg H (2006) Alzheimer's disease. Lancet 368:387–403
95. Cogswell JP, Ward J, Taylor IA, Waters M, Shi Y et al (2008) Identification of miRNA changes in Alzheimer's disease brain and CSF yields putative biomarkers and insights into disease pathways. J Alzheimers Dis 14:27–41
96. Maes OC, Chertkow HM, Wang E, Schipper HM (2009) MicroRNA: implications for Alzheimer disease and other human CNS disorders. Curr Genomics 10:154–168
97. Maes OC, Xu S, Yu B, Chertkow HM, Wang E et al (2007) Transcriptional profiling of Alzheimer blood mononuclear cells by microarray. Neurobiol Aging 28:1795–1809
98. Blalock EM, Chen KC, Stromberg AJ, Norris CM, Kadish I et al (2005) Harnessing the power of gene microarrays for the study of brain aging and Alzheimer's disease: statistical reliability and functional correlation. Ageing Res Rev 4:481–512
99. Nunez-Iglesias J, Liu CC, Morgan TE, Finch CE, Zhou XJ (2010) Joint genome-wide profiling of miRNA and mRNA expression in Alzheimer's disease cortex reveals altered miRNA regulation. PLoS One 5:e8898
100. Hebert SS, Horre K, Nicolai L, Papadopoulou AS, Mandemakers W et al (2008) Loss of microRNA cluster miR-29a/b-1 in sporadic Alzheimer's disease correlates with increased BACE1/beta-secretase expression. Proc Natl Acad Sci U S A 105:6415–6420
101. Hebert SS, Horre K, Nicolai L, Bergmans B, Papadopoulou AS et al (2009) MicroRNA regulation of Alzheimer's Amyloid precursor protein expression. Neurobiol Dis 33:422–428
102. Booton R, Lindsay MA (2014) Emerging role of MicroRNAs and long noncoding RNAs in respiratory disease. Chest 146:193–204
103. Williams AE, Moschos SA, Perry MM, Barnes PJ, Lindsay MA (2007) Maternally imprinted microRNAs are differentially expressed during mouse and human lung development. Dev Dyn 236:572–580
104. Harris KS, Zhang Z, McManus MT, Harfe BD, Sun X (2006) Dicer function is essential for lung epithelium morphogenesis. Proc Natl Acad Sci U S A 103:2208–2213
105. Lu Y, Thomson JM, Wong HY, Hammond SM, Hogan BL (2007) Transgenic over-expression of the microRNA miR-17-92 cluster promotes proliferation and inhibits differentiation of lung epithelial progenitor cells. Dev Biol 310:442–453
106. Jardim MJ, Dailey L, Silbajoris R, Diaz-Sanchez D (2012) Distinct microRNA expression in human airway cells of asthmatic donors identifies a novel asthma-associated gene. Am J Respir Cell Mol Biol 47:536–542
107. Solberg OD, Ostrin EJ, Love MI, Peng JC, Bhakta NR et al (2012) Airway epithelial miRNA expression is altered in asthma. Am J Respir Crit Care Med 186:965–974
108. Tsitsiou E, Williams AE, Moschos SA, Patel K, Rossios C et al (2012) Transcriptome analysis shows activation of circulating CD8+ T cells in patients with severe asthma. J Allergy Clin Immunol 129:95–103
109. O'Connell RM, Rao DS, Baltimore D (2012) microRNA regulation of inflammatory responses. Annu Rev Immunol 30:295–312
110. Pandit KV, Corcoran D, Yousef H, Yarlagadda M, Tzouvelekis A et al (2010) Inhibition and role of let-7d in idiopathic pulmonary fibrosis. Am J Respir Crit Care Med 182:220–229
111. Dakhlallah D, Batte K, Wang Y, Cantemir-Stone CZ, Yan P et al (2013) Epigenetic regulation of miR-17~92 contributes to the pathogenesis of pulmonary fibrosis. Am J Respir Crit Care Med 187:397–405
112. Liu G, Friggeri A, Yang Y, Milosevic J, Ding Q et al (2010) miR-21 mediates fibrogenic activation of pulmonary fibroblasts and lung fibrosis. J Exp Med 207:1589–1597
113. Cushing L, Kuang PP, Qian J, Shao F, Wu J et al (2011) miR-29 is a major regulator of genes associated with pulmonary fibrosis. Am J Respir Cell Mol Biol 45:287–294
114. Yang S, Banerjee S, de Freitas A, Sanders YY, Ding Q et al (2012) Participation of miR-200 in pulmonary fibrosis. Am J Pathol 180:484–493
115. Jiang X, Tsitsiou E, Herrick SE, Lindsay MA (2010) MicroRNAs and the regulation of fibrosis. FEBS J 277:2015–2021
116. Ezzie ME, Crawford M, Cho JH, Orellana R, Zhang S et al (2012) Gene expression networks in COPD: microRNA and mRNA regulation. Thorax 67:122–131
117. Sato T, Liu X, Nelson A, Nakanishi M, Kanaji N et al (2010) Reduced miR-146a increases prostaglandin E(2)in chronic obstructive pulmonary disease fibroblasts. Am J Respir Crit Care Med 182:1020–1029
118. Lewis A, Riddoch-Contreras J, Natanek SA, Donaldson A, Man WD et al (2012) Downregulation of the serum response factor/miR-1 axis in the quadriceps of patients with COPD. Thorax 67:26–34

119. Cunningham F, Amode MR, Barrell D, Beal K, Billis K et al (2015) Ensembl 2015. Nucleic Acids Res 43:D662–D669
120. Lanz RB, McKenna NJ, Onate SA, Albrecht U, Wong J et al (1999) A steroid receptor coactivator, SRA, functions as an RNA and is present in an SRC-1 complex. Cell 97:17–27
121. Rinn JL, Chang HY (2012) Genome regulation by long noncoding RNAs. Annu Rev Biochem 81:145–166
122. Shibayama Y, Fanucchi S, Magagula L, Mhlanga MM (2014) lncRNA and gene looping: what's the connection? Transcription 5:e28658
123. Shi X, Sun M, Liu H, Yao Y, Song Y (2013) Long non-coding RNAs: a new frontier in the study of human diseases. Cancer Lett 339:159–166
124. Zong X, Tripathi V, Prasanth KV (2011) RNA splicing control: yet another gene regulatory role for long nuclear noncoding RNAs. RNA Biol 8:968–977
125. Kretz M, Siprashvili Z, Chu C, Webster DE, Zehnder A et al (2013) Control of somatic tissue differentiation by the long non-coding RNA TINCR. Nature 493:231–235
126. Hacisuleyman E, Goff LA, Trapnell C, Williams A, Henao-Mejia J et al (2014) Topological organization of multichromosomal regions by the long intergenic noncoding RNA Firre. Nat Struct Mol Biol 21:198–206
127. Ponting CP, Oliver PL, Reik W (2009) Evolution and functions of long noncoding RNAs. Cell 136:629–641
128. Nagano T, Mitchell JA, Sanz LA, Pauler FM, Ferguson-Smith AC et al (2008) The Air noncoding RNA epigenetically silences transcription by targeting G9a to chromatin. Science 322:1717–1720
129. Rinn JL, Kertesz M, Wang JK, Squazzo SL, Xu X et al (2007) Functional demarcation of active and silent chromatin domains in human HOX loci by noncoding RNAs. Cell 129:1311–1323
130. Pandey RR, Mondal T, Mohammad F, Enroth S, Redrup L et al (2008) Kcnq1ot1 antisense noncoding RNA mediates lineage-specific transcriptional silencing through chromatin-level regulation. Mol Cell 32:232–246
131. Zhao J, Sun BK, Erwin JA, Song JJ, Lee JT (2008) Polycomb proteins targeted by a short repeat RNA to the mouse X chromosome. Science 322:750–756
132. Mohammad F, Mondal T, Guseva N, Pandey GK, Kanduri C (2010) Kcnq1ot1 noncoding RNA mediates transcriptional gene silencing by interacting with Dnmt1. Development 137:2493–2499
133. Wu Y, Zhang L, Wang Y, Li H, Ren X et al (2015) Long non-coding RNA HOTAIR promotes tumor cell invasion and metastasis by recruiting EZH2 and repressing E-cadherin in oral squamous cell carcinoma. Int J Oncol 46:2586–2594
134. Khalil AM, Guttman M, Huarte M, Garber M, Raj A et al (2009) Many human large intergenic noncoding RNAs associate with chromatin-modifying complexes and affect gene expression. Proc Natl Acad Sci U S A 106:11667–11672
135. Zhao J, Ohsumi TK, Kung JT, Ogawa Y, Grau DJ et al (2010) Genome-wide identification of polycomb-associated RNAs by RIP-seq. Mol Cell 40:939–953
136. Brannan CI, Dees EC, Ingram RS, Tilghman SM (1990) The product of the H19 gene may function as an RNA. Mol Cell Biol 10:28–36
137. Brown CJ, Ballabio A, Rupert JL, Lafreniere RG, Grompe M et al (1991) A gene from the region of the human X inactivation centre is expressed exclusively from the inactive X chromosome. Nature 349:38–44
138. Simon MD, Pinter SF, Fang R, Sarma K, Rutenberg-Schoenberg M et al (2013) High-resolution Xist binding maps reveal two-step spreading during X-chromosome inactivation. Nature 504:465–469
139. Chu C, Qu K, Zhong FL, Artandi SE, Chang HY (2011) Genomic maps of long noncoding RNA occupancy reveal principles of RNA-chromatin interactions. Mol Cell 44:667–678
140. Arab K, Park YJ, Lindroth AM, Schafer A, Oakes C et al (2014) Long noncoding RNA TARID directs demethylation and activation of the tumor suppressor TCF21 via GADD45A. Mol Cell 55(4):604–614
141. Tripathi V, Ellis JD, Shen Z, Song DY, Pan Q et al (2010) The nuclear-retained noncoding RNA MALAT1 regulates alternative splicing by modulating SR splicing factor phosphorylation. Mol Cell 39:925–938
142. Bernard D, Prasanth KV, Tripathi V, Colasse S, Nakamura T et al (2010) A long nuclear-retained non-coding RNA regulates synaptogenesis by modulating gene expression. EMBO J 29:3082–3093
143. Gong C, Maquat LE (2011) lncRNAs transactivate STAU1-mediated mRNA decay by duplexing with 3′ UTRs via Alu elements. Nature 470:284–288

144. Yoon JH, Abdelmohsen K, Srikantan S, Yang X, Martindale JL et al (2012) LincRNA-p21 suppresses target mRNA translation. Mol Cell 47:648–655
145. Carrieri C, Cimatti L, Biagioli M, Beugnet A, Zucchelli S et al (2012) Long non-coding antisense RNA controls Uchl1 translation through an embedded SINEB2 repeat. Nature 491:454–457
146. Zappulla DC, Cech TR (2006) RNA as a flexible scaffold for proteins: yeast telomerase and beyond. Cold Spring Harb Symp Quant Biol 71:217–224
147. Koziol MJ, Rinn JL (2010) RNA traffic control of chromatin complexes. Curr Opin Genet Dev 20:142–148
148. Tsai MC, Manor O, Wan Y, Mosammaparast N, Wang JK et al (2010) Long noncoding RNA as modular scaffold of histone modification complexes. Science 329:689–693
149. Faghihi MA, Modarresi F, Khalil AM, Wood DE, Sahagan BG et al (2008) Expression of a noncoding RNA is elevated in Alzheimer's disease and drives rapid feed-forward regulation of beta-secretase. Nat Med 14:723–730
150. Carrieri C, Forrest AR, Santoro C, Persichetti F, Carninci P et al (2015) Expression analysis of the long non-coding RNA antisense to Uchl1 (AS Uchl1) during dopaminergic cells' differentiation in vitro and in neurochemical models of Parkinson's disease. Front Cell Neurosci 9:114
151. Ishii N, Ozaki K, Sato H, Mizuno H, Saito S et al (2006) Identification of a novel non-coding RNA, MIAT, that confers risk of myocardial infarction. J Hum Genet 51:1087–1099
152. Pasmant E, Laurendeau I, Heron D, Vidaud M, Vidaud D et al (2007) Characterization of a germ-line deletion, including the entire INK4/ARF locus, in a melanoma-neural system tumor family: identification of ANRIL, an antisense noncoding RNA whose expression coclusters with ARF. Cancer Res 67:3963–3969
153. Daughters RS, Tuttle DL, Gao W, Ikeda Y, Moseley ML et al (2009) RNA gain-of-function in spinocerebellar ataxia type 8. PLoS Genet 5:e1000600
154. Khalil AM, Faghihi MA, Modarresi F, Brothers SP, Wahlestedt C (2008) A novel RNA transcript with antiapoptotic function is silenced in fragile X syndrome. PLoS One 3:e1486
155. Prensner JR, Chinnaiyan AM (2011) The emergence of lncRNAs in cancer biology. Cancer Discov 1:391–407
156. Naemura M, Murasaki C, Inoue Y, Okamoto H, Kotake Y (2015) Long noncoding RNA ANRIL regulates proliferation of non-small cell lung cancer and cervical cancer cells. Anticancer Res 35:5377–5382
157. Cai Y, He J, Zhang D (2015) Long noncoding RNA CCAT2 promotes breast tumor growth by regulating the Wnt signaling pathway. Onco Targets Ther 8:2657–2664
158. Zhuang Y, Nguyen HT, Burow ME, Zhuo Y, El-Dahr SS et al (2014) Elevated expression of long intergenic non-coding RNA HOTAIR in a basal-like variant of MCF-7 breast cancer cells. Mol Carcinog. 54(12):1656–1667
159. Gupta RA, Shah N, Wang KC, Kim J, Horlings HM et al (2010) Long non-coding RNA HOTAIR reprograms chromatin state to promote cancer metastasis. Nature 464:1071–1076
160. Kogo R, Shimamura T, Mimori K, Kawahara K, Imoto S et al (2011) Long noncoding RNA HOTAIR regulates polycomb-dependent chromatin modification and is associated with poor prognosis in colorectal cancers. Cancer Res 71:6320–6326
161. Chung S, Nakagawa H, Uemura M, Piao L, Ashikawa K et al (2011) Association of a novel long non-coding RNA in 8q24 with prostate cancer susceptibility. Cancer Sci 102:245–252
162. Calin GA, Pekarsky Y, Croce CM (2007) The role of microRNA and other non-coding RNA in the pathogenesis of chronic lymphocytic leukemia. Best Pract Res Clin Haematol 20:425–437
163. Calin GA, Liu CG, Ferracin M, Hyslop T, Spizzo R et al (2007) Ultraconserved regions encoding ncRNAs are altered in human leukemias and carcinomas. Cancer Cell 12:215–229
164. Khaitan D, Dinger ME, Mazar J, Crawford J, Smith MA et al (2011) The melanoma-upregulated long noncoding RNA SPRY4-IT1 modulates apoptosis and invasion. Cancer Res 71:3852–3862
165. Li L, Feng T, Lian Y, Zhang G, Garen A et al (2009) Role of human noncoding RNAs in the control of tumorigenesis. Proc Natl Acad Sci U S A 106:12956–12961
166. Huarte M, Guttman M, Feldser D, Garber M, Koziol MJ et al (2010) A large intergenic noncoding RNA induced by p53 mediates global gene repression in the p53 response. Cell 142:409–419
167. Yu W, Gius D, Onyango P, Muldoon-Jacobs K, Karp J et al (2008) Epigenetic silencing of tumour suppressor gene p15 by its antisense RNA. Nature 451:202–206

168. Gutschner T, Hammerle M, Eissmann M, Hsu J, Kim Y et al (2013) The noncoding RNA MALAT1 is a critical regulator of the metastasis phenotype of lung cancer cells. Cancer Res 73:1180–1189
169. Tano K, Mizuno R, Okada T, Rakwal R, Shibato J et al (2010) MALAT-1 enhances cell motility of lung adenocarcinoma cells by influencing the expression of motility-related genes. FEBS Lett 584:4575–4580
170. Lopez-Ayllon BD, Moncho-Amor V, Abarrategi A, Ibanez de Caceres I, Castro-Carpeno J et al (2014) Cancer stem cells and cisplatin-resistant cells isolated from non-small-lung cancer cell lines constitute related cell populations. Cancer Med 3:1099–1111
171. Weber DG, Johnen G, Casjens S, Bryk O, Pesch B et al (2013) Evaluation of long non-coding RNA MALAT1 as a candidate blood-based biomarker for the diagnosis of non-small cell lung cancer. BMC Res Notes 6:518
172. Yao Y, Fan Y, Wu J, Wan H, Wang J et al (2012) Potential application of non-small cell lung cancer-associated autoantibodies to early cancer diagnosis. Biochem Biophys Res Commun 423:613–619
173. Guffanti A, Iacono M, Pelucchi P, Kim N, Solda G et al (2009) A transcriptional sketch of a primary human breast cancer by 454 deep sequencing. BMC Genomics 10:163
174. Kan JY, Wu DC, Yu FJ, Wu CY, Ho YW et al (2015) Chemokine (C-C motif) ligand 5 is involved in tumor-associated dendritic cell-mediated colon cancer progression through non-coding RNA MALAT-1. J Cell Physiol 230:1883–1894
175. Fan Y, Shen B, Tan M, Mu X, Qin Y et al (2014) TGF beta induced upregulation of malat1 promotes bladder cancer metastasis by associating with suz12. Clin Cancer Res 20:1531–1541
176. Okugawa Y, Toiyama Y, Hur K, Toden S, Saigusa S et al (2014) Metastasis-associated long non-coding RNA drives gastric cancer development and promotes peritoneal metastasis. Carcinogenesis 35:2731–2739
177. Hu L, Wu Y, Tan D, Meng H, Wang K et al (2015) Up-regulation of long noncoding RNA MALAT1 contributes to proliferation and metastasis in esophageal squamous cell carcinoma. J Exp Clin Cancer Res 34:7
178. Kuo IY, Wu CC, Chang JM, Huang YL, Lin CH et al (2014) Low SOX17 expression is a prognostic factor and drives transcriptional dysregulation and esophageal cancer progression. Int J Cancer 135:563–573
179. Wang X, Li M, Wang Z, Han S, Tang X et al (2015) Silencing of long noncoding RNA MALAT1 by miR-101 and miR-217 inhibits proliferation, migration, and invasion of esophageal squamous cell carcinoma cells. J Biol Chem 290:3925–3935
180. Mohamadkhani A (2014) Long noncoding RNAs in interaction with RNA binding proteins in hepatocellular carcinoma. Hepat Mon 14:e18794
181. Liu SP, Yang JX, Cao DY, Shen K (2013) Identification of differentially expressed long non-coding RNAs in human ovarian cancer cells with different metastatic potentials. Cancer Biol Med 10:138–141
182. Ren S, Liu Y, Xu W, Sun Y, Lu J et al (2013) Long noncoding RNA MALAT-1 is a new potential therapeutic target for castration resistant prostate cancer. J Urol 190:2278–2287
183. Sowalsky AG, Xia Z, Wang L, Zhao H, Chen S et al (2015) Whole transcriptome sequencing reveals extensive unspliced mRNA in metastatic castration-resistant prostate cancer. Mol Cancer Res 13:98–106
184. Wang F, Ren S, Chen R, Lu J, Shi X et al (2014) Development and prospective multicenter evaluation of the long noncoding RNA MALAT-1 as a diagnostic urinary biomarker for prostate cancer. Oncotarget 5:11091–11102
185. Ellis MJ, Ding L, Shen D, Luo J, Suman VJ et al (2012) Whole-genome analysis informs breast cancer response to aromatase inhibition. Nature 486:353–360
186. Ji Q, Zhang L, Liu X, Zhou L, Wang W et al (2014) Long non-coding RNA MALAT1 promotes tumour growth and metastasis in colorectal cancer through binding to SFPQ and releasing oncogene PTBP2 from SFPQ/PTBP2 complex. Br J Cancer 111:736–748
187. Xu C, Yang M, Tian J, Wang X, Li Z (2011) MALAT-1: a long non-coding RNA and its important 3′ end functional motif in colorectal cancer metastasis. Int J Oncol 39:169–175
188. Lin R, Roychowdhury-Saha M, Black C, Watt AT, Marcusson EG et al (2011) Control of RNA processing by a large non-coding RNA over-expressed in carcinomas. FEBS Lett 585:671–676
189. Yang L, Lin C, Liu W, Zhang J, Ohgi KA et al (2011) ncRNA- and Pc2 methylation-dependent gene relocation between nuclear structures mediates gene activation programs. Cell 147:773–788

190. Loewen G, Jayawickramarajah J, Zhuo Y, Shan B (2014) Functions of lncRNA HOTAIR in lung cancer. J Hematol Oncol 7:90
191. Loewen G, Zhuo Y, Zhuang Y, Jayawickramarajah J, Shan B (2014) lincRNA HOTAIR as a novel promoter of cancer progression. J Can Res Updates 3:7
192. Zhuang Y, Wang X, Nguyen HT, Zhuo Y, Cui X et al (2013) Induction of long intergenic non-coding RNA HOTAIR in lung cancer cells by type I collagen. J Hematol Oncol 6:35
193. Svoboda M, Slyskova J, Schneiderova M, Makovicky P, Bielik L et al (2014) HOTAIR long non-coding RNA is a negative prognostic factor not only in primary tumors, but also in the blood of colorectal cancer patients. Carcinogenesis 35:1510–1515
194. Chiyomaru T, Yamamura S, Fukuhara S, Yoshino H, Kinoshita T et al (2013) Genistein inhibits prostate cancer cell growth by targeting miR-34a and oncogenic HOTAIR. PLoS One 8:e70372
195. Xue X, Yang YA, Zhang A, Fong KW, Kim J et al (2016) LncRNA HOTAIR enhances ER signaling and confers tamoxifen resistance in breast cancer. Oncogene 35(21):2746–2755
196. Mourtada-Maarabouni M, Pickard MR, Hedge VL, Farzaneh F, Williams GT (2009) GAS5, a non-protein-coding RNA, controls apoptosis and is downregulated in breast cancer. Oncogene 28:195–208
197. Dimitrova N, Zamudio JR, Jong RM, Soukup D, Resnick R et al (2014) LincRNA-p21 activates p21 in cis to promote Polycomb target gene expression and to enforce the G1/S checkpoint. Mol Cell 54:777–790
198. Cai B, Wu Z, Liao K, Zhang S (2014) Long noncoding RNA HOTAIR can serve as a common molecular marker for lymph node metastasis: a meta-analysis. Tumour Biol 35(9):8445–8450
199. Zheng HT, Shi DB, Wang YW, Li XX, Xu Y et al (2014) High expression of lncRNA MALAT1 suggests a biomarker of poor prognosis in colorectal cancer. Int J Clin Exp Pathol 7:3174–3181
200. de Kok JB, Verhaegh GW, Roelofs RW, Hessels D, Kiemeney LA et al (2002) DD3(PCA3), a very sensitive and specific marker to detect prostate tumors. Cancer Res 62:2695–2698
201. Bussemakers MJ, van Bokhoven A, Verhaegh GW, Smit FP, Karthaus HF et al (1999) DD3: a new prostate-specific gene, highly overexpressed in prostate cancer. Cancer Res 59:5975–5979
202. Nilsson J, Skog J, Nordstrand A, Baranov V, Mincheva-Nilsson L et al (2009) Prostate cancer-derived urine exosomes: a novel approach to biomarkers for prostate cancer. Br J Cancer 100:1603–1607
203. Kogure T, Yan IK, Lin WL, Patel T (2013) Extracellular vesicle-mediated transfer of a novel long noncoding RNA TUC339: a mechanism of intercellular signaling in human hepatocellular cancer. Genes Cancer 4:261–272
204. Zhuang Y, Nguyen HT, Burow ME, Zhuo Y, El-Dahr SS et al (2015) Elevated expression of long intergenic non-coding RNA HOTAIR in a basal-like variant of MCF-7 breast cancer cells. Mol Carcinog 54:1656–1667
205. Pedram Fatemi R, Salah-Uddin S, Modarresi F, Khoury N, Wahlestedt C et al (2015) Screening for small-molecule modulators of long noncoding RNA-protein interactions using AlphaScreen. J Biomol Screen 20:1132–1141
206. Ng SY, Lin L, Soh BS, Stanton LW (2013) Long noncoding RNAs in development and disease of the central nervous system. Trends Genet 29:461–468
207. Ng SY, Johnson R, Stanton LW (2012) Human long non-coding RNAs promote pluripotency and neuronal differentiation by association with chromatin modifiers and transcription factors. EMBO J 31:522–533
208. Modarresi F, Faghihi MA, Patel NS, Sahagan BG, Wahlestedt C et al (2011) Knockdown of BACE1-AS Nonprotein-coding transcript modulates beta-amyloid-related hippocampal neurogenesis. Int J Alzheimers Dis 2011:929042
209. Muddashetty R, Khanam T, Kondrashov A, Bundman M, Iacoangeli A et al (2002) Poly(A)-binding protein is associated with neuronal BC1 and BC200 ribonucleoprotein particles. J Mol Biol 321:433–445
210. Mus E, Hof PR, Tiedge H (2007) Dendritic BC200 RNA in aging and in Alzheimer's disease. Proc Natl Acad Sci U S A 104:10679–10684
211. Morais VA, Verstreken P, Roethig A, Smet J, Snellinx A et al (2009) Parkinson's disease mutations in PINK1 result in decreased Complex I activity and deficient synaptic function. EMBO Mol Med 1:99–111
212. Scheele C, Petrovic N, Faghihi MA, Lassmann T, Fredriksson K et al (2007) The human PINK1 locus is regulated in vivo by a non-coding natural antisense RNA during modulation of mitochondrial function. BMC Genomics 8:74

213. Herriges MJ, Swarr DT, Morley MP, Rathi KS, Peng T et al (2014) Long noncoding RNAs are spatially correlated with transcription factors and regulate lung development. Genes Dev 28:1363–1379
214. Szafranski P, Dharmadhikari AV, Brosens E, Gurha P, Kolodziejska KE et al (2013) Small noncoding differentially methylated copy-number variants, including lncRNA genes, cause a lethal lung developmental disorder. Genome Res 23:23–33
215. Michalik KM, You X, Manavski Y, Doddaballapur A, Zornig M et al (2014) Long noncoding RNA MALAT1 regulates endothelial cell function and vessel growth. Circ Res 114:1389–1397
216. Yoon JH, Abdelmohsen K, Gorospe M (2014) Functional interactions among microRNAs and long noncoding RNAs. Semin Cell Dev Biol 34C:9–14
217. de Giorgio A, Krell J, Harding V, Stebbing J, Castellano L (2013) Emerging roles of competing endogenous RNAs in cancer: insights from the regulation of PTEN. Mol Cell Biol 33:3976–3982
218. Wang Y, Xu Z, Jiang J, Xu C, Kang J et al (2013) Endogenous miRNA sponge lincRNA-RoR regulates Oct4, Nanog, and Sox2 in human embryonic stem cell self-renewal. Dev Cell 25:69–80
219. Liu XH, Sun M, Nie FQ, Ge YB, Zhang EB et al (2014) Lnc RNA HOTAIR functions as a competing endogenous RNA to regulate HER2 expression by sponging miR-331-3p in gastric cancer. Mol Cancer 13:92
220. Ma MZ, Li CX, Zhang Y, Weng MZ, Zhang MD et al (2014) Long non-coding RNA HOTAIR, a c-Myc activated driver of malignancy, negatively regulates miRNA-130a in gallbladder cancer. Mol Cancer 13:156
221. Zhou X, Ye F, Yin C, Zhuang Y, Yue G et al (2015) The interaction between MiR-141 and lncRNA-H19 in regulating cell proliferation and migration in gastric cancer. Cell Physiol Biochem 36:1440–1452
222. Kallen AN, Zhou XB, Xu J, Qiao C, Ma J et al (2013) The imprinted H19 lncRNA antagonizes let-7 microRNAs. Mol Cell 52:101–112
223. Cesana M, Cacchiarelli D, Legnini I, Santini T, Sthandier O et al (2011) A long noncoding RNA controls muscle differentiation by functioning as a competing endogenous RNA. Cell 147:358–369
224. Jeck WR, Sharpless NE (2014) Detecting and characterizing circular RNAs. Nat Biotechnol 32:453–461
225. Hansen TB, Jensen TI, Clausen BH, Bramsen JB, Finsen B et al (2013) Natural RNA circles function as efficient microRNA sponges. Nature 495:384–388

Chapter 2

MicroRNA Expression: Protein Participants in MicroRNA Regulation

Valeria M. King and Glen M. Borchert

Abstract

MiRNAs are ~20 nt small RNAs that regulate networks of proteins using a seed region of nucleotides 2–8 to complement the 3′ UTR of target mRNAs. The biogenesis and function of miRNAs as translational repressors is facilitated by protein counterparts that process primary and precursor miRNAs to maturity (Drosha/DCGR8 and Dicer/TRBP respectively) and incorporate miRNAs into the protein complex RISC to recognize and repress target mRNAs (RISC proteins: Ago/TRBP1/TRBP2/DICER). Similarly, siRNAs through comparable mechanisms are loaded into the protein complex RITS to heterochromatin formation of DNA and suppress transcription of particular genes. MiRNAs are also regulated themselves through many different pathways including transcriptional regulation, post-transcriptional RNA editing, and RNA tailing. Dysregulation of miRNAs and the protein participants that mature them are implicated in the development of a number of diseases, tumorigenesis, and arrested development of embryonic cells. In this chapter, we will explore the biosynthesis, function, and regulation of miRNAs.

Key words Dicer, Drosha, miRNA, mRNA, Protein, RISC, Regulation

1 MicroRNA Production and Activity

MicroRNAs are small noncoding RNAs around 22 nucleotides in length that are involved in the regulation of mRNAs in the cytoplasm via inducing translational repression or message degradation [1]. MiRNAs constitute a broad regulatory network with one miRNA potentially regulating dozens of distinct mRNAs. These regulatory networks control levels of specific proteins and other RNAs like long noncoding RNAs (lncRNAs) in cells. MiRNA misregulation is implicated in cancer, a myriad of other illnesses, and abnormal development [2–4]. The first miRNA was described in 1993 and was initially thought to be a novel molecular species unique to *Caenorhabditis elegans* [5]. In 2001, however, nearly 10 years after their initial discovery, miRNAs were found to occur in several different species including humans [6]. Since that time, novel miRNA discovery has proceeded at a marked rate, and by

Jingshan Huang et al. (eds.), *Bioinformatics in MicroRNA Research*, Methods in Molecular Biology, vol. 1617,
DOI 10.1007/978-1-4939-7046-9_2,

2015, MiRBase.org [7] has detailed significant evidence supporting the expressions of over 2500 unique human miRNAs and well over 28,000 unique miRNAs across species.

1.1 MiRNA Processing

MiRNAs are transcribed from the genome by RNA Polymerase II (Pol II) or Pol III [1]. Transcription results in an initial transcript (called a primary miRNA or pri-miRNA) of variable length containing an unprocessed hairpin [8]. The pri-miRNA is next processed by a ribonuclease protein complex including DROSHA, which targets and cleaves the flanking ends of the hairpin, and DCGR8 that stabilizes the complex on the pri-miRNA. DROSHA processing yields an ~70–100 nt long stem loop called a precursor miRNA or pre-miRNA [9].

Following excision, the pre-miRNA stem loop is transported out of the nucleus and into the cytoplasm via the transport protein exportin-5 using an active transport mechanism with GTP. Once in the cytoplasm, the pre-miRNA is targeted by another ribonuclease, DICER, which cleaves the molecule further by removing the loop portion of the hairpin and leaving an intermediate duplex which consists of the mature miRNA and a semi-complementary sequence referred to as the passenger strand. The intermediate duplex, which is ~22 base pairs in length, is then loaded into an Argonaute (Ago) protein, and the passenger strand discarded [1] (*see* Fig. 1).

1.2 Genomic Loci

MiRNAs can be separated into two broad categories depending on their position in the genome: canonical and noncanonical [1]. Canonical miRNAs are those that are found in intergenic regions and are cleaved by Drosha/DCGR1 to form the precursor miRNA (pre-miRNA) [1, 2]. Noncanonical miRNAs are mitrons or pre-miRNAs that are cleaved from intron sequences using splicing instead of Drosha.

While the evolutionary origin of miRNAs is still largely unknown, significant evidence suggests that miRNAs and their regulatory networks arose from the insertion of transposable elements in the genome [10]. Importantly, the ability of miRNAs to regulate multiple distinct genes may have directly arisen as a consequence of transposons inserting themselves into the UTRs of protein coding genes. Since miRNAs target mRNAs through sequence complementarity, the ability of a miRNA to identify and target a specific mRNA may well be due to a common molecular origin shared by a miRNA locus and its mRNA target sites [10–12] (*see* Fig. 2).

1.3 Translational Repression and Signal Degradation

The mature miRNA in conjunction with the Ago protein is called an RNA-induced silencing complex or RISC. MiRNAs function as protein level regulators by binding target mRNAs and inducing transcriptional repression and in some instances complete signal

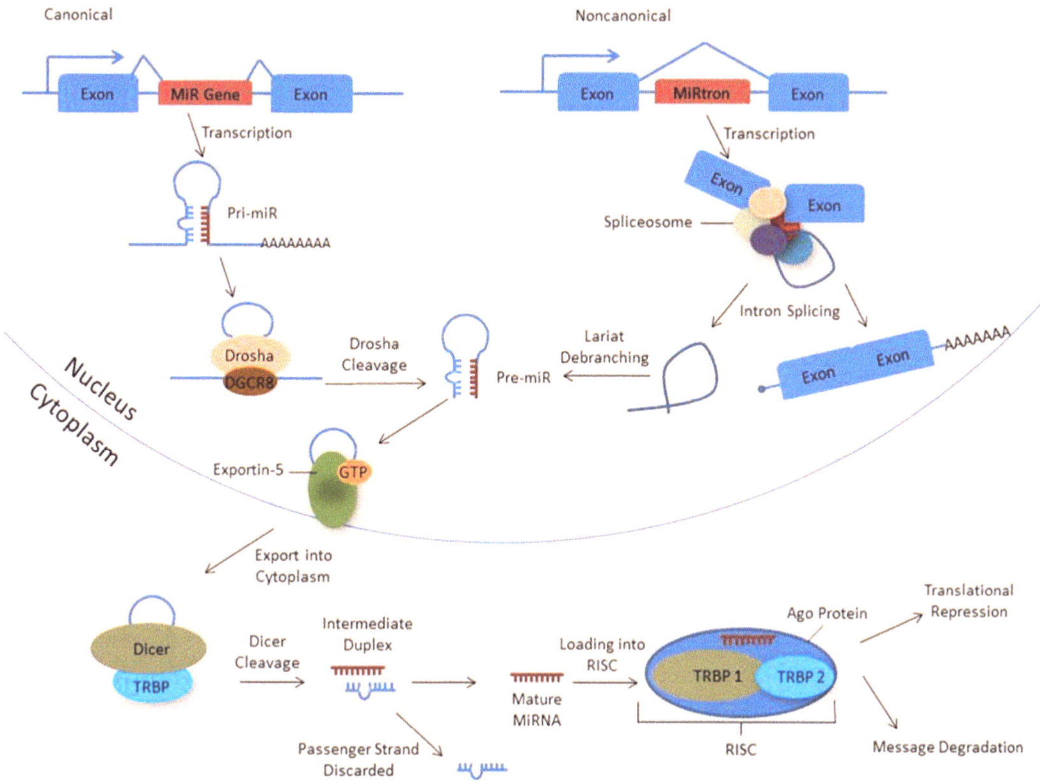

Fig. 1 Canonical and noncanonical miRNA maturation pathways. Cartoon illustrating the transcription of a canonical miRNA, Drosha/DGCR8 processing of the primary hairpin, and the export of the resulting hairpin to the cytoplasm mediated by exportin-5 and GTP. Once in the cytoplasm, the hairpin is recognized and bound by DICER which cleaves the loop off of the stem loop and leaves a double-stranded intermediate duplex. The mature strand bound to the passenger strand is then loaded into an Ago protein complex called RISC. RISC transports the miRNA to a prospective mRNA target which the miRNA recognizes and binds. Once the RISC complex is bound to an mRNA, translation of the mRNA cannot occur and is repressed

degradation. Included in a mature miRNA is a ~7 nt sequence (nts 2–8) called the miRNA seed that perfectly complements a specific region of a mRNA called a seed match usually found in the 3′ UTR. A miRNA seed binds a corresponding seed match in a mRNA, and RISC inhibits its translation. RISC localizes mRNAs that are under transcriptional repression to p-bodies where the mRNA is eventually degraded or released back into the cytoplasm for translation [4]. If the seed is highly complementary to the seed match, the Ago2 protein associated in RISC cleaves the mRNA and results in signal degradation (*see* Fig. 3).

1.4 RISC

The regulation of mRNAs by miRNAs is accomplished by the RNA-induced silencing complex, or RISC. RISC consists of several different proteins, is between 200 and 500 kDa and exhibits

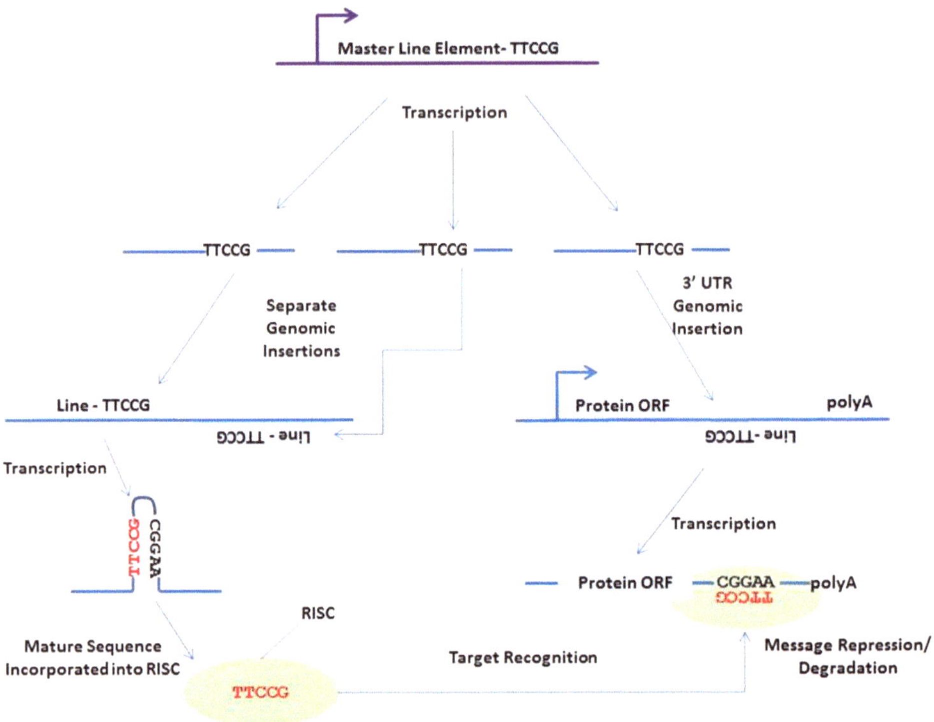

Fig. 2 MiRNA regulatory networks arising from transposable elements. Cartoon depicting transposable line elements being transcribed and inserted into the genome in multiple locations including in the untranslated region of a protein-coding gene. To produce a miRNA hairpin, two line elements are inserted in the genome juxtaposed to each other on different strands. MiRNAs are able to recognize target mRNA seed matches because they each share part of a line element sequence

ribonuclease activity [13]. MRNAs are incorporated into the RISC complex when targeted by miRNAs. AGO proteins in RISC cleave mRNAs that are highly complementary to the incorporated miRNA, whereas mRNAs that are mostly imperfectly bound to the miRNA are silenced by translation inhibition. The best described protein subunits of RISC are the RNases Dicer, Ago 1 and 2. Ago 1 and 2 serve as the central components of RISC and are responsible for translational repression and cleavage/degradation [14]. Also included in RISC are TAR RNA binding proteins, or TARBPs, which comes in two isoforms, TARBP1 and 2. TARBP proteins contain domains that bind double-stranded RNA [15]. TARBP1 functions as a methyltransferase that recruits an Ago protein into RISC [16]. Additionally, TARBP2 loads the miRNA into RISC and exhibits a double-stranded RNA (dsRNA) binding site, which holds the miRNA inside RISC [17, 18].

In addition to loading RNAs into RISC, TRBPs also stabilize Dicer during pre-miRNA processing. After an incorporated miRNA binds to an mRNA, the Ago protein either cleaves the mRNA for degradation, which is usually associated with Ago 2, or the protein

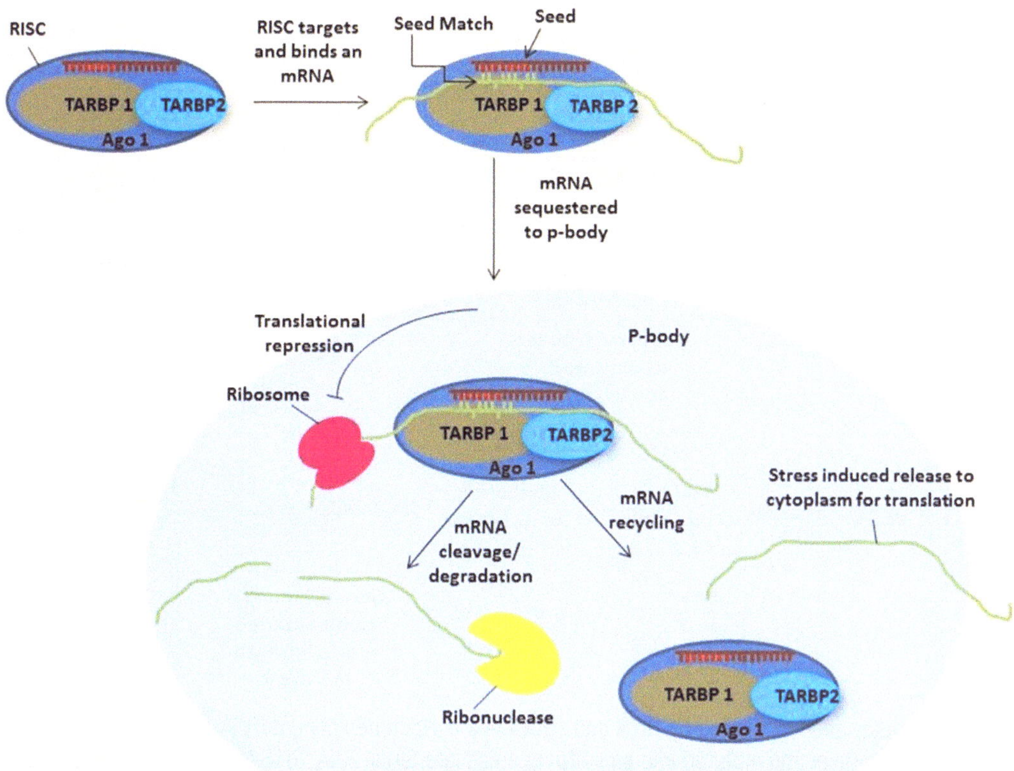

Fig. 3 Translational regulation through seed matching. Cartoon showing the seed region of a mature miRNA incorporated into RISC recognizing and binding to the seed match region of an mRNA. RISC takes the mRNA to the p-body region where it represses translation or cleaves the mRNA for degradation

in conjunction with RISC prevents translation from occurring until the message is degraded or the message is released by RISC through stress-induced pathways and is recycled [19] (*see* Fig. 3).

1.5 SiRNAs and RITS

SiRNAs, or small interfering RNAs, are noncoding RNAs with comparable size and function to miRNAs. SiRNAs differ from miRNAs in several aspects including the pathways from transcription to maturity, and in that while miRNAs generally regulate mRNA networks, siRNAs typically regulate a specific target gene [17]. RITS, or RNA-induced initiation of transcriptional silencing, is a complex of proteins in conjunction with a mature siRNA that inhibits the transcription of specific genes by triggering heterochromatin assembly in centromeric regions.

SiRNA and RITS complexes have been experimentally characterized in fission yeast. In fission yeast the RITS complex consists of Ago1; Chp1, which is a hetero-chromatin-associated protein; and Tas3, a novel protein that is necessary for H3-K9 methylation [20]. This protein complex, in conjunction with a mature siRNA, targets specific regions of DNA and silences them using methylation and heterochromatin biogenesis [21]. Upon being loaded

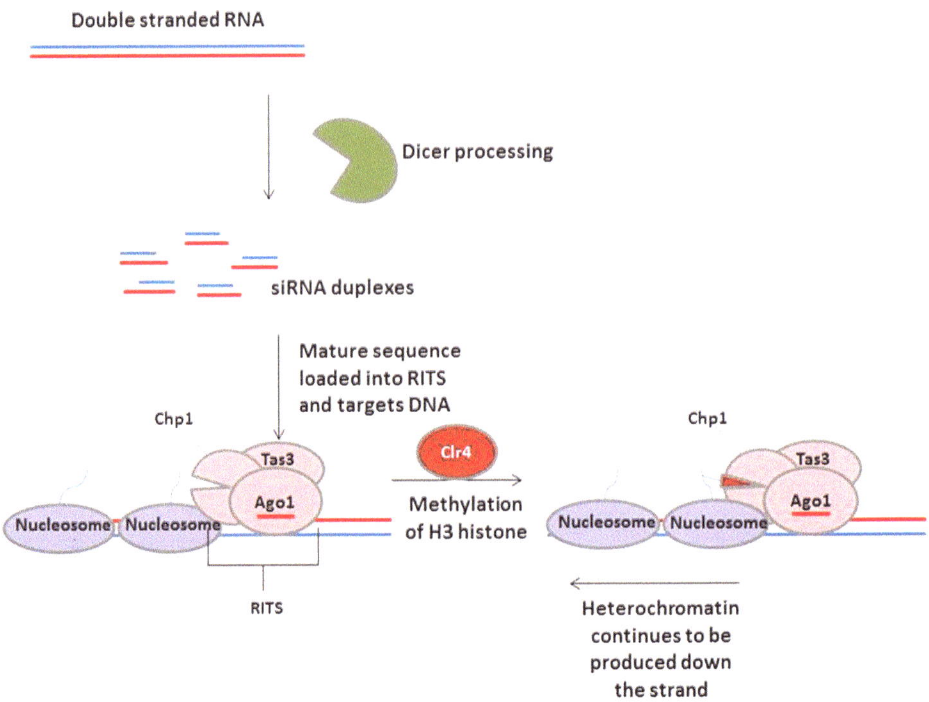

Fig. 4 DNA methylation facilitated by RITS and siRNA is a cartoon depicting dsRNA or double-stranded RNA being cleaved by Dicer and matured into an siRNA or small interfering RNA. RITS is composed of at least three protein components including Ago1, Chp1, and Tas3. The RITS protein complex, in conjunction with the siRNA, binds to a centromeric region of DNA specified by the siRNA and enables methylation of the H3 histone by Clr4, an H3 methyltransferase

into Ago1, a siRNA will bind a complementary centromeric region of DNA in complex with the RITS proteins. Then K9 methylation of the H3 histone is initiated by Clr4 protein, a histone H3 methyltransferase [22]. In response to this methylation, targeted DNA coils tightly around its associated histones thereby preventing transcription of the region (*see* Fig. 4).

2 MiRNA Regulation

Importantly, miRNAs are themselves regulated through several different mechanisms such as transcriptional regulations, single nucleotide polymorphisms (SNPs), RNA editing, miRNA tailing, and miRNA degradation [23]. MiRNA regulation can alter miRNA expressions and protein targets, affect miRNA dosing and miRNA proliferation, and induce miRNA degradation.

2.1 Regulation of MicroRNA Transcription

Transcriptional regulation of miRNAs is perhaps the most well-understood mechanism by which to regulate miRNA biogenesis [24]. MiRNA locus methylation is the untemplated addition of methyl groups to a region of DNA in order to encourage tight heterochromatin folding of DNA that prevents transcription. MiRNAs can be down regulated when regions in the DNA that code for the miRNA and regions that allow the miRNA to be transcribed such as a promoter or transcription factor are silenced by gene inaccessibility [25]. Hypomethylation plays a role in up-regulated levels of miRNAs in the cell.

Regions that are normally inaccessible to transcription can be "opened up" by mechanisms that are as yet not fully understood. Hepatocellular carcinoma (HCC) is associated with the dysregulation of miRNAs by hypermethylating regions of the DNA which include tumor-suppressing miRNAs and hypomethylating regions that are normally constitutively transcribed and causes the up-regulation of miRNAs that can promote tumor growth [26].

Additionally, transcription can also be affected by levels of particular proteins (typically transcription factors) in the cell. For instance, mir-145 has been shown to produce an apoptotic effect in cells following an activation of TP53, a tumor suppressor. The production of TP53 also stimulates the transcription of miRNA-145 creating an apoptosis-promoting loop. Conversely, miRNA-145 under-expression is observed in a variety of cancers including breast, colon, and lung cancers [27].

Further, transcriptional regulation of miRNAs has been shown to play a major role in embryonic stem cell (ES cell) differentiation [28]. Four transcription factors have been implicated in regulating miRNA levels in the cell to induce differentiation in mice: Oct4, Sox2, Nanog, and Tcf3. Using CHIP-seq data and intensive miRNA promoter mapping, Marson et al. were able to show that the transcription factors bind to promoter regions that are responsible for the transcription of at least 81 miRNA genes and inhibit particular miRNAs from being transcribed [29]. This process results in the shift of ES cells from pluripotency to specificity [30]. The transcription factors bind to the promoter regions of miRNA genes and prevent the gene from being polymerized which in turn results in increased expression of proteins that the targeted miRNA regulates.

2.2 Single Nucleotide Polymorphisms

Single nucleotide polymorphisms or SNPs are areas in the genome where a single nucleotide can differ between individuals due to typically benign mutations in the DNA sequence [31]. That said, SNPs can drastically alter miRNA activity in the cell. A SNP in the seed sequence of a miRNA can significantly alter its targets and allow a certain protein to go uninhibited while another protein becomes more stringently regulated. This can cause issues when oncogenes, for example, are no longer being targeted to be a particular miRNA, or if tumor suppressor proteins are severely repressed following the introduction of an SNP in a miRNA that does not normally regulate the tumor suppressor gene [23]. SNPs can also lead to miRNA regulation when it is not localized in the seed region. SNPs in the passenger strand or pri-miRNA stem loop can interfere with Drosha and DICER processing and inhibit the production of a mature miRNA [32].

2.3 RNA Editing

MiRNAs can also be regulated through RNA editing. A protein called ADAR1 can convert adenosine molecules into inosines that preferentially form base pairs with cytosines [33]. RNA editing may affect pri-miRNAs, pre-miRNAs, and mature miRNA sequences, and like SNPs, these edits can alter gene targets or decrease the affinity for Drosha or DICER affecting miRNA processing [34].

Importantly, it is estimated that 16% of human pri-miRNAs are edited by ADAR1 [23], suggesting that ADAR editing may well provide a largely underappreciated layer of complexity in miRNA biogenesis. Although miRNA editing can allow the production of several unique miRNAs with differing targets to be produced from a single genomic locus, the effects of miRNA editing remain largely unexplored.

2.4 MiRNA Tailing

RNA tailing is the post-transcriptional addition of nucleotides to the 3′ end of RNA. Uridylation mainly occurs in pre- and pri-miRNAs. For example, during embryonic stages, members of the let-7 family are suppressed after transcription by LIN28A and its paralogue LIN28B. These proteins bind to the terminal loop of pri-let7 and pre-let-7 respectively, and prevent Drosha and Dicer processing. LIN28 proteins then employ terminal uridylyl transferases TUT4 and TUT7 to signal pre-let-7 for decay by inducing oliguridylation [35, 36]. Next, DIS3L2 exonuclease targets the oligo-U tail and degrades the miRNA. Conversely, when LIN28 is down regulated in cells, TUT7, TUT4, and TUT2 stimulate monouridylation of pre-let-7, which increases let-7 proliferation [37].

Another type of RNA tailing is adenylation, which primarily occurs in mature miRNAs. Adenylation can result in either miRNA stabilization or miRNA decay [38]. As examples, miRNA-122, a hepatic miRNA, is frequently stabilized by adenylation, whereas poxvirus polyadenylation polymerase targets host miRNAs and adenylates them causing their degradation. It remains unclear what causes the difference in response following miRNA polyadenylation [39].

2.5 MiRNA Degradation

Mature miRNA degradation has been observed in several different systems. Though it is unclear how nucleases specify targets, numerous nucleases are suspected of actively degrading miRNAs in humans [18], *C. elegans* [40], and mice [41]. The first reported instance in which miRNAs were rapidly degraded was observed in *Arabidopsis thaliana*, in which mature miRNAs were cleaved and removed by an association of 3′–5′ exonucleases called small-RNA-degrading nuclease [42].

Similarly, it has been shown that viruses destabilize specific miRNAs by using their own RNA that contains a perfectly complementary sequence [43]. For example, T cells that are infected with herpes virus experience a rapid decrease in miRNA-27 due to viral noncoding RNA specifically binding and destabilizing miRNA-27 [44]. Also, mouse cytomegalovirus contains RNA that specifically binds miRNA-27 and facilitates its degradation [45].

3 Concluding Remarks

Though miRNAs genes were almost entirely overlooked until the turn of the millennium, miRNAs have now been shown to play an integral part in the post-transcriptional regulation of many (if not a majority of) protein genes. What is more, our understanding of miRNAs and their functions as regulators continues to broaden with significant new insights continuing to be described. For example, miRNAs were recently shown to target not only mRNAs, but also other noncoding RNAs such as long noncoding RNAs or lncRNAs. Linc-MD1 is a lncRNA that is expressed during myoblast differentiation in muscle cells. MiRNA-133 and -135 down regulate two transcription factors that stimulate muscle-specific gene expression, MAML1 and MEF2C respectively. Linc-MD1 competes with these transcription factors to bind the miRNAs and allow the transcription factors to initiate cell differentiation [46]. As another example, other small RNAs have now been shown to behave like mature miRNAs. For example, many snoRNAs, or small nucleolar RNAs, classically thought to simply chemically modify other RNAs, have now been reported to undergo alternative processing and behave like mature miRNAs. In a recent study, specific snoRNAs were found to be processed into miRNA-like fragments and direct translational repression of target genes [47].

In conclusion, while we have learned a lot about miRNA production and regulation in a very short time, our understanding of these molecules is still in its infancy, and exciting new revelations undoubtedly await.

References

1. Graves P, Zeng Y (2012) Biogenesis of mammalian microRNAs: a global view. Genomics Proteomics Bioinformatics 10:239–245. doi:10.1016/j.gpb.2012.06.004
2. Ha M, Kim VN (2014) Regulation of microRNA biogenesis. Nat Rev Mol Cell Biol 15:509–524. doi:10.1038/nrm3838
3. Krützfeldt J, Stoffel M (2006) MicroRNAs: a new class of regulatory genes affecting metabolism. Cell Metab 4:9–12. doi:10.1016/j.cmet.2006.05.009
4. Nakahara K, Carthew RW (2004) Expanding roles for miRNAs and siRNAs in cell regulation. Curr Opin Cell Biol 16:127–133. doi:10.1016/j.ceb.2004.02.006
5. Lee RC, Feinbaum RL, Ambros V (1993) The *C. elegans* heterochronic gene lin-4 encodes small RNAs with antisense complementarity to

lin-14. Cell 75:843–854. doi:10.1016/0092-8674(93)90529-Y
6. Lee RC, Ambros V (2001) An extensive class of small RNAs in *Caenorhabditis elegans*. Science 294:862–864. doi:10.1126/science.1065329
7. miRBase. http://www.mirbase.org/index.shtml. Accessed 11 Oct 2015
8. Li M, Marin-Muller C, Bharadwaj U et al (2009) MicroRNAs: control and loss of control in human physiology and disease. World J Surg 33:667–684. doi:10.1007/s00268-008-9836-x
9. Yue S-B, Trujillo RD, Tang Y et al (2011) Loop nucleotides control primary and mature miRNA function in target recognition and repression. RNA Biol 8:1115–1123. doi:10.4161/rna.8.6.17626
10. Roberts JT, Cooper EA, Favreau CJ et al (2013) Continuing analysis of microRNA origins: formation from transposable element insertions and noncoding RNA mutations. Mob Genet Elements 3:e27755. doi:10.4161/mge.27755
11. Roberts JT, Cardin SE, Borchert GM (2014) Burgeoning evidence indicates that microRNAs were initially formed from transposable element sequences. Mob Genet Elements 4:e29255. doi:10.4161/mge.29255
12. Filshtein TJ, Mackenzie CO, Dale MD et al (2012) OrbId: origin-based identification of microRNA targets. Mob Genet Elements 2:184–192. doi:10.4161/mge.21617
13. Kobayashi H, Tomari Y (2015) RISC assembly: coordination between small RNAs and Argonaute proteins. Biochim Biophys Acta. doi:10.1016/j.bbagrm.2015.08.007
14. Ouellet DL, Perron MP, Gobeil L-A, Plante P, Provost P (2006) MicroRNAs in gene regulation: when the smallest governs it all. J Biomed Biotechnol 2006:20. doi:10.1155/JBB/2006/69616
15. Parker GS, Maity TS, Bass BL (2008) dsRNA binding properties of RDE-4 and TRBP reflect their distinct roles in RNAi. J Mol Biol 384:967–979. doi:10.1016/j.jmb.2008.10.002
16. Bahubeshi A, Tischkowitz M, Foulkes WD (2011) miRNA processing and human cancer: DICER1 cuts the mustard. Sci Transl Med 3:111ps46. doi:10.1126/scitranslmed.3002493
17. Agrawal N, Dasaradhi PVN, Mohmmed A et al (2003) RNA interference: biology, mechanism, and applications. Microbiol Mol Biol Rev 67:657–685. doi:10.1128/MMBR.67.4.657-685.2003
18. Krol J, Busskamp V, Markiewicz I et al (2010) Characterizing light-regulated retinal microRNAs reveals rapid turnover as a common property of neuronal microRNAs. Cell 141:618–631. doi:10.1016/j.cell.2010.03.039
19. Zhang B, Wang Q, Pan X (2007) MicroRNAs and their regulatory roles in animals and plants. J Cell Physiol 210:279–289. doi:10.1002/jcp.20869
20. Verdel A, Jia S, Gerber S et al (2004) RNAi-mediated targeting of heterochromatin by the RITS complex. Science 303:672–676. doi:10.1126/science.1093686
21. Lam JKW, Chow MYT, Zhang Y, Leung SWS (2015) siRNA versus miRNA as therapeutics for gene silencing. Mol Ther Nucleic Acids 4:e252. doi:10.1038/mtna.2015.23
22. Ivanova AV, Bonaduce MJ, Ivanov SV, Klar AJ (1998) The chromo and SET domains of the Clr4 protein are essential for silencing in fission yeast. Nat Genet 19:192–195. doi:10.1038/566
23. Cai Y, Yu X, Hu S, Yu J (2009) A brief review on the mechanisms of miRNA regulation. Genomics Proteomics Bioinformatics 7:147–154. doi:10.1016/S1672-0229(08)60044-3
24. Lee C-T, Risom T, Strauss WM (2006) MicroRNAs in mammalian development. Birth Defects Res C Embryo Today 78:129–139. doi:10.1002/bdrc.20072
25. Xhemalce B, Robson SC, Kouzarides T (2012) Human RNA methyltransferase BCDIN3D regulates microRNA processing. Cell 151:278–288. doi:10.1016/j.cell.2012.08.041
26. He X-X, Kuang S-Z, Liao J-Z et al (2015) The regulation of microRNA expression by DNA methylation in hepatocellular carcinoma. Mol Biosyst 11:532–539. doi:10.1039/C4MB00563E
27. Schanen BC, Li X (2011) Transcriptional regulation of mammalian miRNA genes. Genomics 97:1–6. doi:10.1016/j.ygeno.2010.10.005
28. Boyer LA, Lee TI, Cole MF et al (2005) Core transcriptional regulatory circuitry in human embryonic stem cells. Cell 122:947–956. doi:10.1016/j.cell.2005.08.020
29. Marson A, Levine SS, Cole MF et al (2008) Connecting microRNA genes to the core transcriptional regulatory circuitry of embryonic stem cells. Cell 134:521–533. doi:10.1016/j.cell.2008.07.020
30. Kanellopoulou C (2005) Dicer-deficient mouse embryonic stem cells are defective in differentiation and centromeric silencing. Genes Dev 19:489–501. doi:10.1101/gad.1248505
31. Sun G, Yan J, Noltner K et al (2009) SNPs in human miRNA genes affect biogenesis and function. RNA 15:1640–1651. doi:10.1261/rna.1560209

32. Lee YS, Nakahara K, Pham JW et al (2004) Distinct roles for Drosophila Dicer-1 and Dicer-2 in the siRNA/miRNA silencing pathways. Cell 117:69–81. doi:10.1016/S0092-8674(04)00261-2
33. Yang W, Chendrimada TP, Wang Q et al (2005) Modulation of microRNA processing and expression through RNA editing by ADAR deaminases. Nat Struct Mol Biol 13:13–21. doi:10.1038/nsmb1041
34. Blow MJ, Grocock RJ, van Dongen S et al (2006) RNA editing of human microRNAs. Genome Biol 7:R27. doi:10.1186/gb-2006-7-4-r27
35. Ameres SL, Zamore PD (2013) Diversifying microRNA sequence and function. Nat Rev Mol Cell Biol 14:475–488. doi:10.1038/nrm3611
36. Pasquinelli AE, Reinhart BJ, Slack F et al (2000) Conservation of the sequence and temporal expression of let-7 heterochronic regulatory RNA. Nature 408:86–89. doi:10.1038/35040556
37. Suh M-R, Lee Y, Kim JY et al (2004) Human embryonic stem cells express a unique set of microRNAs. Dev Biol 270:488–498. doi:10.1016/j.ydbio.2004.02.019
38. Katoh T, Sakaguchi Y, Miyauchi K et al (2009) Selective stabilization of mammalian microRNAs by 3′ adenylation mediated by the cytoplasmic poly(A) polymerase GLD-2. Genes Dev 23:433–438. doi:10.1101/gad.1761509
39. Backes S, Shapiro JS, Sabin LR et al (2012) Degradation of host MicroRNAs by poxvirus poly(A) polymerase reveals terminal RNA methylation as a protective antiviral mechanism. Cell Host Microbe 12:200–210. doi:10.1016/j.chom.2012.05.019
40. Chatterjee S, Fasler M, Büssing I, Grosshans H (2011) Target-mediated protection of endogenous microRNAs in *C. elegans*. Dev Cell 20:388–396. doi:10.1016/j.devcel.2011.02.008
41. Rüegger S, Großhans H (2012) MicroRNA turnover: when, how, and why. Trends Biochem Sci 37:436–446. doi:10.1016/j.tibs.2012.07.002
42. Ramachandran V, Chen X (2008) Degradation of microRNAs by a family of exoribonucleases in Arabidopsis. Science 321:1490–1492. doi:10.1126/science.1163728
43. Suzuki HI, Arase M, Matsuyama H et al (2011) MCPIP1 ribonuclease antagonizes dicer and terminates MicroRNA biogenesis through precursor microRNA degradation. Mol Cell 44:424–436. doi:10.1016/j.molcel.2011.09.012
44. Cazalla D, Yario T, Steitz JA (2010) Down-regulation of a host microRNA by a Herpesvirus saimiri noncoding RNA. Science 328:1563–1566. doi:10.1126/science.1187197
45. Lee S, Song J, Kim S et al (2013) Selective degradation of host MicroRNAs by an intergenic HCMV noncoding RNA accelerates virus production. Cell Host Microbe 13:678–690. doi:10.1016/j.chom.2013.05.007
46. Cesana M, Cacchiarelli D, Legnini I et al (2011) A long noncoding RNA controls muscle differentiation by functioning as a competing endogenous RNA. Cell 147:358–369. doi:10.1016/j.cell.2011.09.028
47. Patterson D (2015) A significant percentage of small nucleolar RNAs are processed into microRNAs. Univeraity of South Alabama

Chapter 3

Viral MicroRNAs, Host MicroRNAs Regulating Viruses, and Bacterial MicroRNA-Like RNAs

Sara-Elizabeth Cardin and Glen M. Borchert

Abstract

As masters of genome-wide regulation, miRNAs represent a key component in the complex architecture of cellular processes. Over the last decade, it has become increasingly apparent that miRNAs have many important roles in the development of disease and cancer. Recently, however, their role in viral and bacterial gene regulation as well as host gene regulation during disease progression has become a field of interest. Due to their small size, miRNAs are the ideal mechanism for bacteria and viruses that have limited room in their genomes, as a single miRNA can target up to ~30 genes. Currently, only a limited number of miRNA and miRNA-like RNAs have been found in bacteria and viruses, a number that is sure to increase rapidly in the future. The interactions of these small noncoding RNAs in such primitive species have wide-reaching effects, from increasing viral and bacterial proliferation, better responses to stress, increased virulence, to manipulation of host immune responses to provide a more ideal environment for these pathogens to thrive. Here, we explore those roles to obtain a better grasp of just how complicated disease truly is.

Key words Bacteria, CRISPR, miRNA, Regulation, sRNA, Virus

1 Viral MicroRNAs

1.1 Viral Life Cycle

Viruses are non-living parasites that are masters in terms of survival and continued replication of their genomes. They can be thought of as glorified transposons that move from host to host, constantly evolving. These invasive mobile genetic elements also represent one of the most abundant entities found on this planet [1, 2]. Several themes are universal among viral structure and function, one such commonality being that they all have one of four types of genomes: ssDNA, ssRNA, dsDNA, or dsRNA. Furthermore, all viral genomes contain genes that serve two functions: genes for replication and genes for viral proteins. Typically, viruses follow the same general scheme for infection and replication. Following initial attachment and penetration, viruses express early viral genes, replicate their nucleic acid (NA), synthesize structural components, then package and assemble new complete virions before exiting the

Jingshan Huang et al. (eds.), *Bioinformatics in MicroRNA Research*, Methods in Molecular Biology, vol. 1617, DOI 10.1007/978-1-4939-7046-9_3, © Springer Science+Business Media LLC 2017

host [2]. However, in the emerging world of bioinformatics and viroinformatics, new information is rapidly becoming available regarding viral genes, namely, the existence of viral microRNAs. As a result, the "life cycle" of viruses has recently become vastly more complicated.

1.2 MicroRNAs and Viral Diseases

MicroRNAs (miRNAs) have a long history with viruses and many are thought to have been introduced into the human genome via retroviruses early in human evolution. With roles in viral infectivity, replication, latency, and immune avoidance, miRNAs are becoming increasingly important to researchers. There are currently 502 known viral miRNAs (Table 1), belonging to several viral families, including herpesviruses, retroviruses, adenoviruses, and polyomaviruses [4]. The function of such miRNAs seems to be quite subtle, acting on numerous host genes to contribute to a prime environment for invasion and persistence within the host. Furthermore, not only do viruses succeed in hijacking host miRNAs to promote their own proliferation, they can also utilize parts of host miRNA pathways to increase levels of those miRNAs. Some viruses are also capable of modulating host miRNAs to combat immune response by downregulating viral defenses, such as interferon [5]. Thus, between promoting their own proliferation and downregulating host response, viral miRNAs may yet prove to be a vital component of the viral replicative machinery.

Unfortunately, viruses are best studied in their natural hosts, but obviously such studies are not ideal for human viruses and investigations of human:viral microRNA interactions are exceptionally challenging. The lack of model systems represents a particularly difficult challenge to overcome with some viruses, such as hepatitis B virus (HBV) [6]. However, some viruses, such as herpes viruses (HSV), already have established effective model systems that can be used for now [4]. Another problem encountered is the extremely rapid evolution of viruses due to constant exchange of nucleic acids, as well as imprecise excision from the genome when coming out of a latent state [7].

Currently, the most well-known miRNA contribution to the persistent nature of viral infections is the miRNA role in the establishment and maintenance of latency (Table 2) [4]. In herpes viruses, there have been a multitude of studies linking viral miRNAs to the persistent nature of those infections. Alpha and gamma herpes viruses, in particular, have been shown to utilize viral miRNAs to establish latency via silencing of trans-activator proteins that are responsible for switching from latent to active infections [7, 8]. Some viruses, such as hepatitis C virus (HCV), also act to stabilize latency by turning off apoptotic genes, thus interfering with apoptosis pathways by upregulating miR-320c and miR-483-5p [9]. Human cytomegalovirus (HCMV) is also known for establishing lifelong latent infections and can cause a number of serious

Table 1
Number of precursor and mature miRNAs made by 29 different viruses [3]

Virus	miR abbreviation	Precursors	Mature
Bandicoot papillopmatosis carcinomatosis virus 1	bpcv1	1	1
Bandicoot papillopmatosis carcinomatosis virus 2	bpcv2	1	1
BK polyomavirus	bkv	1	2
Bovine foamy virus	bfv	2	4
Bovine herpesvirus 1	bhv1	10	12
Bovine herpesvirus2	bhv2	5	5
Bovine leukemia virus	blv	5	10
Duck enteritis virus	dev	24	33
Epstein-Barr virus	ebv	25	44
Herpes B virus	hbv	12	15
Herpes simplex virus 1	hsv1	18	27
Herpes simplex virus 2	hsv2	18	24
Herpesvirus of turkeys	hvt	17	28
Herpesvirus saimiri strain A11	hsva	3	6
Human cytomegalovirus	hcmv	15	26
Human herpesvirus 6B	hhv6b	4	8
Human immunodeficiency virus 1	hiv1	3	4
Infectious laryngotracheitis virus	iltv	7	10
JC polyomavirus	jcv	1	2
Kaposi sarcoma-associated herpesvirus	kshv	13	25
Mareks disease virus 1	mdv1	14	26
Mareks disease virus 2	mdv2	18	36
Merkel cell polyomavirus	mcv	1	2
Mouse cytomegalovirus	mcmv	18	29
Mouse gammaherpesvirus 68	mghv	15	28
Pseudorabies virus	prv	13	13
Rhesus lymphocryptovirus	rlcv	36	68
Rhesus monkey rhadinovirus	rrv	7	11
Simian virus	sv	1	2
		Total	*502*

Table 2
Cellular and viral microRNAs with their putative roles in latency

Role in latency	Type of miRNA	Virus	miRNA	Target	PMID
Latency establishment and reactivation	Cellular miRNAs	EBV	miR-429	ZEB1 and 2	20668090
					20484493
		HCMV	miR-92a	GATA2	21471310
			miR-200b	IE86	24599990
		HIV	miR-155	TRIM32	25873391
		HIV-1	miR-196b	Unknown	26469550
			miR-1290	Unknown	26469550
		HSV	miR-138	ICP0	24721573
	Viral miRNAs	EBV	miR-BART-18-5p	BRLF1 and BZLF1	25012295
			miR-BART-20-5p	MAP3K2	24899173
		HCMV	miR-UL112-1	IE72	17983268
					18378902
		HSV-1	miR-H2-3p	ICP0 and ICP4	19656888
			miR-H6	ICP0 and ICP4	19656888
		HSV-2	miR-H2	ICP0 and ICP34.5	19019961
					21325410
			miR-H3	ICP0 and ICP34.5	19019961
					21325410
			miR-H4	ICP0 and ICP34.5	19019961
					21325410
		KSHV	miR-K12-1	IκBα	20081837
			miR-K12-3	NFIB	20847741
			miR-K12-4-5p	Rbl2	20071580
			miR-K12-5	BCLAF1	19098914
			miR-K12-7	NFIB	20847741
			miR-K12-7-5p	RTA	21283761
			miR-K12-9*	RTA	20006845
			miR-K12-9	BCLAF1	19098914
			miR-K12-10a	BCLAF1	19098914
			miR-K12-10b	BCLAF1	19098914
			miR-K12-11	NFIB	20847741
Survival during and maintenance of latency	Cellular miRNA	EBV	miR-155	Multiple	20844043
					18753206
					18367535
					20427544
	Viral miRNAs	EBV	miR-BHRF1	Multiple	21379335
					23468485
					20808852

(continued)

Table 2
(continued)

Role in latency	Type of miRNA	Virus	miRNA	Target	PMID
Survival during and maintanence of latency	Viral miRNAs	EBV	miR-BHRF2	Multiple	21379335
					23468485
					20808852
			miR-BHRF3	Multiple	21379335
					23468485
					20808852
			miR-BARTs	Multiple	23503461
			miR-BART5	PUMA	18838543
		KSHV	miR-K12-1	IκBα	24385912
			miR-K12-1	CASP3	22174674
			miR-K12-3	CASP3	22174674
			miR-K12-4	IκBα	24385912
			miR-K12-4-3p	CASP3	22174674
			miR-K12-10a	TWEAKR	20844036
			miR-K12-11	IκBα	24385912
			miR-K12-11 (miR-155 orthologue)	Multiple	21813606
					18075594
					23966392
					17881434
		MDV	miR-M4	Multiple	21383974
Immune evasion	Cellular miRNAs	HIV-1	miR-15a	Pur-α	22835829
			miR-15b	Pur-α	22835829
			miR-16	Pur-α	22835829
			miR-28	CD4+ T cells	17906637
			miR-125b	CD4+ T cells	17906637
			miR-150	CD4+ T cells	17906637
			miR-198	Cyclin T1	19148268
			miR-223	CD4+ T cells	17906637
			miR-382	CD4+ T cells	17906637
	Viral miRNAs	EBV	miR-BART2-5P	MICB	19380116
		HCMV	miR-UL112-1	MICB	17641203
			miR-UL112-1	Multiple	24629342
			miR-UL148D-1	RANTES	22412377
			miR-US5-1	Multiple	24629342
			miR-US5-2	Multiple	24629342
		KSHV	miR-K12-7	MICB	19380116
			miR-K12-9	IRAK1 and MyD88	22896623

illnesses [10]. This is in part due to its ability to infect a very wide range of cells, including smooth muscle cells, hepatocytes, endothelial cells, epithelial cells, neuronal cells, stromal cells, monocytes/macrophages, and neutrophils [11]. Currently, there are 26 mature miRNAs encoded by HCMV according to miRbase [3], many of which have roles in the establishment of latency, such as miR-UL112-1, as well as roles in immune evasion, including miR-UL112-1, miR-UL148D-1, miR-US5-1, and miR-US5-2.

Some human miRNAs also are capable of positively regulating viral infections. Interestingly, this was found to be the case in HCV infection with miR-122, a liver-specific miRNA. MiR-122 directly interacts with the ssRNA genome of HCV and facilitates its accumulation and translation [12–14]. Furthermore, HCV hijacks miRNA processing machinery, using Dicer and TRBP to activate HCV replication [15], and also requiring Ago2 for miR-122 regulation of HCV RNA accumulation and translation [16]. Other miRNAs are also reported as having direct interaction with HCV RNA. Murakami et al. reported that miR-199a overexpression inhibits the replication of HCV's genome in HCV 1b or 2a cell lines by binding to the stem-loop II region of HCV 5′ UTR [17]. As miR-199a expression in liver tissue is low, it appears to be another contributing factor for the liver tropism of HCV [18]. Let-7b also results in decrease of HCV replication by targeting the 5′ untranslated region (UTR) and NS5B coding region of the HCV genome, thus downregulating HCV accumulation and reducing its infectivity [19]. Additionally, two more miRNAs, miR-196 and miR-448, target the NS5A coding region and core of the HCV genome, respectively. As a result, overexpression of those two miRNAs significantly reduces HCV replication [20].

1.3 Viral miRNAs and Cancer

Some viruses have long been known to contribute to carcinogenesis in humans, such as human immunodeficiency virus (HIV), human papillomavirus (HPV), Epstein-Barr virus (EBV), and hepatitis B virus (HBV) [6, 21]. However, recently, it has become apparent that virally encoded miRs also play a role in cancer and are thus termed oncomiRs. These viral miRs are thought to contribute to carcinogenesis by silencing tumor suppressor genes within the host genome, allowing proto-oncogenes to become active [22]. MiR-124 is thought to be a tumor suppressor, and so its reduced expression following HCV infection has been attributed to involvement in hepatocellular carcinoma (HCC) [23]. Changes in miRNA levels can also contribute to other progressive virus-associated diseases. HCV infection induces modulation of miRNAs that can lead to related diseases such as cirrhosis, fibrosis, and HCC. Increased levels of miR-155 in particular have been linked to the promotion of the proliferation and progression to HCC by altering Wnt signaling [24].

MiRNAs have also been shown to have roles in cervical carcinoma (CC) caused by HPV. It has long been accepted that high-risk HPV acts to target and inactivate p53 and pRB proteins within the host [22]. One study showed significant overexpression of miR-21, miR-135b, miR-223, and miR-301 in CC tissues compared to normal tissue, with potential to be used to distinguish normal cervical tissue from cervical cancers [25]. MiR-21 was also found to modulate resistance of HPV CC to radiation via its targeting of large tumor suppressor kinase 1 (LATS1) [26]. Another study found that reduced expression of miR-100 aids the development of CC, possibly due to the loss of its target gene Polo-like Kinase1 (PLK1) [27]. HPV16 E7 was also discovered to have a role in CC by elevating miR-27b, thus inhibiting PPARγ expression to promote CC proliferation and invasion [28].

MiRNAs are furthermore implicated in cancers associated with EBV, a major oncogenic virus that is associated with ~10% of gastric carcinomas [29]. One particular EBV-miRNA cluster (miR-BART2, miR-BART4, miR-BART5, miR-BART18, and miR-BART22) was discovered to be linked to the expression of cytokines that hinder host response to cancer [30]. EBV miRNAs are additionally found to be associated with nasopharyngeal carcinoma, including miR-BART3 and miR-BART5 that target genes in TGF-β, Wnt signaling, and p53 pathways [31]. EBV is also capable of inducing expression of host oncogenic miRNAs. Bazot et al. found that EBV proteins together do just that, inducing miR-221/22 cluster, thus diminishing the expression of its target gene p57KIP2, a cyclin-dependent kinase inhibitor [32]. Another study showed that EBV is also capable of inducing miR-21 in malignant B cells. A well-known oncomiR, miR-21, is induced in multiple myeloma, resulting in downregulated p21 and increased cyclin D3 expression [33].

1.4 Research Applications

MiRNAs have numerous applications in research, including, but not limited to, genome editing, delivery of miRNAs using viral vectors, and possible treatment of viral disease and cancers. Viruses have long been used to transform cell lines, contributing to their immortality and allowing them to be continually cultured. Some are also commonly used to introduce specific miRNAs into cell lines, especially cell lines and animal models that otherwise prove difficult to transfect [4].

While some viral miRNAs are able to contribute to carcinogenesis, some viruses can also potentially be used to manipulate miRNA levels in tumors [34]. Such oncolytic viruses show much promise. Viral vectors can be used for exogenous gene expression, including adenovirus, adeno-associated virus, and baculovirus, due to their ability to be controlled therapeutically to enhance treatments by including miRNA response elements (MREs) [35]. Recently, MREs have been employed to control expression of TNF-related apoptosis-inducing ligand (TRAIL), which is a cytokine that selectively activates apoptosis. In preclinical studies, TRAIL has demonstrated robust anticancer activity, and MREs aid in reducing toxicity of TRAIL therapy against prostate, glioma, uveal melanoma, and osteosarcoma models [36, 37]. MiRNA targeting can also be employed in regulating oncolytic viral tropism, enhancing tumor specificity and reducing or eliminating toxicities [38]. Overall, this form of miRNA targeting is incredibly versatile as both DNA and RNA viruses can be used. Thus far, most miRNA-targeted viruses are single-stranded, positive-sense RNA viruses, which have proven highly receptive to this targeting strategy. In contrast, only a few negative-sense RNA viruses, such as influenza A virus (IAV), measles virus (MV), and vesicular stomatitis virus (VSV) have been used as targets for MREs. It is thought to be more difficult due to the viral genome being encapsulated in the capsid as transcription and replication occurs, hindering the accessibility of MREs [34].

2 Host MicroRNAs Regulating Viruses

2.1 MicroRNA Response to Viral Infection

Having numerous roles in human regulatory networks, known miRNA involvements in almost every pathway also extend to responses to viral infection. In the "genome wars" that occur during viral infection, cellular miRNAs offer a line of defense, acting to mediate host responses to inhibit or elicit the appropriate immune response.

2.2 Role in Immunity

The immune system consists of two basic branches: innate and adaptive. Human miRNAs have roles in both branches in regards to response to viral infection. MiRNAs interact with innate responses, which are the body's first line of defense against foreign invaders, in order to both induce and maintain levels of appropriate cells and biochemical mediators, such as cytokines and interferon (IFN) [4]. Though some have suggested that cellular miRNAs directly target viral mRNAs as an antiviral mechanism, the reality is that such a mechanism is highly unlikely due to viruses' ability to rapidly escape through mutation [39]. However, some human miRNAs have been shown to potentially limit viral replication. Bondanese et al. found that miR-128 and miR-155 can decrease the replication of human rhinovirus by binding to viral RNA [40]. Another group also found that eight miRNAs (miR-135b, miR-155, miR-190, miR-422a, miR-489, miR-590, miR-601, and miR-1290) were strongly induced in human enterovirus cardiomyopathy with viral persistence and continuing clinical decline. Those eight miRNAs are predicted to target several immune response genes, thus providing possible clinical application [41]. Furthermore, miR-21 actively reduces HCMV replication by targeting Cdc25a, a cell cycle regulator, in neural cells [42].

Natural killer (NK) cells and interferon are major innate defenses for the human antiviral response against a variety of viral invaders that include HIV, HSV, HCV, HCMV, influenza, and EBV [5, 10]. Interactions between viruses and miRNA regulations have been reported to occur in these defenses. For example, type I IFN acts as a defense against invading viral pathogens [43]. To beat type I IFN's antiviral activity, HCV modifies several miRNAs capable of regulating those signaling pathways. However, some interactions result in a battle for supremacy. IFN enhances miR-196 expression [44, 45], reducing HCV replication, while infection with HCV acts to repress miR-196 expression, thus allowing replication to occur.

Some viruses are also able to avoid the adaptive response. Again, HCMV not only avoids innate immunity, but has also been shown to evade adaptive immunity via regulation of the major histocompatibility complex (MHC) molecule known as HLA-E. Increased surface levels of HLA-E result in higher concentrations of an inhibitory ligand for NK receptor CD94/NKG2A [46]. One group has shown that RNA editing of cellular miR-376a via ADAR1-p110 activity actually downregulates HLA-E, thus avoiding HLA-E-mediated inhibitory action on NK cells [47].

2.3 Downregulation and Destruction of Host MicroRNAs by Viruses

Due to the compact nature of viral genomes, it is remarkable that they are capable of producing not only miRNAs that contribute to their own proliferation, but also miRNAs that interfere with host miRNA responses [48]. What is more, viruses are capable of degrading human miRNAs to manipulate the host immune response. MiR-27 is degraded in this was by herpesvirus saimiri (HVS) and murine cytomegalovirus (MCMV) [48]. As an oncogenic gamma-herpesvirus, HVS is capable of transforming primate and human T cells [49]. In latently infected marmoset T cells, the most plentiful viral transcripts are small U-rich ncRNAs called Herpesvirus saimiri U RNAs (HSURs) [50]. HSUR-1 base-pairs with the marmoset's host miR-27, ultimately resulting in miRNA degradation [51]. Though the exact mechanism is unknown, high-throughput RNA sequencing following cross-linking immunoprecipitation (HITS-CLIP) analysis [52] showed that miR-27 acts on mRNAs that encode parts of the T-cell receptor (TCR) signaling pathways as well as downstream effectors in T cells infected with HVS [53]. MCMV, a beta-herpesvirus, is also capable of degrading host miR-27 by employing an antisense mechanism similarly to HVS [54]. However, the viral agent is an MCMV mRNA instead of a noncoding RNA (ncRNA) in this instance. This mRNA, m169, encompasses a miR-27 target site in its 3′ UTR resulting in rapid degradation of miR-27 [55]. The levels of viral m169 transcript are also reciprocally regulated by miR-27 [56].

3 Bacterial MicroRNA-like RNAs

3.1 sRNAs

Though bacteria do not possess miRNAs per se, many species do produce small RNAs (sRNAs) that are similar to miRNAs in their ability to regulate gene expression through antisense basepairing. These RNAs generally play roles in a bacterium's metabolism and general housekeeping, regulation of outer membrane proteins, stress response, virulence, quorum sensing, biofilm formation, iron homeostasis, host-cell contact, amino acid metabolism, and also possibly contribute to a bacteria's ability to cause cancer [57, 58]. Such sRNAs are typically highly structured, containing multiple stemloops [59, 60], and behave similarly to miRNAs in that they are able to bind to mRNA targets to regulate gene expression. However, some are also capable of modifying the function of bound proteins by imitating the secondary structures of other nucleic acids [61]. SRNAs also differ from miRNAs in that their size varies from ~50 to 450 nucleotides (nts), whereas miRNAs are roughly 22–25 nts long [62].

Small RNAs are a relatively novel class of RNAs that contribute to several regulatory pathways in bacteria. There are four main groups of regulating sRNAs: *cis*-encoded base-pairing NAs, *trans*-encoded base-pairing RNAs, RNAs modulating protein activity, and CRISPRs [63]. *Cis*-encoded sRNAs are located on the DNA strand opposite of the target and typically share ~75 nt complementarity with their mRNA targets [64]. *Trans*-encoded sRNAs, however, have limited complementarity with their targets and have different chromosomal locations (Fig. 1a). *Trans*-encoded sRNAs are one of the most studied of the four groups, with roles as both repressors and activators. SRNA activators of gene expression, such as DsrA, GlmZ, RNAIII, RprA, RyhB, and Qrr, can act as direct translational activators via an antisense mechanism, binding to the 5′ mRNA UTR [65]. *Cis*-encoded sRNAs, however, are the true antisense sRNAs, with their most prevalent role in bacteria being repressors of genes encoding potentially toxic proteins [66]. Furthermore, these antisense sRNAs are also located on both plasmids and bacterial chromosomes, repressing synthesis of a variety of proteins such as Hok protein on *E. coli* R1, R100, and F plasmids, as well as the Fst protein of *Enterococcus faecalis* plasmid pAD1 [61].

Interestingly, in bacteria that cause sepsis, several sRNAs act to downregulate adhesion molecules and granulocyte-macrophage-stimulating factors, as well as regulate the expression of nuclear transport shuttles involved in sepsis [67]. Similarly, extracellular miR-223's action in the sepsis machinery reduces the expression of cellular adhesion molecule 1 and granulocyte-macrophage colony stimulating factor 2 in endothelial cells [68]. Other miRNAs have also been linked to regulation of expression in sepsis, such as miR-181b, which regulates nuclear transport shuttles such as importin α3 [69].

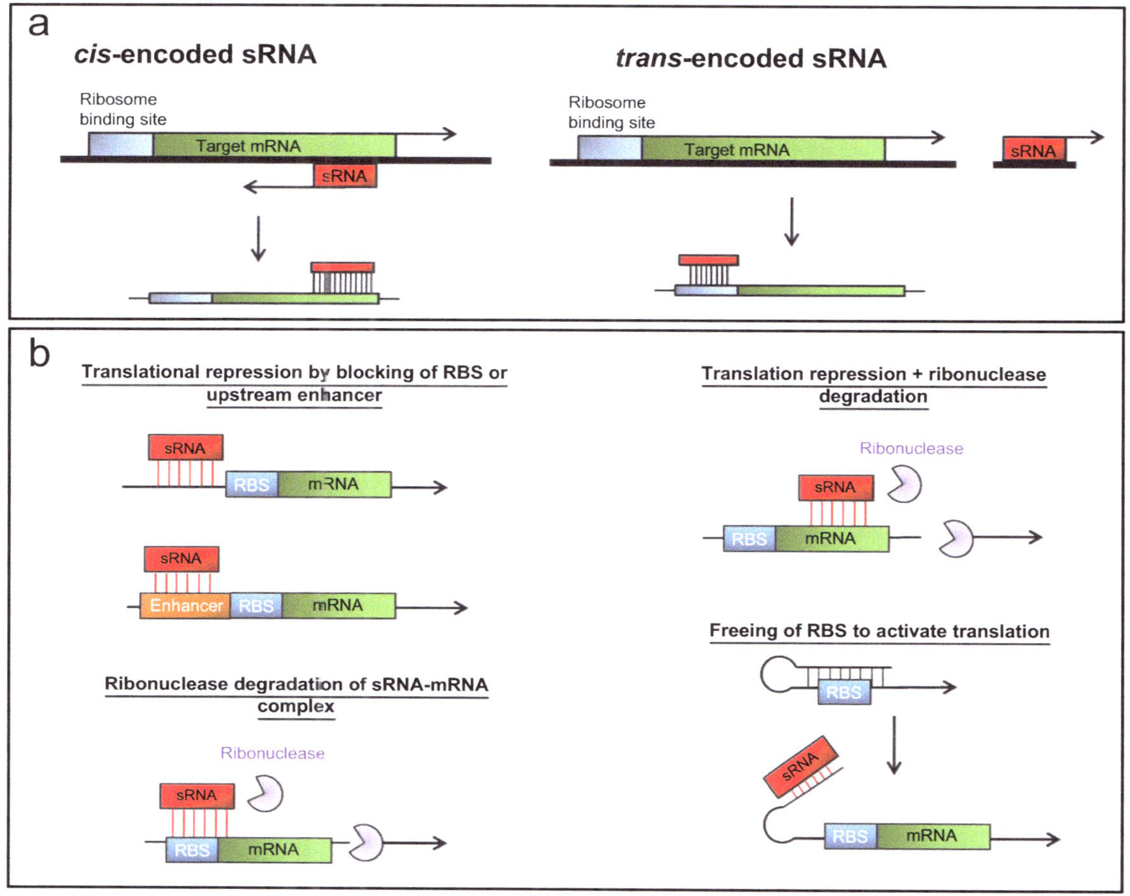

Fig. 1 Bacterial sRNAs. (**a**) Difference of genomic location for *cis*- and *trans*-encoded sRNA. *Cis*-encoded sRNAs (i.e., antisense sRNAs) are located on the opposite strand of the regulated RNA, whereas *trans*-encoded sRNAs are transcribed distantly from their targets. (**b**) Different types of regulation by *trans*-encoded sRNAs. SRNA blocks the ribosome binding site (RBS) to prevent translation; recruitment of ribonucleases by sRNA presence results in degradation of sRNA-mRNA complex; translational repression concurrent with ribonuclease degradation; activation of translation by sRNA binding to free the ribosomal binding site

3.2 CRISPR/Cas System

Clustered regularly interspaced short palindromic repeats (CRISPRs) are portions of bacterial DNA that have short repetitions of base sequences, with small segments of nonidentical "spacer DNA" from previous interaction with a bacteriophage or bacterial plasmid [70]. As such, some subsets of spacer sequences are identical to plasmid DNA and phage sequences [71]. They were first discovered upon sequencing of an *E. coli* chromosomal fragment in 1987 [72], with many other such CRISPRs since found in other prokaryotes. They are also accompanied by CRISPR-associated genes (*cas* genes). The action mechanism (Fig. 2) of CRISPR/Cas can be broken down into three main stages. Stage 1 is the integration of fragments of nucleic acid of invading viruses or other mobile genetic elements as spacers into a CRISPR's locus. In Stage 2, CRISPR gets transcribed as a precursor (pre-crRNA) that is then cleaved by an endoribonuclease and results in mature CRISPR RNAS (crRNAs) that remain associated with a Cas protein complex. Finally, during Stage 3, the crRNA acts as a guide for the Cas complex, directing it to cleave invading nucleic acids [2].

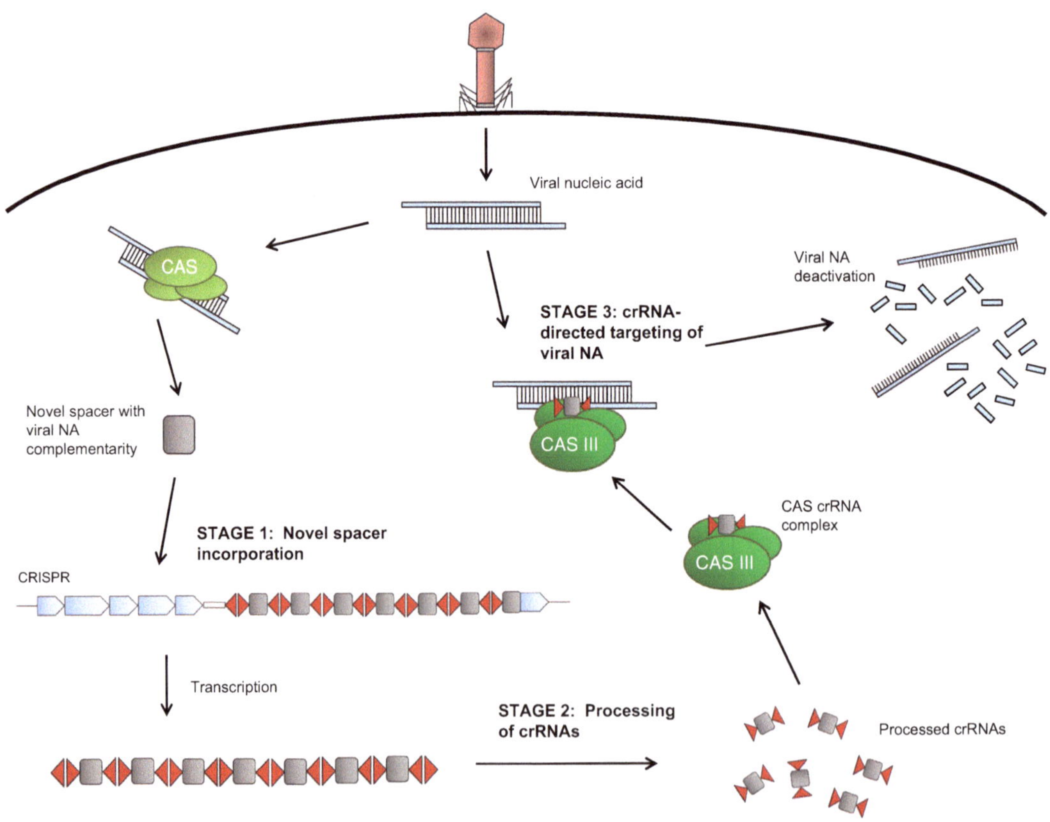

Fig. 2 Mechanism of CRISPR/Cas targeting of viral nucleic acids. Invading NAs are integrated into the CRISPR as novel spacers. Next, they are processed into mature crRNAs, which then associate with Cas proteins. Finally, the crRNA-guided Cas proteins target viral NAs and inactivate them

Because phage infections can ultimately result in host cell lysis, bacteria and some archaea have needed to develop sophisticated tools such as CRISPR to avoid such destruction [61]. CRISPRs/Cas9 systems, therefore, act as a defense mechanism against the disruption of bacterial genes when bacteria are infected by mobile genetic elements, i.e., phages, a mechanism strikingly similar to the proposed function of a significant percentage of miRNAs [73–76]. CRISPRs and their *cas* genes act by incorporating viral nucleic acid fragments into the CRISPR locus, thereby giving protection to the bacterial cell. Those crRNAs then specifically direct the Cas protein machinery to the crRNAs' complementary targets: viral DNA or RNA or plasmids. As a result, the CRISPR/Cas system redirects the virus' NA to act against itself, providing the host with acquired and hereditary resistance (reviewed in [70, 77]).

CRISPRs are also quickly becoming popular for use in genetic research. Complete gene knockout is usually the ultimate goal to elucidate transcript functions and their roles in biological pathways and processes. While some have had success on a small scale, such as with yeast, total knockout of genes on a larger or genome-scale has proven a daunting obstacle. Fortunately, CRISPRs offer a potential remedy by deleting target genes from a particular genome. A quickly advancing field, the CRISPR/Cas9 system, has been shown to be more effective than RNAi in both gain-of-function and loss-of-function screening, targeting both regulatory elements and protein-coding sequences. Some possible targets of this system include long noncoding RNAs (lncRNAs), elements that transcribe miRNAs, promoters, and enhancers [78]. As such, much knowledge is to be gained as researchers continue to delve further into the possibilities offered using CRISPR knockouts.

Strikingly, both the biogenesis and function of crRNAs and their mode of target interference is very similar to that of eukaryotic small regulatory RNAs, such as miRNAs that silence host gene expression and small interfering RNAs (siRNAs) which get involved in viral RNA silencing [2]. All three are derived from larger RNA precursors, form complexes with RISC, and bind to a target via basepairing to degrade it. Furthermore, all three have roles in immune systems, with CRISPRs forming a primitive prokaryotic immunity and miRNAs/siRNAs functioning in human immunity. However, a key difference between the two is that CRISPRs, unlike their RNAi counterparts, prefer to target invading DNA, rather than targeting RNA [79]. Furthermore, crRNAs act as an adaptive immunity, whereas antiviral siRNAs are part of innate immunity in eukaryotes. Still, crRNAs, miRNAs, and siRNAs all arose to combat viral invasion, with miRNAs also continuing on to target endogenous viral retrotransposons [75]. Thus, the running theme among all of these small, noncoding RNAs is a battle against invading mobile genetic elements.

4 Concluding Remarks

As demonstrated, miRNAs and similar miRNA-like regulations are present among not only eukaryotes, but also in bacteria and viruses. Such interactions have far reaching implications, affecting numerous pathways from metabolism to stress response and contributing to virulence and immune responses. Of note, there is now even evidence for interspecies miRNA regulations. For example, Jiang et al. [80] recently demonstrated that rice-rich diets result in rice miRNA presence in human serum, and these miRNAs are capable of regulating human gene expression. Thus, miRNAs across the spectrum of living and even non-living entities reveal that viral and bacterial diseases may be significantly more complicated than currently appreciated. However, characterizing novel microbial microRNAs and similar noncoding regulatory RNAs may well aid in better understanding just how these organisms affect us and ultimately lead to new therapeutic targets.

Currently, studies have revealed only a handful of viral miRNAs and virus-host miRNA interactions. However, that number will likely increase dramatically in the future as new small RNAs are discovered and as our ability to accurately identify their target molecules improves. That said, while only a handful of viruses have so far been shown to encode microRNAs, this will undoubtedly increase as the considerably restricted genome size of viruses makes miRNAs the perfect addition to their arsenals providing unprecedented regulatory capacities corresponding to markedly short genomic sequences. While interspecies RNA:RNA interactions are only beginning to be identified, it is tempting to speculate that the importance of nucleotide interplay between symbiotic species will ultimately prove critical for fully understanding mutualistic and parasitic relationships.

References

1. Bergh O, Borsheim KY, Bratbak G, Heldal M (1989) High abundance of viruses found in aquatic environments. Nature 340(6233):467–468. doi:10.1038/340467a0
2. Jore MM, Brouns SJ, van der Oost J (2012) RNA in defense: CRISPRs protect prokaryotes against mobile genetic elements. Cold Spring Harb Perspect Biol 4(6). doi:10.1101/cshperspect.a003657
3. Kozomara A, Griffiths-Jones S (2014) miRBase: annotating high confidence microRNAs using deep sequencing data. Nucleic Acids Res 42(Database issue):D68–D73. doi:10.1093/nar/gkt1181
4. Grey F (2015) Role of microRNAs in herpesvirus latency and persistence. J Gen Virol 96(Pt 4):739–751. doi:10.1099/vir.0.070862-0
5. Lee CH, Kim JH, Lee SW (2014) The role of microRNAs in hepatitis C virus replication and related liver diseases. J Microbiol 52(6):445–451. doi:10.1007/s12275-014-4267-x
6. Lamontagne J, Steel LF, Bouchard MJ (2015) Hepatitis B virus and microRNAs: complex interactions affecting hepatitis B virus replication and hepatitis B virus-associated diseases. World J Gastroenterol 21(24):7375–7399. doi:10.3748/wjg.v21.i24.7375
7. Goodrum F, Caviness K, Zagallo P (2012) Human cytomegalovirus persistence. Cell Microbiol 14(5):644–655. doi:10.1111/j.1462-5822.2012.01774.x
8. Grundhoff A, Sullivan CS (2011) Virus-encoded microRNAs. Virology 411(2):325–343. doi:10.1016/j.virol.2011.01.002

9. Shwetha S, Gouthamchandra K, Chandra M, Ravishankar B, Khaja MN, Das S (2013) Circulating miRNA profile in HCV infected serum: novel insight into pathogenesis. Sci Rep 3:1555. doi:10.1038/srep01555
10. Goldberger T, Mandelboim O (2014) The use of microRNA by human viruses: lessons from NK cells and HCMV infection. Semin Immunopathol 36(6):659–674. doi:10.1007/s00281-014-0447-3
11. Compton T, Feire A (2007) Early events in human cytomegalovirus infection. In: Arvin A, Campadelli-Fiume G, Mocarski E et al (eds) Human herpesviruses: biology, therapy, and immunoprophylaxis. Cambridge University Press, Cambridge
12. Jopling CL, Yi M, Lancaster AM, Lemon SM, Sarnow P (2005) Modulation of hepatitis C virus RNA abundance by a liver-specific MicroRNA. Science 309(5740):1577–1581. doi:10.1126/science.1113329
13. Niepmann M (2009) Activation of hepatitis C virus translation by a liver-specific microRNA. Cell Cycle 8(10):1473–1477
14. Shimakami T, Yamane D, Welsch C, Hensley L, Jangra RK, Lemon SM (2012) Base pairing between hepatitis C virus RNA and microRNA 122 3′ of its seed sequence is essential for genome stabilization and production of infectious virus. J Virol 86(13):7372–7383. doi:10.1128/JVI.00513-12
15. Zhang C, Huys A, Thibault PA, Wilson JA (2012) Requirements for human Dicer and TRBP in microRNA-122 regulation of HCV translation and RNA abundance. Virology 433(2):479–488. doi:10.1016/j.virol.2012.08.039
16. Wilson JA, Zhang C, Huys A, Richardson CD (2011) Human Ago2 is required for efficient microRNA 122 regulation of hepatitis C virus RNA accumulation and translation. J Virol 85(5):2342–2350. doi:10.1128/JVI.02046-10
17. Murakami Y, Aly HH, Tajima A, Inoue I, Shimotohno K (2009) Regulation of the hepatitis C virus genome replication by miR-199a. J Hepatol 50(3):453–460. doi:10.1016/j.jhep.2008.06.010
18. Pietschmann T (2009) Regulation of hepatitis C virus replication by microRNAs. J Hepatol 50(3):441–444. doi:10.1016/j.jhep.2008.12.007
19. Cheng JC, Yeh YJ, Tseng CP, Hsu SD, Chang YL, Sakamoto N, Huang HD (2012) Let-7b is a novel regulator of hepatitis C virus replication. Cell Mol Life Sci 69(15):2621–2633. doi:10.1007/s00018-012-0940-6
20. Pedersen IM, Cheng G, Wieland S, Volinia S, Croce CM, Chisari FV, David M (2007) Interferon modulation of cellular microRNAs as an antiviral mechanism. Nature 449(7164):919–922. doi:10.1038/nature06205
21. Kuzembayeva M, Hayes M, Sugden B (2014) Multiple functions are mediated by the miRNAs of Epstein-Barr virus. Curr Opin Virol 7:61–65. doi:10.1016/j.coviro.2014.04.003
22. Pedroza-Torres A, Lopez-Urrutia E, Garcia-Castillo V, Jacobo-Herrera N, Herrera LA, Peralta-Zaragoza O, Lopez-Camarillo C, De Leon DC, Fernandez-Retana J, Cerna-Cortes JF, Perez-Plasencia C (2014) MicroRNAs in cervical cancer: evidences for a miRNA profile deregulated by HPV and its impact on radio-resistance. Molecules 19(5):6263–6281. doi:10.3390/molecules19056263
23. Zheng F, Liao YJ, Cai MY, Liu YH, Liu TH, Chen SP, Bian XW, Guan XY, Lin MC, Zeng YX, Kung HF, Xie D (2012) The putative tumour suppressor microRNA-124 modulates hepatocellular carcinoma cell aggressiveness by repressing ROCK2 and EZH2. Gut 61(2):278–289. doi:10.1136/gut.2011.239145
24. Zhang Y, Wei W, Cheng N, Wang K, Li B, Jiang X, Sun S (2012) Hepatitis C virus-induced up-regulation of microRNA-155 promotes hepatocarcinogenesis by activating Wnt signaling. Hepatology 56(5):1631–1640. doi:10.1002/hep.25849
25. Pereira PM, Marques JP, Soares AR, Carreto L, Santos MA (2010) MicroRNA expression variability in human cervical tissues. PLoS One 5(7):e11780. doi:10.1371/journal.pone.0011780
26. Liu S, Song L, Zhang L, Zeng S, Gao F (2015) miR-21 modulates resistance of HR-HPV positive cervical cancer cells to radiation through targeting LATS1. Biochem Biophys Res Commun 459(4):679–685. doi:10.1016/j.bbrc.2015.03.004
27. Li BH, Zhou JS, Ye F, Cheng XD, Zhou CY, Lu WG, Xie X (2011) Reduced miR-100 expression in cervical cancer and precursors and its carcinogenic effect through targeting PLK1 protein. Eur J Cancer 47(14):2166–2174. doi:10.1016/j.ejca.2011.04.037
28. Zhang S, Liu F, Mao X, Huang J, Yang J, Yin X, Wu L, Zheng L, Wang Q (2015) Elevation of miR-27b by HPV16 E7 inhibits PPARgamma expression and promotes proliferation and invasion in cervical carcinoma cells. Int J Oncol. doi:10.3892/ijo.2015.3162
29. Shinozaki-Ushiku A, Kunita A, Isogai M, Hibiya T, Ushiku T, Takada K, Fukayama M

(2015) Profiling of virus-encoded microRNAs in Epstein-Barr virus-associated gastric carcinoma and their roles in gastric carcinogenesis. J Virol 89(10):5581–5591. doi:10.1128/JVI.03639-14
30. Pandya D, Mariani M, He S, Andreoli M, Spennato M, Dowell-Martino C, Fiedler P, Ferlini C (2015) Epstein-Barr virus microRNA expression increases aggressiveness of solid malignancies. PLoS One 10(9):e0136058. doi:10.1371/journal.pone.0136058
31. Wan XX, Yi H, Qu JQ, He QY, Xiao ZQ (2015) Integrated analysis of the differential cellular and EBV miRNA expression profiles in microdissected nasopharyngeal carcinoma and non-cancerous nasopharyngeal tissues. Oncol Rep 34(5):2585–2601. doi:10.3892/or.2015.4237
32. Bazot Q, Paschos K, Skalska L, Kalchschmidt JS, Parker GA, Allday MJ (2015) Epstein-Barr virus proteins EBNA3A and EBNA3C together induce expression of the oncogenic microRNA cluster miR-221/miR-222 and ablate expression of its target p57KIP2. PLoS Pathog 11(7):e1005031. doi:10.1371/journal.ppat.1005031
33. Anastasiadou E, Garg N, Bigi R, Yadav S, Campese AF, Lapenta C, Spada M, Cuomo L, Botta A, Belardelli F, Frati L, Ferretti E, Faggioni A, Trivedi P (2015) Epstein-Barr virus infection induces miR-21 in terminally differentiated malignant B cells. Int J Cancer 137(6):1491–1497. doi:10.1002/ijc.29489
34. Ruiz AJ, Russell SJ (2015) MicroRNAs and oncolytic viruses. Curr Opin Virol 13:40–48. doi:10.1016/j.coviro.2015.03.007
35. Geisler A, Jungmann A, Kurreck J, Poller W, Katus HA, Vetter R, Fechner H, Muller OJ (2011) microRNA122-regulated transgene expression increases specificity of cardiac gene transfer upon intravenous delivery of AAV9 vectors. Gene Ther 18(2):199–209. doi:10.1038/gt.2010.141
36. Bo Y, Guo G, Yao W (2013) MiRNA-mediated tumor specific delivery of TRAIL reduced glioma growth. J Neuro-Oncol 112(1):27–37. doi:10.1007/s11060-012-1033-y
37. Liu J, Ma L, Li C, Zhang Z, Yang G, Zhang W (2013) Tumor-targeting TRAIL expression mediated by miRNA response elements suppressed growth of uveal melanoma cells. Mol Oncol 7(6):1043–1055. doi:10.1016/j.molonc.2013.08.003
38. Kelly EJ, Russell SJ (2009) MicroRNAs and the regulation of vector tropism. Mol Ther 17(3):409–416. doi:10.1038/mt.2008.288
39. Bogerd HP, Skalsky RL, Kennedy EM, Furuse Y, Whisnant AW, Flores O, Schultz KL, Putnam N, Barrows NJ, Sherry B, Scholle F, Garcia-Blanco MA, Griffin DE, Cullen BR (2014) Replication of many human viruses is refractory to inhibition by endogenous cellular microRNAs. J Virol 88(14):8065–8076. doi:10.1128/JVI.00985-14
40. Bondanese VP, Francisco-Garcia A, Bedke N, Davies DE, Sanchez-Elsner T (2014) Identification of host miRNAs that may limit human rhinovirus replication. World J Biol Chem 5(4):437–456. doi:10.4331/wjbc.v5.i4.437
41. Kuehl U, Lassner D, Gast M, Stroux A, Rohde M, Siegismund C, Wang X, Escher F, Gross M, Skurk C, Tschoepe C, Loebel M, Scheibenbogen C, Schultheiss HP, Poller W (2015) Differential cardiac microRNA expression predicts the clinical course in human enterovirus cardiomyopathy. Circ Heart Fail 8(3):605–618. doi:10.1161/CIRCHEARTFAILURE.114.001475
42. Fu YR, Liu XJ, Li XJ, Shen ZZ, Yang B, Wu CC, Li JF, Miao LF, Ye HQ, Qiao GH, Rayner S, Chavanas S, Davrinche C, Britt WJ, Tang Q, McVoy M, Mocarski E, Luo MH (2015) MicroRNA miR-21 attenuates human cytomegalovirus replication in neural cells by targeting Cdc25a. J Virol 89(2):1070–1082. doi:10.1128/JVI.01740-14
43. Takaoka A, Yanai H (2006) Interferon signalling network in innate defence. Cell Microbiol8(6):907–922.doi:10.1111/j.1462-5822.2006.00716.x
44. Hou W, Tian Q, Zheng J, Bonkovsky HL (2010) MicroRNA-196 represses Bach1 protein and hepatitis C virus gene expression in human hepatoma cells expressing hepatitis C viral proteins. Hepatology 51(5):1494–1504. doi:10.1002/hep.23401
45. Bruni R, Marcantonio C, Tritarelli E, Tataseo P, Stellacci E, Costantino A, Villano U, Battistini A, Ciccaglione AR (2011) An integrated approach identifies IFN-regulated microRNAs and targeted mRNAs modulated by different HCV replicon clones. BMC Genomics 12:485. doi:10.1186/1471-2164-12-485
46. Tomasec P, Braud VM, Rickards C, Powell MB, McSharry BP, Gadola S, Cerundolo V, Borysiewicz LK, McMichael AJ, Wilkinson GW (2000) Surface expression of HLA-E, an inhibitor of natural killer cells, enhanced by human cytomegalovirus gpUL40. Science 287(5455):1031
47. Nachmani D, Zimmermann A, Oiknine Djian E, Weisblum Y, Livneh Y, Khanh Le VT, Galun E, Horejsi V, Isakov O, Shomron N, Wolf DG, Hengel H, Mandelboim O (2014) MicroRNA editing facilitates immune elimination of HCMV

infected cells. PLoS Pathog 10(2):e1003963. doi:10.1371/journal.ppat.1003963
48. Guo YE, Steitz JA (2014) Virus meets host microRNA: the destroyer, the booster, the hijacker. Mol Cell Biol 34(20):3780–3787. doi:10.1128/MCB.00871-14
49. Ensser A, Fleckenstein B (2005) T-cell transformation and oncogenesis by gamma2-herpesviruses. Adv Cancer Res 93:91–128. doi:10.1016/S0065-230X(05)93003-0
50. Wassarman DA, Lee SI, Steitz JA (1989) Nucleotide sequence of HSUR 5 RNA from herpesvirus saimiri. Nucleic Acids Res 17(3):1258
51. Cazalla D, Yario T, Steitz JA (2010) Down-regulation of a host microRNA by a Herpesvirus saimiri noncoding RNA. Science 328(5985):1563–1566. doi:10.1126/science.1187197
52. Chi SW, Zang JB, Mele A, Darnell RB (2009) Argonaute HITS-CLIP decodes microRNA-mRNA interaction maps. Nature 460(7254):479–486. doi:10.1038/nature08170
53. Guo YE, Riley KJ, Iwasaki A, Steitz JA (2014) Alternative capture of noncoding RNAs or protein-coding genes by herpesviruses to alter host T cell function. Mol Cell 54(1):67–79. doi:10.1016/j.molcel.2014.03.025
54. Buck AH, Perot J, Chisholm MA, Kumar DS, Tuddenham L, Cognat V, Marcinowski L, Dolken L, Pfeffer S (2010) Post-transcriptional regulation of miR-27 in murine cytomegalovirus infection. RNA 16(2):307–315. doi:10.1261/rna.1819210
55. Libri V, Helwak A, Miesen P, Santhakumar D, Borger JG, Kudla G, Grey F, Tollervey D, Buck AH (2012) Murine cytomegalovirus encodes a miR-27 inhibitor disguised as a target. Proc Natl Acad Sci U S A 109(1):279–284. doi:10.1073/pnas.1114204109
56. Marcinowski L, Tanguy M, Krmpotic A, Radle B, Lisnic VJ, Tuddenham L, Chane-Woon-Ming B, Ruzsics Z, Erhard F, Benkartek C, Babic M, Zimmer R, Trgovcich J, Koszinowski UH, Jonjic S, Pfeffer S, Dolken L (2012) Degradation of cellular mir-27 by a novel, highly abundant viral transcript is important for efficient virus replication in vivo. PLoS Pathog 8(2):e1002510. doi:10.1371/journal.ppat.1002510
57. Papenfort K, Vogel J (2014) Small RNA functions in carbon metabolism and virulence of enteric pathogens. Front Cell Infect Microbiol 4:91. doi:10.3389/fcimb.2014.00091
58. Nishizawa T, Suzuki H (2015) Gastric carcinogenesis and underlying molecular mechanisms: Helicobacter pylori and novel targeted therapy. Biomed Res Int 2015:794378. doi:10.1155/2015/794378
59. Vogel J, Wagner EG (2007) Target identification of small noncoding RNAs in bacteria. Curr Opin Microbiol 10(3):262–270. doi:10.1016/j.mib.2007.06.001
60. Viegas SC, Arraiano CM (2008) Regulating the regulators: how ribonucleases dictate the rules in the control of small non-coding RNAs. RNA Biol 5(4):230–243
61. Gottesman S, Storz G (2011) Bacterial small RNA regulators: versatile roles and rapidly evolving variations. Cold Spring Harb Perspect Biol 3(12). doi:10.1101/cshperspect.a003798
62. Harris JF, Micheva-Viteva S, Li N, Hong-Geller E (2013) Small RNA-mediated regulation of host-pathogen interactions. Virulence 4(8):785–795. doi:10.4161/viru.26119
63. Storz G, Vogel J, Wassarman KM (2011) Regulation by small RNAs in bacteria: expanding frontiers. Mol Cell 43(6):880–891. doi:10.1016/j.molcel.2011.08.022
64. Michaux C, Verneuil N, Hartke A, Giard JC (2014) Physiological roles of small RNA molecules. Microbiology 160(Pt 6):1007–1019. doi:10.1099/mic.0.076208-0
65. Frohlich KS, Vogel J (2009) Activation of gene expression by small RNA. Curr Opin Microbiol 12(6):674–682. doi:10.1016/j.mib.2009.09.009
66. Fozo EM, Hemm MR, Storz G (2008) Small toxic proteins and the antisense RNAs that repress them. Microbiol Mol Biol Rev 72(4):579–589. doi:10.1128/MMBR.00025-08. Table of Contents
67. Hawiger J, Veach RA, Zienkiewicz J (2015) New paradigms in sepsis: from prevention to protection of failing microcirculation. J Thromb Haemost. doi:10.1111/jth.13061
68. Tabet F, Vickers KC, Cuesta Torres LF, Wiese CB, Shoucri BM, Lambert G, Catherinet C, Prado-Lourenco L, Levin MG, Thacker S, Sethupathy P, Barter PJ, Remaley AT, Rye KA (2014) HDL-transferred microRNA-223 regulates ICAM-1 expression in endothelial cells. Nat Commun 5:3292. doi:10.1038/ncomms4292
69. Sun X, Icli B, Wara AK, Belkin N, He S, Kobzik L, Hunninghake GM, Vera MP, Registry M, Blackwell TS, Baron RM, Feinberg MW (2012) MicroRNA-181b regulates NF-kappaB-mediated vascular inflammation. J Clin Invest 122(6):1973–1990. doi:10.1172/JCI61495
70. Marraffini LA, Sontheimer EJ (2010) CRISPR interference: RNA-directed adaptive immunity in bacteria and archaea. Nat Rev Genet 11(3):181–190. doi:10.1038/nrg2749
71. Bolotin A, Quinquis B, Sorokin A, Ehrlich SD (2005) Clustered regularly interspaced short

palindrome repeats (CRISPRs) have spacers of extrachromosomal origin. Microbiology 151(Pt 8):2551–2561. doi:10.1099/mic.0.28048-0
72. Ishino Y, Shinagawa H, Makino K, Amemura M, Nakata A (1987) Nucleotide sequence of the iap gene, responsible for alkaline phosphatase isozyme conversion in *Escherichia coli*, and identification of the gene product. J Bacteriol 169(12):5429–5433
73. Borchert GM, Holton NW, Williams JD, Hernan WL, Bishop IP, Dembosky JA, Elste JE, Gregoire NS, Kim JA, Koehler WW, Lengerich JC, Medema AA, Nguyen MA, Ower GD, Rarick MA, Strong BN, Tardi NJ, Tasker NM, Wozniak DJ, Gatto C, Larson ED (2011) Comprehensive analysis of microRNA genomic loci identifies pervasive repetitive-element origins. Mob Genet Elements 1(1):8–17. doi:10.4161/mge.1.1.15766
74. Filshtein TJ, Mackenzie CO, Dale MD, Dela-Cruz PS, Ernst DM, Frankenberger EA, He C, Heath KL, Jones AS, Jones DK, King ER, Maher MB, Mitchell TJ, Morgan RR, Sirobhushanam S, Halkyard SD, Tiwari KB, Rubin DA, Borchert GM, Larson ED (2012) OrbId: Origin-based identification of microRNA targets. Mob Genet Elements 2(4):184–192. doi:10.4161/mge.21617
75. Roberts JT, Cardin SE, Borchert GM (2014) Burgeoning evidence indicates that microRNAs were initially formed from transposable element sequences. Mob Genet Elements 4:e29255. doi:10.4161/mge.29255
76. Roberts JT, Cooper EA, Favreau CJ, Howell JS, Lane LG, Mills JE, Newman DC, Perry TJ, Russell ME, Wallace BM, Borchert GM (2013) Continuing analysis of microRNA origins: formation from transposable element insertions and noncoding RNA mutations. Mob Genet Elements 3(6):e27755. doi:10.4161/mge.27755
77. Sorek R, Kunin V, Hugenholtz P (2008) CRISPR—a widespread system that provides acquired resistance against phages in bacteria and archaea. Nat Rev Microbiol 6(3):181–186. doi:10.1038/nrmicro1793
78. Li HH, Ma F, Zeng X, Wang JY, Yuan P, Fan Y, Xu BH (2011) Comparison of fluorescence in situ hybridization and immunohistochemistry assessment for Her-2 status in breast cancer and its relationship to clinicopathological characteristics. Zhonghua Yi Xue Za Zhi 91(2):76–80
79. Makarova KS, Grishin NV, Shabalina SA, Wolf YI, Koonin EV (2006) A putative RNA-interference-based immune system in prokaryotes: computational analysis of the predicted enzymatic machinery, functional analogies with eukaryotic RNAi, and hypothetical mechanisms of action. Biol Direct 1:7. doi:10.1186/1745-6150-1-7
80. Jiang M, Sang X, Hong Z (2012) Beyond nutrients: food-derived microRNAs provide cross-kingdom regulation. Bioessays 34(4):280–284. doi:10.1002/bies.201100181

Chapter 4

MicroRNAs: Biomarkers, Diagnostics, and Therapeutics

Weili Huang

Abstract

MicroRNAs (miRNAs) are small noncoding RNAs (21–23 nucleotides in length) that regulate gene expression at translational or posttranslational levels. The major regulatory mechanisms include translational repression or mRNA degradation (Filipowicz et al., Curr Opin Struct Biol 15:331–341, 2005).

Aberrant expression of miRNAs has been found to be associated with a variety of human diseases such as cancers/tumors, diabetes, viral infections, cardiovascular diseases, neurodegenerative diseases, and other diseases (Wang et al., J Cell Physiol 23:25–30, 2016; Lawrie, MicroRNAs in medicine, 2013). The expression of miRNAs is tissue specific and can be used to identify tumor type and its origin (Mishra and Merlino, J Clin Invest 119:2119–2123, 2009). Many investigations suggest that the miRNA-expression profiles are novel diagnostic and prognostic biomarkers for multiple human diseases. Manipulating relevant miRNA expression or function may serve as potential therapeutic strategies for different diseases.

Key words Biomarkers, Diagnostics, miRNA, Prognostics, Regulation, Therapeutics

1 MicroRNAs

MicroRNAs (miRNAs) are small noncoding, single-stranded, 21–23-nucleotide RNAs. MiRNAs regulate expression of many genes by base pairing to complementary sequences of the 3′-untranslated region (3′-UTR), which lead to translation repression. MiRNAs can also regulate gene expressions at transcriptional levels through deadenylation, degradation, and/or destabilization of target mRNAs [1, 2].

MiRNAs are expressed in various tissues and cell types. As biological regulators, miRNAs play important roles in physiological processes such as cell growth, proliferation, differentiation, apoptosis, metabolism, and homeostasis [3–6].

2 MicroRNAs: Disease Biomarkers

MiRNAs are stable and can be detected in plasma, blood, urine, saliva, and other body fluids. Circulating miRNAs secreted from tumor tissues are protected from endogenous RNase activity [7].

Jingshan Huang et al. (eds.), *Bioinformatics in MicroRNA Research*, Methods in Molecular Biology, vol. 1617,
DOI 10.1007/978-1-4939-7046-9_4, © Springer Science+Business Media LLC 2017

Previous studies have indicated that the dysregulated expression levels of circulating miRNAs are associated with cancer/tumors including prostate, breast, cervical, lung, gastric, colorectal cancer as well as leukemia, lymphoma, melanoma, and hepatocellular carcinoma [3, 8]. Besides cancer, the abnormal expression levels of circulating miRNAs are associated with other diseases such as diabetes, ectopic pregnancy, hepatitis C, kidney injury, liver injury, pulmonary tuberculosis, sepsis, systemic lupus, systemic sclerosis, and myocardial disease [3, 8]. Thus, circulating microRNAs are proposed as potential diagnostic and prognostic biomarkers in human diseases.

MiRNAs are also contained in microvesicles (i.e., exosomes), which are 30–120 nm membrane-derived vesicles. The exosomes medicate cellular cross-talk and miRNA secretion. For example, miRNAs in exosomes, secreted from cancer cells, can be engulfed by their surrounding or distant cells, and regulate physiological and immune response of those cells [9]. The regulatory mechanism of miRNA may lead to the development of new personalized treatments for cancer patients. Exosomal miRNAs exosomes are released into body fluids such as blood and urine, and could be used as potential diagnostic biomarkers for diseases.

2.1 MiRNAs as Biomarkers for Cancers/ Tumors

Cancers are diseases caused by uncontrolled growth of abnormal cells which invade healthy cells and tissues. MiRNAs control important cellular processes such as proliferation, differentiation, adhesion, apoptosis, and angiogenesis. Deregulation of the expression of miRNAs may play primary roles in the onset, progression, and metastasis of cancer [3, 10].

Previous studies have demonstrated that the expression of miRNAs is tissue-specific, and plays an important role in maintaining tissue-specific functions and cellular differentiation [11]. MiRNAs are expressed in cancer or tumor tissues from patients with colorectal cancer, breast cancer, hepatocellular carcinoma, melanoma, glioblastomas, lung cancer, pancreatic cancer, papillary thyroid carcinoma, and renal tumor [3, 12].

MiRNA down-regulation and gene deletion in cancer was first reported in 2002. The study showed that microRNA genes (miR-15 and miR-16) are located within a 30 kb region of chromosome 13q14, which is frequently deleted in chronic lymphocytic leukemia (CLL) [13]. The expression profiles of miRNA are altered in a various of cancer types, such as breast cancer [14], leukemia [15, 16], lung adenocarcinoma [17], hepatocellular carcinoma [18, 19], ovarian cancer [20], pancreatic cancer [21, 22], papillary thyroid carcinoma [23, 24], glioblastoma [25], and prostate cancer [26]. MicroRNA expression signatures are reported to reflect developmental origin of the tumor type [11, 27]. Therefore, tumor types and subtypes could be classified by miRNAs according to the origin of tissues and cells [28, 29]. In addition, the genetic alterations in miRNA biogenesis machinery, such as DROSHA, DGCR8, DICER, TARBP2, AGO2, Dicer, and Exportin-5 (XPO5), were reported to be involved in the cellular transformation and carcinogenesis process in different tumor and cancer types [30–32].

MiRNAs can act as oncogenes, and facilitate tumorigenesis including proliferation, angiogenesis, invasion, and migration. MiR-17~92 Cluster, miR-10b, miR-21, miR-103, miR-107, miR-141, miR-155, miR-221, miR-222, miR-372, miR-373, and miR-520c are overexpressed or dysregulated in multiple or different types of malignancies, including lymphomas, leukemia, neuroblastoma, glioblastoma, thyroid carcinoma, testicular tumors, and breast, lung, colon, stomach, colorectal, liver and pancreatic cancers [3, 8, 33]. On the other hand, miRNAs act as tumor suppressors, such as the let-7 family, miR-15a, miRNA-16-1, miR-27b, miR-29, miR-31, miR-34, miR-96, miR-101, miR-125a, miR-125b, miR-126, miR-145, miR-200c, miR-203, and miR-335 [3, 8, 33]. Tumor suppressors regulate the cell cycle, apoptosis, differentiation, DNA repair, angiogenesis, and metastasis. They are silenced or down-expressed in many different types of cancer. Overexpression or reintroduction of those miRNAs as tumor suppressors can inhibit tumor growth, by the control of cancer cell survival, proliferation, invasion, and migration.

MiRNAs can be detected in blood, plasma, serum, urine, saliva, cystic fluid, pancreatic juice, and sputum [3]. An early study showed that serum miRNAs can be used as biomarkers for diffuse large B cell lymphoma (DLBCL), which is an aggressive malignancy that accounts for nearly 40% of all lymphoid tumors [34]. Later, various miRNAs in serum, plasma, urine, and saliva samples have been proposed as diagnostic biomarkers of different types of cancer [35]. For example, serum levels of miR-141 can distinguish patients with prostate cancer from healthy individuals [7], the ratio of miR-126:miR-182 in urine samples can be used to identify urothelial bladder cancer [36], and saliva levels of miR-125a and miR-200a can be used for oral cancer detection [37].

2.2 MiRNAs as Biomarkers for Diabetes

Diabetes is a condition with high blood glucose levels. Chronically exposed to the high concentration of glucose, organs suffer dysfunction and failure due to micro-and macrovascular damage. MiRNAs are critical regulators of the development and physiological state of metabolically active tissues, including insulin release and resistance. In pre-diabetic and diabetic conditions, miRNAs expression profiles in both organs and serum are altered, consequently impairing insulin signaling, glucose, and lipid homeostasis [8].

The expression of serum miRNAs has been investigated in type 1 diabetes patients (T1D). For example, miR-25 was found to be associated with residual beta-cell function and glycemic control during T1D progression [38]. Also, miR-152, miR-30a-5p, miR-181a, miR-24, miR-148a, miR-210, miR-27a, miR-29a, miR-26a, miR-27b, miR-25, and miR-200a were upregulated in T1D patients [38]. With regard to type 2 diabetes (T2D), serum miR-126 was proposed to be used as a biomarker for pre-diabetes and T2D [39]. Also, another study revealed that serum miR-23a was a valuable biomarker for the early detection of T2D and pre-diabetes with normal glucose tolerance [40]. Furthermore, serum miRNAs such as miR-29a, miR-222, and miR-132 were reported to be differentially expressed between gestational diabetes mellitus (GDM) women and controls, and they were suggested as candidate biomarkers for predicting GDM [41].

2.3 MiRNAs as Regulators for Viral Infections

When host is infected by virus, host gene expression including host miRNAs is altered. It was reported that some viruses could reduce host miRNA accumulation, shut down the miRNA machinery, and mediate degradation of cellular miRNAs [8]. Generally, viral miRNAs targets host and viral genes, playing regulatory roles in both cell cycle and viral cycle, including development, growth, homeostasis, immune response, and apoptosis to augment their replication potential [8, 42].

On the contrary, the host miRNAs could control viral infection and replication [3]. For example, miR-199a-3p and miR-210 suppressed hepatitis B virus (HBV) replication [43], miR-199a reduced hepatitis C virus (HCV) RNA replication activity [44], and miR-32 restricted the accumulation of the retrovirus primate foamy virus type 1 (PFV-1) in the human host cells [45]. Additionally, miRNAs can inhibit human immunodeficiency type I virus (HIV-1) production by a novel mechanism, which involves binding to the viral Gag protein and preventing the HIV RNA-mediated assembly into viral particles [46]. These miRNAs may serve as novel targets for antiviral therapy. A recent study reported that circulating miR-122, miR-22, and miR-34a were correlated with the etiology of liver injury in HIV patients, and may serve as biomarkers for liver injury in HIV patients [47].

2.4 MiRNAs as Biomarkers for Cardiovascular Diseases

According to the World Health Organization (WHO), cardiovascular diseases (CVDs) are the number one cause of death in the world. About 17.5 million people died from CVDs in 2012, representing 31% of all global deaths. MiRNAs are key regulators of biological processes related to cardiac development and maintenance, as well as multiple cardiovascular diseases. Altered gene expressions result in pathological changes of the heart. MiRNAs are up or downregulated in the following diseases, such as cardiac hypertrophy, myocardial ischemia, myocardial infarction (MI), arrhythmia, angiogenesis, atherosclerosis, coronary artery disease, vascular disease, heart failure, atrial fibrillation, lipid metabolism, and cardiac fibrosis [3, 8, 48]. MiRNAs in the systemic circulation may reflect tissue damage, and circulating miRNAs such as miR-1, miR-126, miR-197, miR-208a, and miR-223 have been suggested as novel and potential biomarkers for the diagnosis of acute myocardial infarction (AMI) [49–51]. In addition, a panel of four miRNAs (miR-16, miR-27a, miR-101, miR-150) was reported to aid in prognostication of outcome after AMI [52]. Moreover, miR-29, miR-92a, and miR-328 MI are indicated as potential targets for treatment of MI, ischemic disease, and atrial fibrillation, respectively [8].

2.5 MiRNAs as Biomarkers for Neurodegenerative Diseases

Neurodegenerative diseases occur when neurons lose structure or function progressively. MiRNAs regulate gene expression in cell-fate decisions and play critical roles during the development of the nervous system [53]. Aberrant miRNA regulation is involved in neurodegenerative diseases such as Alzheimer's disease, Parkinson's disease, and amyotrophic lateral sclerosis (ALS) [3, 8, 54]. For example, miRNA binding sites were identified in amyloid precursor protein (APP) which may be related to Alzheimer's disease [8]. In addition, miRNAs regulate Aβ biogenesis and the alterations in miRNA population are associated with the disease progression [8]. Furthermore, miR-107 is expressed at a low level in the cortex of Alzheimer's disease patients, and it may accelerate disease progression through regulation of beta-site amyloid precursor protein-cleaving enzyme [3, 55].

With regard to Parkinson's disease, miRNAs regulate α-synuclein gene expression that was related to the disease. A mutation in the miRNA-433 binding site of fibroblast growth factor 20 (FGF20) increased risks for Parkinson's disease by overexpression of α-synuclein [8, 56]. In addition, miR-1, miR-22*, and miR-29 expression levels can be used to distinguish nontreated patients with Parkinson's disease from healthy subjects. It suggests that those miRNAs are potential novel and effective biomarkers for Parkinson's disease [57].

MiRNA expression profiles provide evidence for progression of neurodegenerative diseases, and the control of miRNA expression may serve as a novel tool for therapeutic purposes.

2.6 MiRNA as Biomarkers for Other Diseases

Altered expression of miRNAs is found to be associated with abnormal pregnancy, immune disease, bowel diseases, as well as liver and kidney diseases. MiRNA expression levels may be used as biomarkers for the diagnosis of those diseases. For example, circulating miR-323-3p (with hCG and progesterone) was suggested as a biomarker for the diagnosis of ectopic pregnancy [58]. The expression levels of miR-155 and miR-146a were increased in rheumatoid arthritis [3, 59]. Multiple miRNAs including miR-16, miR-23a, miR-29a, miR-106a, miR-107, miR-126, miR-191, miR-199a-5p, miR-200c, miR-362-3p, and miR-532-3p were expressed at significantly higher levels in the blood from patients with Crohn's disease, compared with the healthy controls [60].

Plasma miR-122 was proposed as a biomarker for viral-, alcohol-, and chemical-related hepatic diseases [61]. In addition, serum levels of miR-34a and miR-122 may be used as novel and noninvasive biomarkers of diagnosis and histological disease severity in patients with hepatitis C infection (CHC) or non-alcoholic fatty-liver disease (NAFLD) [62]. Urinary miRNAs such as miR-1, miR-133, miR-223, and miR-199 were found to be dysregulated in patients with autosomal-dominant polycystic kidney disease, and miRNA profiles can be used as potential biomarkers of disease progression [63]. In addition, circulating miRNAs such as miR-210 was deregulated in critically ill patients with acute kidney injury (AKI) and it predicted mortality in this patient cohort. Thus, it may serve as a novel biomarker for AKI reflecting pathophysiological changes on a cellular level [64].

3 MiRNA-Based Therapeutic Intervention

MiRNAs are important regulators in physiological processes such as cellular development and homeostasis. Because abnormal miRNA expression is associated with many diseases, miRNAs become potential therapeutic targets and manipulation of their expression is used as new clinical treatment strategies. In cancer patients, some tumor suppressor miRNAs are often low expressed in cancer/tumors, whereas oncogene miRNAs are overexpressed in cancer/tumors. Many studies have been conducted to deliver miRNA (i.e., miRNA replacement) to increase miRNA levels to suppress oncogenes; or deliver miRNA inhibitors to decrease miRNA levels for upregulation of tumor suppressor genes [8].

For miRNA replacement, the miRNAs were delivered into animal/xenografts models to block or inhibit tumor growth, such as let-7, miR-26a, miR-34a, miR-29b, miR-143, miR-101, miR-33a, miR-145, miR-15a, miR-16, miR-196a, and miR-502 [3, 8]. On the other hand, designed miRNA inhibitors were delivered in vivo to inhibit target miRNAs including let-7, miR-122, miR-16, miR-194, miR-10b, miR-134, and miR-192 [3, 8]. The miRNA inhibitors include anti-miRs, antagomirs, anti-miRNA oligonucleotides (AMOs), decoys, or sponges.

The miRNA delivery methods include viral and non-viral-based systems. Viral systems use virus such as retrovirus, lentivirus, adenovirus, or adeno-associated virus to transduce cells and tissues with miRNA genes. The non-viral systems include lipid-based systems, polymer-based systems, and inorganic carriers [8, 65, 66].

Fomivirsen (Vitravene) is the first antisense drug approved by US FDA for the treatment of AIDS-related cytomegalovirus (CMV) retinitis. It is a phosphorothioate oligonucleotide that inhibits human CMV replication by pairing to the CMV mRNA [67]. Ipomersen (Kynamro) is another antisense oligonucleotide drug targeted to mRNA for apo B-100. The drug was approved to reduce low-density lipoprotein-cholesterol (LDL-C), apolipoprotein-B (apo B), total cholesterol (TC), and non-high-density lipoprotein–cholesterol in patients with homozygous familial hypercholesterolemia (HoFH) [67].

4 MiRNA Detection Methods

There are several approaches that have been used for miRNA detection and quantitation, including quantitative real-time PCR (qPCR), northern blots analysis, RNase protection assays, in situ hybridization analysis, miRNA microarray, next-generation sequencing (NGS), and the nanotechnology-based assay [3, 68, 69].

5 Conclusion

MiRNAs are expressed in a variety of tissues and associated with different diseases such as cancer, diabetes, viral infections, neurodegenerative diseases, cardiovascular disorders, and other diseases. MiRNAs have been detected and measured in biological fluids, including blood, plasma, serum, urine, and saliva. MiRNAs may serve as novel and noninvasive biomarkers of diseases. In addition, miRNAs can be potential and promising therapeutic targets for disease treatment.

References

1. Giraldez AJ, Mishima Y, Rihel J, Grocock RJ, Van Dongen S, Inoue K, Enright AJ, Schier AF (2006) Zebrafish miR-430 promotes deadenylation and clearance of maternal mRNAs. Science 312:75–79. doi:10.1126/science.1122689
2. Filipowicz W, Jaskiewicz L, Kolb FA, Pillai RS (2005) Post-transcriptional gene silencing by siRNAs and miRNAs. Curr Opin Struct Biol 15:331–341. doi:10.1016/j.sbi.2005.05.006
3. Wang J, Chen J, Sen S (2016) MicroRNA as biomarkers and diagnostics. J Cell Physiol 23:25–30. doi:10.1002/jcp.25056
4. Brennecke J, Hipfner DR, Stark A, Russell RB, Cohen SM (2003) bantam encodes a developmentally regulated microRNA that controls cell proliferation and regulates the proapoptotic gene hid in Drosophila. Cell 113:25–36. doi:10.1016/S0092-8674(03)00231-9
5. Bartel DP (2004) MicroRNAs: genomics, biogenesis, mechanism, and function. Cell 116:281–297. doi:10.1016/S0092-8674(04)00045-5
6. Chen CZ, Li L, Lodish HF, Bartel DP (2004) MicroRNAs modulate hematopoietic lineage differentiation. Science 303:83–86. doi:10.1126/science.1091903
7. Mitchell PS, Parkin RK, Kroh EM, Fritz BR, Wyman SK, Pogosova-Agadjanyan EL, Peterson A, Noteboom J, O'Briant KC, Allen A, Lin DW, Urban N, Drescher CW, Knudsen BS, Stirewalt DL, Gentleman R, Vessella RL, Nelson PS, Martin DB, Tewari M (2008) Circulating microRNAs as stable blood-based markers for cancer detection. Proc Natl Acad Sci U S A 105:10513–10518. doi:10.1073/pnas.0804549105
8. Lawrie CH (2013) MicroRNAs in medicine. John Wiley & Sons, Inc., Hoboken, NJ. doi:10.1002/9781118300312
9. Challagundla KB, Fanini F, Vannini I, Wise P, Murtadha M, Malinconico L, Cimmino A,

Fabbri M (2014) microRNAs in the tumor microenvironment: solving the riddle for a better diagnostics. Expert Rev Mol Diagn 14:565–574. doi:10.1586/14737159.2014.922879
10. Palmero EI, de Campos SG, Campos M, de Souza NC, Guerreiro ID, Carvalho AL, Marques MM (2011) Mechanisms and role of microRNA deregulation in cancer onset and progression. Genet Mol Biol 34:363–370. doi:10.1590/S1415-47572011000300001
11. Mishra PJ, Merlino G (2009) MicroRNA reexpression as differentiation therapy in cancer. J Clin Invest 119:2119–2123. doi:10.1172/JCI40107
12. Garzon R, Fabbri M, Cimmino A, Calin GA, Croce CM (2006) MicroRNA expression and function in cancer. Trends Mol Med 12:580–587. doi:10.1016/j.molmed.2006.10.006
13. Calin GA, Dumitru CD, Shimizu M, Bichi R, Zupo S, Noch E, Aldler H, Rattan S, Keating M, Rai K, Rassenti L, Kipps T, Negrini M, Bullrich F, Croce CM (2002) Frequent deletions and down-regulation of micro-RNA genes miR15 and miR16 at 13q14 in chronic lymphocytic leukemia. Proc Natl Acad Sci U S A 99:15524–15529. doi:10.1073/pnas.242606799
14. Iorio MV, Ferracin M, Liu CG, Veronese A, Spizzo R, Sabbioni S, Magri E, Pedriali M, Fabbri M, Campiglio M, Ménard S, Palazzo JP, Rosenberg A, Musiani P, Volinia S, Nenci I, Calin GA, Querzoli P, Negrini M, Croce CM (2005) MicroRNA gene expression deregulation in human breast cancer. Cancer Res 65:7065–7070. doi:10.1158/0008-5472.CAN-05-1783
15. Calin GA, Liu CG, Sevignani C, Ferracin M, Felli N, Dumitru CD, Shimizu M, Cimmino A, Zupo S, Dono M, Dell'Aquila ML, Alder H, Rassenti L, Kipps TJ, Bullrich F, Negrini M, Croce CM (2004) MicroRNA profiling reveals distinct signatures in B cell chronic lymphocytic leukemias. Proc Natl Acad Sci U S A 101:11755–11760. doi:10.1073/pnas.0404432101
16. Calin GA, Ferracin M, Cimmino A, Di Leva G, Shimizu M, Wojcik SE, Iorio MV, Visone R, Sever NI, Fabbri M, Iuliano R, Palumbo T, Pichiorri F, Roldo C, Garzon R, Sevignani C, Rassenti L, Alder H, Volinia S, Liu CG, Kipps TJ, Negrini M, Croce CM (2005) A microRNA signature associated with prognosis and progression in chronic lymphocytic leukemia. N Engl J Med 352:1667–1676. doi:10.1056/NEJMMoa050995
17. Yanaihara N, Caplen N, Bowman E, Seike M, Kumamoto K, Yi M, Stephens RM, Okamoto A, Yokota J, Tanaka T, Calin GA, Liu CG, Croce CM, Harris CC (2006) Unique microRNA molecular profiles in lung cancer diagnosis and prognosis. Cancer Cell 9:189–198. doi:10.1016/j.ccr2006.01.025
18. Murakami Y, Yasuda T, Saigo K, Urashima T, Toyoda H, Okanoue T, Shimotohno K (2006) Comprehensive analysis of microRNA expression patterns in hepatocellular carcinoma and non-tumorous tissues. Oncogene 25:2537–2545. doi:10.1038/sj.onc.1209283
19. Qi J, Wang J, Katayama H, Sen S, Liu SM (2013) Circulating microRNAs (cmiRNAs) as novel potential biomarkers for hepatocellular carcinoma. Neoplasma 60:135–142. doi:10.4149/neo_2013_018
20. Iorio MV, Visone R, Di Leva G, Donati V, Petrocca F, Casalini P, Taccioli C, Volinia S, Liu CG, Alder H, Calin GA, Menard S, Croce CM (2007) MicroRNA signatures in human ovarian cancer. Cancer Res 67:8699–8707. doi:10.1158/0008-5472.CAN-07-1936
21. Roldo C, Missiaglia E, Hagan JP, Falconi M, Capelli P, Bersani S, Calin GA, Volinia S, Liu CG, Scarpa A, Croce CM (2006) MicroRNA expression abnormalities in pancreatic endocrine and acinar tumors are associated with distinctive pathological features and clinical behavior. J Clin Oncol 24:4677–4684. doi:10.1200/JCO.2005.05.5194
22. Wang J, Sen S (2011) MicroRNA functional network in pancreatic cancer: from biology to biomarkers of disease. J Biosci 36:481–491. doi:10.1007/s12038-011-9083-4
23. He H, Jazdzewski K, Li W, Liyanarachchi S, Nagy R, Volinia S, Calin GA, Liu CG, Franssila K, Suster S, Kloos RT, Croce CM, de la Chapelle A (2005) The role of microRNA genes in papillary thyroid carcinoma. Proc Natl Acad Sci U S A 102:19075–19080. doi:10.1073/pnas.0509603102
24. Pallante P, Visone R, Ferracin M, Ferraro A, Berlingieri MT, Troncone G, Chiappetta G, Liu CG, Santoro M, Negrini M, Croce CM, Fusco A (2006) MicroRNA deregulation in human thyroid papillary carcinomas. Endocr Relat Cancer 13:497–508. doi:10.1677/erc.1.01209
25. Ciafrè SA, Galardi S, Mangiola A, Ferracin M, Liu CG, Sabatino G, Negrini M, Maira G, Croce CM, Farace MG (2005) Extensive modulation of a set of microRNAs in primary glioblastoma. Biochem Biophys Res Commun 334:1351–1358. doi:10.1016/j.bbrc.2005.07.030
26. Porkka KP, Pfeiffer MJ, Waltering KK, Vessella RL, Tammela TLJ, Visakorpi T (2007) MicroRNA expression profiling in prostate cancer. Cancer Res 67:6130–6135. doi:10.1158/0008-5472.CAN-07-0533

27. Lu J, Getz G, Miska EA, Alvarez-Saavedra E, Lamb J, Peck D, Sweet-Cordero A, Ebert BL, Mak RH, Ferrando AA, Downing JR, Jacks T, Horvitz HR, Golub TR (2005) MicroRNA expression profiles classify human cancers. Nat Cell Biol 435:834–838. doi:10.1038/nature03702
28. Rosenfeld N, Aharonov R, Meiri E, Rosenwald S, Spector Y, Zepeniuk M, Benjamin H, Shabes N, Tabak S, Levy A, Lebanony D, Goren Y, Silberschein E, Targan N, Ben-Ari A, Gilad S, Sion-Vardy N, Tobar A, Feinmesser M, Kharenko O, Nativ O, Nass D, Perelman M, Yosepovich A, Shalmon B, Polak-Charcon S, Fridman E, Avniel A, Bentwich I, Bentwich Z, Cohen D, Chajut A, Barshack I (2008) MicroRNAs accurately identify cancer tissue origin. Nat Biotechnol 26:462–469. doi:10.1038/nbt1392
29. Wandt H, Haferlach T, Thiede C, Ehninger G (2010) WHO classification of myeloid neoplasms and leukemia. Blood 115:748–749. doi:10.1182/blood-2009-10-249664
30. Kumar MS, Lu J, Mercer KL, Golub TR, Jacks T (2007) Impaired microRNA processing enhances cellular transformation and tumorigenesis. Nat Genet 39:673–677. doi:10.1038/ng2003
31. Esteller M (2011) Noncoding RNAs in human disease. Nat Rev Genet 12:861–874. doi:10.1038/nrg3074
32. Huang JT, Wang J, Srivastava V, Sen S, Liu SM (2014) MicroRNA machinery genes as novel biomarkers for cancer. Front Oncol 4:113. doi:10.3389/fonc.2014.00113
33. Shenouda SK, Alahari SK (2009) MicroRNA function in cancer: oncogene or a tumor suppressor? Cancer Metastasis Rev 28:369–378. doi:10.1007/s10555-009-9188-5
34. Lawrie CH, Soneji S, Marafioti T, Cooper CDO, Palazzo S, Paterson JC, Cattan H, Enver T, Mager R, Boultwood J, Wainscoat JS, Hatton CSR (2007) MicroRNA expression distinguishes between germinal center B cell-like and activated B cell-like subtypes of diffuse large B cell lymphoma. Int J Cancer 121:1156–1161. doi:10.1002/ijc.22800
35. Etheridge A, Lee I, Hood L, Galas D, Wang K (2011) Extracellular microRNA: a new source of biomarkers. Mutat Res 717:85–90. doi:10.1016/j.mrfmmm.2011.03.004
36. Hanke M, Hoefig K, Merz H, Feller AC, Kausch I, Jocham D, Warnecke JM, Sczakiel G (2010) A robust methodology to study urine microRNA as tumor marker: microRNA-126 and microRNA-182 are related to urinary bladder cancer. Urol Oncol 28:655–661. doi:10.1016/j.urolonc.2009.01.027
37. Park NJ, Zhou H, Elashoff D, Henson BS, Kastratovic DA, Abemayor E, Wong DT (2009) Salivary microRNA: discovery, characterization, and clinical utility for oral cancer detection. Clin Cancer Res 15:5473–5477. doi:10.1158/1078-0432.CCR-09-0736
38. Nielsen LB, Wang C, Sorensen K, Bang-Berthelsen CH, Hansen L, Andersen ML, Hougaard P, Juul A, Zhang CY, Pociot F, Mortensen HB (2012) Circulating levels of microRNA from children with newly diagnosed type 1 diabetes and healthy controls: evidence that miR-25 associates to residual beta-cell function and glycaemic control during disease progression. Exp Diabetes Res 2012:896362. doi:10.1155/2012/896362
39. Liu Y, Gao G, Yang C, Zhou K, Shen B, Liang H, Jiang X (2014) The role of circulating microRNA-126 (miR-126): a novel biomarker for screening prediabetes and newly diagnosed type 2 diabetes mellitus. Int J Mol Sci 15:10567–10577. doi:10.3390/ijms150610567
40. Yang Z, Chen H, Si H, Li X, Ding X, Sheng Q, Chen P, Zhang H (2014) Serum miR-23a, a potential biomarker for diagnosis of pre-diabetes and type 2 diabetes. Acta Diabetol 51:823–831. doi:10.1007/s00592-014-0617-8
41. Zhao C, Dong J, Jiang T, Shi Z, Yu B, Zhu Y, Chen D, Xu J, Huo R, Dai J, Xia Y, Pan S, Hu Z, Sha J (2011) Early second-trimester serum miRNA profiling predicts gestational diabetes mellitus. PLoS One 6:e23925. doi:10.1371/journal.pone.0023925
42. Skalsky RL, Cullen BR (2010) Viruses, microRNAs, and host interactions. Annu Rev Microbiol 64:123–141. doi:10.1146/annurev.micro.112408.134243
43. Zhang GL, Li YX, Zheng SQ, Liu M, Li X, Tang H (2010) Suppression of hepatitis B virus replication by microRNA-199a-3p and microRNA-210. Antivir Res 88:169–175. doi:10.1016/j.antiviral.2010.08.008
44. Murakami Y, Aly HH, Tajima A, Inoue I, Shimotohno K (2009) Regulation of the hepatitis C virus genome replication by miR-199a. J Hepatol 50:453–460. doi:10.1016/j.jhep.2008.06.010
45. Lecellier CH, Dunoyer P, Arar K, Lehmann-Che J, Eyquem S, Himber C, Saib A, Voinnet O (2005) A cellular microRNA mediates antiviral defense in human cells. Science 308:557–560. doi:10.1126/science.1108784
46. Chen AK, Sengupta P, Waki K, Van Engelenburg SB, Ochiya T, Ablan SD, Freed EO, Lippincott-Schwartz J (2014) MicroRNA binding to the HIV-1 Gag protein inhibits Gag

assembly and virus production. Proc Natl Acad Sci U S A 111:E2676–E2683. doi:10.1073/pnas.1408037111

47. Anadol E, Schierwagen R, Elfimova N, Tack K, Schwarze-Zander C, Eischeid H, Noetel A, Boesecke C, Jansen C, Dold L, Wasmuth JC, Strassburg CP, Spengler U, Rockstroh JK, Odenthal M, Trebicka J (2015) Circulating microRNAs as a marker for liver injury in human immunodeficiency virus patients. Hepatology 61:46–55. doi:10.1002/hep.27369
48. Romaine SP, Tomaszewski M, Condorelli G, Samani NJ (2015) MicroRNAs in cardiovascular disease: an introduction for clinicians. Heart 101:921–928. doi:10.1136/heartjnl-2013-305402
49. Ai J, Zhang R, Li Y, Pu JL, Lu YJ, Jiao JD, Li K, Yu B, Li ZQ, Wang RR, Wang LH, Li Q, Wang N, Shan HL, Li ZY, Yang BF (2010) Circulating microRNA as a potential novel biomarker for acute myocardial infarction. Biochem Biophys Res Commun 391:73–77. doi:10.1016/j.bbrc.2009.11.005
50. Zampetaki A, Willeit P, Tilling L, Drozdov I, Prokopi M, Renard JM, Mayr A, Weger S, Schett G, Shah A, Boulanger CM, Willeit J, Chowienczyk PJ, Kiechl S, Mayr M (2012) Prospective study on circulating microRNAs and risk of myocardial infarction. J Am Coll Cardiol 60:290–299. doi:10.1016/j.jacc.2012.03.056
51. Wang GK, Zhu JQ, Zhang JT, Li Q, Li Y, He J, Qin YW, Jing Q (2010) Circulating microRNA: a novel potential biomarker for early diagnosis of acute myocardial infarction in humans. Eur Heart J 31:659–666. doi:10.1093/eurheartj/ehq013
52. Devaux Y, Vausort M, McCann GP, Kelly D, Collignon O, Ng LL, Wagner DR, Squire IB (2013) A panel of 4 microRNAs facilitates the prediction of left ventricular contractility after acute myocardial infarction. PLoS One 8:e70644. doi:10.1371/journal.pone.0070644
53. Fineberg SK, Kosik KS, Davidson BL (2009) MicroRNAs potentiate neural development. Neuron 64:303–309. doi:10.1016/j.neuron.2009.10.020
54. Williams AH, Valdez G, Moresi V, Qi X, McAnally J, Elliott JL, Bassel-Duby R, Sanes JR, Olson EN (2009) MicroRNA-206 delays ALS progression and promotes regeneration of neuromuscular synapses in mice. Science 326:1549–1554. doi:10.1126/science.1181046
55. Wang WX, Rajeev BW, Stromberg AJ, Ren N, Tang GL, Huang QW, Rigoutsos I, Nelson PT (2008) The expression of microRNA miR-107 decreases early in Alzheimer's disease and may accelerate disease progression through regulation of beta-site amyloid precursor protein-cleaving enzyme. J Neurosci 28:1213–1223. doi:10.1523/JNEUROSCI.5065-07.2008
56. Wang G, van der Walt JM, Mayhew G, Li YJ, Züchner S, Scott WK, Martin ER, Vance JM (2008) Variation in the miRNA-433 binding site of FGF20 confers risk for Parkinson disease by overexpression of alpha-synuclein. Am J Hum Genet 82:283–289. doi:10.1016/j.ajhg.2007.09.021
57. Margis R, Margis R, Rieder CR (2011) Identification of blood microRNAs associated to Parkinsonis disease. J Biotechnol 152:96–101. doi:10.1016/j.jbiotec.2011.01.023
58. Zhao Z, Zhao Q, Warrick J, Lockwood CM, Woodworth A, Moley KH, Gronowski AM (2012) Circulating microRNA miR-323-3p as a biomarker of ectopic pregnancy. Clin Chem 58:896–905. doi:10.1373/clinchem.2011.179283
59. Stanczyk J, Pedrioli DM, Brentano F, Sanchez-Pernaute O, Kolling C, Gay RE, Detmar M, Gay S, Kyburz D (2008) Altered expression of MicroRNA in synovial fibroblasts and synovial tissue in rheumatoid arthritis. Arthritis Rheum 58:1001–1009. doi:10.1002/art.23386
60. Paraskevi A, Theodoropoulos G, Papaconstantinou I, Mantzaris G, Nikiteas N, Gazouli M (2012) Circulating MicroRNA in inflammatory bowel disease. J Crohns Colitis 6:900–904. doi:10.1016/j.crohns.2012.02.006
61. Zhang Y, Jia Y, Zheng RY, Guo YJ, Wang Y, Guo H, Fei MY, Sun SH (2010b) Plasma microRNA-122 as a biomarker for viral-, alcohol-, and chemical-related hepatic diseases. Clin Chem 56:1830–1838. doi:10.1373/clinichem.2010.147850
62. Cermelli S, Ruggieri A, Marrero JA, Ioannou GN, Beretta L (2011) Circulating microRNAs in patients with chronic hepatitis C and non-alcoholic fatty liver disease. PLoS One 6:e23937. doi:10.1371/journal.pone.0023937
63. Ben-Dov IZ, Tan YC, Morozov P, Wilson PD, Rennert H, Blumenfeld JD, Tuschl T (2014) Urine microRNA as potential biomarkers of autosomal dominant polycystic kidney disease progression: description of miRNA profiles at baseline. PLoS One 9:e86856. doi:10.1371/journal.pone.0086856
64. Lorenzen JM, Kielstein JT, Hafer C, Gupta SK, Kümpers P, Faulhaber-Walter R, Haller H, Fliser D, Thum T (2011) Circulating miR-210 predicts survival in critically ill patients with

acute kidney injury. Clin J Am Soc Nephrol 6:1540–1546. doi:10.2215/CJN.00430111

65. Aigner A (2008) Cellular delivery in vivo of siRNA-based therapeutics. Curr Pharm Des 14:3603–3619. doi:10.2174/138161208786898815
66. Yang N (2015) An overview of viral and nonviral delivery systems for microRNA. Int J Pharm Investig 5:179–181. doi:10.4103/2230-973X.167646
67. Drug labeling, drugs@FDA. https://www.accessdata.fda.gov/scripts/cder/drugsatfda/
68. Chugh P, Dittmer DP (2012) Potential pitfalls in microRNA profiling. Wiley Interdiscip Rev RNA 3:601–616. doi:10.1002/wrna.1120
69. Wang Y, Zheng D, Tan Q, Wang MX, Gu LQ (2011) Nanopore-based detection of circulating microRNAs in lung cancer patients. Nat Nanotechnol 6:668–674. doi:10.1038/nnano.2011.147

Chapter 5

Relational Databases and Biomedical Big Data

N.H. Nisansa D. de Silva

Abstract

In various biomedical applications that collect, handle, and manipulate data, the amounts of data tend to build up and venture into the range identified as bigdata. In such occurrences, a design decision has to be taken as to what type of database would be used to handle this data. More often than not, the default and classical solution to this in the biomedical domain according to past research is relational databases. While this used to be the norm for a long while, it is evident that there is a trend to move away from relational databases in favor of other types and paradigms of databases. However, it still has paramount importance to understand the interrelation that exists between biomedical big data and relational databases. This chapter will review the pros and cons of using relational databases to store biomedical big data that previous researches have discussed and used.

Key words Relational databases, Big data, Biomedical big data, Data mining

1 Introduction

Since the beginning of the practice of handling biomedical data by computers, it was just a matter of time till biomedical big data would become a hot topic. This is due to the inherent nature of data volume that is associated with biomedical data. It should be noted that there are a very high number of applications that venture into the realm of data velocity as well. With this setting, it is no wonder a discussion about biomedical big data on relational databases is needed. With this setting, it is needed to have a discussion about biomedical big data on relational databases, especially given the widespread usage and simple nature of relational databases in not only biomedical but also other numerous fields. This chapter will give a brief introduction to all the concepts in question; relational databases, big data, and finally biomedical big data. We will be discussing the pros and cons of using relational databases for biomedical big data applications. The discussion will happen exclusively as a series of evidence for the argument and counter argument with rationales extracted from the respective researchers

Jingshan Huang et al. (eds.), *Bioinformatics in MicroRNA Research*, Methods in Molecular Biology, vol. 1617,
DOI 10.1007/978-1-4939-7046-9_5, © Springer Science+Business Media LLC 2017

themselves. We present the evidence in this was so that the reader may evaluate the evidence impartially and adopt a system that the reader may seem fit.

2 Rational Databases

Out of the ways that humans have devised to store digital data, relational databases arguably are a very popular choice. Relational databases are organized on the concept of relational model of data first introduced by E. F. Codd in 1970 [1]. The initial objective was to come up with a tool to help with accounting. But since then, relational databases have transcended that initial objective and have become useful in many avenues in data storage. The relational model is built on first-order predicate logic. In this model, all data is represented in terms of tuples. Tuples are grouped as relations, hence the name relational databases. A tuple in layman's words would be equal to a row of a table and a relation would be akin to the table that is made up by such rows of data. An attribute is a column in the table. In fact, the most popular way to show data from relational databases to humans is in this table form.

There are many software systems that are used to handle and mange relational database systems. They are called Relational Database Management Systems (RDBMS). The method to get information stored in a relational database is to query it. Almost all relational database systems use SQL (Structured Query Language) for both querying and maintaining the database. Microsoft SQL Server, Oracle Database, MySQL, and IBM DB2 are examples for popular Relational Database Management Systems. Out of these, MySQL is popular as a part of the LAMP stack (Linux, Apache, MySQL, PHP) which is widely used for web applications. Others are generally used for large enterprise applications more often than not.

The relational model gives users a declarative method to specify data and queries. In other words, the users directly mention what kind of data the database has and what they want from it. The underlying data structures and data storing/retrieving systems are handled by the Database Management System and are fully transparent to the user. Given below is a sample MySQL query.

SELECT firstName FROM Students WHERE Country = 'USA';

Even a person completely unaware of programming would be able to understand that this query is trying to get the first names of the students who are from USA. This is because of the declarative nature of the Structured Query Languages.

As mentioned earlier, most of the relational databases use a type of SQL for data definition and querying. A table in an SQL database contains a relation, the table name itself maps to a predicate variable in the relational model. Key and other constraints along with the aforementioned queries are mapped to predicates.

"Keys" that were mentioned in the previous paragraph are an integral part of relational databases. Each row of a table must have at least one unique key. A key may contain one or more attributes. For example, in a hospital data management system, the patient id number can be a key. The patient's social security number can also be a key. The combination of full name and address can also be a cumbersome but a mostly valid key. All these keys are valid because they are unique. In the very rare case of two patients with the same name living at the same address, the latter scheme breaks. But logically it is impossible for two people to have the same patient id number because it is generated by the database itself to be unique, so it is a very safe key.

Almost all of the processing done on tables depends on the ability to modify one and only one row at a time. This does not mean that queries that affect multiple rows are impossible. On the contrary, in fact, most practical applications extensively use multiple row manipulation or retrieval. What is discussed here is the inner workings of the database where even the queries that are applied on multiple rows are broken down to the single row level and then applied in batch or in parallel. This requirement of acting on a single row is what demands the usage of keys. Unlike in the case of the patient example given above where we conveniently have a unique id for each individual in the form of the patient id, most tables will not have such pre-existing unique ids. In this scenario, most physical implementations resort to a system-assigned, unique primary key (PK). When new data is added to the table, the system generates a unique value and enters that with the given data as the new row of the table. The system then uses this key to primarily access the table, hence the name. Most systems are performance enhanced for PKs. As mentioned earlier, a table may have other unique keys as single or combinations of attributes. These are called alternate keys (AK). Any primary key or alternate key can and should be able to uniquely identify a row within the table.

Rows in tables are linked to rows in other tables by adding a column of a unique key of the linked row of the linked table to the linking row of the linking table. For example, assume we are modeling a university, we have a professors table and a subjects table. We want to show which professor teaches each subject. The way to do this is to put the professor id from the professors table in a column of the subjects table. Such columns are called foreign keys. It has been proved by Codd that it is possible to represent data relationships of arbitrary complexity using this set of simple concepts.

One thing you may have noted in the previous example of the university modeling is that, while a single subject will be taught by a single professor, there is no restriction to prevent a single professor from teaching multiple subjects. Therefore, the foreign key professor id in the subject table would not necessarily have a unique value. This is an example of a One-to-Many relationship in a relational database. Similarly, there can be other relationships of the types; one-to-one and many-to-many. The person table and the car table might have a one-to-one relationship which shows the ownership of the car. A doctor table and the patient table might have a many-to-many relationship given that many doctors may treat the same patient and each doctor will have more than one patient.

As one might have identified by now, the method of adding a column as a foreign key might work as well for one-to-one as it did for one-to-many but we would be in a conundrum when it comes to many-to-many. Take the doctors and patients examples given above, putting the list of doctor ids for each patient or putting the list of patient ids for each doctor is a cumbersome way to solve the problem. In fact, most relational databases are created and designed in such a way that each column in each row holds only a single value. (This is called values being atomic.) The solution to this problem is to introduce a new link table in between the two tables. This link table will contain primary keys from both tables. Thus, each row of this link table will represent a unique relationship between a doctor and a patient. If we only consider the doctor table and the link table, it is as if we have a one-to-many relationship from doctor table to the link table. If we only consider the patient table and the link table, it is as if we have a one-to-many relationship from patient table to the link table. Therefore no database property is abridged. We have achieved portraying a many-to-many relationship between the doctor table and the patient table.

For the database management systems to operate accurately and safely, four properties are maintained in all transactions. These transactions are called ACID transactions. The A stands for Atomicity. It makes sure that each transaction happens in entirety or not at all. If one part of the transaction fails, no matter how much of the transaction has already executed, the entire transaction is considered failed. If that happens, the database is left unchanged. The database management system must guarantee atomicity under any and all situations, including but not limited to power failures, software or hardware errors, and crashes. An atomic transaction, to the outside world, appears to be an atomic unit. Further, in the case of an aborted transaction, none of its parts should happen. The C in ACID stands for Consistency. This property makes sure that each transaction will convert the database from one valid state to another. Any data written or altered by the said transaction must be valid under the defined rules of the database. One important thing to note here is the fact that this does not guarantee correctness in the way the application programmer might have wished it to be. That responsibility lies beyond database management and in the domain of application level code. What this property guarantees is the fact that programming errors will not result in database violating any of the defined rules. The I in the ACID stands for Isolation. This ensures that in a scenario where multiple transactions happen in parallel (concurrently), at the end, the database ends up in a state that is exactly the same as the state which it will be if the said transactions were executed serially (one after the other). Ensuring this property is the main objective of concurrency control. In concurrency control methods with strict serializability, the effects of incomplete transactions are completely invisible to the other transactions. This is not so in control methods with relaxed serializability. But both methods ensure that the Isolation property is preserved. Finally, the D in the ACID stands for Durability. This means if a transaction is committed, it will remain as committed despite power loss, crashes, or errors. To ensure that Durability is preserved against power loss, transactions or their effects are recorded in non-volatile memory.

3 Big Data

Big data is a blanket term for any data set too large or complex (or both) so much so that traditional data processing applications are proven to be inadequate. These challenges might arise within the realms of; analysis, capture, search, data curation, sharing, storage, transfer, visualization, and information privacy. However, in general usage, the term big data is often used to mean doing predictive analytics or other methods to obtain valuable knowledge from data regardless of the size of the data set. But in correct terminology, that process is data mining. It is possible to do data mining on big data but big data is not just about data mining. The importance of big data is the fact that accuracy in big data can lead to increased confidence in future decision making and thereby grater operational efficiency with reduced cost and risk.

Big data analysis can result in new correlations that help "spot business trends, prevent diseases, combat crime and so on" according to The Economist [2]. Various groups of people have to meet the challenge of big data. This includes governments, advertises, media agencies, business executives, and most importantly, scientists. Scientists encounter problems with large amounts of data in fields such as connectomics, complex physics simulations, genomics, meteorology, biological and environmental research. On the other side, governments, corporations, and political campaigns use big data to take informed decisions about their constituents, customers, and investors. These informed decisions are used to alter or enhance the course of their strategies.

A good example of this is how the 2012 Obama campaign used big data-based analytics done on the fused data from census, voter lists, active outreach, and social media such as Facebook to identify swing voters and ultimately approach and influence them [3]. As it was making waves recently, the National Security Agency (NSA) collects massive amounts of data from phone and Internet service providers and then runs various algorithms on the said data to find patterns that would tag potential terrorists or people of interest. It is mayhap controversial to the same extent and as well known that Google uses the data collected from a user's web history and geographical context to personalize search results. All the above cases have gone beyond just collecting data to the level of linking information to individual human beings. It might be useful to know what percentage of voters have a potential to be swayed. But knowing who they are exactly, can result in a more efficient campaign [4].

The growth of data size can be attributed to the rapid reduction of the price of sensory devices resulting in more numerous deployment of such devices, increased availability of various mobile devices, availability of drones and other aerial remote sensing equipment, radio-frequency identification readers, wireless sensor networks. The widespread use of equipment such as cameras and microphones that are attached to smartphones does a significant contribution as well. One very common, but not so obvious, source of big data for the average person is software logs of various systems; web servers, banking systems, flight reservations, hotel bookings. Almost all well-structured enterprise-level software systems generate logs for security and record-keeping purposes. With the advent of more novel technology, these logs have become both more numerous and more descriptive. According to Hilbert and López the world's technological per-capita capacity to store information has roughly doubled every 40 months since the 1980s [5]. IBM claims that, as of 2012, every day 2.5 exabytes (2.5 × 1018) of data were created [6]. Given that information is power, the question who has access to the company-related big data can disrupt the traditional company power hierarchies. Therefore, large enterprises often face a challenge as to who should own the big data or the associated initiative that straddle the entire organization [7].

It is generally accepted that relational database management systems and desktop-based statistics and visualization packages usually are not competent enough to handle big data. The consensus is that it needs "massively parallel software running on tens, hundreds, or even thousands of servers" [8]. However, it is worthy to note that what one would consider to be big data often varies on the capabilities and capacities of the users and the tools that they are using. Expanding capabilities makes what was considered to be big before, to be considered small or mediocre now. From the perspective of some organizations, hundreds of gigabytes of data can be considered big data; but for some technology giants, even hundreds of terabytes of data are a mundane and negligible load.

4 Biomedical Big Data

It has long been in the wind that big data will bring about an era of efficiency, accountability, and better services in the health care sector [9, 10]. This has not entirely been realized so far. In fact, there are other industries that have reaped better and more abundant benefits from the advent of big data than the biomedical sector. They have been quite successful in integrating their large-scale systems and analyzing heterogeneous data sources to obtain knowledge and value. Figuring out the inherent nature of big data, which makes it transformative once various disparate data sets are linked at individual personal level, has helped these industries to obtain this status. In contrast to this, big biomedical data are divided among institutions and are kept guarded and isolated to honor the patient privacy (which unquestionably is sacred to the medical profession) [4]. The common practice is to anonymize any and every bit of information that leaves the confines of the institution. This results in a situation where linking data from multiple sources becomes impossible. Sharing the anonymization scheme between institutions is not a valid solution because, even though it might prevent other parties from discovering information about individual patents, it will not prevent one institution from reverse engineering data presented by another institution to get to pre anonymized information to which they should not have access. This is akin to having two secure vaults with the same key combination with two people knowing the key combination of one vault. Trivially, both would now have access to both vaults even though initially and by law they should only have access to their own. Technical challenges such as this and other sociopolitical challenges will have to be addressed before we can see good strides in biomedical big data having significant influences on health care. Despite this, medical decision-making is becoming more and more dependent on data analysis, rather than conventional experience and intuition [11].

Linking big data will give access to a plethora of new information that can be used to build and test new hypotheses and ultimately take preventive or supportive action that might have not been possible had the data had still been unlinked and existed behind several layers of secrecy. Some potentially interesting questions would be; what is the correlation between health issues such as high cholesterol, obesity, type 2 diabetes in public health databases to the local patterns of grocery shopping obtained from stores or gym membership information in various areas? How well does the consumption of cholesterol-lowering drugs, correlate with level of exercise done by an individual where the drug details are obtained from the refills at the pharmacy while the level of exercise is obtained from home and individual monitoring devices? How much of an influence does the physical distance from the homes of patients have to hospitals and pharmacies exert on health care facility utilization and claims? How much of an influence do friends of an individual on social media platforms such as Facebook have on lifestyle choices or the willingness to engage in medical treatments by the said individual? It is duly noted that correlation does not apply causality. However, even to begin exploring these questions the ability to link data at the patient level is a prerequisite [12]. It is worthy to note that only then will we be able to gauge whether this type of correlative inferences is possible to be found in big data and how well physicians would be able to use those information.

The first question to answer is identifying the potential sources of health care information that are valuable to link together. This is expected to be done along the different dimensions of "bigness" of data [4]. Some types of big data such as electronic health records (EHRs) can be used to provide depth by including different types of data that may include images and notes in addition to the traditional simple text data. These additional information might most probably be about individual patient encounters. Other types of data such as claims data will provide what is known as longitudinality which is a view of a patient's medical history over an extended period for a narrow range of categories. It is worthy of note that linking data adds value when one fills the gaps present in the other. Biomedical data that are outside the traditional health care system such as social media, credit card purchase information, census records, and other types of data help create a more holistic view of a patient. However, it should not be ignored the fact that these sources have varying degrees of quality. Regardless, the said holistic view can bring to the front the social and environmental factors that might influence the individual's health which might have escaped the notice of individual physicians who are traditionally confined to a small portion of the whole image due to inaccessibility of the rest of the data.

As implied above, one major obstacle in linking data sources to obtain workable big data is the non-existence of a system that would provide a nationwide unique patient identifier (UPI). This is a very valid concern in the United States of America where different healthcare providers use different methods and conventions to store patient information. This has motivated the hospitals and clinics to come up with rather advanced probabilistic linkage algorithms based on other information that are not private such as demographics [10]. It acknowledges that it is probable for two different patients to have the same name, age, zip code, or other characteristics. However, it further reasons that given enough of these variables, it is possible to reduce the risk of erroneous links to an acceptable percentage. These probabilistic linkage methods employed to match different electronic health records of patients can be extended to data sources that are external to health care [4]. Some data sources might not have some variables or might not divulge them due to various policies. This might increase the likelihood of errors. However, the probability of these errors decreases when the number of patients increases to the range of millions [4].

As mentioned in the beginning of this section, privacy and security concerns are ever so present in the case of biomedical big data. More holistic the profile of patients becomes, easier it becomes to identify [13, 14]. Regardless, the reality is the fact that big data is making strides in other industries and it is obviously an important asset to have in the future of the healthcare industry on the perspectives of delivery, monitoring, and marketing. Thus, it can be argued that it is of best interests of the medical establishments to guide social and legislative steps toward this goal. The prudent way forward is to identify and regulate what is legal and ethical, proceed when benefits outweigh the potential risks, and most importantly, include the patients in question in the decision-making process [15]. An easy way out of this legal and ethical maze is to give patients control over their own data. However, the advent of social media has proved that some individuals share private information publicly only to regret it later and in some cases shift the blame to the facility providers that enabled them to share the said data [4].

5 Using Relational Databases for Biomedical Big Data

As explained in the above section on big data, it is generally accepted that relational database management systems usually are not competent enough to handle big data. However, the vague definition of the term big data itself, as explained in the same section, has kept it open for some biomedical big data applications to employ relational database management systems. However, given the easiness of handling, which is inherent to relational database management systems, some biomedical big data applications on relational database management systems do exist.

Most of the clinical data are stored in the Entity-Attribute-Value (EAV) format [16]. In the most common setting, entity column carries a clinical event. It can be taken as a patient ID and date/time stamp pair [17]. The attribute column carries a clinical parameter. The value column carries the clinical parameter's value [18]. These are converted to relational table format by pivoting. For example, the MLBCD [18] system then transforms raw clinical parameters into features. Then one or more predictive models are built on the set of clinical parameters and evaluated. The clinical parameter extraction calls for another famous big data technology, MapReduce framework [19], which in turn paves the way for the biomedical database to be queried by Spark SQL [20].

Multiparameter Intelligent Monitoring in Intensive Care II (MIMIC-II) [21] is a public-access intensive care unit database that contains information of 25,328 intensive care unit stays. This information includes laboratory data, therapeutic intervention profiles such as vasoactive medication drip rates and ventilator settings, nursing progress notes, discharge summaries, radiology reports, provider order entry data, International Classification of Diseases,

9th Revision codes, and, for a subset of patients, high-resolution vital sign trends, and waveforms.

A study done by Wang et al. used a publicly available transcriptomic data set taken from NCBI GEO concerning Multiple Myeloma to do a comparison between relational database management systems against no-SQL databases [22]. The relational database used was tranSMART [23] which holds over 70 million gene expression records. They observed that even database partitioning could not improve the data retrieval performance issues of tranSMART which were inherited from the relational database model. First, they ported one of tranSMART's microarray data tables to MongoDB to store as key-value pairs to compare performance against the original relational database. Further experiments were done on HBase [24]. From their experiments they concluded that the new key-value data model, in particular its implementation in HBase, outperforms the relational model currently implemented in tranSMART.

Ježek and Mouček discuss a Semantic framework for mapping object-oriented model to semantic web languages [25] in which they discuss the problems with existing relational database solutions such as the EEG/ERP Portal (EEGBase) [26] in terms of lack of semantic expressivity. Further, they pointed out that the inflexibility of relational databases restricts the usages that one can obtain from relational databases in the sphere of biomedical big data.

Despite the above few examples of naysayers of the usage of relational databases in biomedical big data, historically, there have been a number of successful implementations. Next, few paragraphs discuss a few of these successful cases and the arguments of the researchers that presented those cases.

Erich J. Baker, discussing the usage of databases in bioinformatics, argues that Traditional relational databases can effectively manage data. However, he points out that relational database model requires in-depth domain knowledge and strong database expertise to produce schemas robust enough to handle scope and integration. Further, he notes that the emergence of NoSQL databases "has caused researchers to reexamine how data is structured and explore flexible alternatives for viewing relationships among differing data types typically encountered in behavioral neuroscience" [27].

Next-generation sequencing (NGS) is a big contributor to biomedical big data in terms of generated data that should be stored and analyzed in various ways. Alexandre G. de Brevern et al., discussing the trends in IT Innovation to manage and analyze next-generation sequencing, argue that given that in biology, concepts and technologies evolve very quickly, and new data formats appear frequently, scientists are forced to reconsider the structure of their data regularly. This, they claim, to go against the very definition of relational database systems because relational database systems need data structuring where an a priori model of the data is required, which effectively freezes the model. Further,

Alexandre G. de Brevern et al. point out the following reasons for relational databases to be unsuitable for biomedical big data; the database cannot adapt to large traffic at an acceptable cost, the number of tables required to maintain the relational model rises too quickly for the corresponding amount of stored data, the relational model no longer meets the performance criteria because the model is no longer adapted to how the system has evolved, the database is subjected to a large number of temporary tables that store intermediate results [28].

Cloudwave is a project that utilizes Hadoop to use distributed processing on Electrophysiological Recordings collected from Epilepsy Clinical Research. This is a very important endeavor given that Epilepsy is the most common serious neurological disorder worldwide. It is currently affecting 50–60 million persons across the globe. European Data Format (EDF) is the de-facto standard based on eXtensible Markup Language (XML) for recording EEG data in commercial equipment and facilitating data interoperability in multi-center research projects. Cloudwave processes and stores EDF data files in a relational database [29].

For pre-surgical evaluation for epilepsy, high-frequency (kHz) and long-duration intracranial monitoring from multiple electrodes is used. The duration extends to days. Thus, the produced data can easily be categorized as big data. Bower et al. discuss using the Multi-scale Annotation Format (MAF) and storing them in relational databases for the benefits given by the relational database model in the realms of data integrity rules and strict schema [30].

e!DAL framework [31] is used to store, share, and publish research data. It used H2 relational database system [32] and concluded that for the data considered for the given use case, relational database systems were able to help in the field of life sciences where there is a big gap between the rate of data collection and the rate of data publication.

Both the Extensible Neuroimaging Archive Toolkit (XNAT) which is a software platform designed to facilitate common management and productivity tasks for neuroimaging and associated data and the mind research network (MRN) rely on open-source, relational database PostgreSQL. COINS is an Innovative Informatics and Neuroimaging Tool Suite built to interface with these implementations [33].

Database-Centric Molecular Simulation (DCMS), a data analytics and management system for molecular simulation, uses relational database management system (DBMS). In a broad definition, Molecular Simulation (MS) is a powerful tool for studying physical/chemical features of large systems. In this case, Molecular Simulation data are stored in a relational database management system (DBMS) to take advantage of the declarative query interface (i.e., SQL), data access methods, query processing, and optimization mechanisms [34].

6 Conclusions

In conclusion, we can claim that biomedical big data is a novel and very useful field to venture into. However, whether or not relational databases should be used in doing so is an open question that should be answered in a case-by-case basis depending on the exact requirements of the user application.

References

1. Codd E (1970) A relational model of data for large shared data banks. Commun ACM 13(6):377–387.doi:10.1145/362384.362685
2. Data, data everywhere. The Economist, 25 Feb 2010
3. Scherer M (2012) Inside the secret world of the data crunchers who helped Obama win. http://swampland.time.com/2012/11/07/inside-the-secret-world-of-quants-and-data-crunchers-who-helped-obama-win/. Accessed 28 Oct 2015
4. Weber GM, Mandl KD, Kohane IS (2014) Finding the missing link for big biomedical data. JAMA 311(24):2479–2480. doi:10.1001/jama.2014.4228
5. Hilbert M, López P (2011) The World's technological capacity to store, communicate, and compute information. Science 332(6025):60–65. doi:10.1126/science.1200970
6. IBM What is big data?—Bringing big data to the enterprise. IBM. http://www.ibm.com/big-data/us/en/. Accessed 27 Oct 2015
7. Oracle and FSN. Mastering big data: CFO strategies to transform insight into opportunity. http://www.fsn.co.uk/channel_bi_bpm_cpm/mastering_big_data_cfo_strategies_to_transform_insight_into_opportunity#.VjBN4NKrT0N. Accessed 27 Oct 2015
8. Jacobs A. The pathologies of big data. ACMQueue. http://queue.acm.org/detail.cfm?id=1563874. Accessed 27 Oct 2015
9. Kayyali B, Knott D, Kuiken S (2013) The big-data revolution in US health care: accelerating value and innovation. McKinsey & Co, Chicago, IL
10. Grannis S, Overhage J, McDonald C (2002) Analysis of identifier performance using a deterministic linkage algorithm. In: Proceeding of the AMIA Symposium, pp 305–309
11. Margolis R, Derr L, Dunn M, Huerta M, Larkin J, Sheehan J, Guyer M, Green E (2014) The National Institutes of Health's big data to knowledge (BD2K) initiative: capitalizing on biomedical big data. J Am Med Inform Assoc 21(6):957–958. doi:10.1136/amiajnl-2014-002974
12. Ayers J, Althouse B, Dredze M (2014) Could behavioral medicine lead the web data revolution? JAMA 311(14):1399–1400. doi:10.1001/jama.2014.1505
13. Sweeney L (2000) Simple demographics often identify people uniquely. Carnegie Mellon University. http://dataprivacylab.org/projects/identifiability/paper1.pdf. Accessed 28 Oct 2015
14. Gymrek M, McGuire A, Golan D, Halperin E, Erlich Y (2013) Identifying personal genomes by surname inference. Science 339(6117):321–324. doi:10.1126/science.1229566
15. Kohane I, Altman R (2005) Health-information altruists. N Engl J Med 353(19):2074–2077. doi:10.1056/NEJMsb051220
16. Dinu V, Nadkarni P (2007) Guidelines for the effective use of entity-attribute-value modeling for biomedical databases. Int J Med Inform 76(11-12):769–779. doi:10.1016/j.ijmedinf.2006.09.023
17. Nadkarni P (2011) Metadata-driven software systems in biomedicine: designing systems that can adapt to changing knowledge. Springer, New York
18. Luo G (2015) MLBCD: a machine learning tool for big clinical data. Health Inf Sci Syst 3:3. doi:10.1186/s13755-015-0011-0
19. Dean J, Ghemawat S (2004) MapReduce: simplified data processing on large clusters. In: OSDI, pp 137–150. doi: 10.1145/1327452.1327492
20. Xin R, Rosen J, Zaharia M, Franklin M, Shenker S, Shark SI (2013) Spark SQL: relational data processing in spark. In: SIGMOD, pp 13–24. doi: 10.1145/2723372.2742797
21. Saeed M, Villarroel M, Reisner A, Clifford G, Lehman L, Moody G, Heldt T, Kyaw T, Moody B, Mark R (2011) Multiparameter intelligent monitoring in intensive care II:

a public-access intensive care unit database. Crit Care Med 39(5):952–960. doi:10.1097/CCM.0b013e31820a92c6
22. Wang S, Pandis I, Chao W, Sijin H, Johnson D, Emam I, Guitton F, Guo Y (2014) High dimensional biological data retrieval optimization with NoSQL technology. BMC Genomics 15(8):S3. doi:10.1186/1471-2164-15-S8-S3
23. Szalma S, Koka V, Khasanova T, Perakslis E (2010) Effective knowledge management in translational medicine. J Transl Med 8:68. doi:10.1186/1479-5876-8-68
24. George L (2008) HBase the definitive guide. O'Reilly Media, California
25. Ježek P, Mouček R (2015) Semantic framework for mapping object-oriented model to semantic web languages. Front Neuroinform 9:3. doi:10.3389/fninf.2015.00003
26. Jezek P, Moucek R (2012) System for EEG/ERP data and metadata storage and management. Neural Network World 22:277–290. doi:10.14311/NNW.2012.22.016
27. Baker EJ (2012) Biological databases for behavioral neurobiology. Int Rev Neurobiol 103:19–38. doi:10.1016/B978-0-12-388408-4.00002-2
28. de Brevern AG, Meyniel J-P, Fairhead C, Cécile N, Malpertuy A (2015) Trends in IT innovation to build a next generation bioinformatics solution to manage and analyse biological big data produced by NGS technologies. Biomed Res Int 2015:904541. doi:10.1155/2015/904541
29. Jayapandian CP, Chen C-H, Bozorgi A, Lhatoo SD, Zhang G-Q, Sahoo SS (2013) Cloudwave: distributed processing of "big data" from electrophysiological recordings for epilepsy clinical research using hadoop. In: AMIA Annual Symposium, pp 691–700
30. Bower MR, Stead M, Brinkmann BH, Dufendach K, Worrell GA (2009) Metadata and annotations for multi-scale electrophysiological data. In: Conference proceeding of the IEEE engineering in medical and biology society, pp 2811–2814. doi: 10.1109/IEMBS.2009.5333570
31. Arend D, Lange M, Chen J, Colmsee C, Flemming S, Hecht D, Scholz U (2014) e!DAL—a framework to store, share and publish research data. BMC Bioinformatics 15:214. doi:10.1186/1471-2105-15-214
32. H2 Database. http://www.h2database.com. Accessed 30 Oct 2015
33. Scott A, Courtney W, Wood D, de la Garza R, Lane S, King M, Wang R, Roberts J, Turner JA, Calhoun VD (2011) COINS: an innovative informatics and neuroimaging tool suite built for large heterogeneous datasets. Front Neuroinform 5:33. doi:10.3389/fninf.2011.00033
34. Kumar A, Grupcev V, Berrada M, Fogarty JC, Tu Y-C, Zhu X, Pandit SA, Xia Y (2015) DCMS: a data analytics and management system for molecular simulation. J Big Data 2(1):9. doi:10.1186/s40537-014-0009-5

Chapter 6

Semantic Technologies and Bio-Ontologies

Fernando Gutierrez

Abstract

As information available through data repositories constantly grows, the need for automated mechanisms for linking, querying, and sharing data has become a relevant factor both in research and industry. This situation is more evident in research fields such as the life sciences, where new experiments by different research groups are constantly generating new information regarding a wide variety of related study objects. However, current methods for representing information and knowledge are not suited for machine processing. The Semantic Technologies are a set of standards and protocols that intend to provide methods for representing and handling data that encourages reusability of information and is machine-readable. In this chapter, we will provide a brief introduction to Semantic Technologies, and how these protocols and standards have been incorporated into the life sciences to facilitate dissemination and access to information.

Key words Semantic Web, Resources, Ontology, Bio-ontology

1 Semantic Web

Created by Berners-Lee and standardized through the World Wide Web Consortium (W3C),[1] the World Wide Web (WWW) is a collection of linked Web resources (e.g., documents) that can be accessed through the Internet. These Web resources mostly consist of documents formatted and annotated in the Hypertext Markup Language (HTML), a language that allows the visualization of content, such as text and images. An important element in HTML is the *hyperlink*, which is a reference to data (or another HTML document) that allows to a user to access it directly. Through the hyperlinks (or simply links), the documents of WWW are connected. Because it is rather simple to publish information, WWW has grown into a very large web of connected documents. The growth in content has led to the situation where it is not possible to review all the available information of any given topic.

[1] https://www.w3.org/.

Jingshan Huang et al. (eds.), *Bioinformatics in MicroRNA Research*, Methods in Molecular Biology, vol. 1617,
DOI 10.1007/978-1-4939-7046-9_6, © Springer Science+Business Media LLC 2017

Such explosive growth of information available in WWW has led to the need of automatic processing methods for interchange and discovery of data. Automation in processing Web information is neither easy nor scalable, however. This limitation has two sources: HTML provides structure to visualize content in a human-readable form and there is not unified format to present information in WWW. Capturing the semantics from plain text and images is far from a trivial process. Both of these media are complex to analyze and, most of the time, they are related to contextual information that is not explicitly expressed within the Web document. The second problem is the lack of a unified structure or representation of information in WWW. Even in the case where we can identify relevant elements based on heuristic mechanisms, such as patterns over the text, the lack of a common structure or format across multiple Web pages limits the capability and efficacy of this approach. Because the same content can be expressed in multiple forms, identifying one piece of information across multiple WWW resources becomes a rather difficult task.

The Semantic Web extends WWW by offering a framework for publishing data on the Web. It establishes standards and protocols (i.e., Semantic Technologies) for representing and handling data that integrates meaning and is machine-readable. The Semantic Web intends to encourage the reuse and exchange of information as well as the use of sophisticated processing methods such as deductive reasoning and inference. These activities should lead to more meaningful results.

2 Semantic Technologies

The W3C has created a set of standards and protocols to describe and exchange data on the Web that extends the Web of documents to a Web of data (i.e., Linked Data) (W3C). These standards and protocols permit storage of data, the creation of vocabularies and knowledge representation models, and the definition of mechanisms to handle data (e.g., query) on the Web. The Semantic Web, through these technologies, will allow the design of more complex software agents that can autonomously navigate this web.

The protocols and standards used in the Semantic Web design are part of W3C's Semantic Web Stack. Some of the elements of the Stack are inherited from the WWW as essential components, such as the Internationalized Resource Identifier (IRI) which provides a unique identifier for Web resources, the eXtended Markup Language (XML) which allows the creation of structured documents, XML Namespaces for the managing of multiple sources, and Unicode for character representation. On top of these basic elements is the Resource Description Framework (RDF) which provides a language to model data as objects with properties. The following layer in the Stack corresponds to knowledge representation languages while rules and query languages form the next layer. The last layers correspond to technologies that have not been standardized, such as user interfaces.

2.1 Resource Description Framework (RDF)

Resource Description Framework (RDF)[2] is a family of specifications for modeling metadata and designed to provide a standard form for data interchange. RDF describes information as statements of resources. These statements are expressed as triples of the form *subject–predicate–object*. For example, the statement "the car is red" in RDF has as subject "the car," as predicate "is," and as object "red."

RDF was developed as a core component for the Semantic Web, with many standards being syntactic and semantic extensions of it. While syntax extensions are mostly expansions to the vocabulary in the form of notations, semantic extensions refer to entailment of the statements. This means that if a statement is valid in RDF it should be also valid in the extension. However, in most cases the extensions of RDF incorporate new constraints, such as OWL languages that we will review later. These new constraints are considered *entailment regimes*. That is, if a statement is valid in RDF, it is valid in the extension unless the extension does not allow the statement. By allowing entailment regimes, RDF permits the specialization of the extension without losing compatibility.

Because of its structure, a set of RDF statements can be represented as a labeled directed graph (i.e., RDF Graph). In the graph, both subject and object can represent vertices while the predicate corresponds to the edge. The direction of the edge is from the subject to the object. Considering a set of RDF statements as a graph permits a more manageable approach for algorithms that process RDF data since it indicates how to connect the different parts of the data set.

2.2 Ontologies

An ontology is an explicit specification of a shared conceptualization [1] that, through concepts, relationships (properties), and individuals, provides both a vocabulary and a model of the domain it represents. An ontology can formally describe the structure of knowledge by providing a hierarchical classification (categorization) of concepts of a domain, with their corresponding properties. In the simplest case, an ontology might be a vocabulary of the domain, while in other cases, it can model hierarchy and properties of concepts and relations. Ontologies are incorporated into the Semantic Web by two standards: RDF Schema (RDFS) and Web Ontology Language (OWL).

[2] https://www.w3.org/RDF/.

RDFS[3] is an extension to RDF that provides basic constructs for describing ontologies. In RDFS, it is possible to define a group of similar resources as classes (rdfs:Class) and subclasses (rdfs:subClassOf). It is also possible to define both domain and range for properties (predicates). The domain of a property corresponds to the class of resources that can be the property's subject, while range corresponds to the class of resources that can be the property's object. With these elements (class, domain, and range), it is possible to describe vocabularies and simple ontologies (taxonomies) in RDFS.

Web Ontology Language (OWL)[4] is a family of languages for knowledge representation (i.e., ontologies). Like RDFS, they also are a semantic extension of RDF, but OWL languages are more expressive than RDFS, allowing a more complex representation of a domain. While OWL is a semantic extension of RDF (and RDFS), its formal semantics are defined (entailment regime) by Description Logic (DL), a mostly decidable fragment of First-Order Logic. Defining OWL's semantics with DL allows the use of DL reasoners, which are sound and complete [2, 3], with OWL ontologies.

Initially, OWL was comprised of three different languages (OWL Full, OWL DL, and OWL Lite) which each had different levels of expressivity. The current OWL specification (OWL2) has three profiles which have been designed to suite different types of real-world applications. OWL2 benefits from significant improvements in description logic which has led to practical reasoners of highly expressive ontologies [3], and to description logic languages that can handle larger sets of instances [4].

While OWL2 was designed for authoring expressive ontologies, OWL2 profiles are designed to offer efficient computing performance in logic reasoning (OWL2-DL) and efficient performance in query-answering (OWL2-EL).

2.3 Query and Rules

Similar to data description and knowledge representation, W3C has considered a few recommendations for handling semantic data. These recommendations intend to offer methods for accessing, sorting, and modifying information stored in RDF and its extensions.

SPARQL Protocol and RDF Query Language (SPARQL) is a semantic query language for retrieving and manipulating RDF data. Inspired by Structured Query Language (SQL), a language for querying databases, SPARQL offers a SQL-like approach to accessing semantic information. Its syntax resembles SQL, offering operations such as JOIN, SORT, and AGGREGATE, but the queries are based on patterns over triples. We can make the analogy of RDF subject as a primary key, with each object value that is related

---

[3] https://www.w3.org/TR/rdf-schema/.

[4] http://www.w3.org/2004/OWL/.

to the subject being a column entrance. However, RDF offers the possibility of multiple values in the column entrees (through subclass relations). Currently there are multiple implementations that can process SPARQL queries [5], or transform them into other languages [6].

Rule Interchange Format (RIF) is an exchange language between rule systems for the Semantic Web. Instead of offering a single and unified language rule to use over knowledge representation and business modeling, RIF offers a set of *translation dialects* that share syntactic and semantic features available in popular paradigms, integrating them with RDF. RIF Basic Logic Dialect (RIF-BLD) is one of the major dialects and it corresponds to Horn logic with extensions, such as frames (as in F-logic), and other Semantic Web elements (e.g., XML Schema). RIF Production Rule Dialect (RIF-PRD) is another major dialect that shares elements with well know production rules such as Jess [7] and Jboss [8]. In contrast, RIF-BLD, RIF-PRD is not based on logic; instead, it uses a more ad hoc approach. RIF Core (RIF-Core) is the subset dialect that results from the intersection of RIF-BLD and RIF-PRD, allowing some exchange between logic-based and production-based rules. There are other RIF dialects that intend to provide specific capabilities, like compatibility with OWL (RIF–RDF+OWL) or XML (RIF+XML–Data).

3 Biomedical Research

The Biomedical Informatics focus is on the optimal use of information through technology for improving health, health care, and research. Researchers study both the development and the use of computer-based methods for knowledge acquisition, data management, and decision-making in clinical context. In the case of biomedical research, biomedical informatics assists researchers in managing the storage and access of data as well as analyzing the large volume of data generated from experiments and trials.

Data management and data access have become a critical challenge for biomedical informatics, especially when considering emerging multidisciplinary research fields that need to exchange experimental data and models. These challenges have led to a strong push by the community to incorporate semantic technologies for representation, storage, and interchange of biomedical information.

3.1 Challenges in Biomedical Research

Data interchange and data accessibility are an issue when validating results with similar studies and with the emergence of multidisciplinary studies that require cross-domain or interdomain analysis. Although the large volume of data generated by biomedical research is problematic, the nature of the data imposes the larger challenges to biomedical informatics. Biomedical data is characterized by its *complexity* and *heterogeneity* [9].

The *complexity* comes from the multiple dimensions that describe the objects of study in life science fields. In biology, organisms can be categorized by their function, their structure, or how they can be affected by malfunction. In the case of pharmacology, the element of analysis can be categorized by its composition, its properties, and its origin. Data representation and categorization cannot always be met with traditional representation models.

Biomedical data *heterogeneity* is caused by the constant change (and improvement) of experimental setups and the use of different approaches (i.e., themes) in the experiments. Biomedical research has strong tradition of making research data available with many public repositories consisting of data generation [10], observations [11], experimental results [12], and publications [13]. In most cases, each of these repositories will have a different representation of the data based on the theme, methodology, and technology used to perform the experiments. This results in little compatibility between repositories for data exchange, merger, or cross source (schema) data analysis.

Now, when considering complexity and heterogeneity, the volume of biomedical data becomes a challenge. The heterogeneity of data can be tackled by *mappings* and *transformation rules.* Mappings can indicate matching attributes across different databases while rules can indicate the type of transformation (e.g., mathematical) necessary to pass data instances from one schema to another one. The creation of mappings and transformation rules requires deep understanding of what the data represents and how the data is structured. This requirement means that both mappings and rules must be manually created with limited automation. As the data and data sources increase in size, handcrafted mappings and transformation rules become more difficult to implement.

Additionally, when addressing complexity in traditional systems, it is very easy to duplicate information to represent the multidimensionality of the data. This factor in combination with both the volume and the heterogeneity of data creates a serious roadblock for the interchange of information.

3.2 Biomedical Solutions Using Semantic Technologies

The challenges in biomedical informatics has led biomedical researchers to become early adopters of Semantic Technologies [14]. The Semantic Web Applications and Tools for Life Sciences (SWAT4LS)[5] Workshop has sparked critical discussions about integrating Semantic Web technologies into the life science domains [15]. It has addressed varied topics from semantic annotation of medical information [16] and analysis of heterogeneous data sources for drug safety risks [17], to modeling drug-drug interactions [18].

[5] http://www.swat4ls.org/.

The approach to Semantic Web used by biomedical informatics that has become best known is the use of ontologies. The National Center for Biomedical Ontologies (NCBO)[6] offers online tools for the access, review, and integration of biomedical and clinical ontologies. The most well-known tool offered by NCBO is BioPortal, a repository for biomedical ontologies. Through BioPortal, it is possible to access more than 400 ontologies. Integrated with BioPortal is the semantic annotation tool: NCBO Annotator. Semantic annotation is the task of labeling or linking data (e.g., terms in a document) with ontological terms. NCBO Annotator can annotate with terms of any of the ontologies available in BioPortal.

Similar to BioPortal, Open Biomedical Ontologies (OBO)[7] Foundry initiative also hosts a large collection of biomedical ontologies. OBO's Basic Formal Ontology (BFO) offers an upper-level ontology on which OBO Foundry is built [19]. OBO's Relations Ontology (RO) offers a collection of ontological relations. RO offers a standardized set of relations across the ontologies in OBO Foundry. Through BFO and RO, OBO promotes integration by reusing knowledge representation and creating a common vocabulary of terms. In OBO Foundry we can find Gene Ontology (GO) and Protein Ontology (PRO), and many others.

With so many available ontologies, specialized semantic search engines have been developed to take advantage of ontologies and annotated data. BioTCM-SE offers information retrieval across Western Medicine and Traditional Chinese Medicine [20]. This engine offers an accurate method to discover implicit knowledge connections across these two approaches to health care. Another semantic search engine is GeneView, which uses a semantically annotated version of PubMed to permit searches based on ontological entities [21]. By relying on the semantic annotation and small ontology, it can retrieve and rank documents based on their relations and the mention of specific concepts. Finally, we have Quertle's commercial biomedical semantic search engine Quetzal.[8] Quetzal searches across a wide range of document repositories, including PubMed, the NIH grants database, and other biomedical related collections. The search is semantic (driven by identifying concepts and relations) and integrates their proprietary linguistic analysis tool, Quantum Logic Linguistic, to produce accurate and meaningful results.

---

6 http://bioportal.bioontology.org/.
7 http://www.obofoundry.org/.
8 https://www.quetzal-search.info/.

4 Conclusions

The Semantic Web is a framework of publishing data, which intends to facilitate the sharing and the linking of information. Based on a set of standards and protocols, the Semantic Web includes languages to represent data and knowledge as well as protocols to query and manipulate them. By incorporating meaning and making the protocols and standards machine-readable, the Semantic Web encourages the reuse of data and introduces sophisticated processing mechanisms such as logic reasoning.

The researchers in life sciences were early adopters of the Semantic Technologies. Because of the challenges of the object of study and the volume of data they generate, the life sciences require the representation of complex entities and the sharing of large volumes of information all while providing mechanisms to link different data sets. Currently, research from the life sciences presents new challenges while improving different aspects of Semantic Technologies.

References

1. Gruber TR (1993) A translation approach to portable ontology specifications. Knowl Acquis 5(2):199–220. doi:10.1006/knac.1993.1008
2. Parsia B, Sirin E (2004) Pellet: an owl dl reasoner. In: 3rd international Semantic Web conference (ISWC2004), Hiroshima, Japan, 2004
3. Motik B, Shearer R, Horrocks I (2009) Hypertableau reasoning for description logics. J Artif Int Res 36(1):165–228
4. Calvanese D, De Giacomo G, Lemho D, Lenzerini M, Rosati R (2005) DL-lite: tractable description logics for ontologies. AAAI Press, Pittsburgh, PA, pp 602–607
5. Barzdins G, Rikacovs S, Zviedris M (2009) Graphical query language as SPARQL frontend. In: 13th east-European conference on advances in databases and information systems (ADBIS-2009), Riga, Latvia, 2009, pp 93–107
6. Bizer C, Seaborne A (2004) D2RQ-treating non-RDF databases as virtual RDF graphs. In: 3rd international Semantic Web conference (ISWC2004), Hiroshima, Japan
7. Hemmer M (2008) Expert systems in chemistry research. CRC Press, Boca Raton, FL
8. Red Hat JBoss Middleware. https://www.redhat.com/en/technologies/jboss-middleware
9. Stevens R, Jupp S, Klein J, Schanstra J (2011) Using Semantic Web technologies to manage complexity and change in biomedical data. Conf Proc IEEE Eng Med Biol Soc 2011:3708–3711. doi:10.1109/IEMBS.2011.6090629
10. Wong N, Wang X (2014) miRDB: an online resource for microRNA target prediction and functional annotations. Nucleic Acids Res 43(D1):D146–D152. doi:10.1093/nar/gku1104
11. Clark K, Vendt B, Smith K, Freymann J, Kirby J, Koppel P, Moore S, Phillips S, Maffitt D, Pringle M, Tarbox L, Prior F (2013) The cancer imaging archive (TCIA): maintaining and operating a public information repository. J Digit Imaging 26(6):1045–1057. doi:10.1007/s10278-013-9622-7
12. National Institute on Drug Abuse Data Share. https://datashare.nida.nih.gov/
13. National Center for Biotechnology Information PubMed. https://www.ncbi.nlm.nih.gov/pubmed/
14. Splendiani A, Burger A, Paschke A, Romano P, Marshall MS (2011) Biomedical semantics in the Semantic Web. J Biomed Semantics 2(Suppl 1):S1. doi:10.1186/2041-1480-2-S1-S1
15. SWAT4LS '11 (2012) Proceedings of the 4th international workshop on Semantic Web applications and tools for the life sciences. ACM, New York, NY

16. Melzi S, Jonquet C (2014) Scoring semantic annotations returned by the NCBO annotator. In: 7th international workshop on Semantic Web applications and tools for life sciences (SWAT4LS2014), Berlin
17. Koutkias V, Jaulent M-C (2014) Leveraging post-marketing drug safety research through semantic technologies: the pharmacovigilance signal detectors ontology. In: 7th international workshop on Semantic Web applications and tools for life sciences (SWAT4LS2014), Berlin
18. Herrero Zazo M, Hastings J, Segura Bedmar I, Croset S, Martínez P, Steinbeck C (2014) An ontology for drug-drug interactions. In: 7th international workshop on Semantic Web applications and tools for life sciences (SWAT4LS2014), Berlin
19. Grenon P, Smith B, Goldberg L (2004) Biodynamic ontology: applying BFO in the biomedical domain. Ontol Med 102:20–38
20. Chen X, Chen H, Bi X, Gu P, Chen J, Wu Z (2014) BioTCM-SE: a semantic search engine for the information retrieval of modern biology and traditional Chinese medicine. Comput Math Methods Med 2014:957231. doi:10.1155/2014/957231
21. Thomas P, Starlinger J, Vowinkel A, Arzt S, Leser U (2012) GeneView: a comprehensive semantic search engine for PubMed. Nucleic Acids Res 40(Web Server issue):W585–W591. doi:10.1093/nar/gks563

Chapter 7

Genome-Wide Analysis of MicroRNA-Regulated Transcripts

David Chevalier and Glen M. Borchert

Abstract

MicroRNAs (miRNAs) are small noncoding RNAs that regulate gene expression by either degrading transcripts or repressing translation. Over the past decade the significance of miRNAs has been unraveled by the characterization of their involvement in crucial cellular functions and the development of disease. However, continued progress in understanding the endogenous importance of miRNAs, as well as their potential uses as therapeutic tools, has been hindered by the difficulty of positively identifying miRNA targets. To face this challenge algorithmic approaches have primarily been utilized to date, but strictly mathematical models have thus far failed to produce a generally accurate, widely accepted methodology for accurate miRNA target determination. As such, several laboratory-based, comprehensive strategies for experimentally identifying all cellular miRNA regulations simultaneously have recently been developed. This chapter discusses the advantages and limitations of both classic and comprehensive strategies for miRNA target prediction.

Key words CLIP, Genome-wide analysis, miRNA, miRNA target prediction, RNA immunoprecipitation

1 Introduction

As we have seen in the previous chapters of this book, microRNAs (miRNAs) are involved in all cellular processes, and their misexpressions or misregulations are linked to many human diseases. While the different steps of synthesis, mechanism of action, and functions of miRNAs are relatively well understood, one aspect of miRNA biology remains largely unresolved: accurate identification of miRNA targets.

Since the discovery of the *lin-4* gene in *Caenorhabditis elegans* and its mechanism of action [1], one of the main focuses of miRNA research is to identify targets—the link between miRNAs and the functions that they regulate. Only the comprehensive identification of a miRNA's targets can fully determine the process(es) regulated by a specific miRNA. That said, the identification of a miRNA's targets remains extremely challenging for several reasons. For example, firstly, the short miRNA nucleotide sequence (seven nucleotides) involved in the recognition of a target mRNA does not provide

Jingshan Huang et al. (eds.), *Bioinformatics in MicroRNA Research*, Methods in Molecular Biology, vol. 1617,
DOI 10.1007/978-1-4939-7046-9_7,

enough sequence specificity to limit the number of potential targets. Secondly, partial complementarity between a miRNA and its targets leads to conflicting models of target interaction. Thirdly, definitively identifying all of a miRNA's targets is complicated by each miRNA regulating the expressions of unique set of multiple genes. Despite these (and other) challenges, the identification of miRNA targets has significantly improved over the past 15 years, and many unique miRNA–mRNAregulations have now been defined. That said, however, while the study of the interaction between a miRNA and one target can bring crucial information about the function of that miRNA, it can also undermine fully understanding a miRNA's broader cellular role as a single miRNA typically regulates multiple target genes simultaneously. As such, genome-wide approaches have now begun to be developed to facilitate the identification of all of the targets of a specific miRNA in parallel.

2 Computational Prediction of miRNA Targets

The in silico prediction of miRNA targets was first developed based on early experiments characterizing the binding of miRNAs to miRNA targets. These first experiments showed that partial sequence complementarity between miRNAs and their targets was sufficient to induce the repression of gene expression [1–4]. However, while the search for long stretches of nucleotides with near perfect matches to known miRNAs was largely successful for identifying miRNA targets in plants, this same strategy did not work well in animals [5], and it was soon found that largely imperfect pairing between miRNAs and their targets predominates in animals [6]. As such, several significantly more complex algorithms based on a multitude of strategies have since been developed to identify miRNA targets in animals. A noncomprehensive list of these algorithms is summarized in Tables 1, 2, and 3. These different algorithms can be classified into the following three groups: first generation, ab initio, based on computational models; second generation, learning-based approaches; and third generation, based on a combination of both machine learning and ab initio approaches. The main caveat when evaluating these different methods is that there has been little experimental validation of any of the putative miRNA–mRNA interactions predicted by these methods. As such, the lack of laboratory verification coupled with the ease of computational predictions has resulted in vastly distinct sets of putative targets and general confusion as to the best method for predicting miRNA targets in the field.

2.1 Ab Initio Algorithms

The first algorithms to identify miRNA targets were based on ab initio approaches (Table 1). The predictions from these algorithms were based on several characteristics of the interactions between

Table 1
List of the ab initio algorithms used for the prediction of miRNA targets

Algorithm	Species	Web server	Reference
Cupid	Animals	http://cupidtool.sourceforge.net/	[64]
DIANA.microT	Animals	http://diana.cslab.ece.ntua.gr/microT/	[65–67]
EIMMO	Animals	http://www.mirz.unibas.ch/ElMMo3/	[68]
HomoTarget	*Homo sapiens*	http://lbb.ut.ac.ir/?p=1190	[69]
Magia	Animals	http://gencomp.bio.unipd.it/magia/start/	[70]
MicroCosm	Animals	http://www.ebi.ac.uk/enright-srv/microcosm/htdocs/targets/v5/#	None
miRanda	Animals	http://www.microrna.org/microrna/home.do	[71]
miRTar	*Homo sapiens*	http://mirtar.mbc.nctu.edu.tw/human/	[72]
PicTar	Animals	http://pictar.mdc-berlin.de/	[73]
PITA	Animals	http://genie.weizmann.ac.il/pubs/mir07/mir07_prediction.html	[74]
psRNATarget	Plants	http://plantgrn.noble.org/psRNATarget/	[75]
RNAhybrid	Any species	http://bibiserv.techfak.uni-bielefeld.de/rnahybrid/	[76]
TargetScan	Mammals	http://www.targetscan.org/	[16, 77–80]

Table 2
Machine learning algorithms for miRNA target prediction

Algorithm	Species	Web server	Reference
GenMir ++	*Homo sapiens*	http://www.psi.toronto.edu/genmir	[81]
MBSTAR	Any species	http://www.isical.ac.in/~bioinfo_miu/MBStar30.htm	[82]
microTar	Any species	http://tiger.dbs.nus.edu.sg/microtar/	[83]
miTarget	Animals	http://cbit.snu.ac.kr/~miTarget	[83]
mirTarget2	Animals	http://mirdb.org	[84]
mirWIP	*Caenorhabditis elegans*	http://146.189.76.171/query.php	[85]
miRror and mirror Suite	Animals	http://www.proto.cs.huji.ac.il/mirror/	[86, 87]
MiRTif	Any species	http://mirtif.bii.a-star.edu.sg/	[88]
NBmirRTar	Any species	http://wotan.wistar.upenn.edu/NBmiRTar	[89]
Piranha	Any species	http://smithlabresearch.org/software/piranha/	[90]
Sylamer	Any species	http://www.ebi.ac.uk/enright/sylamer/	[91]

Table 3
List of the hybrid algorithms used for the prediction of miRNA targets

Algorithm	Species	Web server	Reference
ComiR	Animals	http://www.benoslab.pitt.edu/comir/	[92]
mirSVR	Animals	http://www.microrna.org/microrna/home.do	[93]
miREE	Any species	http://omictools.com/miree-s7507.html	[14]
TargetMiner	Any species	http://www.isical.ac.in/~bioinfo_miu/targetminer20.htm	[94]
MTar	Any species	None	[95]
RegRNA 2.0	Any species	http://regrna2.mbc.nctu.edu.tw/	[96]

miRNAs and their targets. The most widely utilized of these characteristics included: the 5′ seed of the miRNA (nucleotide positions 2–8 of the miRNA) being complementary to the 3′UTR of a mRNA target, the binding sites of a miRNA being highly conserved between species, and the miRNA–mRNA duplex having a higher negative folding energy than the single RNAs themselves. Importantly, algorithms strictly based on these characteristics do not directly require any experimental data to predict miRNA targets. Consequently, the main pitfall of the algorithms based on ab initio approaches is the high number of false positives typically identified for a given miRNA [7, 8]. To limit the number of false positives, accessory restrictions were often included. For example, when the conservation of a predicted miRNA binding site between species is utilized, the algorithm parameters can be restricted to require more evolutionarily distant relationships [6]. Notably, while employing these restrictions help to decrease the number of false positives, they can also lead to the elimination of true targets.

Clearly, as additional algorithms for identifying miRNA targets based on ab initio approaches continue to be developed, it becomes increasingly more difficult to select the best target prediction strategy to utilize. To address this issue, several reports have now performed comparisons of these algorithms based on sensitivity and precision. Of note, Sethupathy et al. were one of the first groups to compare the five leading algorithms and propose integrating them [9]. These authors suggest that the intersections of the results obtained from the five algorithms result in a much higher specificity than any single strategy in isolation. That said, their work actually suggested that the best compromise between sensitivity and specificity was obtained through identifying the common results from TargetScan and PicTar. Also of note, Alexiou et al. [10] similarly reported a comparison of eight algorithms using a data set obtained from a previous study [11] and similarly found that identifying the intersections of the targets obtained from distinct algorithms resulted in a higher frequency of actual target identification. Finally, more recently, Kumar et al. compared four algorithms using CLIP-seq datasets [12] and found the miRanda algorithm had the best sensitivity whereas TargetScan and PicTar had the lowest sensitivity.

2.2 Machine Learning Algorithms

Machine learning algorithms were developed more recently than algorithms based on ab initio approaches (Table 2). These algorithms are directly based on experimental data and require significant laboratory characterizations of the interactions between miRNAs and their targets for their development. These data are used to train a classifier that facilitates the identification of miRNA targets based on similarity with the training data. The classifier of these algorithms uses experimentally characterized miRNA–mRNA interactions to differentiate between positive and negative interactions between miRNAs and mRNAs. That said, few published negative interaction reports are available largely due to the fact that disproven experimental interactions are usually deemed not useful and discarded. As such, the experimental data set of negative interactions to train the classifiers of these algorithms is strikingly limited as compared to the experimental data set of positive interactions. The main pitfall of machine learning algorithms is therefore simply a lack of negative interaction data sets to fully train algorithm classifiers. That said, a report by Baek et al. [13] comparing the machine learning based algorithm mirWIP with five existing ab initio algorithms previously found that mirWIP had significantly lower rates of false positives and higher sensitivity than ab initio algorithms.

Machine learning algorithms, however, are still prone to high numbers of false positives. Recently, Reyes-Herrera et al. [14] compared five machine based algorithms using datasets with strong experimental evidence obtained from public databases and found that each of these algorithms carried various unbalanced results for sensitivity and specificity. In light of this, as well as other problems of the algorithms based on ab initio and computer based approaches, hybrid algorithms employing elements of both strategies have now also been developed (Table 3). These hybrid algorithms integrate the strong features of each of these two approaches avoiding many of their principle pitfalls.

3 Experimental Identification of miRNA Targets

While algorithms such as those described above have been successful in identifying many miRNA targets, they also carry significant limitations. First, there is little overlap in the identified target data sets between algorithms. Second, these predictions do not include the biological context and are therefore not cell specific. To avoid limitations such as these, in vivo and in vitro approaches have been developed to identify legitimate miRNA regulations. These techniques include transcriptome, proteome, and biochemical approaches. Transcriptome and proteome approaches are indirect methods as transcriptome approaches involve the identification of altered RNA expressions while proteome approaches use altered protein levels as a means to identify miRNA targets. In contrast, many biochemical approaches attempt to directly characterize specific interactions between miRNAs and their targets.

3.1 Transcriptome Approaches

Microarray-based techniques were the first to allow the study of changes in gene expression for a high number of genes at the same time as a consequence of miRNA regulation in order to deduce the targets of miRNAs. More recently, high-throughput RNA sequencing (RNA-Seq) has allowed a much more thorough examination of cellular transcriptomes. That said, one strategy for identifying miRNA regulations using transcriptomic analyses involves the overexpression of a specific miRNA [15–18] followed by the determination of significant changes in gene expression to identify targets of a specific microRNA. The overexpression of miRNAs in this manner has several major pitfalls. First, a gene could be mistakenly identified as a target due to the high nonphysiological expression levels of a miRNA saturating the RISC complex preventing the incorporation of other miRNAs into RISC [19]. Secondly, cells used for overexpression analyses are generally not the cell types where a miRNA regulation is endogenously relevant. For example, Hela cells have been employed to study brain-specific miRNAs [18]. As a result, targets can be missed because the genes of interest are not transcribed in the cell type used for the overexpression. Further, some genes that are not normally expressed in the cell type from which the miRNAs originate may be expressed in the cell used for the overexpression leading again to the false identification of a target. A second transcriptomic strategy includes the use of mutant Dicer. Without functional Dicer proteins, pre-miRNAs cannot be processed into functional miRNAs, and miRNAs can therefore not regulate the expression of their targets [20–23]. Finally, another transcriptomic strategy of note includes the isolation of a mutant in a specific miRNA or the knock down of a specific miRNA [24–27]. Techniques to knock down miRNAs include small interfering RNAs (siRNAs) [24], antisense oligonucleotides such as locked nucleic acids (LNA) [28] and antagomirs [26], miRNA sponges [29], and small molecular inhibitors [30, 31].

Transcriptome approaches have thus far proven quite successful in identifying miRNA targets and have helped confirm many early ideas about miRNA functions such as tissue specific gene regulations, the importance of seed sequences in defining miRNA targets, the broad effects of miRNAs on RNA stability, and in agreeing that miRNAs have a large number of targets. That said, however, transcriptome approaches cannot directly characterize miRNA translational repressions. As such, the greatest pitfall associated with examining the expressions of particular mRNAs by microarray or RNA-Seq is unquestionably that many microRNAs regulate their targets through translational repression.

3.2 Proteome Approaches

As with transcriptome approaches, proteome approaches also represent indirect methods to identify miRNA targets. In contrast, however, these approaches allow for the identification of miRNA targets regulated at the translation level. The first proteome approaches involved translation profiles which do not directly measure protein levels but instead estimate translation rates. Two different methods can be utilized for translation profiling: polyribosome profiling and ribosome profiling. The first report employing these methods identified translational changes due to miRNAs through characterizing transcripts that were released from translational repression after knock down of a specific miRNA via polyribosome profiling [24]. That said, similar to computational strategies, this approach has been found to generate a high rate of false positives. As an example, this strategy led Hendrickson et al. [32] to report the identification of around 600 potential targets of miR-124. The second method of translation profiling is ribosome profiling or ribosome foot printing. This method involves the treatment of samples with RNAse I after the addition of cyclohexamide and cell lysis [33]. RNAase I degrades all mRNAs not protected by ribosomes after which the surviving mRNAs are sequenced. Highly similar to polyribosome profiling, ribosome profiling also produces a large numbers of false positives and still only represents an indirect method of miRNA target identification.

In contrast to these strategies, other approaches have now been developed to directly measure the changes in proteins levels in response to miRNAs. For example, stable isotope labeling by amino acids in cell culture (SILAC) has been successfully used to identify changes in proteins in response to miRNAs [11, 13, 18, 34, 35]. Another approach directly examining changes in proteins levels involves two-dimensional differentiation in-gel electrophoresis (2D-DIGE). This approach includes the electrophoresis of two different sets of proteins labeled with different dyes on a single gel. Differentially expressed proteins between two data sets are determined by identifying differences in gel migrations followed by mass spectrometry. This approach can successfully identify miRNA targets by comparing proteomes with or without treatment with miRNA inhibitors [36, 37].

Importantly, proteome approaches such as these can successfully facilitate genome-wide identifications of regulations of translation by miRNAs. As many miRNA targets are only regulated at the translation level, proteome analyses are instrumental to describing these relationships. That said a combinatorial transcriptome and proteome analysis is perhaps the best currently available method for the genome-wide identification of microRNA targets. Also, by analyzing the mRNA sequences of targets regulated at the translational level, the rules for miRNA targeting derived from both algorithms and transcriptome approaches can be better examined [13].

3.3 RNA Immunoprecipitation (RIP) Approaches

Neither transcriptome nor proteome approaches can identify miRNA targets directly as these strategies instead use the levels of transcripts or proteins as a read out of miRNA activity. Therefore, in order to directly ascertain miRNA targets, researchers have now developed several biochemical approaches to characterize miRNA–target interactions directly.

RNA immunoprecipitation (RIP) approaches are based on the immunoprecipitation of proteins that bind miRNAs followed by the sequencing of bound RNAs. This approach was originally successfully used to identify mRNAs bound to specific RNA-binding proteins [38]. That said, for the identification of miRNA targets, a protein component of the RISC complex is typically used to immunoprecipitate a miRNA directly in complex with a target [25, 39–43]. While the overall approach remains the same, researchers have customized the immunoprecipitation techniques to specifically identify miRNA targets. Firstly, the protein that is immunoprecipitated varies: different Argonaute proteins or TNRC6 can be used. Secondly, various methods of tagging the RISC complex proteins including HA-tagged, *c*-myc, and FLAG can be employed. Finally, the determination of the sequence of the miRNA target is now commonly performed using RNA-Seq.

Importantly, RIP has now been successfully employed in identifying known and new miRNA targets and has proven significantly more effective at identifying legitimate miRNA targets than any combination of classic algorithmic or transcriptomic approaches [40–42]. That said, RIP is not without problems. The RIP approach requires cells to be lysed before RIP and therefore disturbs cellular compartmentalizations. As a result, RNAs and proteins initially in different cellular compartments can potentially interact and produce false positives [44]. In addition, the RIP approach requires a sufficient level of interaction between a miRNA and its targets to maintain their association. It is unknown whether some weak interactions between miRNAs and targets are lost during the immunoprecipitation process.

3.3.1 CLIP, HITS-CLIP

To address the potential drawbacks of the RIP approach and to ensure that immunoprecipitation results really reflect true cellular interactions an additional step can be added to RIP. This modified approach called cross-linking immunoprecipitation (CLIP) was originally developed to identify RNA–protein interactions [45]. In this strategy, a UV cross-linking step is used to induce the formation of covalent bonds between a RNA and its targets prior to immunoprecipitation [7, 46, 47]. More recently, the combination of CLIP with RNA-Seq has resulted in the development of a new approach: high-throughput sequencing of RNA isolated by cross-linking immunoprecipitation (HITS-CLIP) or cross-linking immunoprecipitation sequencing (CLIP-Seq). Importantly, HITS-CLIP enables the identification of miRNA targets and the location of miRNA binding sites both within the 3′UTR and the coding sequence of target mRNAs [7]. However, despite being a powerful approach, HITS-CLIP too is not without limitations. Of note, the crosslinking efficiency between proteins and RNAs is fairly low potentially resulting in a loss of potential targets [48]. In addition, this approach only identifies a target region of around 100 base pairs on an mRNA instead of a specific target site [48].

3.3.2 PAR-CLIP

In an attempt to improve the cross-linking between RNA and proteins, a modification of the CLIP approach has recently been developed. This method, photoactivatable-ribonucleoside-enhanced cross-linking and immunoprecipitation (PAR-CLIP), has now proven to be significantly more efficient at crosslinking proteins and RNAs than CLIP [48, 49]. In this method, cells are incubated with a photoactivatable nucleoside such as the 4-thiouridine, resulting in a higher frequency of transitions from thymidine to cytidine in the cross-linked sites as compared to the non-cross-linked regions. When compared to CLIP, this change improves the amount of RNA recovered after immunoprecipitation by 100- to 1000-fold and allows for the identification of specific interaction sites between miRNAs and their mRNA targets [50].

3.3.3 iCLIP

While CLIP and related approaches provide powerful data, each of these strategies is significantly hindered by the inefficiency of cDNA library production from immunoprecipitated RNAs. The cDNA libraries generated from these techniques are often of low complexity due to low amounts of recovered RNAs. In addition, the inefficiency of two RNA ligation steps in the preparation of the cDNA libraries as well as the formation of truncated cDNAs (which are usually lost during the formation of the cDNA libraries) also contribute to the low complexity of these cDNA libraries. To address this, a new technique called individual-nucleotide resolution CLIP (iCLIP) has now been developed [51]. In iCLIP, one of the RNA ligation steps with low efficiency is replaced by a more efficient intramolecular cDNA circularization and truncated cDNAs are also sequenced [52].

3.3.4 CLASH

The cross-linking, immunoprecipitation, and sequencing of hybrids (CLASH) approach is also a recent modification of the traditional CLIP approach [53, 54]. The CLASH approach includes an additional step that ensures the capture of both miRNAs and their targets: the miRNAs and targets are ligated together with the RISC complex. After immunoprecipitation, the miRNA–target complex is sequenced. This approach is unique in that it leaves little doubt as to which mRNA a miRNA is regulating.

3.4 PARE

One final strategy of note is the parallel analysis of RNA ends (PARE) (also called degradome-seq or genome-wide mapping of uncapped transcripts (GMUCT)). PARE has recently been used to identify the mRNA degradation products produced by miRNA regulations at a genome-wide scale. Using a modified 5′ RNA ligase mediated-rapid amplification of cDNA ends, the cleavage products of miRNAs are specifically reversed transcribed, amplified and sequenced after addition of adaptors [55, 56]. Importantly, while this approach has proven successful in identifying numerous cleavage sites in plants [57–59], it has proven less successful in animals in animals [60–62]. Importantly, miRNA-directed cleavage of mRNAs requires extensive base pairing between miRNAs and their targets, and while extensive base pairing and degradation of miRNA targets frequently occurs in plants, this is much less prevalent in animals. As such, PARE analysis is generally only suited for studies of plant species [63].

4 Conclusion

As outlined in this chapter, numerous strategies for identifying microRNA-regulated transcripts on a genome-wide scale have now been developed. Importantly, while each strategy boasts significant advantages, each also carries specific limitations. As such the best possible strategy for the genome-wide identification of microRNA targets has likely yet to be developed but will most likely consist of a combinatorial computational approach partnered with comprehensive transcriptomic, proteomic, and/or immunoprecipitation-based approaches.

References

1. Lee RC, Feinbaum RL, Ambros V (1993) The *C. elegans* heterochronic gene lin-4 encodes small RNAs with antisense complementarity to lin-14. Cell 75(5):843–854
2. Wightman B, Ha I, Ruvkun G (1993) Posttranscriptional regulation of the heterochronic gene lin-14 by lin-4 mediates temporal pattern formation in *C. elegans*. Cell 75(5): 855–862
3. Reinhart BJ, Slack FJ, Basson M, Pasquinelli AE, Bettinger JC, Rougvie AE, Horvitz HR, Ruvkun G (2000) The 21-nucleotide let-7 RNA regulates developmental timing in *Caenorhabditis elegans*. Nature 403(6772):901–906. doi:10.1038/35002607
4. Moss EG, Lee RC, Ambros V (1997) The cold shock domain protein LIN-28 controls developmental timing in *C. elegans* and is regulated by the lin-4 RNA. Cell 88(5):637–646
5. Rhoades MW, Reinhart BJ, Lim LP, Burge CB, Bartel B, Bartel DP (2002) Prediction of plant microRNA targets. Cell 110(4):513–520
6. Lewis BP, Shih IH, Jones-Rhoades MW, Bartel DP, Burge CB (2003) Prediction of mammalian microRNA targets. Cell 115(7):787–798
7. Chi SW, Zang JB, Mele A, Darnell RB (2009) Argonaute HITS-CLIP decodes microRNA-mRNA interaction maps. Nature 460(7254): 479–486. doi:10.1038/nature08170
8. Bartel DP (2009) MicroRNAs: target recognition and regulatory functions. Cell 136(2):215–233. doi:10.1016/j.cell.2009.01.002
9. Sethupathy P, Megraw M, Hatzigeorgiou AG (2006) A guide through present computational approaches for the identification of mammalian microRNA targets. Nat Methods 3(11):881–886. doi:10.1038/nmeth954
10. Alexiou P, Maragkakis M, Papadopoulos GL, Reczko M, Hatzigeorgiou AG (2009) Lost in translation: an assessment and perspective for computational microRNA target identification. Bioinformatics 25(23):3049–3055. doi:10.1093/bioinformatics/btp565
11. Selbach M, Schwanhausser B, Thierfelder N, Fang Z, Khanin R, Rajewsky N (2008) Widespread changes in protein synthesis induced by microRNAs. Nature 455(7209):58–63. doi:10.1038/nature07228
12. Kumar A, Wong AK, Tizard ML, Moore RJ, Lefevre C (2012) miRNA_Targets: a database for miRNA target predictions in coding and non-coding regions of mRNAs. Genomics 100(6):352–356. doi:10.1016/j.ygeno.2012.08.006
13. Baek D, Villen J, Shin C, Camargo FD, Gygi SP, Bartel DP (2008) The impact of microRNAs on protein output. Nature 455(7209): 64–71. doi:10.1038/nature07242
14. Reyes-Herrera PH, Ficarra E, Acquaviva A, Macii E (2011) miREE: miRNA recognition elements ensemble. BMC Bioinformatics 12:454. doi:10.1186/1471–2105–12-454
15. Lim LP, Lau NC, Garrett-Engele P, Grimson A, Schelter JM, Castle J, Bartel DP, Linsley PS, Johnson JM (2005) Microarray analysis shows that some microRNAs downregulate large numbers of target mRNAs. Nature 433(7027): 769–773. doi:10.1038/nature03315
16. Grimson A, Farh KK, Johnston WK, Garrett-Engele P, Lim LP, Bartel DP (2007) MicroRNA targeting specificity in mammals: determinants beyond seed pairing. Mol Cell 27(1):91–105. doi:10.1016/j.molcel.2007.06.017
17. Linsley PS, Schelter J, Burchard J, Kibukawa M, Martin MM, Bartz SR, Johnson JM, Cummins JM, Raymond CK, Dai H, Chau N, Cleary M, Jackson AL, Carleton M, Lim L (2007) Transcripts targeted by the microRNA-16 family cooperatively regulate cell cycle progression. Mol Cell Biol 27(6):2240–2252. doi:10.1128/MCB.02005-06
18. Vinther J, Hedegaard MM, Gardner PP, Andersen JS, Arctander P (2006) Identification of miRNA targets with stable isotope labeling by amino acids in cell culture. Nucleic Acids Res 34(16):e107. doi:10.1093/nar/gkl590
19. Hobert O (2007) miRNAs play a tune. Cell 131(1):22–24. doi:10.1016/j.cell.2007.09.031
20. Grishok A, Pasquinelli AE, Conte D, Li N, Parrish S, Ha I, Baillie DL, Fire A, Ruvkun G, Mello CC (2001) Genes and mechanisms

related to RNA interference regulate expression of the small temporal RNAs that control *C. elegans* developmental timing. Cell 106(1):23–34

21. Hutvagner G, McLachlan J, Pasquinelli AE, Balint E, Tuschl T, Zamore PD (2001) A cellular function for the RNA-interference enzyme dicer in the maturation of the let-7 small temporal RNA. Science 293(5531): 834–838. doi:10.1126/science.1062961
22. Ketting RF, Fischer SE, Bernstein E, Sijen T, Hannon GJ, Plasterk RH (2001) Dicer functions in RNA interference and in synthesis of small RNA involved in developmental timing in *C. elegans*. Genes Dev 15(20):2654–2659. doi:10.1101/gad.927801
23. Knight SW, Bass BL (2001) A role for the RNase III enzyme DCR-1 in RNA interference and germ line development in *Caenorhabditis elegans*. Science 293(5538):2269–2271. doi:10.1126/science.1062039
24. Nakamoto M, Jin P, O'Donnell WT, Warren ST (2005) Physiological identification of human transcripts translationally regulated by a specific microRNA. Hum Mol Genet 14(24): 3813–3821. doi:10.1093/hmg/ddi397
25. Easow G, Teleman AA, Cohen SM (2007) Isolation of microRNA targets by miRNP immunopurification. RNA 13(8):1198–1204. doi:10.1261/rna.563707
26. Krutzfeldt J, Rajewsky N, Braich R, Rajeev KG, Tuschl T, Manoharan M, Stoffel M (2005) Silencing of microRNAs in vivo with 'antagomirs'. Nature 438(7068):685–689. doi:10.1038/nature04303
27. Rodriguez A, Vigorito E, Clare S, Warren MV, Couttet P, Soond DR, van Dongen S, Grocock RJ, Das PP, Miska EA, Vetrie D, Okkenhaug K, Enright AJ, Dougan G, Turner M, Bradley A (2007) Requirement of bic/microRNA-155 for normal immune function. Science 316(5824): 608–611. doi:10.1126/science.1139253
28. Orom UA, Kauppinen S, Lund AH (2006) LNA-modified oligonucleotides mediate specific inhibition of microRNA function. Gene 372:137–141. doi:10.1016/j.gene.2005.12.031
29. Ebert MS, Neilson JR, Sharp PA (2007) MicroRNA sponges: competitive inhibitors of small RNAs in mammalian cells. Nat Methods 4(9):721–726. doi:10.1038/nmeth1079
30. Thomas JR, Hergenrother PJ (2008) Targeting RNA with small molecules. Chem Rev 108(4):1171–1224. doi:10.1021/cr0681546
31. Zhang S, Chen L, Jung EJ, Calin GA (2010) Targeting microRNAs with small molecules: from dream to reality. Clin Pharmacol Ther 87(6):754–758. doi:10.1038/clpt.2010.46
32. Hendrickson DG, Hogan DJ, McCullough HL, Myers JW, Herschlag D, Ferrell JE, Brown PO (2009) Concordant regulation of translation and mRNA abundance for hundreds of targets of a human microRNA. PLoS Biol 7(11):e1000238. doi:10.1371/journal.pbio.1000238
33. Guo H, Ingolia NT, Weissman JS, Bartel DP (2010) Mammalian microRNAs predominantly act to decrease target mRNA levels. Nature 466(7308):835–840. doi:10.1038/nature09267
34. Ong SE, Blagoev B, Kratchmarova I, Kristensen DB, Steen H, Pandey A, Mann M (2002) Stable isotope labeling by amino acids in cell culture, SILAC, as a simple and accurate approach to expression proteomics. Mol Cell Proteomics 1(5):376–386
35. Zhu H, Pan S, Gu S, Bradbury EM, Chen X (2002) Amino acid residue specific stable isotope labeling for quantitative proteomics. Rapid Commun Mass Spectrom 16(22):2115–2123. doi:10.1002/rcm.831
36. Zhu S, Si ML, Wu H, Mo YY (2007) MicroRNA-21 targets the tumor suppressor gene tropomyosin 1 (TPM1). J Biol Chem 282(19):14328–14336. doi:10.1074/jbc.M611393200
37. Muniyappa MK, Dowling P, Henry M, Meleady P, Doolan P, Gammell P, Clynes M, Barron N (2009) MiRNA-29a regulates the expression of numerous proteins and reduces the invasiveness and proliferation of human carcinoma cell lines. Eur J Cancer 45(17):3104–3118. doi:10.1016/j.ejca.2009.09.014
38. Tenenbaum SA, Carson CC, Lager PJ, Keene JD (2000) Identifying mRNA subsets in messenger ribonucleoprotein complexes by using cDNA arrays. Proc Natl Acad Sci U S A 97(26):14085–14090. doi:10.1073/pnas.97.26.14085
39. Meier J, Hovestadt V, Zapatka M, Pscherer A, Lichter P, Seiffert M (2013) Genome-wide identification of translationally inhibited and degraded miR-155 targets using RNA-interacting protein-IP. RNA Biol 10(6):1018–1029. doi:10.4161/rna.24553
40. Beitzinger M, Peters L, Zhu JY, Kremmer E, Meister G (2007) Identification of human microRNA targets from isolated argonaute protein complexes. RNA Biol 4(2):76–84
41. Karginov FV, Conaco C, Xuan Z, Schmidt BH, Parker JS, Mandel G, Hannon GJ (2007) A biochemical approach to identifying microRNA targets. Proc Natl Acad Sci U S A 104(49):19291–19296. doi:10.1073/pnas.0709971104
42. Hendrickson DG, Hogan DJ, Herschlag D, Ferrell JE, Brown PO (2008) Systematic identi-

fication of mRNAs recruited to argonaute 2 by specific microRNAs and corresponding changes in transcript abundance. PLoS One 3(5):e2126. doi:10.1371/journal.pone.0002126
43. Zhang L, Ding L, Cheung TH, Dong MQ, Chen J, Sewell AK, Liu X, Yates JR 3rd, Han M (2007) Systematic identification of *C. elegans* miRISC proteins, miRNAs, and mRNA targets by their interactions with GW182 proteins AIN-1 and AIN-2. Mol Cell 28(4):598–613. doi:10.1016/j.molcel.2007.09.014
44. Mili S, Steitz JA (2004) Evidence for reassociation of RNA-binding proteins after cell lysis: implications for the interpretation of immunoprecipitation analyses. RNA 10(11):1692–1694. doi:10.1261/rna.7151404
45. Ule J, Jensen KB, Ruggiu M, Mele A, Ule A, Darnell RB (2003) CLIP identifies Nova-regulated RNA networks in the brain. Science 302(5648):1212–1215. doi:10.1126/science.1090095
46. Zisoulis DG, Lovci MT, Wilbert ML, Hutt KR, Liang TY, Pasquinelli AE, Yeo GW (2010) Comprehensive discovery of endogenous argonaute binding sites in *Caenorhabditis elegans*. Nat Struct Mol Biol 17(2):173–179. doi:10.1038/nsmb.1745
47. Zhang C, Darnell RB (2011) Mapping in vivo protein-RNA interactions at single-nucleotide resolution from HITS-CLIP data. Nat Biotechnol 29(7):607–614. doi:10.1038/nbt.1873
48. Hafner M, Landthaler M, Burger L, Khorshid M, Hausser J, Berninger P, Rothballer A, Ascano M Jr, Jungkamp AC, Munschauer M, Ulrich A, Wardle GS, Dewell S, Zavolan M, Tuschl T (2010a) Transcriptome-wide identification of RNA-binding protein and microRNA target sites by PAR-CLIP. Cell 141(1):129–141. doi:10.1016/j.cell.2010.03.009
49. Hafner M, Landthaler M, Burger L, Khorshid M, Hausser J, Berninger P, Rothballer A, Ascano M, Jungkamp AC, Munschauer M, Ulrich A, Wardle GS, Dewell S, Zavolan M, Tuschl T (2010b) PAR-CliP--a method to identify transcriptome-wide the binding sites of RNA binding proteins. J Vis Exp 41:2034. doi:10.3791/2034
50. Kishore S, Jaskiewicz L, Burger L, Hausser J, Khorshid M, Zavolan M (2011) A quantitative analysis of CLIP methods for identifying binding sites of RNA-binding proteins. Nat Methods 8(7):559–564. doi:10.1038/nmeth.1608
51. Konig J, Zarnack K, Rot G, Curk T, Kayikci M, Zupan B, Turner DJ, Luscombe NM, Ule J (2011) iCLIP—transcriptome-wide mapping of protein-RNA interactions with individual nucleotide resolution. J Vis Exp 50:2638. doi:10.3791/2638
52. Broughton JP, Pasquinelli AE (2013) Identifying argonaute binding sites in *Caenorhabditis elegans* using iCLIP. Methods 63(2):119–125. doi:10.1016/j.ymeth.2013.03.033
53. Helwak A, Kudla G, Dudnakova T, Tollervey D (2013) Mapping the human miRNA interactome by CLASH reveals frequent noncanonical binding. Cell 153(3):654–665. doi:10.1016/j.cell.2013.03.043
54. Travis AJ, Moody J, Helwak A, Tollervey D, Kudla G (2014) Hyb: a bioinformatics pipeline for the analysis of CLASH (crosslinking, ligation and sequencing of hybrids) data. Methods 65(3):263–273. doi:10.1016/j.ymeth.2013.10.015
55. Gregory BD, O'Malley RC, Lister R, Urich MA, Tonti-Filippini J, Chen H, Millar AH, Ecker JR (2008) A link between RNA metabolism and silencing affecting Arabidopsis development. Dev Cell 14(6):854–866. doi:10.1016/j.devcel.2008.04.005
56. Addo-Quaye C, Miller W, Axtell MJ (2009) CleaveLand: a pipeline for using degradome data to find cleaved small RNA targets. Bioinformatics 25(1):130–131. doi:10.1093/bioinformatics/btn604
57. German MA, Luo S, Schroth G, Meyers BC, Green PJ (2009) Construction of parallel analysis of RNA ends (PARE) libraries for the study of cleaved miRNA targets and the RNA degradome. Nat Protoc 4(3):356–362. doi:10.1038/nprot.2009.8
58. German MA, Pillay M, Jeong DH, Hetawal A, Luo S, Janardhanan P, Kannan V, Rymarquis LA, Nobuta K, German R, De Paoli E, Lu C, Schroth G, Meyers BC, Green PJ (2008) Global identification of microRNA-target RNA pairs by parallel analysis of RNA ends. Nat Biotechnol 26(8):941–946. doi:10.1038/nbt1417
59. Li YF, Zheng Y, Addo-Quaye C, Zhang L, Saini A, Jagadeeswaran G, Axtell MJ, Zhang W, Sunkar R (2010) Transcriptome-wide identification of microRNA targets in rice. Plant J 62(5):742–759. doi:10.1111/j.1365-313X.2010.04187.x
60. Bracken CP, Szubert JM, Mercer TR, Dinger ME, Thomson DW, Mattick JS, Michael MZ, Goodall GJ (2011) Global analysis of the mammalian RNA degradome reveals widespread miRNA-dependent and miRNA-independent endonucleolytic cleavage. Nucleic Acids Res 39(13):5658–5668. doi:10.1093/nar/gkr110
61. Karginov FV, Cheloufi S, Chong MM, Stark A, Smith AD, Hannon GJ (2010) Diverse endonucleolytic cleavage sites in the mammalian transcriptome depend upon microRNAs, Drosha, and additional nucleases. Mol Cell 38(6):781–788. doi:10.1016/j.molcel.2010.06.001

62. Shin C, Nam JW, Farh KK, Chiang HR, Shkumatava A, Bartel DP (2010) Expanding the microRNA targeting code: functional sites with centered pairing. Mol Cell 38(6):789–802. doi:10.1016/j.molcel.2010.06.005
63. Eckardt NA (2009) Investigating translational repression by microRNAs in Arabidopsis. Plant Cell 21(6):1624. doi:10.1105/tpc.109.210613
64. Chiu HS, Llobet-Navas D, Yang X, Chung WJ, Ambesi-Impiombato A, Iyer A, Kim HR, Seviour EG, Luo Z, Sehgal V, Moss T, Lu Y, Ram P, Silva J, Mills GB, Califano A, Sumazin P (2015) Cupid: simultaneous reconstruction of microRNA-target and ceRNA networks. Genome Res 25(2):257–267. doi:10.1101/gr.178194.114
65. Maragkakis M, Reczko M, Simossis VA, Alexiou P, Papadopoulos GL, Dalamagas T, Giannopoulos G, Goumas G, Koukis E, Kourtis K, Vergoulis T, Koziris N, Sellis T, Tsanakas P, Hatzigeorgiou AG (2009) DIANA-microT web server: elucidating microRNA functions through target prediction. Nucleic Acids Res 37(Web Server issue):W273–W276. doi:10.1093/nar/gkp292
66. Maragkakis M, Vergoulis T, Alexiou P, Reczko M, Plomaritou K, Gousis M, Kourtis K, Koziris N, Dalamagas T, Hatzigeorgiou AG (2011) DIANA-microT Web server upgrade supports Fly and Worm miRNA target prediction and bibliographic miRNA to disease association. Nucleic Acids Res 39(Web Server issue):W145–W148. doi:10.1093/nar/gkr294
67. Paraskevopoulou MD, Georgakilas G, Kostoulas N, Vlachos IS, Vergoulis T, Reczko M, Filippidis C, Dalamagas T, Hatzigeorgiou AG (2013) DIANA-microT web server v5.0: service integration into miRNA functional analysis workflows. Nucleic Acids Res 41(Web Server issue):W169–W173. doi:10.1093/nar/gkt393
68. Gaidatzis D, van Nimwegen E, Hausser J, Zavolan M (2007) Inference of miRNA targets using evolutionary conservation and pathway analysis. BMC Bioinformatics 8:69. doi:10.1186/1471-2105-8-69
69. Ahmadi H, Ahmadi A, Azimzadeh-Jamalkandi S, Shoorehdeli MA, Salehzadeh-Yazdi A, Bidkhori G, Masoudi-Nejad A (2013) HomoTarget: a new algorithm for prediction of microRNA targets in *Homo sapiens*. Genomics 101(2):94–100. doi:10.1016/j.ygeno.2012.11.005
70. Sales G, Coppe A, Bisognin A, Biasiolo M, Bortoluzzi S, Romualdi C (2010) MAGIA, a web-based tool for miRNA and genes integrated analysis. Nucleic Acids Res 38(Web Server issue):W352–W359. doi:10.1093/nar/gkq423
71. Enright AJ, John B, Gaul U, Tuschl T, Sander C, Marks DS (2003) MicroRNA targets in drosophila. Genome Biol 5(1):R1. doi:10.1186/gb-2003-5-1-r1
72. Hsu JB, Chiu CM, Hsu SD, Huang WY, Chien CH, Lee TY, Huang HD (2011) miRTar: an integrated system for identifying miRNA-target interactions in human. BMC Bioinformatics 12:300. doi:10.1186/1471-2105-12-300
73. Krek A, Grun D, Poy MN, Wolf R, Rosenberg L, Epstein EJ, MacMenamin P, da Piedade I, Gunsalus KC, Stoffel M, Rajewsky N (2005) Combinatorial microRNA target predictions. Nat Genet 37(5):495–500. doi:10.1038/ng1536
74. Kertesz M, Iovino N, Unnerstall U, Gaul U, Segal E (2007) The role of site accessibility in microRNA target recognition. Nat Genet 39(10):1278–1284. doi:10.1038/ng2135
75. Dai X, Zhao PX (2011) psRNATarget: a plant small RNA target analysis server. Nucleic Acids Res 39(Web Server issue):W155–W159. doi:10.1093/nar/gkr319
76. Rehmsmeier M, Steffen P, Hochsmann M, Giegerich R (2004) Fast and effective prediction of microRNA/target duplexes. RNA 10(10):1507–1517. doi:10.1261/rna.5248604
77. Lewis BP, Burge CB, Bartel DP (2005) Conserved seed pairing, often flanked by adenosines, indicates that thousands of human genes are microRNA targets. Cell 120(1):15–20. doi:10.1016/j.cell.2004.12.035
78. Friedman RC, Farh KK, Burge CB, Bartel DP (2009) Most mammalian mRNAs are conserved targets of microRNAs. Genome Res 19(1):92–105. doi:10.1101/gr.082701.108
79. Garcia DM, Baek D, Shin C, Bell GW, Grimson A, Bartel DP (2011) Weak seed-pairing stability and high target-site abundance decrease the proficiency of lsy-6 and other microRNAs. Nat Struct Mol Biol 18(10):1139–1146. doi:10.1038/nsmb.2115
80. Agarwal V, Bell GW, Nam JW, Bartel DP (2015) Predicting effective microRNA target sites in mammalian mRNAs. eLife 4:e05005. doi:10.7554/eLife.05005
81. Huang JC, Babak T, Corson TW, Chua G, Khan S, Gallie BL, Hughes TR, Blencowe BJ, Frey BJ, Morris QD (2007) Using expression profiling data to identify human microRNA targets. Nat Methods 4(12):1045–1049. doi:10.1038/nmeth1130
82. Bandyopadhyay S, Ghosh D, Mitra R, Zhao Z (2015) MBSTAR: multiple instance learning for predicting specific functional binding sites in microRNA targets. Sci Rep 5:8004. doi:10.1038/srep08004

83. Thadani R, Tammi MT (2006) MicroTar: predicting microRNA targets from RNA duplexes. BMC Bioinformatics 7(Suppl 5):S20. doi:10.1186/1471-2105-7-S5-S20
84. Wang X, El Naqa IM (2008) Prediction of both conserved and nonconserved microRNA targets in animals. Bioinformatics 24(3):325–332. doi:10.1093/bioinformatics/btm595
85. Hammell M, Long D, Zhang L, Lee A, Carmack CS, Han M, Ding Y, Ambros V (2008) mirWIP: microRNA target prediction based on microRNA-containing ribonucleoprotein-enriched transcripts. Nat Methods 5(9):813–819. doi:10.1038/nmeth.1247
86. Friedman Y, Karsenty S, Linial M (2014) miRror-suite: decoding coordinated regulation by microRNAs. Database (Oxford) 2014:bau043. doi:10.1093/database/bau043
87. Friedman Y, Naamati G, Linial M (2010) MiRror: a combinatorial analysis web tool for ensembles of microRNAs and their targets. Bioinformatics 26(15):1920–1921. doi:10.1093/bioinformatics/btq298
88. Yang Y, Wang YP, Li KB (2008) MiRTif: a support vector machine-based microRNA target interaction filter. BMC Bioinformatics 9(Suppl 12):S4. doi:10.1186/1471-2105-9-S12-S4
89. Yousef M, Jung S, Kossenkov AV, Showe LC, Showe MK (2007) Naive Bayes for microRNA target predictions--machine learning for microRNA targets. Bioinformatics 23(22):2987–2992. doi:10.1093/bioinformatics/btm484
90. Uren PJ, Bahrami-Samani E, Burns SC, Qiao M, Karginov FV, Hodges E, Hannon GJ, Sanford JR, Penalva LO, Smith AD (2012) Site identification in high-throughput RNA-protein interaction data. Bioinformatics 28(23):3013–3020. doi:10.1093/bioinformatics/bts569
91. van Dongen S, Abreu-Goodger C, Enright AJ (2008) Detecting microRNA binding and siRNA off-target effects from expression data. Nat Methods 5(12):1023–1025. doi:10.1038/nmeth.1267
92. Coronnello C, Benos PV (2013) ComiR: Combinatorial microRNA target prediction tool. Nucleic Acids Res 41(Web Server issue):W159–W164. doi:10.1093/nar/gkt379
93. Betel D, Koppal A, Agius P, Sander C, Leslie C (2010) Comprehensive modeling of microRNA targets predicts functional non-conserved and non-canonical sites. Genome Biol 11(8):R90. doi:10.1186/gb-2010-11-8-r90
94. Bandyopadhyay S, Mitra R (2009) TargetMiner: microRNA target prediction with systematic identification of tissue-specific negative examples. Bioinformatics 25(20):2625–2631. doi:10.1093/bioinformatics/btp503
95. Chandra V, Girijadevi R, Nair AS, Pillai SS, Pillai RM (2010) MTar: a computational microRNA target prediction architecture for human transcriptome. BMC Bioinformatics 11(Suppl 1):S2. doi:10.1186/1471-2105-11-S1-S2
96. Chang TH, Huang HY, Hsu JB, Weng SL, Horng JT, Huang HD (2013) An enhanced computational platform for investigating the roles of regulatory RNA and for identifying functional RNA motifs. BMC Bioinformatics 14(Suppl 2):S4. doi:10.1186/1471–2105-14-S2-S4

Chapter 8

Computational Prediction of MicroRNA Target Genes, Target Prediction Databases, and Web Resources

Justin T. Roberts and Glen M. Borchert

Abstract

MicroRNA (miRNA) mediated silencing and repression of mRNA molecules requires complementary base pairing between the "seed" region of the miRNA and the "seed match" region of target mRNAs. While this mechanism is fairly well understood, accurate prediction of valid miRNA targets remains challenging due to factors such as imperfect sequence specificity, target site availability, and the thermodynamic stability of the mRNA structure itself. As knowledge of what genes are being targeted by each miRNA is arguably the most important facet of miRNA biology, many approaches have been developed to address the need for reliable prediction and ranking of putative targets, with most using a combination of various strategies such as evolutionary conservation, statistical inference, and distinct features of the target sequences themselves. This chapter reviews the pros and cons of a number of different prediction algorithms, showcases some databases that store experimentally validated miRNA targets, and also provides a case study that profiles some of the potential microRNA–mRNA interactions predicted by each methodology for various human genes.

Key words MicroRNA, mRNA, Target prediction, Algorithms, Databases, Resources

1 Introduction

Since the initial discovery of these small regulatory molecules in the early 1990s [1], the number of reported microRNAs has increased exponentially. MiRBase [2], the chief data repository for microRNAs, currently contains over 28,000 sequences, with approximately 2600 in humans alone. However, despite the fact that new miRNA and microRNA-like molecules are identified every year, the vast majority of annotated miRNAs have no accurately characterized targets. This is primarily due to three factors: (1) the high difficulty and expense of experimentally validating miRNA mediated gene regulation, (2) the ability for multiple microRNAs to regulate the same mRNA target [3] (and conversely a single miRNA's ability to regulate multiple mRNAs [4]), and arguably most importantly, (3) the lack of a proven, widely accepted

Jingshan Huang et al. (eds.), *Bioinformatics in MicroRNA Research*, Methods in Molecular Biology, vol. 1617,
DOI 10.1007/978-1-4939-7046-9_8, © Springer Science+Business Media LLC 2017

prediction algorithm that can overcome the sheer computational complexity required to generate reliable targets [5]. Despite these challenges, however, the need for accurate miRNA target prediction remains high as increasingly more cellular processes and pathologies are being reported to have some degree of microRNA mediated regulation [6].

The induction of gene silencing and repression via microRNAs typically requires complementary base pairing between specific regions of the miRNA and its target mRNA. Known as the "seed" region within the microRNA, nucleotides 2–7 are the canonical positions that must match to complementary sites within the mRNA in order to be regulated [7] (Fig. 1a). However, while this specific pairing is necessary in most cases, there are reported examples of other types shown to be sufficient for functional regulation [8]. For instance some studies have found that non Watson–Crick pairing with G–U wobbles or mismatches may be acceptable [9], and very extensive pairing to the 3′ region of the miRNA can also compensate for a wobble or mismatch to some of the seed positions [10] (Fig. 1b). Nevertheless, these non-canonical binding sites are extremely rare, and the vast majority of reports [4, 11, 12] show that strict seed pairing is the most reliable predicator for functional target repression, and therefore, most prediction strategies require seed complementary in their algorithms. That said, because the seed only spans six or seven nucleotides, many putative target matches will occur over a given mRNA just by chance giving rise to hundreds of possible targets for most miRNAs. Indeed, some estimates report that as much as 90% of all human genes are regulated by miRNAs [13], with some targets being regulated by a number of different miRNAs [3]. Given that the impetus for undertaking miRNA target prediction is often the need to generate a reliable yet concise list of targets for experimental validation, biologically meaningful ranking of the high number of possible targets is highly desired. Therefore, when

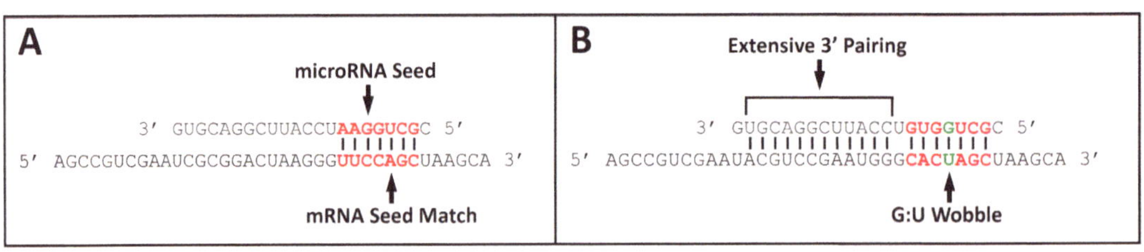

Fig. 1 Mechanism of microRNA mediated gene regulation. (**a**) MicroRNA induced gene silencing and repression generally requires base pairing between a specific region within the miRNA (referred to as the "seed") and a complementary "seed match" area within the mRNA. These regions are shown in *red* in the figure above, with base pairing indicated by *bold vertical lines*. (**b**) In rare cases, noncanonical pairings such as G–U wobbles (shown in *green*) may still be acceptable for functional regulation if they occur along with very extensive base pairing to the 3′ region of the miRNA

evaluating the various target prediction algorithms the ability not only to predict microRNA–mRNA interactions but also to accurately compare and rank them should be considered as well.

2 Target Prediction

While there are many different factors that affect a miRNA's ability to bind to its target, in terms of prediction strategies, the features can broadly be categorized into four groups: attributes of the mRNA sequence itself, thermodynamic stability of the microRNA–mRNA duplex, evolutionary conservation, and statistical inference based machine learning. Most target prediction algorithms typically utilize a combination of these strategies, with some relying more heavily on certain groups and others being more balanced. It should be noted that there is not a one size fits all approach; for instance, if the microRNA in question is highly conserved among species, then a prediction strategy that favors that facet should be considered, whereas more recently discovered miRNAs might require a different methodology. Below, each major strategy is discussed along with a brief profile of a relevant tool that utilizes that approach. A comprehensive table of many other target prediction algorithms (Table 1) is also provided with the specific strategies they incorporate indicated.

2.1 Sequence Features

Detailed analysis of conserved microRNA–mRNA interactions has shown that sequence features within the seed region as well the immediate surrounding area have a distinct effect on the efficacy of miRNA induced gene repression, and thus these features have been incorporated into target prediction strategies to increase their accuracy. Specifically, several classes of targets sites have been identified [7], with the most effective canonical sites (listed in order of decreasing preferential conservation and regulatory efficiency) being the 8mer Watson–Crick match to miRNA positions 2–8 with an "A" opposite position 1, followed by the 7mer site (position 2–8 match without the "A" opposite position 1), and the 7mer A1 site (position 2–7 match with an A opposite position 1) [33]. Multiple experiments have shown that the preference for an adenosine opposite position 1 is due to the specific recognition of the target adenosine within the Argonaute protein [34] and is independent of the nucleotide identity within the miRNA [11, 12, 35]. Two other site types, each associated with lower conservation and efficacy [36], are the 6mer site (position 2–7 match) [33] and the offset 6mer site (position 3–8 match) [36] (Fig. 2).

Further, while the type of the target site (as discussed above) does strongly influence the strength of gene repression, the number of sites and their relative location has also been shown to be an important factor in miRNA induced silencing. Multiple target sites

Table 1
List of microRNA target prediction algorithms and databases with the type(s) of utilized strategies indicated

	Sequence features	Thermo stability	Evolutionary conservation	Machine learning	Webserver	References
ANTAR				✓	http://servers.binf.ku.dk/antar/	Wen et al. [14]
ComiR				✓	http://www.benoslab.pitt.edu/comir/	Coronnello and Benos [15]
DIANA-microT		✓	✓	✓	http://diana.cslab.ece.ntua.gr/microT/	Paraskevopoulou et al. [16]
ElMMo			✓		http://www.mirz.unibas.ch/ElMMo2/	Gaidatzis et al. [17]
HOCTAR	✓				http://hoctar.tigem.it/	Gennarino et al. [18]
MBStar				✓	http://www.isical.ac.in/~bioinfo_miu/MBStar30.htm	Bandyopadhyay et al. [19]
MicroTar	✓	✓			http://tiger.dbs.nus.edu.sg/microtar/	Thadani and Tammi [20]
miRanda	✓	✓	✓		http://www.microrna.org/microrna/	John et al. [21]
miRiam		✓			http://ferrolab.dmi.unict.it/miriam.html	Laganà et al. [22]
miRmap	✓	✓	✓	✓	http://mirmap.ezlab.org/	Vejnar and Zdobnov [23]
miRNA_Targets	✓	✓	✓		http://mamsap.it.deakin.edu.au/mirna_targets/	Kumar et al. [24]
MIRZA-G	✓	✓	✓		http://www.clipz.unibas.ch/index.php?r=tools/sub/mirza_g	Gumienny and Zavolan [25]
OrBId			✓		http://borchertlab.com/orbid	Filshtein et al. [26]
PACMIT		✓	✓		http://paccmit.epfl.ch/	Marin and Vanicek [27]
PicTar		✓	✓		http://pictar.mdc-berlin.de/	Krek et al. [28]
PITA		✓			http://genie.weizmann.ac.il/pubs/mir07/mir07_prediction.html	Kertesz et al. [29]
RNA22				✓	https://cm.jefferson.edu/rna22/	Loher and Rigoutsos [30]
RNAhybrid		✓			http://bibiserv.techfak.uni-bielefeld.de/rnahybrid	Kruger and Rehmsmeier [31]
TargetScan	✓		✓		http://targetscan.org	Agarwal et al. [32]

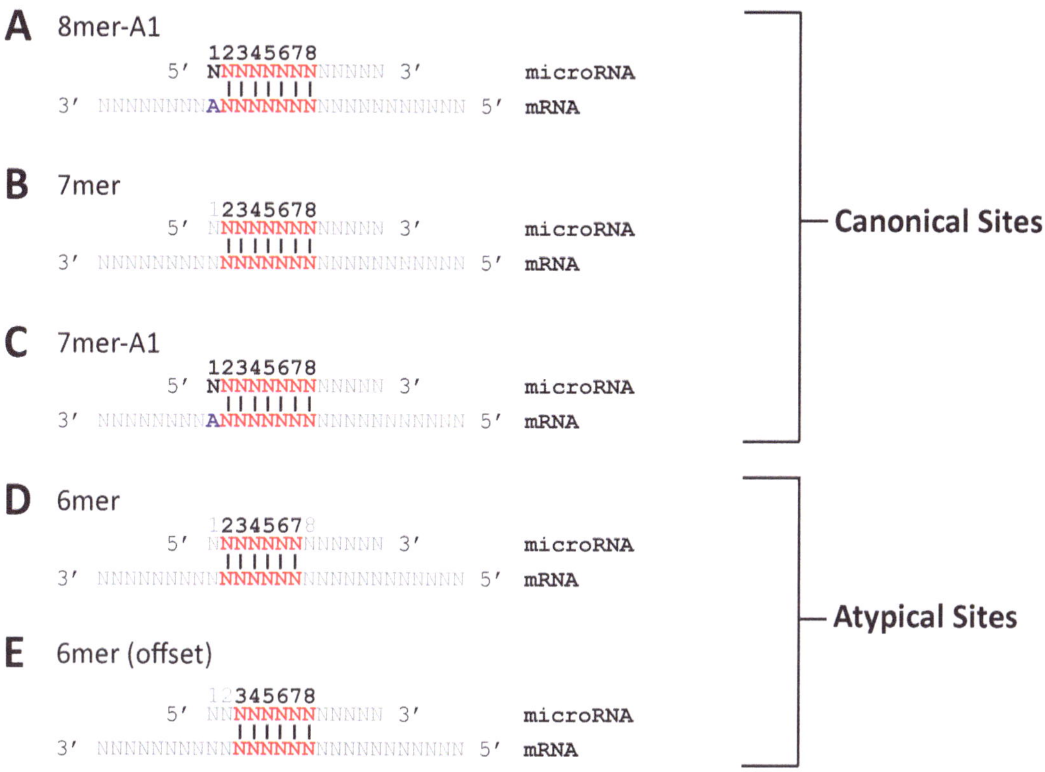

Fig. 2 Types of miRNA target sites. (**a–c**) Canonical target sites are between 7 and 8 nucleotides with many having a preference for an "A" opposite position 1 (shown in *blue*). (**d, e**) Atypical sites are shorter (6mer) and generally have reduced efficacy and conservation. *Vertical dashes* depict complementary Watson–Crick pairing, and the numbers above the microRNA sequences indicate positions from the 5′ end

within 10–50 nucleotides of each other have been shown to induce enhanced repression, whereas sites too close to one another (less than 8 nt) tend to act competitively [11, 35]. Other site context sequence features of note include the positioning of the site outside of the path of the ribosome [11], the positioning of the site within more accessible 3′ UTR segments [35], high AU content along the length of the 3′ UTR [37], shorter overall 3′ UTR length [38], and shorter distance from a 3′ UTR terminus [39]. These sequence features help explain why a given site is more effective in one target mRNA than in another and are thus very informative when utilized to build quantitative models within target prediction algorithms.

One such algorithm, TargetScan [32] (v7.0; targetscan.org), does exactly this by incorporating many of the attributes mentioned above into its prediction strategy. Its scoring model considers over 14 different sequence features and ranks the most effectively targeted mRNAs accordingly. In addition, it also allows for the incorporation of other prediction approaches mentioned later in the chapter including evolutionary conservation, structural stability, and statistical modeling, and it can be implemented on a number of different model organisms including human, mouse, zebrafish, *D. melanogaster*, and *C. elegans*. That said, although the algorithm is very comprehensive, its usability is hindered by choosing to default to only displaying those sites that are conserved among species. This gives the initial impression that only a limited number of miRNAs are targeting a given mRNA and might tempt the user to disregard less conserved miRNAs even though they have higher scores.

2.2 Thermodynamic Stability

While sequence features such as the ones discussed above are obviously very informative in terms of predicting microRNA–mRNA interactions, the secondary structure, or folding, of the mRNA also contributes to target recognition as there is an energetic cost to the free base pairing interactions within the mRNA molecule ultimately necessary to make the target accessible for microRNA binding. That said, many target prediction algorithms incorporate thermodynamic stability assessments into their analysis, most commonly by comparing minimum free energy states of the predicted miRNA–mRNA duplexes, using tools such as Mfold [40], and then determining the most energetically favorable hybridization sites between the miRNA and the target mRNA. While some algorithms only incorporate these stability measures to confirm initial sequence based predictions, others rely on them completely for their initial considerations.

One such algorithm, RNAhybrid [31] (http://bibiserv.techfak.uni-bielefeld.de/rnahybrid/), utilizes thermodynamic stability as its primary means of microRNA target prediction. The method itself is an extension of a classical secondary structure prediction algorithm [41] that used known structural energy data to compute minimum free energies of single RNA conformations. RNAhybrid builds on this approach by applying the same methodology to two sequences and essentially calculating the minimum free energy of all possible hybridizations between a miRNA and its target mRNA. By coupling these results with robust statistical analysis the program provides meaningful predictions of microRNA targets based on the thermodynamic stability of miRNA–mRNA association. Advantages to this strategy include that it can be used to predict noncanonical binding sites and does not require conservation of target sites across species (an extremely important consideration for species-specific miRNAs). However, one potential drawback of this strategy is that the algorithm itself relies on free energy calculations based on computational models of nucleotide association. Further, in terms of usability, the program does not rank the targets by default and thus requires manual manipulation of the output file in order to effectively identify the top predictions.

2.3 Evolutionary Conservation

Due to the sheer number of possible targets for each microRNA (as previously described), prediction strategies often incorporate methodologies that attempt to minimize the number of false positives reported by the algorithm. One such approach is to use sequence conservation between different species to limit the number of predicted miRNA–mRNA interactions to those based on homology. This idea is based on the notion that miRNA regulations with advantageous biological functions are selected for and maintained over the course of evolution [42]. Typically these types of algorithms use comparative sequence analysis to predict miRNA targets conserved across multiple genomes. Given a conserved miRNA and a set of orthologous 3'UTR sequences, these strategies search for targets that exhibit perfect complementarity with the miRNA seed region. However, while this approach does reduce the number of predicted false positives, it is also limiting in the fact that it can only search for targets of evolutionary conserved miRNAs. What's more, previous studies [43] show that at least 30% of experimentally validated microRNA targets are NOT conserved, strongly suggesting that homology alone is not a sufficient strategy for miRNA target prediction.

That said, in contrast to specifically requiring target site conservation, alternative prediction methodologies that utilize other sequence homologies and relationships have now also been developed. One such algorithm, OrBId [26] (http://borchertlab.com/orbid) contrasts itself to other evolution based approaches by attempting to predict targets through identifying the molecular origins of individual microRNAs. This algorithm was developed in light of recent evidence characterizing the parallel formation of both microRNAs and their target sites from the insertions of related transposable elements (TEs) [44, 45]. Through limiting target searches to mRNA transcripts that contain the TE from which a microRNA arose, when compared to other algorithms, this strategy predicts significantly fewer false positives greatly increasing the overall confidence that predicted targets are real. That said, in stark contrast to other conservation based algorithms which are typically more effective at predicting targets for older miRNAs, OrBId is instead ideally suited for predicting targets of "younger," often taxon-specific, miRNAs that were formed more recently. Likely due to degeneration of nonessential sequences over time, OrBId is poorly suited for examining older, more conserved miRNAs. As such, employing a combination of strategies that considers both target site conservation and evolutionarily origins of recently formed miRNAs can be advantageous to studies examining multiple miRNAs.

2.4 Machine Learning

Machine learning approaches attempt to identify miRNA targets by comparing them to miRNA–mRNA interactions with known biological relevance instead of making "de novo" predictions based on sequence data or secondary structure stability. Machine learning in general is a specialty within computer science that strives to develop algorithms that can "learn" from given datasets and use that knowledge to make predictions on similarly unseen data. These strategies are typically based on pattern recognition and utilize computationally based statistical inferences to distinguish between positive and negative datasets [46]. By training algorithms on experimentally verified microRNA–mRNA interactions and artificially generated negative examples, machine learning software attempts to identify patterns that distinguish actual targets from false ones. Thus when presented with a new previously unseen dataset, a machine learning algorithm can use these patterns to categorize whether or not a target is "real." This approach is useful in that like conservation based methods it similarly limits the number of false positives but is not limited to older conserved microRNAs. Importantly, machine learning also allows for the identification of noncanonical binding sites such as those within coding regions since it is not preprogrammed to require strict seed matches within 3′ UTRs. That said, the primary limitation of machine learning is that it learns by example so only results similar to those examples can be found.

MBStar [19] (http://www.isical.ac.in/~bioinfo_miu/MBStar30.htm) is a recently developed machine learning based target prediction algorithm that implements the basic strategy outlined above. MBStar is trained on over 9000 biologically validated interacting miRNA–mRNA pairs (and roughly 1000 non interacting pairs) confirmed by RISC associated immunoprecipitation data. After extracting 40 features that identified positive miRNA–target interactions, the developers of MBStar built a classifier model achieving the highest accuracy rate (as compared to other popular prediction strategies) when employed to predict targets in validated experimental data sets. However, while the machine learning approach does convey some advantages in terms of target predictability, this specific tool's usability is again limited in that it requires manual manipulation of input files which can become very time consuming and tedious if multiple interactions are analyzed.

3 MiRNA Databases

The need for centralized and easy to access databases containing predicted and validated microRNA targets is clearly evidenced by the sheer number of microRNA target prediction algorithms that have been deployed over the last several years (Table 1). Indeed, several relevant repositories have emerged to address this with many of them containing advanced search and filtering capabilities that allow researchers to rapidly retrieve info on genes of interest. Some deploy artificial data mining algorithms on miRNA literature and datasets while others manually curate experimentally validated regulations. High throughput analysis of CLIP-seq experiments has also been used to provide archives of known interactions between microRNAs and RISC proteins such as AGO. Given that new discoveries involving microRNAs are made with ever increasing frequency this data is only going to increase, and with it so too does the need for reliable and maintainable databases to store it. Some of the largest and most widely accessed of these repositories are briefly profiled below.

3.1 MiRDB

MiRDB (http://mirdb.org/miRDB/) [47] is an online database for miRNA target prediction and functional annotations. All MiRDB targets were predicted by the bioinformatics tool, MirTarget [48], which was developed by analyzing thousands of miRNA–target interactions from high-throughput sequencing experiments. MiRDB hosts predicted miRNA targets in five species: human, mouse, rat, dog, and chicken. That said, a recent update has now additionally provided an interface for users to upload their own sequences for customized target prediction.

3.2 MiRTarBase

Consisting of more than 360,000 potential miRNA–target interactions (MTIs), regulations described in miRTarBase (http://mirtarbase.mbc.nctu.edu.tw/) [49] were collected by data mining research articles and manually surveying pertinent literature related to functional studies of miRNAs. For inclusion in miRTarBase, MTIs had to have been reported as being validated experimentally by reporter assay, western blot, microarray, and/or next-generation sequencing experiments.

3.3 TarBase

TarBase (http://www.microrna.gr/tarbase) [50] claims to house the largest manually curated collection of experimentally tested miRNA targets available, having indexed more than half a million miRNA–gene interactions from published experiments on 356 different cell types from 24 species. TarBase target regulations were typically derived from analyses of high throughput experiments such as microarrays and proteomics with specific attention paid to those from NGS sequencing. Each interaction is described with respect to the regulating miRNA, the gene in which it occurs, the nature of the experiments that were conducted to test it, the sufficiency of the site to induce translational repression and/or cleavage, and the paper from which all these data were extracted.

4 Case Study

In order to illustrate the differences between the various target prediction algorithms and databases discussed in this chapter, a small case study was performed whereby four unrelated human genes were used as input in order to identify potential microRNA–mRNA interactions. By limiting the possible target sites to these genes (as opposed to searching for genome wide targets of specific microRNAs), the individual advantages and limitations of each strategy are highlighted. Wherever possible the actual transcript identifier was used as opposed to the gene name as some genes have a multitude of transcripts (though many of these algorithms do not consider this possibility which likely contributes to the perceived discrepancies between them). Results are depicted in Table 2, with the top five predicted miRNA regulators listed for each gene as derived from the four prediction algorithms and three databases previously mentioned. What should be particularly obvious is the lack of overlap between the strategies. With the first gene, DFFA, for instance, there is not a single miRNA that is predicted by more than one algorithm; though it should be reiterated that only the top miRNAs are listed and that more overlap would occur if less ideal predictions were also compared. That said, given the particular criteria that each of these different strategies favor, when multiple algorithms do agree it should warrant increased attention, as is the case with the SOX9 and SNAI2 genes.

When taken as a whole, it becomes clear based off of these limited results that there is not one strategy that is capable of accurately predicting targets for all possible circumstances. Rather, a more robust approach would be to utilize each algorithm according to the individualized needs of the experiment at hand. For instance, if the microRNA in question is relatively less conserved then strategies based primarily on homology across species should not be considered. Secondary structure centered algorithms should also be limited to feasibility tests and confirmations rather than a means of de novo prediction, as evidenced by the fact that none of the miRNAs predicted by RNAhybrid are immediately listed in the experimentally validated databases. Indeed, algorithms that incorporate as much information as possible, whether from the sequence itself or from thermostability or from actual validation, are the ones seemingly most primed to generate accurate predictions.

5 Conclusions

With increasing evidence indicating that most human genes are regulated by microRNAs [13], the need for precise and reliable prediction of targets is strikingly evident. Current approaches for target discovery however tend to produce a significant number of false positives due to the high probability of having complementarity between mRNAs and the short seed regions of miRNAs. Further complicating the matter, other genetic events such as RNA editing and alternative splicing can fundamentally alter the target site and dramatically affect potential miRNA binding and regulation [51, 52].

Table 2
Case study listing microRNAs predicted by the various algorithms and databases discussed in this chapter

Gene	TargetScan	RNAhybrid	OrBId	MBStar	miRDB	miRTarBase	TarBase
DFFAENST00000377036	miR-193a-5p	miR-4436b-5p		miR-30c-1-3p	miR-6778-3p	miR-145-5p	miR-575
	miR-103-3p/107	miR-4722-5p		miR-1273g-3p	miR-485-5p	miR-196a-5p	miR-651
	miR-212-5p	miR-612		miR-892a	miR-6884-5p	let-7b-5p	miR-769-5p
	miR-200bc-3p/429	miR-4763-3p		miR-126-5p	miR-504-3p	miR-216a-5p	miR-361-3p
	miR-429	miR-6727-5p		miR-4648	miR-1184	miR-3613-3p	miR-876-3p
PIPOX ENST00000323372	miR-375	miR-623	miR-619-5p*	miR-3671	miR-298	miR-197-3p*	miR-197-3p*
		miR-4323	miR-5096	miR-5697	miR-1910-3p		miR-18a-5p
		miR-4685-5p	miR-1285-5p	miR-4461	miR-4316		miR-18b-5p
		miR-619-5p*	miR-5095	miR-4517	miR-6090		
		miR-6749-3p	miR-545-3p	miR-6500-5p	miR-7159-5p		
SOX9ENST00000245479	miR-101-3p*	miR-6749-5p	miR-4459	miR-302b-3p*	let-7-3p	miR-124-3p*	miR-296-3p
	miR-1-3p/206/613	miR-6775-5p	miR-1202	miR-519b-3p	miR-98-3p	let-7b-5p	miR-590-3p
	miR-145-5p/5195-3p	miR-762*	miR-762*	miR-373-3p	miR-588	miR-199a-5p	miR-935
	miR-302-3p/520-3p*	miR-4787-5p	miR-3686	miR-4643	miR-30-5p	miR-101-3p*	miR-942
	miR-124-3p/506-3p*	miR-4763-3p		miR-4426	miR-6826-3p	miR-1-3p	miR-548n
SNAI2ENST00000020945	miR-203-3p*	miR-6786-5p	miR-574-5p	miR-520e	miR-124-3p*	miR-124-3p*	miR-566
	miR-200bc-3p/429	miR-6089	miR-3149	miR-490-5p	miR-506-3p	miR-204-5p	miR-614
	miR-124-3p*	miR-4763-3p		miR-1269b	miR-203-3p*	miR-1-3p*	miR-630
	miR-1-3p/206/613*	miR-4741		miR-487b	miR-586	miR-182-5p	miR-542-3p
	miR-182-5p	miR-3620-5p		miR-4652-3p	miR-890	miR-203a-3p*	miR-147b

Notes: Where applicable, the top five miRNAs were chosen based on that particular strategy's ranking methodology. If no default ranking occurs then the miRNAs listed are the first five displayed to the user. * indicates a miRNA that is predicted by more than one algorithm. Actual Ensembl transcript identifiers were used whenever possible. TargetScan results are only from "conserved sites for miRNA families broadly conserved among vertebrates" as described by their website. While the algorithm does generate results for other nonconserved miR families this is not the default display and thus was not taken into account. RNAhybrid was ran from the command line with the following parameters: -m 5000 -s 3utr_human –e 40 -p 0.1 -f 2,8. The "e" and "p" values were adjusted for each gene to limit candidates until only five remained. OrBId defines significant alignments between miRNAs and TEs as having ≥88% identity for ≥17 bp hits or 100% identity for 12–16 bp hits which resulted in less than five top predictions for three of the four genes. MBStar uses RefSeq identifiers for genes not specific to individual transcripts; therefore, in some instances transcript identifiers other than those listed were used

Given that validating mRNA targets experimentally is difficult, time-consuming, and expensive, accurate and concise target predictions are extremely valuable in terms of experimental design. That said, each one of the prediction strategies discussed in this chapter has its own benefits and limitations that should be taken into account when deciding on a specific tool. For instance, energetically favorable interactions are meaningless if the target site is not accessible by RISC. Context is key in these situations, and given that in the end all the methods are computational algorithms that still ultimately require experimental validation, the best results will likely come from initially utilizing a combination of tools to identify targets that are agreed upon by multiple approaches.

As we continue to gain better insight into miRNA regulatory pathways, there is no doubt that novel prediction strategies will be devised to more accurately understand these small molecules and the genes they target. Even now, new technologies such as next generation sequencing coupled with immunoprecipitation like CLIP-seq are giving researchers increased ability to see what specific microRNAs are bound to RISC and what specific mRNAs they are regulating across entire transcriptomes [14, 53]. Such technologies allow for much quicker experimental validation and may be the way of the future as they allow unprecedented views into what is actually present in the cell at a given time. What's more, new prediction strategies will also likely need to incorporate the recent evidence pointing to microRNA binding and regulating of noncanonical regions such as ORFs and 5′ UTR [54] as well as new evidence suggesting some miRNAs actually target lncRNAs instead of mRNAs [55].

References

1. Lee RC, Feinbaum RL, Ambros V (1993) The *C. elegans* heterochronic gene lin-4 encodes small RNAs with antisense complementarity to lin-14. Cell 75:843–854. doi:10.1016/0092-8674(93)90529-Y
2. Kozomara A, Griffiths-Jones S (2014) miRBase: annotating high confidence microRNAs using deep sequencing data. Nucleic Acids Res 42:D68–D73. doi:10.1093/nar/gkt1181
3. Wu S, Huang S, Ding J et al (2010) Multiple microRNAs modulate p21Cip1/Waf1 expression by directly targeting its 3′ untranslated region. Oncogene 29:2302–2308. doi:10.1038/onc.2010.34
4. Selbach M, Schwanhäusser B, Thierfelder N et al (2008) Widespread changes in protein synthesis induced by microRNAs. Nature 455:58–63. doi:10.1038/nature07228
5. Barbato C, Arisi I, Frizzo ME et al (2009) Computational challenges in miRNA target predictions: to be or not to be a true target? J Biomed Biotechnol 2009:803069. doi:10.1155/2009/803069
6. He L, Hannon GJ (2004) MicroRNAs: small RNAs with a big role in gene regulation. Nat Rev Genet 5:522–531. doi:10.1038/nrg1379
7. Bartel DP (2009) MicroRNAs: target recognition and regulatory functions. Cell 136:215–233. doi:10.1016/j.cell.2009.01.002
8. Brennecke J, Stark A, Russell RB, Cohen SM (2005) Principles of MicroRNA–target recognition. PLoS Biol 3:e85. doi:10.1371/journal.pbio.0030085
9. Didiano D, Hobert O (2006) Perfect seed pairing is not a generally reliable predictor for miRNA-target interactions. Nat Struct Mol Biol 13:849–851. doi:10.1038/nsmb1138
10. Doench JG, Sharp PA (2004) Specificity of microRNA target selection in translational repression. Genes Dev 18:504–511. doi:10.1101/gad.1184404

11. Grimson A, Farh KK-H, Johnston WK et al (2007) MicroRNA targeting specificity in mammals: determinants beyond seed pairing. Mol Cell 27:91–105. doi:10.1016/j.molcel.2007.06.017
12. Baek D, Villén J, Shin C et al (2008) The impact of microRNAs on protein output. Nature 455:64–71. doi:10.1038/nature07242
13. Miranda KC, Huynh T, Tay Y et al (2006) A pattern-based method for the identification of MicroRNA binding sites and their corresponding heteroduplexes. Cell 126:1203–1217. doi:10.1016/j.cell.2006.07.031
14. Wen J, Parker BJ, Jacobsen A, Krogh A (2011) MicroRNA transfection and AGO-bound CLIP-seq data sets reveal distinct determinants of miRNA action. RNA 17:820–834. doi:10.1261/rna.2387911
15. Coronnello C, Benos PV (2013) ComiR: combinatorial microRNA target prediction tool. Nucleic Acids Res 41:W159–W164. doi:10.1093/nar/gkt379
16. Paraskevopoulou MD, Georgakilas G, Kostoulas N et al (2013) DIANA-microT web server v5.0: service integration into miRNA functional analysis workflows. Nucleic Acids Res 41:W169–W173. doi:10.1093/nar/gkt393
17. Gaidatzis D, van Nimwegen E, Hausser J, Zavolan M (2007) Inference of miRNA targets using evolutionary conservation and pathway analysis. BMC Bioinformatics 8:69. doi:10.1186/1471-2105-8-69
18. Gennarino VA, Sardiello M, Mutarelli M et al (2011) HOCTAR database: a unique resource for microRNA target prediction. Gene 480:51–58. doi:10.1016/j.gene.2011.03.005
19. Bandyopadhyay S, Ghosh D, Mitra R, Zhao Z (2015) MBSTAR: multiple instance learning for predicting specific functional binding sites in microRNA targets. Sci Rep 5:8004. doi:10.1038/srep08004
20. Thadani R, Tammi MT (2006) MicroTar: predicting microRNA targets from RNA duplexes. BMC Bioinformatics 7(Suppl 5):S20. doi:10.1186/1471-2105-7-S5-S20
21. John B, Enright AJ, Aravin A et al (2004) Human microRNA targets. PLoS Biol 2:e363. doi:10.1371/journal.pbio.0020363
22. Laganà A, Forte S, Russo F et al (2010) Prediction of human targets for viral-encoded microRNAs by thermodynamics and empirical constraints. J RNAi Gene Silencing 6:379–385
23. Vejnar CE, Zdobnov EM (2012) MiRmap: comprehensive prediction of microRNA target repression strength. Nucleic Acids Res 40:11673–11683. doi:10.1093/nar/gks901
24. Kumar A, Wong AK-L, Tizard ML et al (2012) miRNA_targets: a database for miRNA target predictions in coding and non-coding regions of mRNAs. Genomics 100:352–356. doi:10.1016/j.ygeno.2012.08.006
25. Gumienny R, Zavolan M (2015) Accurate transcriptome-wide prediction of microRNA targets and small interfering RNA off-targets with MIRZA-G. Nucleic Acids Res 43:1380–1391. doi:10.1093/nar/gkv050
26. Filshtein TJ, Mackenzie CO, Dale MD et al (2014) OrbId: origin-based identification of microRNA targets. Mob Genet Elements 2:184–192. doi:10.4161/mge.21617
27. Šulc M, Marín RM, Robins HS, Vaníček J (2015) PACCMIT/PACCMIT-CDS: identifying microRNA targets in 3′ UTRs and coding sequences. Nucleic Acids Res 43:W474–W479. doi:10.1093/nar/gkv457
28. Krek A, Grün D, Poy MN et al (2005) Combinatorial microRNA target predictions. Nat Genet 37:495–500. doi:10.1038/ng1536
29. Kertesz M, Iovino N, Unnerstall U et al (2007) The role of site accessibility in microRNA target recognition. Nat Genet 39:1278–1284. doi:10.1038/ng2135
30. Loher P, Rigoutsos I (2012) Interactive exploration of RNA22 microRNA target predictions. Bioinformatics 28:3322–3323. doi:10.1093/bioinformatics/bts615
31. Kruger J, Rehmsmeier M (2006) RNAhybrid: microRNA target prediction easy, fast and flexible. Nucleic Acids Res 34:W451–W454. doi:10.1093/nar/gkl243
32. Agarwal V, Bell GW, Nam J-W, Bartel DP (2015) Predicting effective microRNA target sites in mammalian mRNAs. eLife. doi:10.7554/eLife.05005
33. Lewis BP, Burge CB, Bartel DP (2005) Conserved seed pairing, often flanked by adenosines, indicates that thousands of human genes are microRNA targets. Cell 120:15–20. doi:10.1016/j.cell.2004.12.035
34. Schirle NT, Sheu-Gruttadauria J, MacRae IJ (2014) Structural basis for microRNA targeting. Science 346:608–613. doi:10.1126/science.1258040
35. Nielsen CB, Shomron N, Sandberg R et al (2007) Determinants of targeting by endogenous and exogenous microRNAs and siRNAs. RNA 13:1894–1910. doi:10.1261/rna.768207
36. Friedman RC, Farh KK-H, Burge CB, Bartel DP (2009) Most mammalian mRNAs are

conserved targets of microRNAs. Genome Res 19:92–105. doi:10.1101/gr.082701.108
37. Robins H, Press WH (2005) Human microRNAs target a functionally distinct population of genes with AT-rich 3′ UTRs. Proc Natl Acad Sci 102:15557–15562. doi:10.1073/pnas.0507443102
38. Hausser J, Zavolan M (2014) Identification and consequences of miRNA-target interactions—beyond repression of gene expression. Nat Rev Genet 15:599–612. doi:10.1038/nrg3765
39. Majoros WH, Ohler U (2007) Spatial preferences of microRNA targets in 3′ untranslated regions. BMC Genomics 8:152. doi:10.1186/1471-2164-8-152
40. Zuker M (2003) Mfold web server for nucleic acid folding and hybridization prediction. Nucleic Acids Res 31:3406–3415. doi:10.1093/nar/gkg595
41. Zuker M, Stiegler P (1981) Optimal computer folding of large RNA sequences using thermodynamics and auxiliary information. Nucleic Acids Res 9:133–148. doi:10.1093/nar/9.1.133
42. Lewis BP, Shih I, Jones-Rhoades MW et al (2003) Prediction of mammalian microRNA targets. Cell 115:787–798
43. Sethupathy P, Corda B, Hatzigeorgiou AG (2006) TarBase: a comprehensive database of experimentally supported animal microRNA targets. RNA 12:192–197. doi:10.1261/rna.2239606
44. Roberts JT, Cooper EA, Favreau CJ et al (2013) Continuing analysis of microRNA origins: formation from transposable element insertions and noncoding RNA mutations. Mob Genet Elements 3:e27755. doi:10.4161/mge.27755
45. Roberts JT, Cardin SE, Borchert GM (2014) Burgeoning evidence indicates that microRNAs were initially formed from transposable element sequences. Mob Genet Elements 4:e29255. doi:10.4161/mge.29255
46. Boser BE, Guyon IM, Vapnik VN (1992) A training algorithm for optimal margin classifiers. In: Proceedings of the 5th annual ACM workshop on computational learning theory, Pittsburgh, PA, 27–29 July 1992. ACM, New York, pp 144–152. ISBN:0-89791-497-X. doi:10.1145/130385.130401
47. Wong N, Wang X (2015) miRDB: an online resource for microRNA target prediction and functional annotations. Nucleic Acids Res 43:D146–D152. doi:10.1093/nar/gku1104
48. Wang X, El Naqa IM (2008) Prediction of both conserved and nonconserved microRNA targets in animals. Bioinformatics 24:325–332. doi:10.1093/bioinformatics/btm595
49. Hsu S-D, Tseng Y-T, Shrestha S et al (2014) miRTarBase update 2014: an information resource for experimentally validated miRNA-target interactions. Nucleic Acids Res 42:D78–D85. doi:10.1093/nar/gkt1266
50. Vlachos IS, Paraskevopoulou MD, Karagkouni D et al (2015) DIANA-TarBase v7.0: indexing more than half a million experimentally supported miRNA:mRNA interactions. Nucleic Acids Res 43:D153–D159. doi:10.1093/nar/gku1215
51. Borchert GM, Gilmore BL, Spengler RM et al (2009) Adenosine deamination in human transcripts generates novel microRNA binding sites. Hum Mol Genet 18:4801–4807. doi:10.1093/hmg/ddp443
52. Yang X, Zhang H, Li L (2012) Alternative mRNA processing increases the complexity of microRNA-based gene regulation in Arabidopsis. Plant J 70:421–431. doi:10.1111/j.1365-313X.2011.04882.x
53. Clark PM, Loher P, Quann K et al (2014) Argonaute CLIP-seq reveals miRNA targetome diversity across tissue types. Sci Rep 4:5947. doi:10.1038/srep05947
54. Lee I, Ajay SS, Jong IY et al (2009) New class of microRNA targets containing simultaneous 5′-UTR and 3′-UTR interaction sites. Genome Res 19:1175–1183. doi:10.1101/gr.089367.108
55. Jalali S, Bhartiya D, Lalwani MK et al (2013) Systematic transcriptome wide analysis of lncRNA-miRNA interactions. PLoS One 8:e53823. doi:10.1371/journal.pone.0053823

Chapter 9

Exploring MicroRNA::Target Regulatory Interactions by Computing Technologies

Yue Hu, Wenjun Lan, and Daniel Miller

Abstract

MiRNA genes (miRNA precursor genes) share some common structural elements with protein genes. As with protein genes, the promoters of miRNA genes are necessary to regulate the expression of miRNA. The computation methods used to find the promoter regions of the protein genes have been applied to miRNA genes and some methods have been designed specifically to find the promoter regions of miRNA genes. The transcription factors (TFs), miRNA, and the targeted genes can form complex regulatory networks in the cells that can be divided into circuits. The miRNA-mediated feed-forward loop (FFL) is the most commonly encountered circuit. The miRNAs can also regulate targeted genes in a collaborative way. Some tools to study these circuits are discussed in this chapter as are some examples of their use.

Key words Transcription factor, miRNA, Promoter, Circuit, Feed forward loop, Synergistic

1 Introduction

In the microRNA (miRNA) research, bioinformatics has played a critical role in the prediction of the target of microRNAs [1, 2] and in the prediction of precursor of microRNAs [3, 4]. There are many other aspects of microRNA research that computational technologies can impact. The first aspect is the study of miRNA expression and decay regulation. The number and, to some extent, content of miRNAs control the level of gene expression. miRNAs with abnormal content may lead to serious diseases and developmental deformities, so it is useful to study the expression and decay of miRNAs. In this aspect, some important transcription factors (TFs) [5] have played a critical role in the expression of the miRNA and the regulation region of the miRNAs gene. Bioinformatics has several tools to study those aspects. The control of miRNA decay is also significant as it determines the time during which the miRNAs can function. In this chapter, we focus on the definition of the promoter regions of miRNA genes.

Jingshan Huang et al. (eds.), *Bioinformatics in MicroRNA Research*, Methods in Molecular Biology, vol. 1617, DOI 10.1007/978-1-4939-7046-9_9, © Springer Science+Business Media LLC 2017

The second aspect is the interactions between miRNAs. miRNAs do not necessarily function alone: groups of miRNAs can play synergistic roles in regulating gene expression [6]. They can also interact with other gene regulation elements such as transcription factors (TFs). These regulatory elements together can function as a local network that can play a global role in the transcription process. The local network can be viewed as a circuit. The type of circuit can control the robustness of the gene's expression. In this chapter, we will focus on those aspects.

2 The Promoter Region of miRNA Genes

Promoter prediction can help with finding genes and delineating other important gene structures. The promoter region typically consists of a few thousand base pairs immediately upstream of the transcription start site (TSS) and it contains enhancers or silencers. A small section of the promoter region, often called the core promoter region, consists of the ~35 base pairs leading up to the TSS. The promoter region has unique features, such as the CG islands near the TSS. Machine learning methods, such as Hidden Markov Models (HMM) and the Discriminate Analysis method, have been used to identify the promoter region based on these features. These methods often use the sequence information and need a training dataset, but both the sequence information and the training dataset have their limitations. Sequence information just reflects the local features and the training datasets can vary across species.

To address these shortcomings, Thomas Abeel [7] developed an algorithm that can predict the gene's promoter region by the features of its structure. Using the GC content and other DNA structural properties, Abeel developed the Easy Promoter Prediction Program (E3P) to find the promoter region in a whole-genome background. It does not need any training data, adapts to many different species, and performs well compared to other programs using strict validation criteria (500 bp maximum distance). Each point of the DNA base pairs is transformed into number profiles by the GC content and structural properties. From those numerical patterns, the features can be used to define the promoter region. The test dataset contains protein-coding genes: small nuclear RNA (snRNA), ribosomal RNA (rRNA), microRNA (miRNA), small nucleolar RNA (snoRNA), and transfer RNA (tRNA). While EP3 does overcome some of the limitations of HMM and Discriminate Analysis, it demonstrates lower performance when identifying the core promoter region of miRNA. For miRNA and tRNA promoters, better results are achieved by using tools specifically designed and trained for these RNA types. Zhou et al. perform a comparison of such tools in their proposal of CoVote [8].

The promoter regions of miRNA genes can be found in different areas relative to the gene. The miRNA genes and miRNA precursors can either be located outside of, or within, a protein gene (a miRNA-targeted gene). In the first instance, the promoter region is the (−900/+100) nontranscribed spacers (nts) upstream of the TSS of the miRNA gene, which is the same as the protein-coding gene (the miRNA-targeted gene). In the second instance, the miRNA gene is inside the protein-coding gene. miRNA genes can also be transcribed both with, and against, the direction of the protein-coding gene. If the miRNA gene transcription direction is opposite to that of the protein-coding gene, those two classes of genes are in a different DNA strand and the promoter region of the miRNA gene is located upstream of the miRNA gene TSS, placing the promoter region of protein-coding gene and the miRNA gene in separate locations. If the direction of the miRNA gene transcription is the same as that of the protein-coding gene, the promoter region will be shared by those two genes. In this case, those two classes of genes can be regulated by the same TFs. The promoters of miRNAs are mostly of type POLII as opposed to type POLI, which synthesizes rRNA, and type POL III, which synthesizes tRNAs, rRNA, and other small RNAs.

3 Interactions Between miRNAs and TFs

The regulatory interactions that govern a gene's expression are very complex. miRNA is a type of small noncoding RNA, which can act as a negative regulator in the expression of genes. The products of a gene's expression are often proteins. TFs can regulate genes with miRNA in pairs. Viewed simply, the TFs only play a role in the progress of the transcription of genes expression and the miRNA only play a part in the progress of the translation (or post-transcription) of a gene's expression from mRNAs to proteins. However, those pairs (TF and miRNA) can form a complicated network that regulates a gene's expression.

We can model these regulatory interactions as a network, albeit a complex one. Many efforts have been made to research these complex networks. Shai S. Shen-Orr et al. [9] in 2002 analyzed the transcription regulation network of *Escherichia coli*. They discovered some basic common structures, which they called network motifs, that could represent the local topology of the transcription regulation network. To identify these motifs, they looked for the occurrence of the motifs in sequence data as compared to the random networks under the assumption that the frequency of occurrences of the network motifs should be much higher in the biological networks than in random networks. In the transcription regulation network of E. coil, they found three frequently occurring motifs. The first motif is the Feed Forward Loop (FFL) that contains a master TF, a medial

TF, and the target gene. The master TF can regulate the targeted gene directly or through a medial TF. The second motif, the Single Input Module (SIM), has one common TF that can regulate many targeted genes. The third motif, Dense Overlapping Regulations (DORs), has many TFs that regulate many genes in a collaborative approach. Consequently, they posit that these complex biological networks can be decomposed into network motifs or circuits that can simplify the analysis of these complex networks.

Matteo Osella et al. used numerical simulation methods to compare three miRNAs-TFs-gene circuits [10]. Those three elements form a complex network to control the expression of proteins. The translation and transcription of the genes are not isolated; The TFs and microRNAs form special motifs that can regulate the expression of proteins efficiently. The complex network is very robust which keeps the cell in a stable state and is tolerant to fluctuations in the concentrations of participants in the regulatory networks. The gene's expression is fine-tuned by these complex networks. The authors demonstrated via their simulation that the microRNA-mediated feed forward loop was the best in reducing noise of the three motifs.

3.1 Tools for Studying the Network Motifs Related to miRNAs

There are many programs and web-based applications that use network motifs to study miRNAs. Zhenyu Yan et al. [11] proposed the dChip-GemiNI[1] method that can integrate the miRNA and gene expression information and give clues regarding the interactions among TFs, miRNAs, and targeted genes. It ranks the related FFLs by their ability to explain the differential gene expressions between normal tissue and cancer tissue. In the examples of six cancers (liver, kidney, prostate, lung, and germ cell), the top-rank FFLs explain a significant amount of change. This method gives a new means to find the tumor markers.

Mohamed Hamed et al. in their paper, "TFmiR: a web server for constructing and analyzing disease-specific transcription factor and miRNA co-regulatory networks," created a web-based application called TFmiR[2] to analyze TF and miRNA gene regulation of gene expressions both individually and collectively [12]. It checks for four different types of regulation against several databases: TF regulation of a gene (TRANSFAC database, OregAnno database, and TRED database), miRNA regulation of a gene (miRTarBase database, TarBase database, miRecords database, and starBase database), TF regulation of miRNA (TransmiR database, PMID20584335 database, and ChipBase database), and miRNA regulation of miRNA (PmmR database). These databases store results from experimental and computational methods. With this tool, the authors integrate the databases incorporating the four interaction types to define synergistic regulatory networks.

---

[1] http://www.canevolve.org/dChip-GemiNi.
[2] http://service.bioinformatik.uni-saarland.de/tfmir.

In all, the TFmiR collects 10,000 genes, 1856 miRNAs, approximately 3000 diseases, and 111,000 interactions. Its analysis relays many results: the disease-specific network disorder in those types of regulation, the disease-related genes and miRNAs, TFs-miRNA regulatory circuit, an overrepresentation analysis (ORA) like the GO analysis, the KEGG pathway enrichment analysis, and so on. As the FFL is an important motif, they also emphasized on this type circuit. They define four types of FFLs:

1. The co-regulation FFL: the TF promotes the gene expression, while the miRNA represses it, but there is no interaction between the TF and miRNA.
2. The TF-FFL: the TF promotes the gene and miRNA expression while the miRNA represses the gene expression. The TF plays the primary role in regulation.
3. The miRNA-FFL: the TF promotes the gene expression, while the miRNA represses the gene expression; the TF promotes the miRNA expression, while the repress the TF expression. The miRNA plays the main role.
4. The composite-FFL: the TF promotes the gene expression, while the miRNA represses the gene expression; the TF promotes the miRNA expression, while the repress the TF expression. The TF and miRNA struggle for the dominance.

In the case study of breast cancer research, they found 53 FFL circuits: 42 co-regulation FFLs, 2 TF-FFLs, 6 miRNA-FFLs, and 3 composite-FFLs. To test the significance of their results, they compared their results to a random network with the same node degrees.

Olivier Friard et al. presented CircuitsDB[3]: a web application devoted to identifying and analyzing interactions of TFs and miRNAs in humans and mice [13]. The regulatory network is studied within the context of local network motifs or circuits. Mixed miRNA/TF FFLs are one of the key circuits that are discussed. The total number of promoters of pre-miRNA genes is relatively small when compared to the total number of promoters of protein-coding genes (130 vs. 21,316 in human, 130 vs. 21,814 in mice). The dataset for CircuitsDB was constructed from a combination of the TF-regulated transcription networks and miRNA-regulated post-transcription networks. TFs regulate the promoter of the protein-coding gene and pre-miRNA genes, so finding the promoters of the protein-coding genes is the first step. miRNA recognizes the 3′ UTR of the protein-coding genes, so the initial step of identifying the post-transcription network is finding the 3′ UTR. Those two networks are then compared between human and mouse by oligo analysis to get the conserved-overrepresentation,

[3] http://biocluster.di.unito.it/circuits/.

then integrated. The raw FFLs were finally functionally annotated by their relevance to cancer and other diseases according to the GO database, Cancer Gene Census catalog, OMIM catalog, and HMDD miRNA-disease database.

3.2 Applications of TF-miRNA Network

The TF-miRNA circuit has been used in many fields. Three examples are given below to show the importance of TF-miRNA networks: their roles in mouse lung development; their roles in the root development of two species of plants; their roles in skeletal myogenesis in mice.

Juan Liu et al. researched the regulation mechanisms for lung development in mice and analyzed the related miRNA-TF-mRNA circuits active during tumor production [14]. They generated lists of genes and TFs from study GSE20954 and used the miRNA list from study GSE201152. These lists were processed to remove those elements that demonstrated little variance during lung development yielding 8299 genes, 50 TFs, and 118 miRNAs. These lists were submitted pairwise to look for known regulatory relationships: TF-gene pairs from Tred, KEGG, and CircuitDB, miRNA-gene pairs from TargetScan, miRanda, and CircuitDB, and miRNA-TF pairs from CircuitDB. The results from these searches were combined which yielded 64,760 candidates circuits that were then checked for significant activity during lung development. Based on these results, they divided the development process of the lung into stages as defined by the active regulation circuits. They also found that some of the genes controlled by these circuits were incorrectly expressed in lung tumor samples, which could explain their formation. They concluded that these circuits may provide additional targets for drug development that could lead to more effective treatments for lung cancer.

Yijun Meng et al. review the miRNAs that participate in the root development of two model plants: rice (*Oryza sativa*) and Arabidopsis (*Arabidopsis thaliana*) [15, 16]. Several signaling pathways involved in the growth and development of the roots are mediated by miRNAs. This review focuses on the auxin signaling, nutrition metabolism, and stress response. In Arabidopsis, miR160, miR164, miR167, miR390, and miR393 mediated the Auxin signaling pathway and miR395, miR398, miR399 mediated the nutrition metabolism pathway. In Rice, miR160, miR164, miR167, and miR390 mediated the auxin signaling, miR399 takes a part in the nutrition metabolism pathway, and miR1169 takes a part in the stress response pathway. The miRNA can be categorized into conservative families that exist in the same signaling pathways across species. Signaling pathways can interact with each other through miRNAs. The miRNAs participating in several signaling pathways could be regarded as the hub. miR167 was shown to mediate both auxin signaling and nitrogen availability showing that miRNA have many targets. Feedback circuits were also identified: miRNA 167 and auxin response factor (ARF) form a feedback circuit controlling the auxin signaling pathway in rice.

Leina Lu et al. performed a study on skeletal myogenesis in mice. Yin Yang 1 and miRNAs can form circuits to regulate the development and differentiation of the skeletal myoblasts [17]. YY1 targets the promotor region of several miRNAs, with miR-1 and miR-133 being of particular interest. miR-1 was shown to downregulate YY1 forming a negative feedback loop. The feedback loop was shown to regulate the corresponding genes with precision. YY1 was also shown to have stronger regulatory effects on miR-133 than on miR-1. The authors proposed two possible explanations: (1) there are three YY1 targeted sites on the promoter region of miR133, while there are two YY1 targeted sites on the promoter region of miR1, and (2) YY1 may exert its regulatory effect at different stages in the transcription process resulting in varying amounts of influence.

4 miRNA Synergistic Interactions

One miRNA can regulate many genes and one gene can be regulated by many miRNAs in a synergistic way [18]. Complex diseases, such as cancer and diabetes, can be caused by the dysfunction of these synergistic miRNAs regulations; thus, it is meaningful to research these regulatory mechanisms. Juan Xu et al. [19] give three criteria to determine if two miRNAs have a synergistic relationship. First, the two miRNA must target the same gene. Second, two miRNAs must have the same functional enrichment as determined by GO analysis: the two miRNAs must perform similar functions. Third, genes in the co-regulated gene set should be located in relative proximity to each other. In their paper, they give two applications of this synergistic function. In the Alzheimer's disease, hsa-miR-101 and hsa-miR-511 compose a synergistic network regulating an enzyme linked to the receptor protein signaling pathway, protein kinase cascade, JAK-STAT cascade, and transmember receptor protein tyrosine kinase signaling pathways. In cardiac hypertrophy, hsa-miR-1, hsa-miR-30b, and hsa-miR-30c regulated vesicle-mediated transport.

In another example, Ming Lu et al. collected the human microRNA-disease association data from 3511 papers to find the Human microRNA Disease Database (HMDD)[4] [20, 21]. In the June 14, 2014 update, this database stores the important associations between 378 miRNA-related diseases and 572 miRNA genes. They suggest that the upregulation and downregulation actions of miRNA have same pattern in similar diseases. Cancers show this pattern in miRNA expression level. For example, the miR-21 has

[4] http://cmbi.bjmu.edu.cn/hmdd.

an upregulation function in most cancers, while the miR-125a serves as a downregulation role. Most miRNAs can be actors in many diseases, but there are some miRNAs that have tissue and disease specificity. They also found that the probability of single nucleotide polymorphisms (SNP) of miRNAs is low (0.0847) illustrating a conservation of diseases-related miRNAs which the authors suggest is related to disease susceptibility.

5 Conclusion

As demonstrated in the examples of the TF and miRNA networks above, there is evidence of circuits in the regulatory interactions of miRNA. Examination of miRNA regulators can be conducted with different focuses. One method is to examine the interactions between TFs and miRNA via predicted or empirical data sets. Another method focuses on the direct regulatory action by locating the promoter region for the targeted miRNA or predicting the TF based on expression. It has also been shown that multiple miRNA can synergistically regulate a target gene. miRNAs can serve as the hub of the synergistic regulatory network with some miRNAs enhancing the regulation. Using a systematic biological view of miRNA could lead to more efficient research efforts.

References

1. Krek A, Grün D, Poy MN, Wolf R, Rosenberg L, Epstein EJ, MacMenamin P, da Piedade I, Gunsalus KC, Stoffel M (2005) Combinatorial microRNA target predictions. Nat Genet 37(5):495–500
2. Rajewsky N (2006) MicroRNA target predictions in animals. Nat Genet 38:S8–S13
3. Adai A, Johnson C, Mlotshwa S, Archer-Evans S, Manocha V, Vance V, Sundaresan V (2005) Computational prediction of miRNAs in *Arabidopsis thaliana*. Genome Res 15(1):78–91
4. Jiang P, Wu H, Wang W, Ma W, Sun X, Lu Z (2007) MiPred: classification of real and pseudo microRNA precursors using random forest prediction model with combined features. Nucleic Acids Res 35(Suppl 2):W339–W344
5. Qiu C, Wang J, Yao P, Wang E, Cui Q (2010) MicroRNA evolution in a human transcription factor and microRNA regulatory network. BMC Syst Biol 4(1):90
6. Sengupta D, Bandyopadhyay S (2011) Participation of microRNAs in human interactome: extraction of microRNA–microRNA regulations. Mol Biosyst 7(6):1966–1973
7. Abeel T, Saeys Y, Bonnet E, Rouzé P, Van de Peer Y (2008) Generic eukaryotic core promoter prediction using structural features of DNA. Genome Res 18(2):310–323
8. Zhou X, Ruan J, Wang G, Zhang W (2007) Characterization and identification of microRNA core promoters in four model species. PLoS Comput Biol 3(3):e37
9. Shen-Orr SS, Milo R, Mangan S, Alon U (2002) Network motifs in the transcriptional regulation network of *Escherichia coli*. Nat Genet 31(1):64–68
10. Osella M, Bosia C, Corá D, Caselle M (2011) The role of incoherent microRNA-mediated feedforward loops in noise buffering. PLoS Comput Biol 7(3):e1001101
11. Yan Z, Shah PK, Amin SB, Samur MK, Huang N, Wang X, Misra V, Ji H, Gabuzda D, Li C (2012) Integrative analysis of gene and miRNA expression profiles with transcription factor–miRNA feed-forward loops identifies regulators in human cancers. Nucleic Acids Res 40(17):e135

12. Hamed M, Spaniol C, Nazarieh M, Helms V (2015) TFmiR: a web server for constructing and analyzing disease-specific transcription factor and miRNA co-regulatory networks. Nucleic Acids Res 43(W1):W283–W288
13. Friard O, Re A, Taverna D, De Bortoli M, Corá D (2010) CircuitsDB: a database of mixed microRNA/transcription factor feed-forward regulatory circuits in human and mouse. BMC Bioinformatics 11(1):435
14. Liu J, Ye X, Wu F-X (2013) Characterizing dynamic regulatory programs in mouse lung development and their potential association with tumourigenesis via miRNA-TF-mRNA circuits. BMC Syst Biol 7(Suppl 2):S11
15. Meng Y, Huang F, Shi Q, Cao J, Chen D, Zhang J, Ni J, Wu P, Chen M (2009) Genome-wide survey of rice microRNAs and microRNA–target pairs in the root of a novel auxin-resistant mutant. Planta 230(5):883–898
16. Yoon EK, Yang JH, Lim J, Kim SH, Kim S-K, Lee WS (2009) Auxin regulation of the microRNA390-dependent transacting small interfering RNA pathway in Arabidopsis lateral root development. Nucleic Acids Res 38(4):1382–1391
17. Lu L, Zhou L, Chen EZ, Sun K, Jiang P, Wang L, Su X, Sun H, Wang H (2012) A novel YY1-miR-1 regulatory circuit in skeletal myogenesis revealed by genome-wide prediction of YY1-miRNA network. PLoS One 7(2):e27596
18. Forrest AR, Kanamori-Katayama M, Tomaru Y, Lassmann T, Ninomiya N, Takahashi Y, de Hoon MJ, Kubosaki A, Kaiho A, Suzuki M (2010) Induction of microRNAs, mir-155, mir-222, mir-424 and mir-503, promotes monocytic differentiation through combinatorial regulation. Leukemia 24(2):460–466
19. Xu J, Li C-X, Li Y-S, Lv J-Y, Ma Y, Shao T-T, Xu L-D, Wang Y-Y, Du L, Zhang Y-P (2011) MiRNA–miRNA synergistic network: construction via co-regulating functional modules and disease miRNA topological features. Nucleic Acids Res 39(3):825–836
20. Li Y, Qiu C, Tu J, Geng B, Yang J, Jiang T, Cui Q (2014) HMDD v2. 0: a database for experimentally supported human microRNA and disease associations. Nucleic Acids Res 42(D1):D1070–D1074
21. Lu M, Zhang Q, Deng M, Miao J, Guo Y, Gao W, Cui Q (2008) An analysis of human microRNA and disease associations. PLoS One 3(10):e3420

Chapter 10

The Limitations of Existing Approaches in Improving MicroRNA Target Prediction Accuracy

Rasiah Loganantharaj and Thomas A. Randall

Abstract

MicroRNAs (miRNAs) are small (18–24 nt) endogenous RNAs found across diverse phyla involved in post-transcriptional regulation, primarily downregulation of mRNAs. Experimentally determining miRNA–mRNA interactions can be expensive and time-consuming, making the accurate computational prediction of miRNA targets a high priority. Since miRNA–mRNA base pairing in mammals is not perfectly complementary and only a fraction of the identified motifs are real binding sites, accurately predicting miRNA targets remains challenging. The limitations and bottlenecks of existing algorithms and approaches are discussed in this chapter.

A new miRNA–mRNA interaction algorithm was implemented in Python (TargetFind) to capture three different modes of association and to maximize detection sensitivity to around 95% for mouse (mm9) and human (hg19) reference data. For human (hg19) data, the prediction accuracy with any one feature among evolutionarily conserved score, multiple targets in a UTR or changes in free energy varied within a close range from 63.5% to 66%. When the results of these features are combined with majority voting, the expected prediction accuracy increases to 69.5%. When all three features are used together, the average best prediction accuracy with tenfold cross validation from the classifiers naïve Bayes, support vector machine, artificial neural network, and decision tree were, respectively, 66.5%, 67.1%, 69%, and 68.4%. The results reveal the advantages and limitations of these approaches.

When comparing different sets of features on their strength in predicting true hg19 targets, evolutionarily conserved score slightly outperformed all other features based on thermostability, and target multiplicity. The sophisticated supervised learning algorithms did not improve the prediction accuracy significantly compared to a simple threshold based approach on conservation score or combining the results of each feature with majority agreements. The targets from randomly generated UTRs behaved similar to that of noninteracting pairs with respect to changes in free energy. Availability of additional experimental data describing noninteracting pairs will advance our understanding of the characteristics and the factors positively and negatively influencing these interactions.

Key words MicroRNA, Transcript regulation, Interacting miRNA–target genes, Pattern matching, Hybridization energy, Thermostability, UTR binding sites

Abbreviations

ANN Artificial neural network
PWM Position weighted matrix
ROC Receiver operating characteristic

Jingshan Huang et al. (eds.), *Bioinformatics in MicroRNA Research*, Methods in Molecular Biology, vol. 1617,
DOI 10.1007/978-1-4939-7046-9_10, © Springer Science+Business Media LLC 2017

SOM Self-organizing map
SVM Support vector machine
UTR Untranslated region

1 Introduction

MicroRNAs (miRNAs) are nearly ubiquitous in eukaryotes, acting as an important component of posttranscriptional regulation. Determining miRNA–mRNA interactions with a high degree of specificity remains challenging despite the effort that the computational community has devoted to this task. A major bottleneck of existing algorithms and methodology is the high rate of false positive prediction rates. Herein we have developed a new miRNA prediction tool and use it to examine the importance of the various features that need consideration during miRNA prediction and highlight the limitations of current approaches.

Identification of experimentally verified miRNAs across diverse species is steadily increasing and the recently released version of miRBase [1] (June 2013 version 20) has 24,521 entries including 2578 and 1908 verified human and mouse miRNA sequences, respectively. Additional experimentally verified targets are maintained in Tarbase [2, 3] and miRecords [4]. The latest release of miRecords on April 2013 has 1814 and 427 interactions in human and mouse genomes. Tarbase 6.0 integrates entries from miRecords, miRTarBase [5], and miR2Disease [6] in addition to maintaining entries using text mining assisted literature curation.

The accurate computational prediction of miRNA targets remains a high priority. Many prediction algorithms are based on base pairing of the seed region of a miRNA with the mRNA 3′ untranslated region (UTR). The core seed region of a miRNA consists of nucleotides 2–7 of the miRNA 5′ end; the rest of the sequence is considered to be non-seed region (*see* Subheading 2 for formal description). The majority of published computational prediction algorithms can be viewed as consisting of two phases: motif findings followed by refinements of targets to minimize the false positive rates. The motif finding algorithms in the context of miRNA target finding are broadly classified into the following groups: (1) structure based prediction, (2) supervised learning, (3) unsupervised learning, and (4) rule-based pattern matching (complementary pairing). Kertesz et al. [7] have shown that the prediction of StarMir [8], which is of the first group and based on secondary structure of mRNA, had poor correlation with experimental results. A supervised learning algorithm for motif prediction starts with a positive training set derived from known binding sites and a negative training set from noninteracting miRNA UTR pairs. Hidden Markov model and profile hidden Markov models are examples of supervised learning models. While an unsupervised learning approach such as a self-organizing map (SOM) is quite appealing to target prediction in the presence of few or no negative examples, it has practical computational challenges in training a large number of mature miRNA and UTRs. For small genomes such as *C. elegans*, mirSOM [9] which was based on SOM has been successful. During the training phase of mirSOM [9] the base pairing score of the seed region was taken into consideration when positioning the target miRNA pair into the underlying grid of the SOM. The results of the potential targets are then refined by changes of free energy in the second phase.

A large number of tools for miRNA target prediction find plausible targets by base pairing. These plausible targets are subsequently refined to reduce the false positive rates. Liu et al. [10] have used a support vector machine (SVM) to refine the plausible targets to reduce the false positive rates. Among the large number of features they have used, the most successful at reducing the false positive rates includes conservation score, number of matches, accessibility energy, and hybridization energy. The targets generated by miRanda [11] are refined by machine learning algorithms such as naïve Bayes [12] and random forest [13] using experimentally determined interacting and noninteracting miRNA–mRNA pairs. Table 1 shows representative features and approaches of the tools for finding miRNA targets.

Table 1
Comparison of representative miRNA target prediction tools

	Base pairing		Thermostability				
Software or method	**Seed region**	**Non-seed**	$\wedge G_{duplox}$	$\wedge G_{opon}$	$\wedge\wedge G$	**Conservation**	**Comment**
PicTar [14]	×		×			×	Pattern matching
PITA [7]	×				×	×	Pattern matching
MirTarget2 [15]	×					×	Supervised learning
Target Scan [16, 17]	×		×			×	Pattern matching
miRanda [18]	×		×			×	Pattern matching
RNAhybrid [16, 19]	×		×				Pattern matching
SVMicro [10]	×	×	×			×	Supervised learning (SVM)
miRmap [20]	×		×	×	×	×	Probabilistic matching
RFMirTarget [13]	×		×			×	Supervised learning (random forest)
MREdictor [21]	×	×	×	×	×		Basic seed match and PWM
Our approach	×	×	×	×	×	×	Pattern matching

Some approaches have combined target finding and refinement phases together. Wang et al. [15] have used SVM with 131 training features to predict miRNA targets in animals.

In this study, we examine the influence of each of the following features in reducing the false positive rate and maximizing the true prediction rate: accessibility energy, hybridization energy, changes in potential energy, conservation score, and multiplicity of targets. Further, we examine the paradigm of using a machine learning approach with all these features to understand the effectiveness and the limitations of machine learning approaches in reducing the false positive rate while improving the overall prediction accuracy.

2 Methods

2.1 Improving Sensitivity

miRNA target prediction tools such as PicTar [22], TargetScan [16], and MiRanda [18] have focused on perfect seed base pairing and its variations. The core seed region is defined as miRNA nucleotide positions 2–7. The definition of seed region defined in [10, 17, 23] and elsewhere is reproduced here for convenience.

Seed match type	Description
6mer	If p_2 through p_7 is W-C complement
7mer-A1	If p_2 through p_7 is W-C complement and p_1 is A
7mer-m1	If p_1 through p_7 is W-C complement
7mer-m8	If p_2 through p_8 is W-C complement
8mer-A1	If p_2 through p_8 is W-C complement and p_1 is A
8mer-m8	If p_1 through p_8 is W-C complement

where W-C stands for Watson–Crick base pairing. Note these definitions of these terms are not disjoint, for example, all the 8mers and 7mers contain the same 6mer.

Brennecke et al. [24] have shown with in vivo experiments in *C. elegans* that perfect base pairing in the seed region is neither necessary nor sufficient for miRNA and UTR interaction. They reveal two other modes of base pairing, namely 5′ dominant and 3′ compensatory. In the canonical mode, strong base pairing taking place in both the seed and non-seed regions. In the 3′ compensatory mode, strong 3′ base pairing compensates for weak 5′ base pairing, while in 5′ dominant mode a strong base pairing in the seed region is associated with a weak base pairing in the non-seed region. For the purpose of the prediction of miRNA targets, we consider all three variations of base pairing. To increase the sensitivity, we allow G–U pairing in both the seed region and the 3′ non-seed regions of the miRNA. The definition of base pairing as used in this work is shown below.

Canonical site	Strong base pairing at the 5′ seed region (at least six nucleotide base pairing including at most one G–U pairing in the seed region) and at the 3′ non-seed region of the miRNA
5′ dominant	Strong base pairing at the 5′ seed region with a weak base pairing at the 3′ non-seed region of the miRNA
3′ compensatory	Weak base pairing at the 5′ seed region with a strong base pairing at the 3′ end of the miRNA (at least ten contiguous nucleotide base pairing in the 3′ non-seed region including at most a single G–U pairing, and at least five contiguous base pairing in the 5′ seed region of the miRNA including at most one G–U pairing)

2.2 Improving Selectivity or Minimizing False-Positive Error Rate

The objective of our approach is to maximize sensitivity while minimizing the false positive error rate. We define all the relevant notations and terms such as sensitivity, specificity, and prediction accuracy.

Notations			
TP	Predicted true instance is called true positive		
TN	Predicted true negative is called true negative		
P	Total number of positive		
N	Total number of negative instances		
FP	False positive (the ones falsely found to be positive), which is equal to N-TN		
Terms			
Sensitivity or true positive rate	= TP/P	Specificity or true negative rate	= TN/N
Prediction accuracy	= (TP + TN)/(P + N)	False discovery rate	= FP/(FP + TP)

As the sensitivity increases with broadening of a decision boundary, the false positive rate increases. The threshold that maximizes the true positive rate while minimizing the false positive rate is called the *optimal threshold* and it occurs at the intersection of true positive rate and the true negative rate in a single feature space scenario. The prediction accuracy, another metric in target prediction, is not necessarily maximized at the optimal threshold.

As the sensitivity is increased with our flexible base pairing strategy, the false positive rate may also be increased. To refine the potential targets so as to achieve the increased selectivity, some combination of the following methods has been used in the literature: variations of thermostability measures, multiple targets, and targets in evolutionarily conserved regions.

To visually illustrate and to quantify the impacts of a feature in predicting targets, true positive rate is plotted against false positive rate, and the area under the curve is computed to quantify the impact of the chosen feature on predicting true targets. When the area under the Receiver Operating Characteristic (ROC) curve is closer to 1, the feature creates a decision boundary enclosing most of the positive instances and least of the negative instances, while the area 0.5 indicates about 50% of the positive and negative instances are within the decision boundary.

2.2.1 Thermostability

Interactions within a miRNA–target duplex are at least partially governed by the thermodynamic considerations. The stable miRNA–target duplex is expected to have a very low free energy compared to an unstable pair. The hybridizing or the binding energy of the miRNA–target duplex is indirectly measured by the free energy of the bound structure, which is denoted by ΔG_{hybrid}. Kertesz et al. [7] have shown that the hybridization energy of a miRNA–target duplex has a poor correlation with observed degree of repression in their experiment. These observations clearly indicate that other binding factors such as the energy required to open the folded structure surrounding the target must also be considered, and such energy is denoted by ΔG_{open}. The thermodynamic affinity score for the binding of a miRNA–target duplex is denoted by $\Delta\Delta G$.

$$\Delta\Delta G = G_{hybrid} - G_{open} \tag{1}$$

Lekprasert et al. [25] have successfully used thermal energy based features alone to predict miRNA targets accurately. A strong correlation between $\Delta\Delta G$ and the observed degree of depression was demonstrated, thus providing evidence for $\Delta\Delta G$ as a factor in reducing the false positive error rate. In PITA [7] the energy associated with multiple targets in a UTR for a miRNA was computed by combining the $\Delta\Delta G$ of all the sites as defined by $-\log(\Sigma e^{-\Delta\Delta G^{k}})$ to represent the statistical weight of all potential targets in which exactly one site will bind with the miRNA. $\Delta\Delta G_{k}$ represents the changes in free energy of site *k*. The combined $\Delta\Delta G$ of all the potential binding sites of a UTR for a miRNA closely follow the lowest $\Delta\Delta G$ among the potential binding sites. We compare the effectiveness of target prediction using the minimum $\Delta\Delta G$ with combined $\Delta\Delta G$ among the targets in a UTR. The ΔG_{hybrid} is computed by the cofold module of the Vienna RNA package [26, 27]. When considering the opening energy of the surrounding target, a decision must be made on the length of the flanking region. We limit the longest flank to 70 nt and the shortest flank to 15 nt to model secondary structure. The opening energy of the secondary structure surrounding the target can be computed by the RNAup module of the Vienna RNA package [28]. In addition to finding the opening energy of a context, RNAup also finds the best hybridization energy of a target within the context with a given miRNA.

2.3 Evolutionarily Conserved Region

Since the seed region of a mature miRNA family is conserved among related species, the binding sites of the corresponding UTR are also likely conserved in orthologous genes [17]. Such an assumption leads miRNA target prediction tools including PicTar [14], PITA [7], miRmap [20], and miRanda [18] to use evolutionarily conserved regions to refine targets so as to decrease the false positive rate. In these tools, multiple sequence alignments of UTRs of selected species have been used as a proxy for conserved regions. Quantitative measures on the extent that this feature improves the overall performance have not been undertaken for complex datasets such as human and mouse.

2.4 Data

Unique 3′ UTRs from mouse and human were downloaded using Biomart [29] keeping only the longest UTR if more than one transcript associated for a gene was available. Additionally, UTRs shorter than 80 nt were excluded. Mature miRNA sequences were downloaded from miRBase (Release 17, April 2011) and interacting miRNA–gene pairs were downloaded from miRecords [4] (Release November 25, 2010). The set of 250 interacting miRNA–gene pairs for the mouse genome consists of 98 miRNAs and 180 genes. One hundred and sixty-two pairs were recovered using these filters. One thousand five hundred and eleven human interacting miRNA–gene pairs consisting of 193 miRNAs and 1035 genes yielded 1070 post filter pairs. While databases such as Tarbase [3] and miRecords [4] maintain interacting miRNA–gene pairs, they contain no informative noninteracting miRNA–gene pairs. Without such information, it is very difficult to evaluate prediction strategies. In the absence of an experimental strategy for determining noninteracting pairs, they can be inferred or UTRs can be randomly simulated and be assumed to have no targets for miRNAs. We have randomly generated 500 UTRs for each genome having a nucleotide composition similar to known 3′ UTRs of mouse and human. The length distribution of the simulated UTRs matches with that of real 3′ UTRs of both genomes.

Alternatively, noninteracting miRNA–target pairs can be derived from miRNA overexpressed microarray data. Those mRNAs overexpressed even in the presence of an overexpressed miRNA can be considered to be noninteracting pairs. Based on this notion Liu et al. [10] have created a dataset of 3542 noninteracting miRNA–gene pairs from 20 different miRNA overexpression microarray datasets. This dataset was also examined.

For consistency and reproducibility, the precomputed multiple sequence alignment tables *phastCons46wayPrimates* and *phastCons30way* from the UCSC Genome Browser were used in deriving conservation scores in target locations in human (hg19) and mouse (mm9) genomes respectively.

2.5 Algorithm

Commonly used motif finding algorithms include position weight matrices, hidden Markov models, profile hidden Markov models, and base pairing. To compute the position weighted matrix, or to train

Table 2
The pseudo code of the TargetFind algorithm

Procedure TargetFind (utr, miRna)
For each 21mer of utr
Find the 6mer of seed region with at least 5 perfect pairing
If successful find 7mer and 8mers
Check for all 3 base pairing modes
Collect the pairing location, scores
Return results

Table 3
The pseudo code of the target find algorithm

Procedure TargetFind (UTR_set, miRNA_set)
For utr ∈ UTR_set
For miRna ∈ miRNA_set
feasiblePairs ← TargetFind(utr,miRna)
For each feasible pair
Find the context surrounding the target and the corresponding ΔΔG
Collect multiple target information
Obtain intersection of the seed region with conserved region
Return results

the hidden Markov model or to compute the transition weight in a profile hidden Markov model, a large number of training examples of the binding sites and non-binding sites are required. Unfortunately only a limited number of experimentally verified sites are available. All the plausible binding sites of a miRNA with a UTR were generated using a base pairing method by aligning the miRNA reverse complement with the UTR. The algorithm named TargetFind in Table 2 takes two parameters, UTR sequence, say *utr*, and miRNA sequence, say *mirna*, as inputs and finds all potential binding sites (all three modes) in the UTR sequence for the miRNA. Each 21 mer of the *utr* is aligned with the reverse complement of the *mirna* with position specific weights on alignment score and gap penalty. The alignment is first done at the seed regions and continued to the rest of the regions as described in the pseudo code in Table 2.

Once the potential targets in a given UTR for a miRNA are obtained by TargetFind, the hybridization energy of each target with the miRNA, the accessibility energy of the context of the targets, and the evolutionarily conservation score of the targets are computed by TargetFind as shown in Table 3. The algorithm runs with two options: with or without finding conservation scores in the binding sites of UTRs. To run the algorithm for finding the conservation score, the genomic coordinates of UTRs must be provided in bed format. With bed format, the corresponding UTRs are extracted from the reference genomic sequences such as mm9 or hg19. In the absence of mature miRNA sequences as input to the program, the set of mature miRNA sequences that are known to interact with UTRs of the given genome are taken as the set of miRNAs.

The $\Delta\Delta G$ in the algorithm TargetFind is computed by the Vienna RNA package [26, 27] as shown in Equation 1. The hybridization energy from both cofold and RNAup were determined for comparison. The intersection of the interval seed region with the conserved region is efficiently computed by bedtools [30].

Alternatively, some variation of dynamic programming similar to the one used for local alignment can be used to implement all three different modes of base pairing efficiently. The efficiency of finding plausible targets will not affect the limitations of existing approaches in maximizing sensitivity while minimizing the false positive rate.

The algorithm produces all the necessary features such as $\Delta\Delta G$, information on multiple targets, and the conservation score for the seed region. When multiple features are used simultaneously, the decision boundary will become complex and may not even be linearly separable. To understand the effectiveness of combined features in improving the overall prediction accuracy, we have used supervised learning algorithms such as Naïve Bayes, multilayer perceptrons (artificial neural networks), decision tree, and support vector machine from the Weka package [31, 32]. Note that these learning algorithms are capable of learning a complex decision boundary that maximizes the prediction accuracy with a representative training set. Some reviews and details of these machine learning algorithms and others are available in [33–35]. Linear regression has also been used to combine features to make prediction in a package such as mirMap [20] to combine multiple features.

When the target prediction accuracy, p, of each feature in a set is greater than 50%, the predicted results of these features can be combined with majority agreement to increase overall prediction accuracy. The features, conservation score of a target, multiple targets in a UTR, and changes in free energy are independent and thus can be modeled as binomial distribution with the probability of each making correct decision p. Using a binomial distribution, the probability of the majority out of three features making correct prediction is given by the following formula:

$$Majority\,agreement - 1 - \sum_{r=0}^{1} \binom{3}{r} p^r (1 \quad p)^{3-r}$$

3 Results

In the absence of direct experimental validation of noninteracting miRNA–gene pairs, such information can be derived from miRNA overexpressed microarray datasets. We use the Liu dataset (described above) as a set of noninteracting pairs to (1) validate our assumption that a randomly generated set of UTRs behave similar to UTRs of noninteracting targets, and (2) test the effectiveness of the selected features in predicting targets. To highlight any possible differences between the information content between the real UTRs and the randomly generated set, 6mer counts multiple sequence alignment tables of the real and simulated data were plotted as shown in Figs. 1 and 2. In contrast to the 6mer occurrences in real UTRs, appearance of 6mer counts in the randomly generated UTRs resembles wide noise.

3.1 miRNA Targets

Considering the three different types of base pairing taking place in the experimental findings reported in [7], the proposed algorithm encodes some variations of these three different modes of base pairing for finding potential targets in the UTRs. The details are provided in a section on improving sensitivity. The tool takes all possible combinations of information related to miRNAs and target genes as shown in below:

The input format for the tool:		
miRNA sequence file in fasta		UTR sequence in fasta
Or		Or
Name of the genome	×	BED file of the UTRs and the genome
Or		Or
Names of miRNA and the genome		Names of genes and the genome

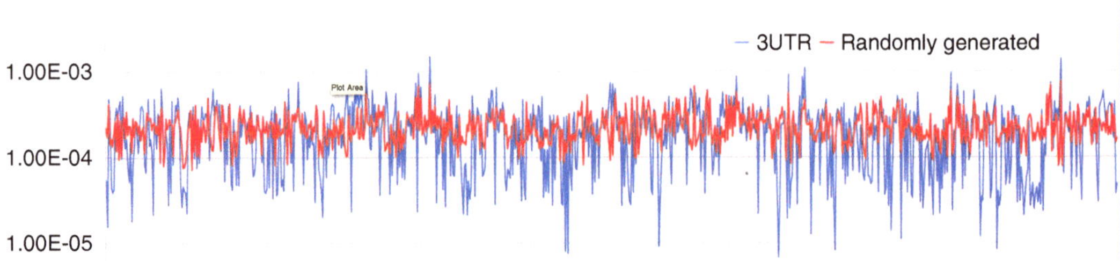

Fig. 1 Comparing 6mer frequency counts in 3′ UTRs of human genome (hg19) with that of simulated UTR. The log scale 6mer frequency counts in 3′ UTR of hg19 (shown in *red*) is compared with that of in simulated UTR (shown in *blue*)

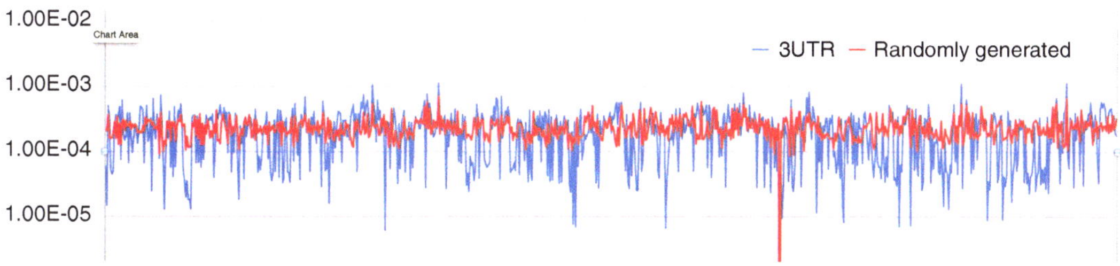

Fig. 2 Comparing 6mer frequency counts in 3′ UTRs of mouse genome (mm9) with that of simulated UTR. The log scale 6mer frequency counts in 3′ UTR of mm9 (shown in *red*) is compared with that of in simulated UTR (shown in *blue*)

Table 4
UTR target prediction results

Genome	Known interaction	Plausible interaction	Predicted interaction	Sensitivity, %
Human (hg19)	1511	1070	1018	95.14
Mouse (mm9)	250	162	153	94.44

The targets for the given set of mature miRNAs were searched among the human and mouse 3′ UTRs and known interactions were downloaded from miRecords [4]. Predicted results and sensitivity are shown in Table 4. Out of 1070 human miRNA–mRNA pairs, the algorithm TargetFind found 1018. The sensitivity for target prediction in human genome is 95.14%. The algorithm found 153 miRNA–mRNA pairs from 162 plausible pairs 94.44% in the mouse data.

To examine specificity, the algorithm was tested on the noninteracting miRNA–target pairs [10]. Out of the 3452 plausible noninteracting human pairs, the algorithm predicted 2361, and thus returned a false positive error rate of 68.4%, emphasizing the need to minimize false positive rates with increased sensitivity.

In order to minimize the false positive rate or to maximize the selectivity, one or more of the following strategies and their variations was applied by target prediction algorithms: thermodynamic equilibrium, targets in conserved regions, and multiple targets.

To investigate the effectiveness of each feature in predicting the real target, we normalize the data such that the sensitivity as well as selectivity varies from 0 to 100% in opposite directions as the selected feature value changes.

3.2 Thermodynamic Equilibrium

The stability of the interaction between a miRNA and its target is partially, if not fully, influenced by the thermodynamic equilibrium. The binding energy or the hybridization energy of the interacting duplex denoted by ΔG_{hybrid} is indirectly measured by the free energy of the folded structure (the lower the energy, the higher the stability). Hybridization energy has been used directly or indirectly in tools such as PicTar, TargetScan, and miRanda to rank the targets and to reduce the false positive rates. When a miRNA has many potential targets in a UTR, the lowest hybridization energy as well as the combined hybridization energy in all targets of a UTR are kept for each miRNA–mRNA pair. We also find the targets from randomly generated UTRs which could be used as a proxy for noninteracting miRNA–mRNA pairs. Figure 3a shows

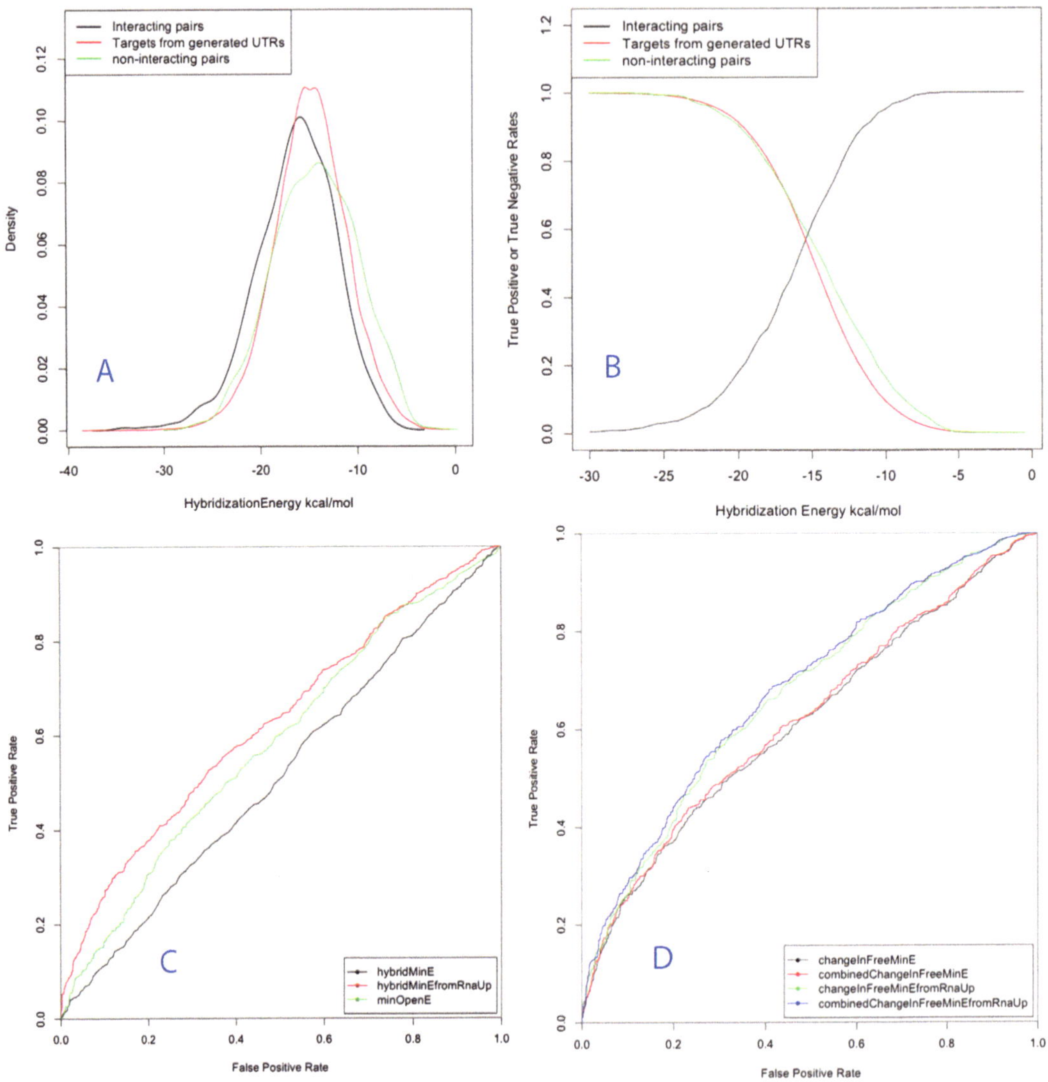

Fig. 3 Examination of hg19 data for thermodynamic features. (**a**) Density of minimum hybridizing energy of interacting, noninteracting, and randomly generated UTR target pairs in hg19. (**b**) Variation of true positive and true negative rates with the hybridization energy in hg19. (**c**) The ROC curves for comparing minimum hybridization energy from cofold and RNAup with the opening energy in hg19. The area under the curves of hybridMinE, hybridMinEfromRnaUp, and minOpenE are, respectively, 0.516, 0.626, and 0.583. (**d**) ROC curves for comparing of changes in free energy (hybridization energy from cofold and RNAup) in hg19. The area under the curves of changeInFreeMinE, combinedChangeInFreeMinE, changesInFreeMinEfromRnaUp, and combinedChangesInFreeMinEfromRnaUp are respectively 0.615, 0.623, 0.672, and 0.683

the density distribution of minimum hybridization energy for the known interacting, noninteracting, and randomly generated UTR target pairs in the human genome (hg19). The prediction accuracy at the optimal threshold for the hybridization energy is 0.58 (*see* Fig. 3b). Note that the true negative rate from randomly generated pairs is closely following the true negative rates of noninteracting pairs.

Before a miRNA can interact with the target, the folded structure surrounding the target has to be opened and it is denoted by ΔG_{open} and is computed by RNAup of Vienna RNA package. To compare the predictive power of opening energy and hybridization energy from either cofold or RNAup, ROC curves are created as shown in Fig. 3c. The area under the curve for minimum hybridization energy from cofold, RNAup, and opening energy are, respectively, 0.516, 0.626 and 0.583. The opening energy by itself is not a better predictor than hybridization energy from RNAup. Some variations of changes in free energy, denoted by $\Delta\Delta G$, have been used in target prediction tools so as to minimize the false positive rate. In our approach we use the definition shown in Equation 1 in the section on thermostability for potential energy change. Based on these data, we will use the hybridization energy value obtained from RNAup instead of from cofold due to its higher effectiveness in discriminating true positives from false positives. When there are multiple targets in a UTR for a miRNA, there are two different ways of handling changes in free energy in all the putative binding sites: (1) to maintain the lowest changes in free energy or (2) to combine them as shown in the section on thermostability to represent statistical weight of all potential targets. The ROC curves from these two options for the changes in free energy are shown in Fig. 3d and the area under the ROC curves are demonstrated in Table 5.

Combining the changes of free energy in all the targets has a minor advantage over maintaining the minimum energy out of all

Table 5
The area under the ROC curves in thermodynamic equilibrium

	Area under the curve	
	Minimum value of changes in free energy	**Combined value of changes in free energy in all the targets**
Changes in free energy (hybridization energy is from RNAup)	0.672	0.683
Changes in free energy (hybridization energy is from cofold)	0.615	0.623

the sites. In either option of calculating the changes in free energy, the hybridization energy from RNAup has a better impact on target prediction.

The feature "changes in free energy" discriminates the interacting and noninteracting pairs better than the feature "hybridization energy." The true positive rate at the optimal threshold for the feature changes in free energy is 63.5% as shown in Fig. 4a

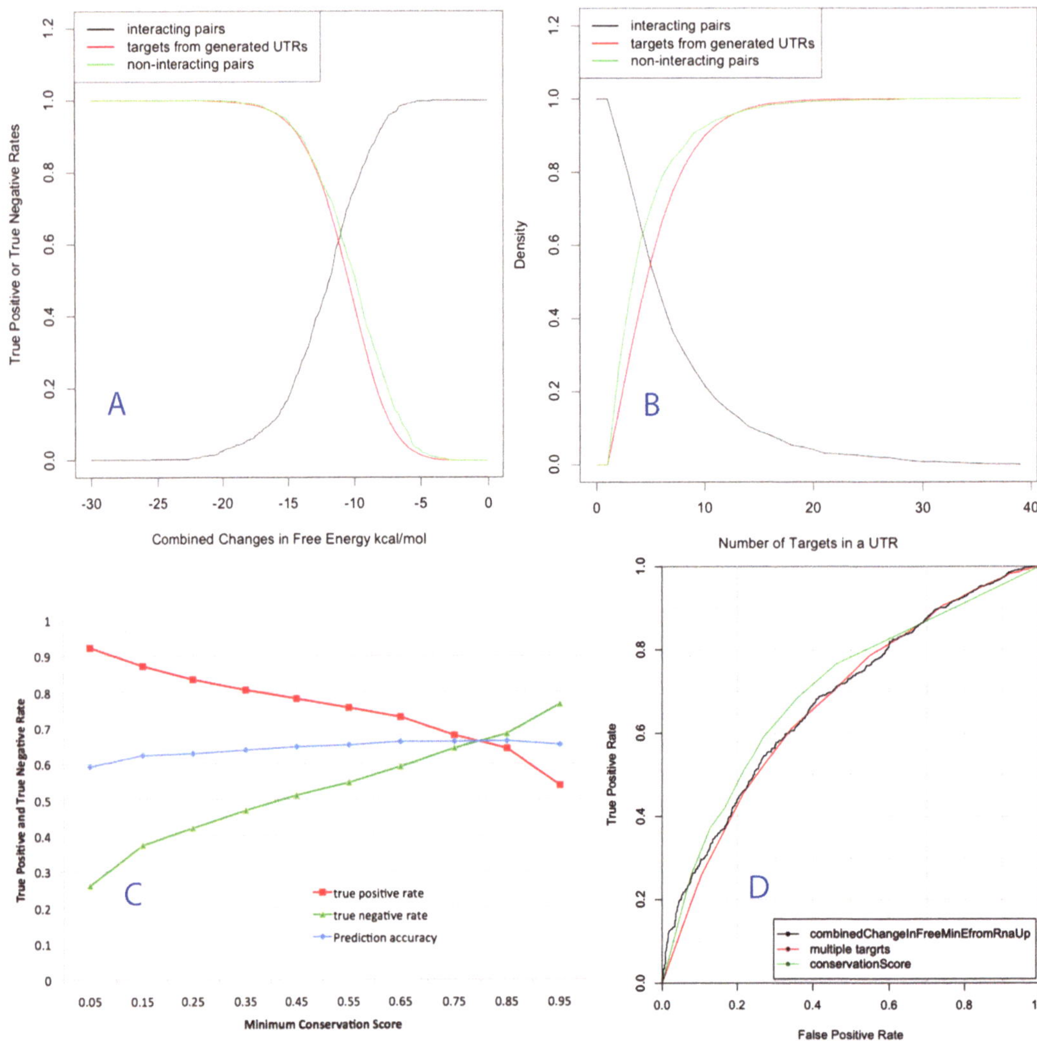

Fig. 4 Comparing different features for their ability of predicting true targets. (**a**) The variation of true positive and true negative rates with the combined changes in free energy in all the miRNA targets in a UTR in hg19. The optimal true prediction rate is 63.5%. (**b**) The variation of true positive and true negative rates with the number of miRNA targets in a UTR that are associated with less than 0 changes in free energy. (**c**) True positive and negative rates with the changes in minimum conservation score of the seed region of the targets in all UTRs in hg19. (**d**) The important three features, changes in free energy, multiple targets, and conservation scores are compared with ROC curves. The area under the cures of these features in the order listed at the legend is 0.683, 0.675, and 0.701

compared to 58% for the feature hybridization energy (Fig. 3b). Thus using changes in free energy as a feature may help to separate false positives from the true positives.

3.3 Multiple Targets

Multiple potential targets in a UTR are expected to increase the affinity of a miRNA to bind a UTR and many tools provide an option to use this as a parameter for refining the potential targets. With the known interacting and noninteracting miRNA–target pairs in human genome, we calculate the number of targets in a UTR for each miRNA from the interacting or noninteracting pairs. All those targets that have negative changes in free energy are considered to be potential targets. When the number of targets in a UTR for a miRNA is greater or equal to the threshold, it is considered to be a real target. The variation of true positive rates and true negative rates with the number of targets are shown in Fig. 4b. At the optimal threshold of four targets, the true prediction rate is 65.8% (the prediction accuracy is also 65.8% assuming that the number of positive and negative instances are the same). Note that the targets found in randomly generated UTRs behave slightly different with the optimal threshold of 5 and has lower prediction accuracy.

3.4 Targets in Conserved Region

It has been shown that the core seed region (p_2 through p_7) and the close neighborhood around the region (p_1 and p_8) is evolutionarily conserved [17]. It is conceivable that the base pairing regions in 3′ UTR may also be conserved. To study the extent to which the base pairing regions in UTR is conserved, we have downloaded appropriate multiple sequence alignments of related species from the UCSC Genome Browser (*phastCons46wayPrimates* and *phastCons30way*) for human and mouse. We preprocess the conserved scores in these alignments (0 through 1) into 10 overlapping bins having minimum conserved scores of 0.05–0.95.

Among the 1070 known interacting miRNA–target pairs in the human genome, 1018 are predicted, while among the 3452 noninteracting miRNA–target pairs only 2361 (false positive) are predicted. The Fig. 4c shows true positive and negative rates with the distribution of targets in bins with different conservation scores. The derived prediction accuracy assuming the balanced training set is also shown. At optimum threshold (the conservation score of 0.8 or better), the true positive rate and the prediction accuracy is 66.1%. Additionally, Table 6 includes extra information regarding targets from interacting and noninteracting sets found in conserved region.

3.5 Comparison of Features

We have looked at individual features and their impact on reducing false positive rate separately. At the optimal threshold, the prediction accuracy of the features changes in free energy, multiple targets, and conservation scores are respectively 63.5%, 65.8%, and 66.1%. The ROC curves for these features are shown in Fig. 4d and the areas

Table 6
Targets from interacting and noninteracting sets found in conserved region

	Interacting pairs (out of 1018 predicted pairs)		Noninteracting pairs (out of 2361 predicted pairs)	
Minimum conserved score	**Number of targets found**	**True positive rate in %**	**Number of targets found**	**False positive rate in %**
0.05	748	73.48	761	32.23
0.15	701	68.86	648	27.45
0.25	674	66.21	593	25.12
0.35	652	64.05	544	23.04
0.45	625	61.39	499	21.14
0.55	603	59.23	470	19.91
0.65	580	56.97	413	17.49
0.75	547	53.73	368	15.59
0.85	504	49.51	323	13.68
0.95	411	40.37	217	9.19

under the curves of these features changes in free energy, multiple targets, and conservation scores are, respectively, 0.682, 0.675, and 0.701. The individual prediction accuracy and as well as the area under the ROC curves of these features vary within a very small range.

Since these features are independent predictors of true positive and the best prediction accuracy is at least better than 63.5%, the results of the prediction of each feature can be combined in a majority agreement basis as outlined in the section on algorithm. The lowest prediction accuracy among the features is 0.635 (p) and the number of features is 3 (n). The result of majority agreement will be 69.7%, which is better than the outcome of any one of these features.

The interacting and noninteracting UTRs are mapped onto the reference genome (hg19) using BLAT [36] to get the coordinates so as to find the conservation scores on the seed target regions. We kept only the unique mapping onto the reference genome, which reduced the plausible miRNA–mRNA pairs. The algorithm found 827 miRNA–mRNA pairs out of the 871 plausible interacting pairs, and 1089 miRNA–mRNA pairs out of 1592 plausible noninteracting pairs. The sensitivity is 94.95%, while the false positive rate is 68.4%.

We set the thresholds for the features changes in hybridization energy, multiple targets, and conservation scores to their respective optimal values, which are −11, 4. and 0.75, respectively, and tested for majority agreements. When the predicted results of each feature are combined, 578 interacting miRNA–mRNA pairs have the majority agreement out of 827 predicted pairs (871 plausible). On the other hand, out of 1089 predicted noninteracting pairs (1592 plausible), 378 were claimed to be true targets, which are false positives. The false positive rate was reduced to 23.74% from 68.4%, while the true positive rate was reduced to 66.36%. In the normalized scale, that is, without factoring into the plausible pairs, the positive rate will become 69.89%, while the false positive rate will become 34.71%. The overall prediction accuracy was 67.6% for the normalized data set and 70.3% for the non-normalized data set, which is better than the results using any one of the features alone. Here the prediction accuracy was computed as the average of true positive and true negative rates with the assumption that positive instances are the same as that of negative instances.

The prediction metrics with changes in free energy and multiple targets without any normalization is shown in Fig. 5a, b. The prediction accuracy at the optimal threshold is about 68.7% for either combined changes in free energy or multiple targets.

3.6 Application of Supervised Learning

We have examined the following factors and their influence in reducing the false positive rate: hybridization energy, opening energy, changes in free energy ($\Delta\Delta G$), multiple targets of a miRNA in a UTR, and presence of a target's seed region within a conserved region. These factors can be used as features in a supervised learning algorithm to improve the overall prediction accuracy. A learned model must be flexible enough to classify new instances (never been used in training) correctly. We use tenfold cross validation to assess the utility of the learned model, and the effectiveness of features for classification. In tenfold cross validation, this dataset is divided into ten equal subsets and nine subsets are used to train and the other subset is tested; this is repeated ten times and the average scores are taken over all the runs. To minimize bias, we have created a dataset with equal number of positive and negative instances. Since we have large numbers of noninteracting miRNA–mRNA pairs in human genome, we have created five different negative subsets randomly extracted from the whole set to match the number of positive instances, and for each subset we ran machine learning algorithm with tenfold cross validation. We have used the machine learning algorithms such as support vector machine (SVM), multilayer perceptrons (ANN), and decision tree. For a baseline comparison, we have used naïve Bayes.

For the purpose of comparing the effectiveness of features under supervised learning, we have created two sets, namely s1 and s2. The set s1 has all the features except the conservation score, while s2 has all the features. The prediction accuracy of each of these feature combinations was tested with each of the abovementioned machine learning algorithms. We also have created five

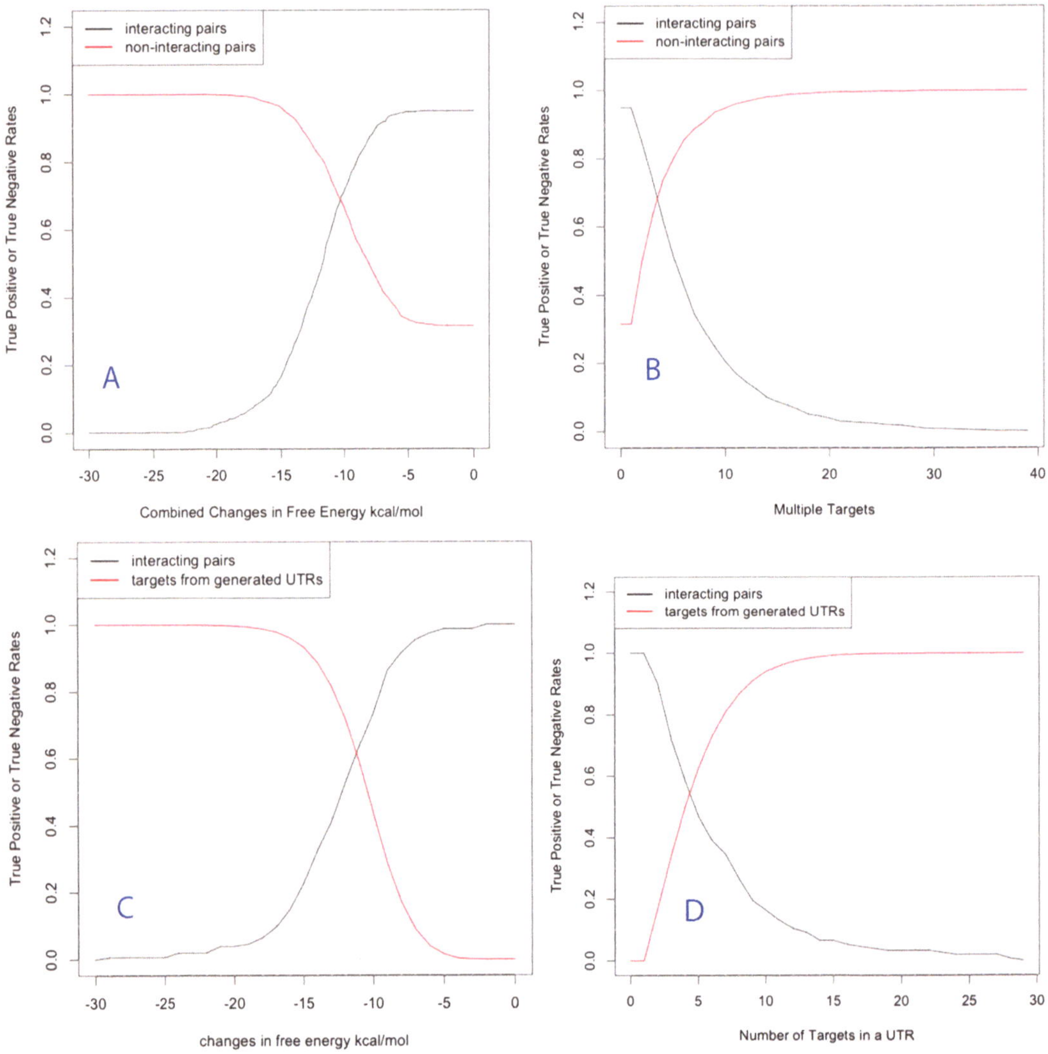

Fig. 5 Comparing thermal energy features and multiple targets in mm9 data. (**a**) The variation of true positive and true negative rates with the combined changes in free energy in all the miRNA targets in all UTRs in hg19 without normalizing. The optimal true prediction rate is 68.7%. (**b**) The variation of true positive and true negative rates with the number of miRNA targets in a UTR in hg19 without normalization. The optimal true prediction rate is 68.7%. (**c**) The variation of true positive and true negative rates with the combined changes in free energy in all the miRNA targets in a UTR for in mm9. The true positive rate is 61.4% at −11.2 kcal/mol. (**d**) Variation of true positive and true negative rates with the number of miRNA targets in a UTR associated with negative changes in free energy in mm9. The prediction accuracy optimal threshold 4 is 55%

different data sets for each feature combination as outlined in Subheading 2. The average of prediction accuracy of each set with tenfold cross validation for each classifier is shown in Fig. 6. The dataset is comparable to the normalized data set used in single feature space. The details are provided in Table 7. The average best prediction accuracy was 69% from ANN followed by the results

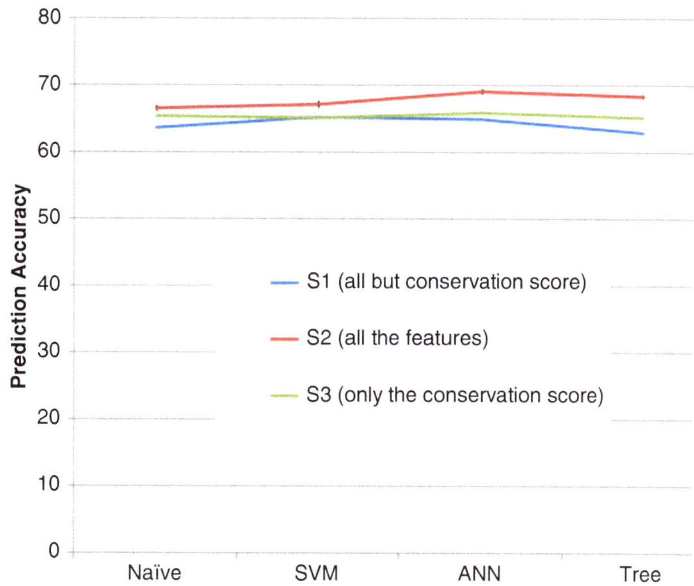

Fig. 6 Comparing prediction accuracy of machine learning algorithms. Average prediction accuracy (measured with tenfold cross validation) of the targets in hg19 3′UTR with different combinations of features using the following supervised learning algorithms: naïve Bayes, SVM, ANN, and decision tree. The ANN algorithm outperformed others when all the three features are used. The data in set S1 has four features: hybridization energy, opening energy, changes in free energy, and target counts, while the data in set S2 has the features of the data in S1 and conservation score. The data in set S3 has conservation score as the only feature

Table 7
The prediction accuracy of tenfold cross validation with feature sets S1 and S2

	Naïve		SVM		ANN		Decision tree	
	S_1	S_2	S_1	S_2	S_1	S_2	S_1	S_2
1	62.7	65.84	64.57	66.2	63.72	68.74	62.09	68.4
2	63.42	66.32	65.05	67.41	64.09	68.5	62.57	68.08
3	64.02	66.44	66.02	67.47	65.54	69.23	62.94	68.56
4	64.33	66.99	65.84	67.17	66.02	69.04	63.6	68.74
5	63.66	66.93	64.69	67.41	65.29	69.71	63.54	67.96
Mean	63.66	66.5	65.23	67.13	64.93	69.04	62.95	68.35
Std	0.622	0.47	0.66	0.53	0.98	0.47	0.64	0.33

The feature set S1 has hybridization energy, open energy, $\Delta\Delta G$, and multiple targets. The set S2 has the features of S1 and the conservation score from decision tree at 68.35%. The results from the sophisticated machine learning algorithms with all the features are not significantly better than the prediction accuracy of 67.6%, which is obtained by simply combining threshold based outcome from each feature with majority agreement.

3.7 Plausibility of Using Targets from Randomly Generated UTRs as a Proxy for Noninteracting Pairs

We do not expect to find any real targets in randomly generated UTRs and therefore the targets found in these generated UTRs are considered to be true negative as are those in the noninteracting pairs. When hybridization energy from RNAup is used as a discriminating parameter, the features of randomly generated UTR behave very similar to that of noninteracting pairs as illustrated in the density plot of Fig. 3a (the changes in true negative rate with hybridization energy). A similar observation can be made from the plot in Fig. 4a showing the true negative rates with changes in free energy. The true negative rates at the optimal threshold as shown in Fig. 4a are 63.5% and 60.7% respectively for noninteracting pairs, and for the targets from randomly generated UTRs. The behavior of the targets on randomly generated UTRs with respect to the feature "number of targets" is way off from the behavior of noninteracting targets as shown in Fig. 4b. The true negative rates at the optimal threshold as shown in Fig. 4b are 65.8% and 54.3%, respectively, for noninteracting pairs and for the targets from randomly generated UTRs. When applying multiple targets as a feature it is possible to get error when using targets from randomly generated UTRs as a proxy for noninteracting pairs.

3.8 Target Prediction in the Mouse Genome

As has been described in the section on data, UTRs of the mouse genomes were simulated to mimic of a nucleotide composition similar to known 3′ UTRs. The length distribution of the simulated UTRs matches with that of real 3′ UTRs. In the human genome, the predicted targets from the simulated UTRs behaves similar to that of noninteracting data set of Liu et al. [10] with respect to energy features, we may conclude that the targets from randomly generated UTRs for house are indeed a good proxy for noninteracting targets.

Figure 5a shows the variation of true positive and true negative (targets from randomly generated UTRs as proxy) with the combined changes in free energy as a feature. At the optimal threshold of −11.2 kcal/mol, the prediction accuracy is 61.4%, which is somewhat closer to the optimal prediction accuracy of 63.5% in human genome using the known noninteracting pairs. The variation of true positive and true negatives against the number of targets in a UTR was shown in Fig. 5b. The optimal prediction accuracy is 55% which is also very close to what we have obtained in human genome with the targets from randomly generated UTRs (54.3%).

4 Discussion

Accurately predicting miRNA targets is still very challenging due to the fact that mature miRNAs are quite small (18–24 nt) and base pairing with the target UTRs is not perfect. The core seed region of a miRNA (positions 2 through 7) and its close neighborhood (position 1 and 8) has been shown to be evolutionarily conserved among related species [17]. The *p*-value in finding a match to a seed region of length of 6 nt in an average UTR is quite high and is open to high rate of false positives. The objective of our approach is to maximize the sensitivity while minimizing the false positive error rate. Perfect base pairing in the seed region alone is not sufficient to reach high sensitivity in mammalian genomes. Brennecke et al. [24] have shown with in vivo experiments in *C. elegans* the existence of other types of base pairing. To increase the sensitivity of our algorithm, TargetFind, we have adapted their experimental findings by recognizing weak 3′ compensatory base pairing in the seed region as a potential target. Further, the constraints on perfect seed region base pairing were relaxed as outlined in the Methods. Our target prediction algorithm identified 95% of the known interaction pairs reported in miRBase [1] in human and mouse genomes.

In order to quantify the false positive rate or to assess the overall prediction accuracy of an algorithm, it is necessary to have a set of validated or derived noninteracting miRNA–target pairs. We validated predicted targets with a derived noninteracting miRNA–target set for human genome from Liu et al. [10]. Additionally, randomly generated UTR sequences mimicking the nucleotide composition and length distribution of real 3′ UTRs of the human and mouse genomes were examined as a proxy for noninteracting pairs.

Many target prediction tools have used one or more of the following strategies to reduce the false positive error rate: thermal energy equilibrium, multiple targets, and targets in the conserved region. Having noninteracting data sets will help to quantify the role of each feature in reducing the false positive rate. Thermodynamic features such as hybridization, opening and changes in free energy are computed by the Vienna Package [27]. When there are multiple targets in a UTR for a miRNA, either the minimum value of the changes in free energy among multiple targets, or the combination of the value of the changes in free energy of all the targets can be used as outlined in the section on the algorithm. The ROC curves of Fig. 3d show the minor advantage of combining the value of free energy over the entire targets as opposed to maintaining the minimum value of the changes in free energy among all the targets in a UTR. For TargetFind, the combined value of changes in free energy in all the targets in a UTR for a miRNA was used. At the optimal threshold, the true positive rate as well as the prediction accuracy is 63.5% when combined values of changes in free energy is used as

Table 8
Summary of the true prediction rate at the optimal threshold and the best prediction accuracy in the human genome (hg19) using interaction and noninteracting pairs, and targets from randomly generated UTRs

	True prediction rate at optimal threshold with noninteracting targets, %	True prediction rate at optimal threshold with targets from generated UTRs, %
Target counts	65.8	54.3
Hybridization Energy from RNAup	58	59
Change in free Energy	63.5	60.7
Conservation score	66.1	NA

a feature as shown in Fig. 4a. The prediction accuracy or the true positive rate at the optimal threshold for each of these features in the human genome is given in Table 8. Using hybridization energy as a predictor for true targets resulted in prediction accuracy of 58%, while using changes in free energy as a predictor has better sensitivity of 63.5% at the optimal threshold. Thus the feature "changes in free energy" is a viable predictor for real targets. The experimental evidence in [7] also shows that hybridization energy alone is not the best predictor of real targets.

The seed region of a mature miRNA is conserved across multiple species and hence the binding seed region of the corresponding targets in a UTR is expected to be conserved. Confounding prediction, targets do not always fall into conserved regions and not all the seed regions have a perfect seed pairing. This favors base pairing on multiple sites within a UTR and we may expect such multiplicity may have a positive impact on reducing the false positive rate. As expected, the feature "multiple targets" has a prediction accuracy of 65.8% at the optimal threshold as shown in Fig. 4b, and it also plays a role as an individual predictor of real targets.

The conservation score of a binding site was derived from the tables *phastCons46wayPrimates* and *phastCons30way* for human (hg19) and mouse (mm9) respectively. Figure 4c shows the metric of true positive and negative rates with the changes in minimum conservation score of the seed region of the targets in 3′UTRs in the human genome (hg19). At the optimal threshold of an 80% conservation score, the true positive rate and the prediction accuracy is 66.1%. The individual prediction accuracy at the optimal threshold for these three features changes in free energy, multiple targets, and conservation energy varies within a narrow range from 63.5% to 66.1%. Using majority agreement as outlined in Methods, the results of these individual predictors were combined to improve the overall prediction accuracy. When the threshold of each feature was set to the optimal values, the overall prediction accuracy was 67.6% which is better than any the results from any one the feature alone.

Supervised learning algorithms can take multiple features of interacting and noninteracting targets and learn a flexible model to discriminate true targets from false ones. We have used the classifiers of support vector machine, multilayer perceptrons, decision tree and Naïve Bayes on different combinations of features with data sets in s1, s2 and s3. The best average prediction accuracy with the feature combination of s1 (hybridization energy, opening energy, changes in free energy, and target counts) is 65.23%, which was not more predictive than conservation score alone, which was about 66.1%. When all the features are combined together in s2, the multilayer perceptrons achieved the best average prediction accuracy of 69.04%, followed by the decision tree at 68.35%. The data in set s3 has conservation score as the only feature and achieved prediction accuracy 66.1% with the multilayer perceptrons.

SVMicro [10] implemented a three-stage approach to maximize the prediction accuracy while minimizing the false positive rate. It is a two-phase process in which a flexible base pairing strategy in the seed region to maximize the sensitivity is followed by two different filtering processes based on a support vector machine learning algorithm to reduce the false positive rates. A large number of features from binding sites as well as from the entire UTRs were extracted for training. Their top performing features include matching in the seed region (1), accessibility energy (8), number of targets (11), hybridization energy (12), and conservation score (13). The value in the brackets denotes the priority of the respective feature. In our discussion, the value of changes in free energy is the summation of accessibility energy and hybridization energy thus capturing these highly ranked features of SVMicro. Our findings are consistent with theirs. We conclude the ranking order of features in predicting the true targets is (1) conservation score, (2) targets counts in a UTR, and (3) changes in free energy. While SVMicro has outperformed other target prediction system such as PicTar, miRanda, mirTarget, PITA, and TargetScan, their overall prediction accuracy is still not high as expected due to the same limiting factors as we have pointed out.

Figures 3a, b and 4a show that targets from randomly generated UTRs have similar characteristics to noninteracting pairs in terms of hybridization energy and changes in free energy. Tables 8 and 9 show the true prediction rate at the optimal threshold for the human genome and the mouse genome, respectively. Notice that the sensitivity at the optimal threshold for noninteracting targets and that targets from randomly generated UTRs differ as high as 11.5% for the target count feature and by 2.8% for changes in free energy. Therefore, appropriate error correction has to be done when using randomly generated UTRs as a proxy for noninteracting pairs in other genomes for the feature targets counts. Without validated noninteracting targets in the mouse genome, it is very difficult to perform correction using simulated UTRs.

Table 9
Summary of the true prediction rate at the optimal threshold in the mouse genome (mm9) using interaction and the targets from randomly generated UTRs

Features	True prediction rate at optimal threshold
Target counts	55
Change in free Energy	61.4

5 Conclusions

We have designed and implemented an algorithm (TargetFind) in Python incorporating some recent experimental findings in miRNA target binding site prediction. As limiting the target search to the seed region is not sufficient in mammalian genomes, finding potential targets is based on a combination of base pairing in the seed region as well as compensatory pairing in the 3′ region of the miRNA. This is outlined in the Methods. We find that searching for multiple targets in a UTR will reduce the false positive rate of finding motifs. Beyond simply finding motifs, it is imperative to reduce the false positive error rate in predicting targets. Combinations of the following parameters have been used to reduce the false positive rate: thermostability, multiple targets in a UTR, and seeking targets in evolutionarily conserved regions. The optimal prediction accuracy for each of these features varies within a narrow range from 55.8 to 66.1%. Since combining the outcome of these features with majority agreement improves the overall prediction accuracy, TargetFind will do this as default. The optimal threshold values for these features are set as defaults; however, a user can set their own parameters.

The ANN reached the highest prediction accuracy of 69.4% among the set of classifiers that were studied with different combination of features. This result was not significantly higher than majority agreement based aggregation of the results of threshold based decision. An interesting alternative to looking at single miRNA or a gene for their corresponding binding partners, ensembles of miRNAs or genes are used as input in MiRror [37] and the results are refined using hypergeometrical distribution with a cutoff *p*-value. MiRror gets putative targets for a miRNA from ensembles of targets prediction algorithms or programs such as TargetScan, PicTar, DIANA-MicroT, PITA, EIMMO-MirZ, and miRanda.

In order to achieve significant progress in accurate target prediction, we need to have a better understanding of the biological process in a specific miRNA–mRNA interaction.

Some recent advances in miRNA mediated gene expression high-throughput experiments [22, 38, 39] and software tools such as PARma [40] and miRNAmRNA [41] to identify targets from the experimental data accurately will help us in the future to study and understand the miRNA–mRNA interaction computationally.

Acknowledgments

Our sincere thanks to Hui Liu for sharing the noninteracting data set that they have collected on human genome.

References

1. Griffiths-Jones S, Saini HK, van Dongen S, Enright AJ (2008) miRBase: tools for microRNA genomics. Nucleic Acids Res 36(Database issue):D154–D158
2. Vergoulis T, Vlachos IS, Alexiou P, Georgakilas G, Maragkakis M, Reczko M, Gerangelos S, Koziris N, Dalamagas T, Hatzigeorgiou AG (2012) TarBase 6.0: capturing the exponential growth of miRNA targets with experimental support. Nucleic Acids Res 40(Database issue):D222–D229
3. Sethupathy P, Corda B, Hatzigeorgiou AG (2006) TarBase: a comprehensive database of experimentally supported animal microRNA targets. RNA 12(2):192–197
4. Xiao F, Zuo Z, Cai G, Kang S, Gao X, Li T (2009) miRecords: an integrated resource for microRNA-target interactions. Nucleic Acids Res 37(Database issue):D105–D110
5. Hsu SD, Lin FM, Wu WY, Liang C, Huang WC, Chan WL, Tsai WT, Chen GZ, Lee CJ, Chiu CM et al (2011) miRTarBase: a database curates experimentally validated microRNA-target interactions. Nucleic Acids Res 39(Database issue):D163–D169
6. Jiang Q, Wang Y, Hao Y, Juan L, Teng M, Zhang X, Li M, Wang G, Liu Y (2009) miR2Disease: a manually curated database for microRNA deregulation in human disease. Nucleic Acids Res 37(Database issue):D98–104
7. Kertesz M, Iovino N, Unnerstall U, Gaul U, Segal E (2007) The role of site accessibility in microRNA target recognition. Nat Genet 39(10):1278–1284
8. Long D, Lee R, Williams P, Chan CY, Ambros V, Ding Y (2007) Potent effect of target structure on microRNA function. Nat Struct Mol Biol 14(4):287–294
9. Heikkinen L, Kolehmainen M, Wong G (2011) Prediction of microRNA targets in *Caenorhabditis elegans* using a self-organizing map. Bioinformatics 27(9):1247–1254
10. Liu H, Yue D, Chen Y, Gao SJ, Huang Y (2010) Improving performance of mammalian microRNA target prediction. BMC Bioinformatics 11:476
11. Enright AJ, John B, Gaul U, Tuschl T, Sander C, Marks DS (2003) MicroRNA targets in drosophila. Genome Biol 5(1):R1
12. Yousef M, Jung S, Kossenkov AV, Showe LC, Showe MK (2007) Naive Bayes for microRNA target predictions—machine learning for microRNA targets. Bioinformatics 23(22):2987–2992
13. Mendoza MR, da Fonseca GC, Loss-Morais G, Alves R, Margis R, Bazzan AL (2013) RFMirTarget: predicting human MicroRNA target genes with a random Forest classifier. PLoS One 8(7):e70153
14. Krek A, Grun D, Poy MN, Wolf R, Rosenberg L, Epstein EJ, MacMenamin P, da Piedade I, Gunsalus KC, Stoffel M et al (2005) Combinatorial microRNA target predictions. Nat Genet 37(5):495–500
15. Wang X, El Naqa IM (2008) Prediction of both conserved and nonconserved microRNA targets in animals. Bioinformatics 24(3):325–332
16. Rehmsmeier M, Steffen P, Hochsmann M, Giegerich R (2004) Fast and effective prediction of microRNA/target duplexes. RNA 10(10):1507–1517
17. Lewis BP, Burge CB, Bartel DP (2005) Conserved seed pairing, often flanked by adenosines, indicates that thousands of human genes are microRNA targets. Cell 120(1):15–20

18. John B, Enright AJ, Aravin A, Tuschl T, Sander C, Marks DS (2004) Human MicroRNA targets. PLoS Biol 2(11):e363
19. Nam S, Kim B, Shin S (2008) Lee S: miRGator: an integrated system for functional annotation of microRNAs. Nucleic Acids Res 36(Database issue):D159–D164
20. Vejnar CE, Zdobnov EM (2012) MiRmap: comprehensive prediction of microRNA target repression strength. Nucleic Acids Res 40(22):11673–11683
21. Incarnato D, Neri F, Diamanti D, Oliviero S (2013) MREdictor: a two-step dynamic interaction model that accounts for mRNA accessibility and Pumilio binding accurately predicts microRNA targets. Nucleic Acids Res 41(18):8421–8433
22. Chi SW, Zang JB, Mele A, Darnell RB (2009) Argonaute HITS-CLIP decodes microRNA-mRNA interaction maps. Nature 460(7254):479–486
23. Bartel DP (2009) MicroRNAs: target recognition and regulatory functions. Cell 136(2):215–233
24. Brennecke J, Stark A, Russell RB, Cohen SM (2005) Principles of microRNA-target recognition. PLoS Biol 3(3):e85
25. Lekprasert P, Mayhew M, Ohler U (2011) Assessing the utility of thermodynamic features for microRNA target prediction under relaxed seed and no conservation requirements. PLoS One 6(6):e20622
26. Hofacker IL (2004) RNA secondary structure analysis using the Vienna RNA package. Curr Protoc Bioinformatics Chapter 12:Unit 12
27. Gruber AR, Lorenz R, Bernhart SH, Neubock R, Hofacker IL (2008) The Vienna RNA websuite. Nucleic Acids Res 36(Web Server issue):W70–W74
28. Muckstein U, Tafer H, Hackermuller J, Bernhart SH, Stadler PF, Hofacker IL (2006) Thermodynamics of RNA-RNA binding. Bioinformatics 22(10):1177–1182
29. Haider S, Ballester B, Smedley D, Zhang J, Rice P, Kasprzyk A (2009) BioMart central portal—unified access to biological data. Nucleic Acids Res 37:23–27
30. bedtools (2012) In., 2.16.2 edn: http://code.google.com/p/bedtools/
31. Ivanciuc O (2008) Weka machine learning for predicting the phospholipidosis inducing potential. Curr Top Med Chem 8(18):1691–1709
32. Frank E, Hall M, Trigg L, Holmes G, Witten IH (2004) Data mining in bioinformatics using Weka. Bioinformatics 20(15):2479–2481
33. Pereira F, Mitchell T, Botvinick M (2009) Machine learning classifiers and fMRI: a tutorial overview. NeuroImage 45(1 Suppl):S199–S209
34. Baldi P, Brunak S (2001) Bioinformatics: the machine learning approach, 2nd edn. MIT Press, Cambridge, MA
35. Mitchell TM (1997) Machine learning. McGraw-Hill, New York, NY
36. Kent WJ (2002) BLAT—the BLAST-like alignment tool. Genome Res 12(4):656–664
37. Friedman Y, Naamati G, Linial M (2010) MiRror: a combinatorial analysis web tool for ensembles of microRNAs and their targets. Bioinformatics 26(15):1920–1921
38. Baek D, Villen J, Shin C, Camargo FD, Gygi SP, Bartel DP (2008) The impact of microRNAs on protein output. Nature 455(7209):64–71
39. Selbach M, Schwanhausser B, Thierfelder N, Fang Z, Khanin R, Rajewsky N (2008) Widespread changes in protein synthesis induced by microRNAs. Nature 455(7209):58–63
40. Erhard F, Dolken L, Jaskiewicz L, Zimmer R (2013) PARma: identification of microRNA target sites in Argonaute PAR-CLIP data. Genome Biol 14(7):R79
41. van Iterson M, Bervoets S, de Meijer EJ, Buermans HP, Hoen PA, Menezes RX, Boer JM (2013) Integrated analysis of microRNA and mRNA expression: adding biological significance to microRNA target predictions. Nucleic Acids Res 41(15):e146

Chapter 11

Genomic Regulation of MicroRNA Expression in Disease Development

Feng Liu

Abstract

MiroRNAs (miRNAs) are an abundant class of regulators of gene expression. Through base paring with messenger RNAs, miRNAs repress the expression levels of other genes, including those encoding transcription factors. On the other hand, the spatial and temporal patterns of miRNAs transcription are subject to regulation by transcription factors. The inter-regulation between miRNAs and TFs integrates two gene regulatory networks—at transcriptional level and post-transcriptional level to fine-tune the gene expression pattern in the development of multicellular organisms. Aberrant regulation at either of these two levels of gene regulation can lead to developmental disorder and disease.

Key words MicroRNA, Transcription factor, Promoter, Gene regulatory network

1 Introduction

MicroRNAs (miRNA) are one of three major types of regulatory noncoding RNAs in metazoans (the other two are lincRNA and piRNA) [1]. Through base pairing with messenger RNAs (mRNAs), each miRNA acts as a guide to recruit the Argonaute (AGO) family proteins and their associated factors to induce mRNA deadenylation, mRNA decay, and translational repression [2]. It is estimated that more than 60% of human protein-coding genes contain at least one conserved miRNA-target site, placing miRNAs as a major class of intracellular regulators of gene expression in the cell [3]. Currently, an intense area of the study of systems biology is to comprehensively characterize miRNA-mediated gene regulatory network to achieve a panoramic view of the molecular mechanisms governing cellular phenotypes.

While mature functional miRNAs are relatively short (~22 nucleotides), initial primary miRNAs transcripts (pri-miRNAs) are several hundreds to thousands of nucleotides long [2]. The conversion of pri-miRNAs to mature miRNAs is carried out by multiple endonucleases, including Drosha and Pasha in the nucleus, and

Jingshan Huang et al. (eds.), *Bioinformatics in MicroRNA Research*, Methods in Molecular Biology, vol. 1617, DOI 10.1007/978-1-4939-7046-9_11, © Springer Science+Business Media LLC 2017

Dicer in the cytoplasm [2]. Since their discovery, the biogenesis of miRNAs is largely focused on these post-transcriptional RNA processing steps. Nevertheless, the tissue and stage-specific expression patterns of individual miRNAs are subject to control by discrete cis-regulatory elements (e.g., promoters and enhancers) in the genome. Indeed, transcriptional regulation miRNAs is an integrative part of the molecular interaction networks governing proper cell fate in development. Conversely, aberrant miRNA transcription is associated with a variety of human diseases, including congenital developmental defect, heart disease, and cancer.

2 The Structure of miRNA Genes

Based on their relative locations to protein-coding sequences (i.e., genes), miRNAs can be broadly classified into two groups. The first group includes those encoded by untranslated sequences of other genes—introns and 5′- and 3′-end untranslated regions (UTR). These miRNAs and their "host" genes are initially transcribed as a single transcript; only later do they separate by RNA splicing events. By contrast, the second group of miRNAs are located in intergenic regions. Some miRNAs of this group have their own coding sequences, thus producing stand-alone transcripts, whereas others belonging to the same family (i.e., those with identical sequences at nucleotides 2–8 of the mature miRNA) are clustered in the same genomic loci, presumably due to gene duplication during evolution [4]. Clustered miRNAs are often co-transcribed in a long poly-cistronic transcript unit, from which individual miRNAs are subsequently spliced out by post-transcriptional mechanisms [2].

Regardless of their respective structural features, the vast majority of miRNAs genes are associated with canonical gene promoters and are transcribed RNA polymerase II [5, 6], with only a few exceptions of viral miRNAs transcribed by RNA Pol III [7]. A canonical promoter is empirically defined as DNA fragments of about 100 bp (−50, +50) in length centering on transcriptional start sites (TSS) (Fig. 1). Within this region, three types of short DNA sequence motifs are often present, which serve as binding sites for different transcription factors: (1) general transcription factor binding sites, such as the TFIIB recognition element (BRE) and the TATA-box at the 5′ end TATA binding boxes, (2) the initiator (Inr) sequences at around the TSS, and (3) downstream promoter element (DPE) 3′ to the TSS. Upon binding with these sequence motifs, multiple general transcription factors form the preinitiation complex (PIC), including the RNA Pol II, at the core promoter to start transcription [8].

In eukaryotic cells, DNA is wrapped by histones, proteins capable of condensing the DNA polymer into chromatins and chromosomes. The tight association between histones and DNA presents a

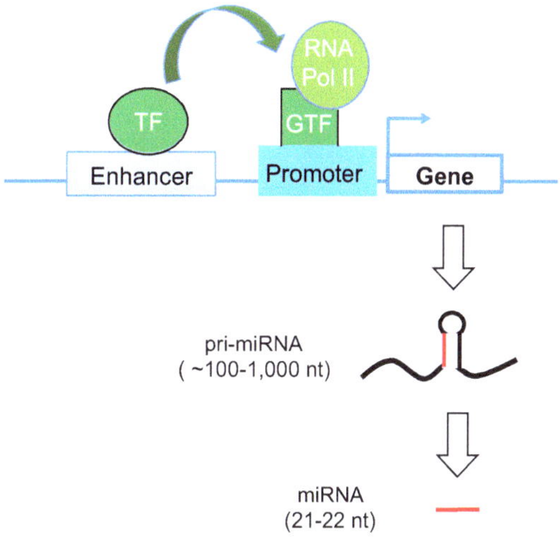

Fig. 1 Schematic illustration of miRNA biosynthesis. Coding sequences of miRNAs are transcribed by RNA polymerase II (RNA Pol II), which recognizes the promoter sequence at the transcription start site. The spatial and temporal specificity (time, level, and cell type) of miRNA transcription is dependent on distal cis-regulatory elements, called enhancers. Promoter and enhancer contain DNA sequence motifs that serve as binding sites for transcription factors. The initial transcripts of miRNAs are several hundreds to thousands long, which are gradually trimmed down to 21–22 nucleotides by multiple RNA endonucleases to form the mature miRNA. *TF* transcription factor. *GTF* general transcription factor

significant barrier for transcription regulators. As a result, certain distal cis-regulatory elements, called enhancers, are usually required to activate detectable gene expression in vivo [9]. Like promoters, enhancers also harbor many short DNA sequence motifs (6–20 bp) that serve as specific binding sites of TFs. Most enhancers and their associated TFs are active at restricted cell types at different stages of development; together, they determine the spatial and temporal specific gene expression patterns in multicellular organisms [10].

3 Transcriptional Control of miRNAs

A paradigm of transcriptional regulation of miRNA is illustrated by the study of the *lethal-7* (*let-7*) expression in the model organism *C. elegans* (Fig. 2). Let-7 was one of the first microRNAs discovered in the early 1990s [11]. During development, the let-7 locus produces two distinct transcripts (~1730 bp and ~890 bp, respectively) [12, 13]. Fine mapping of the cis-regulatory activity of *let-7* promoter revealed two promoter-proximal elements that are critical for the expression of *let-7* in different tissue types. One element, called TRE, activates *let-7* expression in the hypoderm, whereas the other element, LTE, activates expression in the intestine. In many other tissues, such as in the neuronal system and the muscle, both TRE and LTE are required for the expression of let-7 [13].

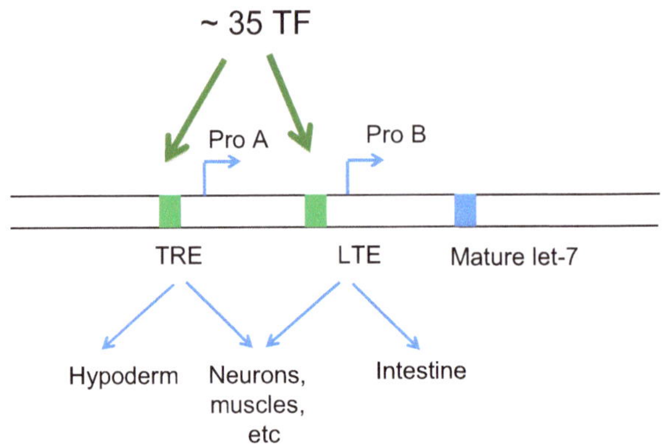

Fig. 2 A paradigm of transcriptional regulation of miRNA. The *let-7* miRNA is transcriptionally regulated during development of *C. elegans*. The *let-7* locus contains two promoters (Pro A and Pro B). Near these two promoters are two cis-regulatory elements TRE and LTE, control *let-7* transcription in different tissues. In the hypoderm and the intestine, *let-7* is respectively regulated by TRE and LTE. In other tissues such as the nervous system and muscles, *let-7* transcription depends on both TRE and LTE

As mentioned earlier, spatial and temporal-specific activities of cis-regulatory elements (i.e., promoters and enhancers) are dependent on sequence-specific DNA binding transcription factors. In an RNAi screen of TFs regulating *let-7* promoters' activities in *C. elegans*, ~35 genes were found to let-7 promoter's activity expression in development, including both positive and negative transcriptional regulators [13]. Complex regulation of miRNAs by TFs is not unique to *C. elegans*. Other notable TFs such as p53, MYC, and MYOD1 have been found to control the transcription from the *miR-34*, *miR-17*, and *miR-1* clusters, respectively [2, 14].

4 Cross-Regulation Between miRNA and Transcription Factors

That miRNAs are controlled by transcription factors indicates a cross-talk between these two families of gene regulators. Notably, this cross-talk is reciprocal, because miRNAs can target TFs' transcripts as well. For example, for the aforementioned miRNA-regulating TFs, such as p53 and Myc, each is subject to repression by miRNAs in various cell types and experimental conditions [2].

In multicellular organisms, microRNAs and transcription factors are the two largest families of trans-acting factors of gene regulation (~600 TFs and ~2600 miRNAs in humans). Given such large numbers, cross-regulations of TFs and miRNAs consist of a complex molecular interaction network. It has been shown that certain recurrent, molecular interaction patterns, called network motifs, are inherit to networks composed of a large number of nodes (e.g., TFs and miRNAs in the gene regulatory network) [15]. Common network motifs include negative/positive feed-back loops and feed-forward loops, each of which mediates distinct dynamical patterns of gene expression. For example, negative feedback loops act as a homeostasis controller to maintain the target gene expression level in the presence of variations of the upstream regulator. By contrast, positive feedback loop and feed-forward loops can start long-term gene expression pattern after a brief expression of the upstream factor [15].

The involvement of network motifs in TF-miRNA-mediated gene regulatory networks was elegantly studied in the diversification of neuronal subtype specifications in *C. elegans* [16] (Fig. 3). For example, two functionally distinct gustatory neurons—ASE left (ASEL) and ASE right (ASER)—express different sets of taste receptor genes. This molecular distinction is dependent on antagonist action of *lsy-6*, a miRNA, and *cog-1*, a transcription factor. Specifically, lsy-6 is preferentially expressed in ASEL, where it prevents cog-1 from being activated in that cell. On the other hand, the absence of *lsy-6* in ASER allows for high levels of *cog-1* therein [17]. The antagonistic regulation of a TF and miRNA molecular switch thus forms a negative feedback loop that controls distinct cell types [16].

One theme that has emerged from the study of transcriptional regulations is the pervasive use of combinatorial control—that is, multiple transcription factors converge on the regulation of one target gene. In some cases, these TFs play a largely redundant role, whereby no one factor is absolutely required for the regulation of the target; in other cases, however, multiple factors work together to regulate the target. Interestingly, combinatorial control is also a common strategy deployed by miRNA-mediated gene regulation. That is, target transcripts often harbor a number of seed sequences capable of paring with different miRNA species [18].

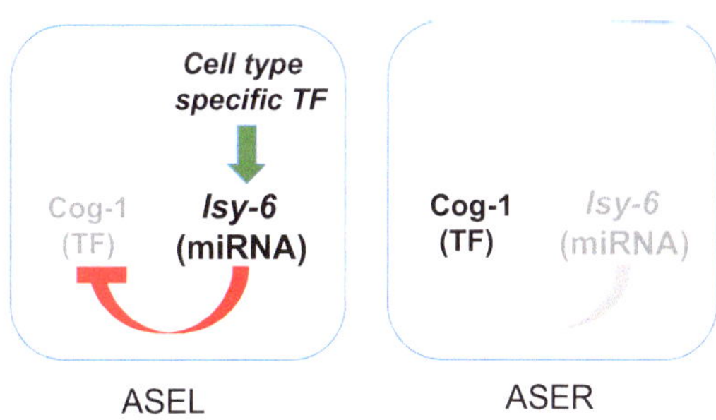

Fig. 3 Reciprocal regulation between TF and miRNA controls cell fate specification. In the nervous system of *C. elegans*, two gustatory neurons (ASEL and ASER) are systemically located in the anterior part of the body. Yet, they express different sets of taste receptor genes. This is molecular distinction that is regulated by an miRNA, lsy-6. Lsy-6 is specifically expressed in ASEL, where it represses a TF named cog-1. In the ASER, the absence of lsy-6 allows for high-level expression of Cog-1, which activates ASER-specific taste receptor genes. In ASEL, non-Cog-1 TFs activate ASEL-specific taste receptor genes

5 miRNA-Mediated Gene Regulatory Networks in Development and Disease

Thus far, the importance of miRNAs in gene regulation is well accepted. Nevertheless, in large loss-of-function studies, only 10% of miRNA mutants/knockdowns led to noticeable change of cellular morphology, function, or cell death [2]. The seemingly minor effect on cellular phenotype masks a hidden role of miRNAs controlling the robustness of genomic activities. Interestingly, this role can be studied in situations where the animal is subject to stresses induced by environmental perturbation [19]. For example, in *Drosophila*, loss of the *miR-27* gene has a negligible effect on the differentiation of sensory neurons in uniform temperature conditions. But when *miR-27* mutant flies were subject to even moderate temperature fluctuations in the laboratory, significant defect in sensory neuron differentiation ensued, suggesting that *miR-9* plays a critical role in normal gene expression and robust neuronal differentiation [20]. In a similar vein, *miR-8* mutation flies exhibit more severe pigmentation defect when cultured in elevated temperatures [21]. These studies suggested that miRNAs usually create thresholds of gene expressing and thus suppress "noisy" gene expressions during environmental changes. When such a buffering role is abolished, the gene expression profiles in the cell are more vulnerable to random changes of the base level of certain genes, such as those targeted by miRNAs. One implication from these studies is that individuals carrying mutations in miRNAs or their target sequences are inherently less resilient against environmental changes. Consequently, they carry a higher risk to develop common diseases, such as developmental disorders, heart disease, and cancer [22–24].

6 Genome-Wide Characterization of miRNA-Mediated Gene Regulatory Network

Because each miRNA interacts with its target transcript via base pairing, the nucleotide sequence of each miRNA can be used to predict its target transcripts with high confidence [1]. Indeed, a number of algorithms have been developed to perform such genome-wide analysis of the target transcriptome of miRNAs [25]. These tools are useful for globally analyzing miRNA-regulated gene expression network.

On the other hand, recent years have seen tremendous growth of high-throughput sequencing technologies, which have allowed for genome-wide identification of the promoters and enhancers of every gene/transcript, including those coding miRNAs [26]. These technologies take advantage of the discovery that the chromatin of active CREs (e.g., promoters and enhancers) is in a relatively "open" configuration and the histones at these loci are chemically modified in special ways (e.g., acetylation and methylation at specific lysines in the Histone 3) [27]. By preferentially targeting these open chromatins using DNase I (DNase-seq), transposase (ATAC-seq), or histone modification-specific antibodies (ChIP-seq), high-throughput sequencing analysis can globally identify CREs active in a particular tissue or cell type. When such information is aligned with the coding sequences in the genome, the promoters and enhancers near individual genes (protein-coding genes and noncoding genes such as miRNA genes) can be deduced and subsequently be used to identify the cohort of transcription factor binding sites [27]. These analyses provide valuable information regarding the classes of TFs capable of interacting with the CREs of miRNAs. This transcription factor-centered analysis, when combined with miRNA-centered analysis, will provide a comprehensive view of the gene regulatory network in the cell (Fig. 4).

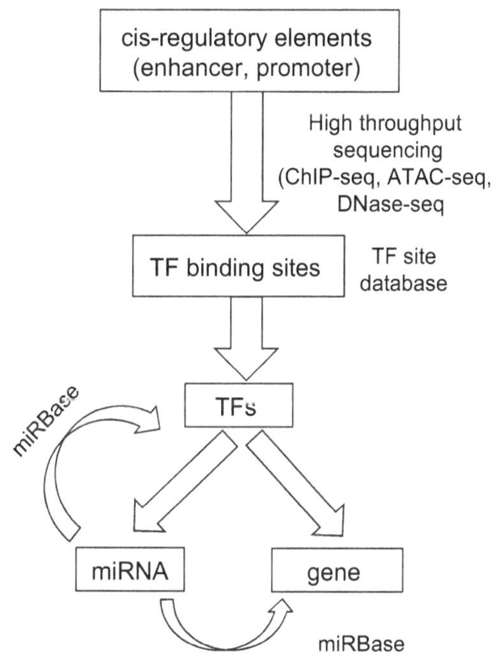

Fig. 4 Integrative analysis of gene regulatory networks involving both TFs and miRNAs. High-throughput sequencing-based techniques, including ChIP-seq, ATAC-seq, and DNase-seq, allow for genome-wide identification of cis-regulatory elements, such as promoters and enhancers. Bioinformatics analysis of the sequences of these elements can lead to the discovery of TFs interacting with these elements. Genes and miRNAs regulated by these TFs can be determined by transcriptome analysis through RNA-seq. Gene regulatory networks further downstream of these miRNAs can be computationally inferred using miRNA-target databases, such as miRBase

7 Conclusion

Since their discovery in the early 1990s, miRNAs have been firmly established as a major class of cellular regulators in the cell. One particular insight from these studies is that miRNAs, like TFs, interact with specific cis-regulatory elements associated with their targets (DNA sequence motifs for TFs and RNA seed sequences for miRNAs) [16]. Moreover, due to cross-regulation between miRNAs and TFs, the miRNA-mediated gene regulatory network is intimately weaved into the large molecular interaction networks in the cell. In this context, a significant challenge for the researchers of miRNA biology today is to define the role of individual miRNAs and miRNA families play in this large molecular interaction network.

References

1. Kozomara A, Griffiths-Jones S (2014) miRBase: annotating high confidence microRNAs using deep sequencing data. Nucleic Acids Res 42(Database issue):D68–D73
2. Kim VN (2005) MicroRNA biogenesis: coordinated cropping and dicing. Nat Rev Mol Cell Biol 6(5):376–385
3. Friedman RC et al (2009) Most mammalian mRNAs are conserved targets of microRNAs. Genome Res 19(1):92–105
4. Chiang HR et al (2010) Mammalian microRNAs: experimental evaluation of novel and previously annotated genes. Genes Dev 24(10):992–1009
5. Cai X, Hagedorn CH, Cullen BR (2004) Human microRNAs are processed from capped, polyadenylated transcripts that can also function as mRNAs. RNA 10(12):1957–1966
6. Lee Y et al (2004) MicroRNA genes are transcribed by RNA polymerase II. EMBO J 23(20):4051–4060
7. Pfeffer S et al (2005) Identification of microRNAs of the herpesvirus family. Nat Methods 2(4):269–276
8. Smale ST, Kadonaga JT (2003) The RNA polymerase II core promoter. Annu Rev Biochem 72:449–479
9. Levine M, Cattoglio C, Tjian R (2014) Looping back to leap forward: transcription enters a new era. Cell 157(1):13–25
10. Levine M (2010) Transcriptional enhancers in animal development and evolution. Curr Biol 20(17):R754–R763
11. Reinhart BJ et al (2000) The 21-nucleotide let-7 RNA regulates developmental timing in *Caenorhabditis elegans*. Nature 403(6772):901–906
12. Johnson SM, Lin SY, Slack FJ (2003) The time of appearance of the *C. elegans* let-7 microRNA is transcriptionally controlled utilizing a temporal regulatory element in its promoter. Dev Biol 259(2):364–379
13. Kai ZS et al (2013) Multiple cis-elements and trans-acting factors regulate dynamic spatio-temporal transcription of let-7 in *Caenorhabditis elegans*. Dev Biol 374(1):223–233
14. Krol J, Loedige I, Filipowicz W (2010) The widespread regulation of microRNA biogenesis, function and decay. Nat Rev Genet 11(9):597–610
15. Alon U (2007) Network motifs: theory and experimental approaches. Nat Rev Genet 8(6):450–461
16. Hobert O (2006) Architecture of a microRNA-controlled gene regulatory network that diversifies neuronal cell fates. Cold Spring Harb Symp Quant Biol 71:181–188
17. Johnston RJ, Hobert O (2003) A microRNA controlling left/right neuronal asymmetry in *Caenorhabditis elegans*. Nature 426(6968):845–849
18. Hobert O (2004) Common logic of transcription factor and microRNA action. Trends Biochem Sci 29(9):462–468
19. Posadas DM, Carthew RW (2014) MicroRNAs and their roles in developmental canalization. Curr Opin Genet Dev 27:1–6
20. Li X et al (2009) A microRNA imparts robustness against environmental fluctuation during development. Cell 137(2):273–282
21. Kennell JA et al (2012) The microRNA miR-8 is a positive regulator of pigmentation and eclosion in Drosophila. Dev Dyn 241(1):161–168

22. Im HI, Kenny PJ (2012) MicroRNAs in neuronal function and dysfunction. Trends Neurosci 35(5):325–334
23. Lujambio A, Lowe SW (2012) The microcosmos of cancer. Nature 482(7385):347–355
24. Zhao Y et al (2007) Dysregulation of cardiogenesis, cardiac conduction, and cell cycle in mice lacking miRNA-1-2. Cell 129(2):303–317
25. Agarwal V et al (2015) Predicting effective microRNA target sites in mammalian mRNAs. eLife 4:e05005
26. Consortium EP (2012) An integrated encyclopedia of DNA elements in the human genome. Nature 489(7414):57–74
27. Rivera CM, Ren B (2013) Mapping human epigenomes. Cell 155(1):39–55

Chapter 12

Next-Generation Sequencing for MicroRNA Expression Profile

Yue Hu, Wenjun Lan, and Daniel Miller

Abstract

Sequencing technologies have made considerable advancements. From the Sanger sequencing method to the next-generation sequencing (NGS) methods, and from the NGS methods to the third-generation sequencing methods, we can see the development thread of the sequencing technology. Currently, NGS is the main contender in the sequencing market. NGS technologies provide an opportunity to research the microRNA (miRNA) expression profiles in detail. The NGS platforms have their own special characteristics, but share some main ideas. DNA sequencing via NGS is fundamental for RNA sequencing and miRNA sequencing. MiRNA sequencing has special characteristics. The pipeline of miRNA sequencing by NGS is explained in detail from the wet experiment to the dry experiment.

Key words Next-generation sequencing, MicroRNA expression profile, 454, Illumina, Ion Torrent, SOLiD

1 Introduction

The microRNA expression profile can be detected by reverse transcription qualitative PCR (RT-qPCR), microarray (hybridization-based detection), and next-generation sequencing (NGS) technologies. In 2009, Hanni Willenbrock et al. compared microarrays with NGS techniques in the paper of "Quantitative miRNA expression analysis: comparing microarrays with next-generation sequencing." [1]. They found that microarray expression profiling was highly sensitive and performed comparably to NGS technologies. Performance comparisons were relative to quantification and reproducibility. They also suggested the NGS technologies had advantages such as finding variants in the miRNA sequence. In 2010, Anna Git, et al. compared three methods of miRNA expression profiling in the paper of "Systematic comparison of microarray profiling, real-time PCR, and next-generation sequencing technologies for measuring differential microRNA expression." [2]. They examined the

Jingshan Huang et al. (eds.), *Bioinformatics in MicroRNA Research*, Methods in Molecular Biology, vol. 1617,
DOI 10.1007/978-1-4939-7046-9_12, © Springer Science+Business Media LLC 2017

utility of microarrays and NGS to research differential miRNA expression profiles. They also examined real-time RT-PCR and challenged its status as a benchmark for studying miRNA expression profiling. They pronounced that they were the first to compare the relative performance of those methods. In 2014, Pieter Mestdagh et al. compared 12 different commercial platforms for microRNA expression profiling in the paper of "Evaluation of quantitative miRNA expression platforms in the microRNA quality control (miRQC) study" [3] in the journal of Nature Methods. They found that each method has its advantages and disadvantages and that the choice of method should depend on the aims of the study. In this chapter, we will not compare the various methods of miRNA expression profiling, we will focus on the details of miRNA expression profiling by next-generation sequencing methods.

Next-generation sequencing [4–8] is the second-generation sequencing relative to the Sanger sequencing method [9] which can be referred to as the first-generation sequencing method. The Sanger sequencing method is the classical method that reaches almost 100% accuracy. It was the pioneering work by which humankind began to discover the genes of all creatures, including ourselves. It was a low-throughput and high-cost method. Limited to the use of this classical method, the Human Genome Project cost almost three billion U.S. dollars to fund the human genome draft map. However, everyone has a unique genome. The differences can be the allele combinations or even single nucleotide point mutations that are called the single nucleotide polymorphisms (SNP). New sequencing technologies were badly needed at that time and the NGS time was coming. The NGS or the second-generation sequencing is characterized by high throughput and low cost and is now the most used method in sequencing. The DNA from the original sample or the RNA reverse transcription is amplified (replicated) in many times in parallel. The amplified DNA is sequenced multiple times simultaneously and the signal can also be amplified. The amplified signal ensures the accuracy of the reads. Different nucleotides or dinucleotides can be added to give characteristic signals that can be detected and interpreted to determine the sequence. There are several widely used sequencing systems for NGS: 454 [10–12], Illumina [13], Ion Torrent [14–16], SOLiD. Ion Torrent and SOLiD are produced by the same company: Life Technologies. We give a detailed introduction in the following sections.

Third-generation sequencing is single molecular sequencing without the DNA amplification. It is not widely used, but has a promising future. Third-generation sequencing techniques include SMRT (single molecule Real-Time) [17] sequencing, tSMS (true single molecule sequencing) [18], Nanopore [19], and so on. SMRT (single molecule Real-Time) sequencing uses a single molecular fluorescent technology. This system uses four fluorescent dyes, marked dNTP, and a nanostructure called a zero-mode waveguide (ZMW). The ZMW is a nanoscale hole much smaller than the fluoresced light wavelength. Only fluorescent signals generated at the bottom of the hole are detected outside the ZMW. The DNA polymerases are anchored at the bottom of this hole and the fluorescent dye marked dNTP that are added to the sequence will react on the DNA polymerases there. This fluorescent signal of the reacting dNTP is detected and the fluorescent signals of the free dissociated dNTP that are not near the bottom of the hole will not be detected. The nucleotide type is determined from the light emitted by different fluorescent dyes. The method is limited by the low intensity of single molecular fluorescence, but as the depth of the sequence increases, the accuracy of the sequencing increases. The other advantages of the SMRT sequencing are that it gives the longest read of all the sequencing methods (about 30Kb). This makes this technique well suited for assembling genomes.

The tSMS (true single molecule sequencing) method also uses single molecular fluorescent technology. This method is much like the Illumina sequencing system, but it does not have a PCR amplification step. The reverse terminated dNTPs are added in the system. There are four types of fluorescent dyes of the dNTP. At the beginning of the elongation, one nucleotide is added, and a fluorescent signal is captured. But as a chemical terminator is linked to the nucleotide, the next nucleotide will not be added. Thus, the fluorescent signal detected is only produced by attached nucleotide. After the chemical terminator is removed, another reversible terminated dNTP can be added and detected. By repeating the process, the sequence can be determined. This method is also limited by the weak fluorescent signal and is more expensive. The company that first sought to develop this method into a commercially viable product is bankrupt.

Compared with those two fluorescent methods of the single molecular sequencing method, the Nanopore sequencing method takes another route to determine the sequence information. The strand of the DNA (the double strands should be open) or RNA is passed through a nanopore. Each nucleotide that passes through the nanopore induces a different change in voltage. Those changes can be used to determine the sequence information.

2 The Major Second-Generation Sequencing Technology Platforms (a.k.a. NGS)

In this section, we will describe the processes in several widely NGS sequencing platforms: 454, Illumina, Ion Torrent, and SOLiD.

2.1 454 Platform

The 454 Life Sciences company first unveiled the 454 sequencing platform. It is also the first commercial second-generation sequencing method. The 454 sequencing system utilizes the four fluorescent dyes of dNTP to detect the sequence order. The DNA fragments are amplified to enhance the fluorescent signals. The main procedures of the second-generation sequencing methods have many of the same aspects. In this section, we outline 454 sequencing to illustrate the main processes of this second-generation sequencing method.

2.1.1 DNA Preparation and Fragmentation

The DNA that will be sequenced is extracted from the cell or tissue and then broken into fragments. In this process, different methods can be used (enzyme degradation, ultrasound, and so on) to break the DNA into fragments of the desired length. The length of the pieces of the DNA should be limited. In sequencing terms, a fragment or piece of the DNA is called a "read." The 454 sequencing system has the longest read of all the second-generation sequencing methods (about 1 kb).

2.1.2 DNA Fragments Are Linked with Adaptor

The fragments or pieces of the DNA are then linked with the adaptors. The adaptors are short single strand DNAs that have special sequences designed to promote PCR amplification. The adaptors are different, so each read has special adaptors.

2.1.3 Amplification and Anchor the DNA to Beads

The DNA fragments are then amplified with the help of the adaptors by PCR. As the adaptors are different from each other, the same adaptor will be linked with the same DNA fragments. Small beads are mixed into the system. The beads that have primer sequences mapped onto them that are complementary with the special adaptors. By doing so, the fragments of the DNA (or read) are anchored to the beads. Beads that do not have attached DNA are filtered from the mix. The anchored double-stranded DNA are then denatured to a single strand form.

2.1.4 One Bead One Well and Sequencing

One bead is put into each well of the microarray. The DNA polymerases, buffers, and PCR primers are also added into those wells. As the read or DNA fragments are in the single strand form, the sequencing is determined by synthesizing the other strand. One type of the four fluorescent dyes of dNTPs is added once in the sequencing and then those dNTPs are washed out. Four fluorescent dyes of dNTPs are added in order (T, A, G, and C for example) and cycles. If the dNTPs are synthesizing in the read, their signals are noted. Before the end of the synthesizing, there always fluorescent signals could be detected in one cycle (T, A, G, and C added in order). The multiple nucleotide additions can also detected as the intensity of the fluorescence is linearly scaled with that of a single nucleotide.

2.1.5 Analyzing the Sequencing Data

The sequencing result of the wet experiments of the 454 sequencing system is the sequencing of reads. The reads are assembled to recover the original DNA sequence. Generally, the sequence of a DNA is covered several times to enhance the accuracy of the sequencing.

The number of times is referred to as the sequencing depth. Sequencing depth is the total number of bases that are sequenced in the NGS (the total length of all the reads) divided by the length of the sequence which we want to measure. Sequencing coverage is the percentage of the sequence that has been measured by NGS.

2.2 Illumina Platform

The Illumina sequencing system sees worldwide application due to its lower cost and high accuracy. The read length is about 100 bp, which is much shorter than the 454 platform. The fragments of the DNA that linked with the adaptors anchor to a slide. The function of this slide is similar to the bead in 454 platform. Those fragments are amplified by PCR with DNA polymerase and other materials. As in the 454 platform, the copies of a fragment will enhance the fluorescent signals. The double-stranded DNA are denatured into the single strand form. The sequencing is achieved in the process of synthesizing the other DNA strand, which is called "sequencing by synthesis." The nucleotides used in the Illumina platform are different from that used on the 454 platform. Those nucleotides are reverse terminators. A chemical unit is added to the nucleotides that are used to stop elongation. So when one type of dNTP is added to the sequence, only one nucleotide is actually added. After the added base is recorded, the chemical unit on the nucleotide is removed, so the new nucleotide could link other nucleotides.

2.3 Ion Torrent

The Ion Torrent is also a "sequencing by synthesis" method like 454 platform and Illumina platform. However, unlike fluorescent signals used in the two methods above, Ion Torrent sequencing detects the proton (H+) change. When a dNTP is added to the DNA sequence by a polymerase, a H+ ion will be released. When one type of dNTP is added into the sequence, the number of H+ could be used to define the number of dNTPs that is added. This situation is like that in the 454 platform but not like that in the Illumina platform. The read length for Ion Torrent sequencing is about 200 bp, which is between the length of read in the 454 platform and the Illumina platform.

2.4 SOLiD

SOLiD sequencing technology is different than the three methods introduced above. It is a "sequencing by ligation" approach. The main reactant used in the SOLiD sequencing is using the DNA ligase, not the DNA polymerase. In every ligation reaction, 8-mer oligonucleotides are added in the sequence. Bases six to eight are cleaved from the sequence. The first two bases make up one of 16 nucleotide combinations, which can be detected by their fluorescent signal. The fluorescent labels linked with the bases three to five are not known. The 16 combinations of dinucleotides are labeled by four fluorescent dyes, thus the dinucleotide type is not defined in one ligation progress. After five rounds of ligation, every base is read twice in the retained five bases. In principal, if one base is defined the other bases could be defined.

3 MicroRNA Sequencing by NGS Methods

The basic process of sequencing RNA [20–23] is the same as with the sequencing described above but, there are several additional procedures that should be done to sequence RNA. First, the RNA should be extracted from cells or tissues. For certain types of RNA, the enrichment method may be different. Then the single stranded RNAs are transformed into the double-stranded cDNA by the process of reverse transcription. From the point of the cDNA, the procedure is the same with DNA sequencing. The main platforms introduced above (Illumina, SOLiD, and Ion Torrent) have a commercial RNA sequencing application.

3.1 Wet Experiment for miRNA Sequencing by NGS Method

The reads are the raw data which were gotten from the sequencing equipment. The main procedure of microRNA sequencing [24–26] is similar to the messenger RNA (mRNA) sequencing, but the details of the library preparation for microRNA sample are different from that for mRNA sample. MicroRNAs normally require an enrichment by gel electrophoresis. Through the classical size of the microRNAs, the right segments of the gel are cut for sequencing in the next steps. Details regarding that process have already been described.

The RNA or microRNA are extracted from cells or tissues to make a library. 3′ Adapter Ligation and 5′ Adapter Ligation can be performed simultaneously or in series. By reverse transcription, the cDNA is acquired. The cDNA are then amplified by PCR. As the microRNA has a particular length, the microRNA could be easily acquired by gel purification. Generally, the libraries are sent to the sequencing company.

3.2 Data Analysis (Dry Experiment) of miRNA Sequencing by NGS Method

After acquiring the raw data from the NGS sequencing process, the data must be analyzed. Here, we will give an introduction in the bioinformatics analysis process.

3.2.1 Raw Data

The reads are the raw data which were gotten from the sequencing equipment. Depending on the platform used in the sequencing, the length of the reads differs. Longer reads may be preferable if the goal of the analysis is to assemble a genome.

3.2.2 Quality Control

There are several quantities that we can measure to ascertain the quality of sequencing. The most often used metric is the quality score. Every base is given a quality score by the sequencing platform during the process of base calling (base recognition). The quality score is computed from the error rate of base calling: $Q = -10\log E$, where Q is the quality score and E is the error rate. $Q10$, $Q20$, and $Q30$ represent the percentage of bases that their quality scores are equal to or greater than 10, 20, and 30 respectively. For example, the $Q20$ represents that error rate of base calling is 1% or the rate of correct base calling is 99%.

3.2.3 Data Filter or Clean

First, the low quantity reads (having more than five bases with quality scores below 20) and adaptors that were added for sequencing and PCR are removed. In miRNA sequencing, the adaptors are often much longer to address the short lengths of miRNAs. As NGS sequencing methods are able to capture many reads at the same time, many samples may be sequenced at the same time (mixed sequencing). The variable region of the adaptors can be used to define the sources of each sample. The statistical sequence length distribution is then checked to ensure it is close to the classical length of the mature miRNA: 20–25 nt.

3.2.4 Analysis of the Clean Data

The sequence data are given annotations by aligning them with the known miRNA databases. The most famous miRNA annotation database is the miRBase [27] (http://www.mirbase.org/). It contains the known miRNA of human, mouse, and several other species. PMRD [28] is a miRNA database that is designed particularly for plants. It contains the most species of model plants (http://bioinformatics.cau.edu.cn/PMRD).

The process is different when the miRNA is not found in a known database. First, the miRNA is compared with the other small RNA databases, piRNA for example. Rfam [29, 30] is often used in this procedure. Rfam is a database of the noncoding RNAs (http://www.sanger.ac.uk/Software/Rfam/ and http://rfam.wustl.edu/). The data that cannot be aligned will be put into the de novo miRNA discovery procedure. The miRDeep2 [31] is often used software to discover new miRNA. miRcat is a tool in the sRNA toolkit [32] to perform the same function. The reads are mapped to the genome of the sequenced species and the precursor sequence of miRNA can be extracted from the mapped region. The folding model can help to define new miRNA. The new miRNA candidates are often on the stem of the stem-loop structure.

3.3 Advantages of miRNA Sequencing Using NGS

High resolution: SNP in genes can be detected by the NGS method. The differences in a single base of miRNA also can be detected by the NGS method.

High throughout: It is the main characteristic of the NGS method. NGS is also called high-throughput sequencing. Ordinarily, as the throughout is so high, the sample that we send to the sequencing company would sequence at the same time as other samples that are sent from other groups (mixed sequencing). The sequencing company gives an index to mark the sources of the samples.

De novo miRNA discovery: hybridization methods such as microarray can only detect miRNA known by the designed probe. By comparing known miRNA database and incorporating prediction methods, de novo miRNA can be discovered by the NGS method.

High accuracy: the high-depth sequencing guarantees that every base is sequenced many times. This characteristic enhances the accuracy of the sequencing.

4 Conclusion

New sequencing methods have sprung up in the last decade. The NGS methods and third-generation sequencing methods constitute the majority of sequencing done today. Third-generation (single molecular) sequencing technologies have their technological advantages, but their cost is high. In commercial sequencing, NGS methods are the mainstream. In this chapter, several NGS platforms have been introduced and their main processes have been described. Additional steps required for miRNA expression profiling by NGS have also been described.

References

1. Willenbrock H, Salomon J, Sokilde R, Barken KB, Hansen TN, Nielsen FC, Moller S, Litman T (2009) Quantitative miRNA expression analysis: comparing microarrays with next-generation sequencing. RNA 15(11):2028–2034. doi:10.1261/rna.1699809
2. Git A, Dvinge H, Salmon-Divon M, Osborne M, Kutter C, Hadfield J, Bertone P, Caldas C (2010) Systematic comparison of microarray profiling, real-time PCR, and next-generation sequencing technologies for measuring differential microRNA expression. RNA 16(5):991–1006. doi:10.1261/rna.1947110
3. Mestdagh P, Hartmann N, Baeriswyl L, Andreasen D, Bernard N, Chen C, Cheo D, D'Andrade P, DeMayo M, Dennis L (2014) Evaluation of quantitative miRNA expression platforms in the microRNA quality control (miRQC) study. Nat Methods 11(8):809–815
4. Schuster SC (2007) Next-generation sequencing transforms today's biology. Nature 200(8):16–18
5. Mardis ER (2008) The impact of next-generation sequencing technology on genetics. Trends Genet 24(3):133–141
6. Morozova O, Marra MA (2008) Applications of next-generation sequencing technologies in functional genomics. Genomics 92(5):255–264
7. Metzker ML (2010) Sequencing technologies—the next generation. Nat Rev Genet 11(1):31–46
8. Shendure J, Ji H (2008) Next-generation DNA sequencing. Nat Biotechnol 26(10):1135–1145
9. Sanger F, Nicklen S, Coulson AR (1977) DNA sequencing with chain-terminating inhibitors. Proc Natl Acad Sci U S A 74(12):5463–5467
10. Rothberg JM, Leamon JH (2008) The development and impact of 454 sequencing. Nat Biotechnol 26(10):1117–1124
11. Taylor KH, Kramer RS, Davis JW, Guo J, Duff DJ, Xu D, Caldwell CW, Shi H (2007) Ultradeep bisulfite sequencing analysis of DNA methylation patterns in multiple gene promoters by 454 sequencing. Cancer Res 67(18):8511–8518
12. Wicker T, Schlagenhauf E, Graner A, Close TJ, Keller B, Stein N (2006) 454 sequencing put to the test using the complex genome of barley. BMC Genomics 7(1):275
13. Quail MA, Kozarewa I, Smith F, Scally A, Stephens PJ, Durbin R, Swerdlow H, Turner DJ (2008) A large genome center's improvements to the Illumina sequencing system. Nat Methods 5(12):1005–1010
14. Quail MA, Smith M, Coupland P, Otto TD, Harris SR, Connor TR, Bertoni A, Swerdlow HP, Gu Y (2012) A tale of three next generation sequencing platforms: comparison of Ion Torrent, Pacific Biosciences and Illumina MiSeq sequencers. BMC Genomics 13(1):341
15. Merriman B, Torrent I, Rothberg JM, Team D (2012) Progress in ion torrent semiconductor chip based sequencing. Electrophoresis 33(23):3397–3417
16. Liu L, Li Y, Li S, Hu N, He Y, Pong R, Lin D, Lu L, Law M (2012) Comparison of next-generation sequencing systems. Biomed Res Int 2012:251364
17. Eid J, Fehr A, Gray J, Luong K, Lyle J, Otto G, Peluso P, Rank D, Baybayan P, Bettman B, Bibillo A, Bjornson K, Chaudhuri B, Christians F, Cicero R, Clark S, Dalal R, Dewinter A, Dixon J, Foquet M, Gaertner A, Hardenbol P, Heiner C, Hester K, Holden D, Kearns G, Kong X, Kuse R, Lacroix Y, Lin S, Lundquist P, Ma C, Marks P, Maxham M, Murphy D, Park I, Pham T, Phillips M, Roy J, Sebra R, Shen G, Sorenson J, Tomaney A, Travers K, Trulson M, Vieceli J, Wegener J, Wu D, Yang A, Zaccarin D, Zhao P, Zhong

F, Korlach J, Turner S (2009) Real-time DNA sequencing from single polymerase molecules. Science 323(5910):133–138. doi:10.1126/science.1162986
18. Harris TD, Buzby PR, Babcock H, Beer E, Bowers J, Braslavsky I, Causey M, Colonell J, Dimeo J, Efcavitch JW, Giladi E, Gill J, Healy J, Jarosz M, Lapen D, Moulton K, Quake SR, Steinmann K, Thayer E, Tyurina A, Ward R, Weiss H, Xie Z (2008) Single-molecule DNA sequencing of a viral genome. Science 320(5872):106–109. doi:10.1126/science.1150427
19. Clarke J, Wu HC, Jayasinghe L, Patel A, Reid S, Bayley H (2009) Continuous base identification for single-molecule nanopore DNA sequencing. Nat Nanotechnol 4(4):265–270. doi:10.1038/nnano.2009.12
20. Ozsolak F, Milos PM (2011) RNA sequencing: advances, challenges and opportunities. Nat Rev Genet 12(2):87–98
21. Auer PL, Doerge R (2010) Statistical design and analysis of RNA sequencing data. Genetics 185(2):405–416
22. Trapnell C, Pachter L, Salzberg SL (2009) TopHat: discovering splice junctions with RNA-Seq. Bioinformatics 25(9):1105–1111
23. Martin JA, Wang Z (2011) Next-generation transcriptome assembly. Nat Rev Genet 12(10):671–682
24. Friedländer MR, Chen W, Adamidi C, Maaskola J, Einspanier R, Knespel S, Rajewsky N (2008) Discovering microRNAs from deep sequencing data using miRDeep. Nat Biotechnol 26(4):407–415
25. Creighton CJ, Reid JG, Gunaratne PH (2009) Expression profiling of microRNAs by deep sequencing. Brief Bioinform 10(5):490–497
26. Bar M, Wyman SK, Fritz BR, Qi J, Garg KS, Parkin RK, Kroh EM, Bendoraite A, Mitchell PS, Nelson AM (2008) MicroRNA discovery and profiling in human embryonic stem cells by deep sequencing of small RNA libraries. Stem Cells 26(10):2496–2505
27. Griffiths-Jones S, Grocock RJ, Van Dongen S, Bateman A, Enright AJ (2006) miRBase: microRNA sequences, targets and gene nomenclature. Nucleic Acids Res 34(suppl 1):D140–D144
28. Zhang Z, Yu J, Li D, Zhang Z, Liu F, Zhou X, Wang T, Ling Y, Su Z (2010) PMRD: plant microRNA database. Nucleic Acids Res 38(suppl 1):D806–D813
29. Griffiths-Jones S, Bateman A, Marshall M, Khanna A, Eddy SR (2003) Rfam: an RNA family database. Nucleic Acids Res 31(1):439–441
30. Gardner PP, Daub J, Tate JG, Nawrocki EP, Kolbe DL, Lindgreen S, Wilkinson AC, Finn RD, Griffiths-Jones S, Eddy SR (2009) Rfam: updates to the RNA families database. Nucleic Acids Res 37(suppl 1):D136–D140
31. Friedländer MR, Mackowiak SD, Li N, Chen W, Rajewsky N (2012) miRDeep2 accurately identifies known and hundreds of novel microRNA genes in seven animal clades. Nucleic Acids Res 40(1):37–52
32. Moxon S, Schwach F, Dalmay T, MacLean D, Studholme DJ, Moulton V (2008) A toolkit for analysing large-scale plant small RNA datasets. Bioinformatics 24(19):2252–2253

Chapter 13

Handling High-Dimension (High-Feature) MicroRNA Data

Yue Hu, Wenjun Lan, and Daniel Miller

Abstract

High-dimensional data, or high-feature variables, are often used to describe the characteristics of microRNA sequence and microarray data. As a consequence, the curse of high dimension often becomes a problem. High-dimension variables lead to many difficulties in processing and can be hard to understand. On the other aspect, as the sample size rather limited, the more variables, the more statistical error would be produced in the data processing. For the purpose of decreasing the dimension of variables, a degenerated *k*-mer method was suggested. To enhance the statistical robustness, the gapped *k*-mer method was introduced. In the last part of this chapter, some traditional supervised and unsupervised mathematical methods that used to decrease the dimensionality of the data are also described.

Key words High-dimension, miRNA, Degenerated *k*-mer, Gapped *k*-mer, Dimension decreasing

1 Introduction

The microRNA or the miRNA plays a significant role in gene expression by negatively regulating transcription [1–4]. The original miRNA precursor will form the mature miRNA through processing. The mature state of the miRNA is a single short sequence, which usually contains 20 ~ 25 nucleotides. Compared with messenger RNA, it is a type of small noncoding RNA. The mature miRNA combines with its target genes by binding with complementary sequences, thereby reducing those genes' expression. Combinations of different miRNA regulation pathways in the cell can form networks. Many complex diseases, like cancers [5] or diabetes [6–8], are caused by improper expression of miRNA. Consequently, miRNA is an attractive research subject for many groups.

The cornerstone of researching an entity is extracting its features. MiRNA and its precursors can be described in many ways, nucleotide compositions for example. While nucleotide composition is an intuitive way of representing miRNA, it is often not sufficient. K-tuple or Kmer [9] is a more general means to define features of miRNAs and other biological sequences [10, 11]. It is

Jingshan Huang et al. (eds.), *Bioinformatics in MicroRNA Research*, Methods in Molecular Biology, vol. 1617,
DOI 10.1007/978-1-4939-7046-9_13, © Springer Science+Business Media LLC 2017

a sequential string of letters from an alphabet *k*. If the alphabet table represents the four types of nucleotides (adenine, cytosine, guanine, and uracil), there will be four letters, {A, C, G, U}. Note that the alphabet table is not confined to the four types of nucleotides. It is an unbiased systematical method to represent miRNAs. Nevertheless, as the cardinality of k is limited what can be represented by single character, K-tuples or Kmers only represent the local sequence arrangement. A parallel type of Pseudo-dinucleotide composition (pPseDNC) and a series type of pseudo-dinucleotide composition (sPseDNC) consider the dinucleotide correlations of 22 physiochemical properties [12–15]. By using different sequence distances, the long-range interaction could be taken into account via a hierarchical pattern (called tiers). Other methods such as Triplet [16] and Pseudo-structure status composition (PseSSC) describe the properties of a miRNA by its structure information, which also considers the long-range sequence information [17]. In this chapter, we focus on the Kmer and variant Kmer. First, we will give a brief introduction of those basic Kmer systems that were used to represent miRNAs.

The more features (dimensions) extracted from miRNA, the more useful the results of the analysis. There is, however, redundant information into those features (dimensions). And the dimension disaster is often like a ghost in the era of information. The curse of dimensionality becomes more serious in big data problems than in classical computing challenges. Handing high-dimensional big data often requires large amounts of memory and calculation. The resource demands of some calculations are impossible to meet with current technology. Developments in high-throughput biology experiments, like the second-generation sequencing [18, 19], mean that biological big data is easy to acquire in using inexpensive techniques. High-dimension and big microRNA data poses an open problem for researchers.

To overcome the curse of dimensionality, we should analyze the high-dimension data itself. The dimensions (features) of the miRNA are not independent, thus we could use important, but smaller, number of dimensions to represent the full data set by space transformation. There are many methods that can be used for dimension reduction. Those methods are pure mathematical technologies. In the last part of this chapter, we will discuss those mathematical technologies. The application of those mathematical technologies is not only being used in miRNA, but also the other biological big data processing. While analysis of the reduced feature space of miRNA can yield meaningful results, explanation of those results should reference the original feature space to explain the relevant properties of the miRNA and there is often not a direct and easy way of reverting to the old feature space. Another technique would be to combine important features that describe the miRNA in a biological view. In the first part of this chapter, we first recommend a degenerate Kmer method using this idea.

The other serious problem when we are handing the high-dimension miRNA data is the statistical errors. When confining the research to some specific field, it is often the case that the training data set is small. As the number of the features is increasing, the counts of every feature are decreasing. Therefore, it is error-prone to estimate the frequencies of every feature. Micheal A. Beer et al. proposed a gapped *k*-mer method to give a much robust estimation of the frequencies of the features. We will cover this method in Subheading 3.2.

2 Features Related to miRNAs (Basic K-Tuple or Kmer)

K-tuples or Kmers are subsequences of a full sequence (miRNA, mRNA, DNA for example), which contain k tandem nucleotides. There are four types of nucleotides in a miRNA from which we can generate an alphabet table (U, G, C, A) to construct the Kmer. For this alphabet, there are $4k$ different arrangements for a Kmer.

Given a miRNA sequence R with the length of L.

$$R = r_1 r_2 r_3 r_4 r_5 r_6 r_7 \ldots r_L$$

With the sequence "*CCGUUGCAAGG*" and k set to 2, the frequencies of the 2-mer are:

$$f(UU) = 0.1, f(UG) = 0.1, f(UC) = 0, f(UA) = 0,$$
$$f(GU) = 0.1, f(GG) = 0.1, f(GC) = 0.1, f(GA) = 0,$$
$$f(CU) = 0, f(CG) = 0.1, f(CC) = 0.1, f(CA) = 0.1,$$
$$f(AU) = 0, f(AG) = 0.1, f(AC) = 0, f(AA) = 0.1.$$

Note that the alphabet table is not confined to four types of nucleotides. Therefore, using Kmers to describe a miRNA, the number of k is limited. Under most conditions, the occurrences frequencies of Kmers only reflect the local sequence information of a miRNA. In the next section, long-range information is considered.

As the limitation of the length of Kmers, the Kmers usually reflect the local sequences arrangements of miRNA. The local sequences of a miRNA form higher rank structures and the broader interaction is very important to the structure of a miRNA. The stem-loop structure of a miRNA is very important to its function, so missing the long range information will lead to problems when we process a miRNA. The correlations between the local sequences could be used to reflect the long-range information. Auto-correlation and cross-correlation of the physicochemical properties of two dinucleotides are often considered. The dinucleotides correlations are considered in tiers. Use the sequence

"CCGUUGCAAGG" as an example. For first-tier correlation, we will consider those dinucleotides correlation functions: cor(CC,CG),cor(CG,GU),cor(GU,UU),cor(UU,UG),cor(UG,GC), cor(GC,CA),cor(CA,AA),cor(AA,AG),cor(AG,GG). For second-tier correlation, we will consider those dinucleotides correlation functions: cor(CC,GU),cor(CG,UU),cor(GU,UG),cor(UU,GC), cor(UG,CA),cor(GC,AA),cor(CA,AG),cor(AA,GG). The higher rank tier correlation can be considered similarly. pPseDNC and sPseDNC consider those dinucleotide correlations in parallel or series respectively [12–15].

3 Decreasing the Number of Features

3.1 Degenerate Kmer

The Kmer is the most popular feature system used to represent miRNA and other sequences. As mentioned previously, the length of Kmers is generally limited to several nucleobases as longer Kmers will lead to the exponential increases in complexity. The classical lengths of miRNAs range from 20 to 25 nucleobases and the miRNAs precursors are even longer. By the application of Kmers, the side effect misses the long-range information. When finding miRNAs precursors, this situation is even worse as the precursor would form a stem-loop structure. The long-range information has an important role in predicting those precursors. Therefore, there is an urgent need to use longer Kmers that could represent miRNA. To break through the limitation of the length of Kmers, several groups have carried out research in this field. Gaining inspiration from quantum mechanics, Liu et al. have proposed a Kmer variant, the degenerate Kmer, which is similar to "degenerate energy levels" [9]. Per their definition, two Kmers can be considered equivalent if they each have identical subsequences that contain at least two base pairs. By using that notation, the length of *k*-mers can decrease dramatically. Assuming four types of nucleotides as the basis for the alphabet table, the dimension of the deKmer composition vector is reduced from 4^k dimensions to:

$$\Omega = 4^2 C_k^2 = 4^2 \frac{k!}{(k-2)!2!}.$$

3.2 Gapped Kmer

Another fundamental limitation of using Kmers to describe features of a miRNA is that as the length of Kmers is increased, the small training data may not give a statistically significant frequency count. The possibility of over-fitting of the training data increases as the number of features increases, thus is prone to an inaccurate distribution estimate. By using gapped Kmers, Micheal et al. have made a meaningful attempt to define the features of genes [20–22]. The prospects of using this method in miRNA research are good, particularly for tasks such as finding miRNA precursors.

They use the observed gapped *k*-mer counts profile to estimate the ungapped *l*-mer frequencies. This method is more robust when utilizing smaller training data. Here, *k* and *l* are different numbers and, in most cases, *k* is less than *l*. The optimal function maximizes the entropy of *l*-mer frequencies, but this requires prohibitive numerical computation. As a good choice, the optimal function could be the minimum L2-norm estimate of *l*-mer frequencies. Giving an observed set of gapped *k*-mer frequencies, they derive an equation for the estimate. They prove that the method gives a more accurate estimate of the *l*-mer frequencies in benchmarks and real biological applications.

4 Ordinary Dimension Reduction Technologies

While the degenerate and gapped *k*-mer methods reduce the dimension of the miRNA data by biological reasoning, the problem can also be handled mathematically. Dimension reduction [23–30] is an interesting issue that bridges mathematics and information science. Those methods have been used to reduce the dimensionality of biological microarray data such as microarray expression data [31–33]. MiRNA microarray profiling has been used to detect many cancers [34].

There are many methods that have been developed that use multivariate statistical analysis to reduce the dimensionality. Methods can be divided into two categories: supervised methods and unsupervised methods. The differentiating factor between the two categories is whether or not a response vector is used. In the case of a binary classification problem, such as predicting the miRNA precursor, if we have a training data set and training data is classified, we can create a vector that contains zero and one (whether or not) to represent the classification result. This vector is called response vector. In the supervised dimension reduction methods, the response vector will "supervise" the dimension reduction process. It is a standard against which to judge the importance of the input variables in this process. Classified training sets do not always exist, however, so unsupervised dimension reduction techniques are widely used. In this section, we will give a short introduction to those dimension reduction technologies.

4.1 Supervised Methods

Sliced inverse regression or SIR [26, 28–30] is complex but useful method to achieve dimension reduction. It utilizes the response variable $X = [x_1, x_2, x_3, \ldots, xn]T$ that are the old variables, and $Y = [y_1, y_2, y_3, \ldots, yn]T$ are the new variables. $U = [u_1, u_2, u_3, \ldots, un]T$ is the orthonormalized transition matrix ($u_i^T u_i = 1, u_i^T u_j = 0$, $i \neq j$). The $z\ (p \times 1)$ are response vectors. Under some conditions, the information in $X = [x_1, x_2, x_3, \ldots, xn]T$ about z could be retained. If those conditions could be represented as a transformation matrix $\eta = (\eta 1, \eta 2, \ldots, \eta q)$ $(p \times q)$, and if $q \leq p$, with this progress, we could implement dimension reduction. The new feature vectors can be represented as ηTX. The space spanned by η could be called a dimension reduction subspace, and the center of all those spaces is the central subspace denoted as $S_{z|X}$. Li et al. have proven that the space $S_{E(X|z)} \subseteq S_{z|X}$, thus by using the conditional expectation E(X|z), $S_{z|X}$ could be determined easily. The conditional expectation E(X|z) is the expectation of the inverse regression. It could be computed as follows: slicing the response vector z, computing the expectation of X on every slice, and computed the mean of the X of all the slices as E(X|z).

Partial Least Squares or PLS is a supervised method to dimension reduction [23, 27]. Partial Least Squares need the response variable when training the data. Partial Least Squares produces several new vectors that are linear combinations of the old vectors. And those new vectors will most likely to produce the response variable. $X = [x_1, x_2, x_3, \ldots, xn]T$, $Y = [y_1, y_2, y_3, \ldots, yn]T$, $U = [u_1, u_2, u_3, \ldots, un]T$ are defined as before. The z is noted as the response vector. The yi and ui are obtained step by step like the progress in PCA (more details in the next section), but the optimized function is max(cov(Xui,z)).

4.2 Unsupervised Methods

Principal component analysis (PCA) is a commonly used method of dimension reduction [35–37]. The key idea of PCA is transforming the space of variables into a new space; in this new space the first few variables will retain a large part of the variation of the original variables. Viewed mathematically, those new variables are the linear combination of the old variables. As those first few variables represent most of the variation present in the data, those variables could be regarded as the principal components of the features of the data set, thus contributing the most to the changes in the data. X, Y, and U are defined as above. The y_i and u_i are obtained step by step where $y_1 = Xu_1$ and it optimizes max(var(Xu_1)), which means it has the largest variation. The resulting u_2 should be orthogonal to u_1, and satisfies the optimization of max (var(Xu_2)), which means that it has the second largest variation. The other transition vectors are obtained in the same manner. This transition matrix can be calculated by the eigen-decomposition of the covariance matrix of X.

Factor analysis supposes the observed variables are primarily defined by few unobserved variables and error [38]. Those unobserved variables are called factors. The observed variables were equal to the linear combinations of those factors and plus random errors. The factor analysis is looking for those common factors. PCA is often used to find those factors, but other methods like maximum likelihood can be used as well.

5 Conclusion

In this chapter, we have described some approaches to handle the high dimensionality of microRNA data. By using degenerated *k*-mers to describe the microRNA precursor, the length of the *k*-mer is dramatically decreased. By using gapped *k*-mer, the statistical error is decreased in the processing of high-dimension data. Some ordinary mathematical methods are also covered here. Those methods can be used to handle the microarray data of miRNA, the prediction of the miRNA precursor, and so on. Sliced inverse regression and Partial Least Squares are supervised dimensionality reduction methods, which need response vectors. Principal component analysis and factor analysis are unsupervised methods that can be applied in a much broader field.

References

1. Lee RC, Feinbaum RL, Ambros V (1993) The *C. elegans* heterochronic gene lin-4 encodes small RNAs with antisense complementarity to lin-14. Cell 75(5):843–854
2. Pritchard CC, Cheng HH, Tewari M (2012) MicroRNA profiling: approaches and considerations. Nat Rev Genet 13(5):358–369
3. Reinhart BJ, Slack FJ, Basson M, Pasquinelli AE, Bettinger JC, Rougvie AE, Horvitz HR, Ruvkun G (2000) The 21-nucleotide let-7 RNA regulates developmental timing in *Caenorhabditis elegans*. Nature 403(6772):901–906
4. Wightman B, Ha I, Ruvkun G (1993) Posttranscriptional regulation of the heterochronic gene lin-14 by lin-4 mediates temporal pattern formation in *C. elegans*. Cell 75(5):855–862
5. Lu J, Getz G, Miska EA, Alvarez-Saavedra E, Lamb J, Peck D, Sweet-Cordero A, Ebert BL, Mak RH, Ferrando AA (2005) MicroRNA expression profiles classify human cancers. Nature 435(7043):834–838
6. Herrera B, Lockstone H, Taylor J, Ria M, Barrett A, Collins S, Kaisaki P, Argoud K, Fernandez C, Travers M (2010) Global microRNA expression profiles in insulin target tissues in a spontaneous rat model of type 2 diabetes. Diabetologia 53(6):1099–1109
7. Pandey AK, Agarwal P, Kaur K, Datta M (2009) MicroRNAs in diabetes: tiny players in big disease. Cell Physiol Biochem 23(4–6):221–232
8. Zampetaki A, Kiechl S, Drozdov I, Willeit P, Mayr U, Prokopi M, Mayr A, Weger S, Oberhollenzer F, Bonora E (2010) Plasma microRNA profiling reveals loss of endothelial miR-126 and other microRNAs in type 2 diabetes. Circ Res 107(6):810–817
9. Liu B, Fang L, Wang S, Wang X, Li H, Chou K-C (2015) Identification of microRNA precursor with the degenerate K-tuple or Kmer strategy. J Theor Biol 385:153–159
10. Li A, Zhang J, Zhou Z (2014) PLEK: a tool for predicting long non-coding RNAs and messenger RNAs based on an improved k-mer scheme. BMC Bioinformatics 15(1):311
11. Zhang Y, Wang X, Kang L (2011) A k-mer scheme to predict piRNAs and characterize locust piRNAs. Bioinformatics 27(6):771–776
12. Chen W, Lei T-Y, Jin D-C, Lin H, Chou K-C (2014) PseKNC: a flexible web server for generating pseudo K-tuple nucleotide composition. Anal Biochem 456:53–60
13. Chen W, Zhang X, Brooker J, Lin H, Zhang L, Chou K-C (2014) PseKNC-general: a cross-platform package for generating various modes of pseudo nucleotide compositions. Bioinformatics 31(1):119–120
14. Chou K-C (2005) Using amphiphilic pseudo amino acid composition to predict enzyme subfamily classes. Bioinformatics 21(1):10–19
15. Chou KC (2001) Prediction of protein cellular attributes using pseudo-amino acid composition. Proteins 43(3):246–255
16. Xue C, Li F, He T, Liu G-P, Li Y, Zhang X (2005) Classification of real and pseudo microRNA precursors using local structure-sequence features and support vector machine. BMC Bioinformatics 6(1):310

17. Liu B, Fang L, Liu F, Wang X, Chen J, Chou K-C (2015) Identification of real microRNA precursors with a pseudo structure status composition approach. PLoS One 10:e0121501
18. Koboldt DC, Steinberg KM, Larson DE, Wilson RK, Mardis ER (2013) The next-generation sequencing revolution and its impact on genomics. Cell 155(1):27–38
19. Liu L, Li Y, Li S, Hu N, He Y, Pong R, Lin D, Lu L, Law M (2012) Comparison of next-generation sequencing systems. Biomed Res Int 2012:11
20. Ghandi M, Lee D, Mohammad-Noori M, Beer MA (2014) Enhanced regulatory sequence prediction using gapped k-mer features. PLoS Comput Biol 10(7):e1003711
21. Ghandi M, Mohammad-Noori M, Beer MA (2014) Robust k-mer frequency estimation using gapped k-mers. J Math Biol 69(2):469–500
22. Lee D, Gorkin DU, Baker M, Strober BJ, Asoni AL, McCallion AS, Beer MA (2015) A method to predict the impact of regulatory variants from DNA sequence. Nat Genet 47(8):955–961
23. Boulesteix A-L (2004) PLS dimension reduction for classification with microarray data. Stat Appl Genet Mol Biol 3(1):1–30
24. Dai JJ, Lieu L, Rocke D (2006) Dimension reduction for classification with gene expression microarray data. Stat Appl Genet Mol Biol 5(1)
25. Hero AO Dimension reduction for classification[J]
26. Li L, Simonoff JS, Tsai C-L (2007) Tobit model estimation and sliced inverse regression. Stat Modelling 7(2):107–123
27. Liu Y, Rayens W (2007) PLS and dimension reduction for classification. Comput Stat 22(2):189–208
28. Lue H-H (2009) Sliced inverse regression for multivariate response regression. J Stat Plan Inference 139(8):2656–2664
29. Wang H, Xia Y (2008) Sliced regression for dimension reduction. J Am Stat Assoc 103(482):811–821
30. Wu Q, Mukherjee S, Liang F (2009) Localized sliced inverse regression. In: Advances in neural information processing systems. MIT Press, Cambridge MA, pp 1785–1792
31. Li L, Li H (2004) Dimension reduction methods for microarrays with application to censored survival data. Bioinformatics 20(18):3406–3412
32. Hisaoka M, Matsuyama A, Nagao Y, Luan L, Kuroda T, Akiyama H, Kondo S, Hashimoto H (2011) Identification of altered MicroRNA expression patterns in synovial sarcoma. Genes Chromosomes Cancer 50(3):137–145
33. Li W, Ruan K (2009) MicroRNA detection by microarray. Anal Bioanal Chem 394(4):1117–1124
34. Konishi H, Ichikawa D, Komatsu S, Shiozaki A, Tsujiura M, Takeshita H, Morimura R, Nagata H, Arita T, Kawaguchi T (2012) Detection of gastric cancer-associated microRNAs on microRNA microarray comparing pre-and post-operative plasma. Br J Cancer 106(4):740–747
35. Abdi H, Williams LJ (2010) Principal component analysis. Wiley Interdiscip Rev Comput Stat 2(4):433–459
36. Jolliffe I (2002) Principal component analysis. Wiley Online Library, New Jersey
37. Wold S, Esbensen K, Geladi P (1987) Principal component analysis. Chemom Intell Lab Syst 2(1):37–52
38. Quackenbush J (2001) Computational analysis of microarray data. Nat Rev Genet 2(6):418–427

Chapter 14

Effective Removal of Noisy Data Via Batch Effect Processing

Ryan G. Benton

Abstract

In order to have faith in the analysis of data, a key factor is to have confidence that the data is reliable. In the case of microRNA, reliability includes understanding the collection methods, ensuring that the analysis is appropriate, and ensuring that the data itself is accurate. A key element in ensuring data accuracy is the removal of noise. While there can be several sources of noise, a common source of noise is the batch effect, which can be defined as systematic variability in the data caused by non-biological factors. This chapter will present various techniques designed to remove variability caused by batch effects and the potential effectiveness.

Key words MicroRNA, Batch effects, Normalization, Knowledge Discovery in Databases, Noise Removal

1 Introduction

Knowledge Discovery in Databases (KDD) is the process of collecting, cleaning, processing, and analyzing data for the purpose of obtaining nontrivial and usable knowledge and information [1]. The KDD process is loosely composed of five major steps: Selection, Preprocessing (Data Cleaning and Preparation), Transformation, Data Mining, and Interpretation/Evaluation. Of those five steps, one study indicated that 89% of 189 data miners spent 41% or more of their efforts on data cleaning/preparation part; 64% claimed they spent more than 60% of their time on data cleaning and preprocessing [2]. Other sources quote that preprocessing takes approximately 80% of the effort [3, 4]. Given the amount of time typically spent on preprocessing, it follows that this step has a great impact upon the trustworthiness of outcome of the KDD process; namely, that the knowledge obtained is truly reliable and useful. In addition, it also follows that ensuring that the preprocessing is done in an efficient manner will have a direct and disproportionate impact on the time required to obtain useable information.

A key component within the preprocessing stage is the removal of noise [5]. While the sources of the noise can vary, each cause of the noise can be viewed as a shift away from the actual value. This, in turn,

Jingshan Huang et al. (eds.), *Bioinformatics in MicroRNA Research*, Methods in Molecular Biology, vol. 1617, DOI 10.1007/978-1-4939-7046-9_14, © Springer Science+Business Media LLC 2017

can lead to a loss of information and a distortion within the analysis. Hence, it is desirable to remove the noise artifacts. In this chapter, we will be concentrating on how to handle a major type of noise typically encountered when utilizing microRNA: the batch effect.

2 Batch Effect

Batch effects have been defined as technical sources of variation obtained due to sampling [6], as the systematic non-biological variability that results from the sample processing and design of microarray experiments [7], or as additive-independent confounding factors [8]. The key concept is that the batch effects are caused by non-biological source and, assuming the factors/causes of it can be isolated, the data can be adjusted accordingly. Hence, the primary trick is how to effectively estimate the noise generated by the batch effects. In this section, we will introduce several methods used to treat batch effects; this list is not exhaustive but should provide an overview of many of the popular techniques. After discussing the batch effect removal techniques, we will detail several studies that compare the effectiveness of the approaches.

2.1 Batch Effects Techniques

2.1.1 Mean-Centering

One straightforward approach is to conduct mean-centering, which is the simplest type of Location and Scale (L/S) family of methods to remove batch effects. This calculates, for each batch, the mean of each feature. After the means are calculated, the values in each sample are then reduced by the mean [7]; this is shown in Eq. 1.

$$\tilde{\Upsilon}_{ijr}^{0} = \Upsilon_{ijr} - \overline{\Upsilon_{ij}} \quad (1)$$

$$\overline{\Upsilon_{ij}} = \frac{1}{n_i}\sum_{r=1}^{n_i}\Upsilon_{ijr} \quad (2)$$

where i is the batch number, N is the number of examples in the batch, n_i is the number of samples in the batch, j is the jth feature, $\tilde{\Upsilon}_{ijr}^{0}$ is the value for the rth sample of the ith batch for the jth feature, and $\overline{\Upsilon_{ij}}$ is the mean value of the jth feature for the ith batch. Technically, this is a zero-centering approach, as described in [9]. To approach a global mean-centered, the global mean across all batches would be calculated before the zero-centering occurred; one would then add the global mean to each zero-centered value [9]. It is possible to formally normalize the data by dividing by the standard deviation for each batch [10]; however, this appears to be optional. A variation of this approach is median-centering, in which the median value is used in place of mean [6]. The median-centering approach, in turn, has yet another variation [11], in which a median is calculated from a vector composed of the $\overline{\Upsilon_{ij}}$ values; this value is $\bar{\Upsilon}$. At that point, the $\tilde{\Upsilon}_{ijr}^{0}$ values are calculated via Eq. 3.

$$\tilde{\Upsilon}_{ijr}^{0} = \Upsilon_{ijr} - \left(\overline{\Upsilon}_{ij} - \overline{\Upsilon}\right) \tag{3}$$

2.1.2 Ratio-Based

Another approach is to create a ratio between a feature value and the feature mean, as seen in Eq. 4, where the mean could be either the arithmetic and geometric mean, as shown in Eq. 5. A study [12] generally indicated that using the ratio method using the geometric mean was generally preferable. Another study [7] generally indicated a preference for geometric mean, but did indicate preference for using the arithmetic mean whenever a number of values tended to be zero.

$$\tilde{\Upsilon}_{ijr}^{0} = \frac{\Upsilon_{ijr}}{\overline{\Upsilon}_{ij}} \tag{4}$$

$$\overline{\Upsilon_{ij}} = \left(\prod_{r=i}^{n_i} \Upsilon_{ijr}\right)^{\frac{1}{n_i}} \tag{5}$$

2.1.3 Quantile Normalization

In mean-centering, the goal was to adjust each variable such that the mean of each variable is zero and the standard deviation is between −1 and 1. For quantile normalization, the idea is to ensure each variable has the same distribution [13]. It is inspired by a quantile-quantile plot, where two different features have the same distribution if the plot shows a straight, diagonal line. The authors of [13] reasoned that, if one had J features, also called dimensions, each with the same distribution, the resulting plot would have a straight, diagonal line with a unit vector of $\left(\frac{1}{\sqrt{J}}, \ldots, \frac{1}{\sqrt{J}}\right)$; this unit vector is labeled as $\boldsymbol{d}$. This, in turn, suggested that a set of data (examples) could be transformed to ensure that they have the same distribution if the J features could be projected onto the same diagonal line represented by the unit vector $\boldsymbol{d}$. To accomplish this, a four-step process is required.

The first step is to create a matrix X, which has J rows and N columns, where each row is a feature and each column is an example. The second step is to create a new matrix, X_{sort}. X_{sort} is created by sorting each column such that the lowest value is in the first row, the second lowest is in the second row, and so forth. The third step calculates the mean across each row of X_{sort}; the values in each row are then replaced by that row's mean. The fourth step is to form $X_{\text{normalized}}$ by reordering each column of X_{sort} sort back to the original ordering of X. The matrix $X_{\text{normalized}}$ is then utilized for any analysis or learning rather than the original matrix X.

Some enhancements to the quantile normalization have been proposed over the years. Enhanced Quantile Normalization [14] presents the case that quantile normalization can be viewed as the decomposition of the original data into a normalized matrix

($X_{\text{normalized}}$) and a residual matrix (X_{residual}). The contention is that (a) the residual matrix may still contain some relevant information and (b) the normalization matrix may still contain noise. To resolve this, the residual matrix is also decomposed using quantile normalization again, resulting in a pure noise matrix (residual matrix of X_{residual}) and the matrix X_{rn}, which may contain potentially useful information. At this point, through the judicious use of SVD, a final matrix X_c is generated, which keeps the relevant substructure of $X_{\text{normalized}}$ while incorporating selected useful information from X_{rn}. Experiments in [14] indicated that the resulting matrix X_c was generally smaller than the $X_{\text{normalized}}$ while enhancing the subsequent analytical results.

Two other enhancements to the quantile normalization process are Subset Quantile Normalization [15] and Conditional Quantile Normalization [16]. Both start with the premise that, unlike Quantile Normalization, only subsets of the data should be used to determine the quantile information. In the case of Subset Quantile Normalization, once the negative samples were selected, the values were calculated as a weighted average of a parametric cumulative distribution function (CDF) and an empirical CDF. Conditional Quantile Normalization utilizes Subset Quantile Normalization but also has the ability to explicitly incorporate outside factors that cause systematic errors.

2.1.4 Surrogate Variable Analysis

Surrogate variable analysis (SVA) [17] was developed initially for gene expression analysis, where it was assumed that many factors, including those unknown and/or unmeasured, could have a strong detrimental impact. SVA is effectively a combination of a linear model with singular value decomposition, where the linear model is designed to incorporate both the known (primary) variables and the estimated (surrogate variables) to create a predictive model that estimates the target variable (dependent variable).

To construct the surrogate variables, a two-step process is required. In the first step, one must first calculate a basic model, as shown in Eq. 6; the residuals from that model are then calculated, which are used to create a residual matrix R.

$$x_{ij} = \mu_i + f(y_i) + e_{ij} \tag{6}$$

where x_{ij} is the jth value for output prediction i, μ_i is the expected baseline value, $f(y_i)$ is the mapping between the y_i, the variable of interest, and the output, and e_{ij} is random noise (typically with a mean of 0). Singular value decomposition is then performed on the residual matrix. At this point, a set of steps, based upon work in parallel analysis [18], are executed to determine which eigenvalues are a significant signature of the residuals. The end result is a set of K eigenvalues, which are then feed into step two, which constructs the surrogate variables. In step two, each eigenvalue is subject to regression to determine how associated it is with respect to the final prediction. A statistical test [19] is performed to determine which eigenvalues are sufficiently associated with the final predictions. At this point, using the eigenvalues that survived the testing, along with the information about the final targets, another round of transformations is done to construct the final surrogate variables. The final model then becomes Eq. 7,

$$x_{ij} = \mu_i + f(y_i) + \sum_{k=1}^{K} (\lambda_{ki} h_{kj}) + e_{ij} \tag{7}$$

where λ_{ki} is the weight with h_{kj} surrogate variable. It should be noted, SVA, unlike the previous approaches, assumes that the user knows what the final predictions are to be. Hence, SVA is not applicable for unsupervised techniques.

2.1.5 Combating Batch Effects When Combing Batches of Gene Expression Microarray Data

Combating Batch Effects when Combing Batches of Gene Expression Microarray Data (ComBat) [20] is an empirical Bayes method that is able to remove both additive and multiplicative batch effects. ComBat can be considered a type of the Location and Scale family of methods, abet using a slightly more complicated framework than that discussed in Subheading 2.1.1. For ComBat, the base equation is assumed to be

$$Y_{ijg} = \alpha_g + X\beta_g + \gamma_{ig} + \delta_{ig}\varepsilon_{ijg} \tag{8}$$

where Y_{ijg} represents the gth output for sample j from batch i, α_g is the overall base value for the gth output, X is a design matrix for the sample conditions, and β_g is the vector of the regression coefficients for X. The additive and multiplicative batch effects are represented by γ_g and δ_{ig} respectively, and the random noise by ε_{ijg} which is assumed to be centered at zero and has a variance of σ_g^2. Hence, in theory, to obtain the batch-corrected values Y_{ijg}^*, Eq. 9 could be utilized.

$$Y_{ijg}^* = \frac{Y_{ijg} - \hat{\alpha}_g - X\hat{\beta}_g - \hat{\gamma}_{ig}}{\hat{\delta}_{ig}} + \hat{\alpha}_g + X\hat{\beta}_g \tag{9}$$

where $\hat{\alpha}_g, X\hat{\beta}_g, \hat{\gamma}_{ig}$, and $\hat{\delta}_{ig}$ are the estimators of the respective parameters.

To find the estimators, three phases are required. The first phase seeks to standardize the data, which is composed of three steps. First, the parameters $\hat{\alpha}_g, \hat{\beta}_g$, and $\hat{\gamma}_{ig}$ are estimated using an ordinary least-squares approach. Next, the $\hat{\sigma}_g^2$ is estimated using Eq. 10, where N is the total number of samples. Finally, the standardized data is then calculated as Eq. 11.

$$\hat{\sigma}_g = \frac{1}{N}\sum_{ij}\left(\Upsilon_{ijg} - \hat{\alpha}_g - X\hat{\beta}_g - \hat{\gamma}_{ig}\right)^2 \quad (10)$$

$$Z_{ijg} = \frac{\Upsilon_{ijg} - \hat{\alpha}_g - X\hat{\beta}_g}{\hat{\sigma}_g} \quad (11)$$

The second phase seeks to determine the batch effect parameter estimates using the standardized data. A key assumption is that the standard data follows a normal distribution, as seen in Eq. 12.

$$Z_{ijg} \sim N\left(v_{ig}, \delta_{ig}^2\right) \quad (12)$$

At this point, two options exist for estimating the v_{ig} *and* δ_{ig}^2. The first option assumes that the parameters follow known distributions, which are $v_{ig} \sim N\left(v_i, \tau_i^2\right)$ and $\delta_{ig}^2 \sim \textit{Inverse Gamma}\left(\lambda_i, \theta_i\right)$. Estimating the parameters uses a combination of estimators and a method of moments. The second option is to utilize a nonparametric prior method; this is necessary when data does not fit the assumptions of a normal distribution for v_{ig} and an inverse gamma distribution for δ_{ig}^2. Whether the parametric approach is utilized or the nonparametric approach is utilized, the estimated parameters v_{ig}^* and δ_{ig}^{2*} are then utilized in the third phase.

The third phase is the simplest of the three as it adjusts the standardized data for the batch effects. However, instead of using Eq. 9, Eq. 13 is utilized instead to incorporate the Empirical Bayes estimated batch effects.

$$Z_{ijg}^* = \frac{\hat{\sigma}_g}{\hat{\delta}_{ig}}\left(Z_{ijg} - \hat{\varpi}_{ig}^*\right) + \hat{\alpha}_g + X\hat{\beta}_g \quad (13)$$

2.1.6 Cyclic Loess

While Cyclic Loess [21] was initially utilized to normalize cDNA microarray data, it has become a standard tool for normalization for microarray data, including microRNA. The basis of the method is based upon M and A plots, where $M_k = \log_2(x_{ki}/x_{kj})$, $A_k = \frac{1}{2}\log_2\left(x_{ki}x_{kj}\right)$, k is the kth feature out of J features, and i and j indicate examples, where $i \neq j$. A normalization curve is then fitted to the M versus A plot, using a local regression technique called Loess [22]. Once the normalization curve is calculated, the fits, $\hat{M}_k$, can be obtained from the curve, which allows the M_k value to be undergone a normalization adjustment, as seen in Eq. 14. From there, x_{ki} and x_{kj} can then be adjusted, using Eqs. 15 and 16 respectively.

$$M_k' = M_k - \hat{M}_k \quad (14)$$

$$x'_{ki} = 2^{A_k + \frac{M'_k}{2}} \tag{15}$$

$$x'_{kj} = 2^{A_k - \frac{M'_k}{2}} \tag{16}$$

As can be seen, the adjustments are based on two examples. To deal with multiple examples (arrays), as explained in [13], normalizations are carried out for all pair combinations, where the adjustments are recorded for each pair. After each iteration, the adjustments for each example are weighted equally and applied. According to [13], typically only a couple of iterations were required before any adjustments became small; it was acknowledged that the process for multiple examples could be time-consuming.

2.2 Effectiveness

A number of methods have been proposed for handling batch effects. Hence, a natural question would be which method should be utilized? Ideally, the answer would depend on the problem and ideally be guided by domain expertise. In practice, however, there may not be enough information to guide the selection. Hence, a number of studies have been conducted to determine the effectiveness of different techniques for removing batch effects. This section will present some of those studies and their conclusions.

In a recent thesis [7], a comparative study of different batch effect removal strategies was conducted on three datasets. The five strategies evaluated include mean-centering, both the parametric and nonparametric ComBat methods, SVA and ratio-based methods. The datasets were (a) a head and neck data, (b) melanoma methylation data, and (c) lung cancer microRNA data. The head and neck data was extracted from 29 head and neck cell lines, which was divided into two groups, namely normal cell fibroblast and tumor cell-associated fibroblast. Two batches of data were processed; the first batch contained 17 tumor samples and 10 normal samples while the second contained 12 tumor samples. With respect to the melanoma data, all 84 samples were tumor samples; the cause of the batch effects was the tissue-processing methods. Sixty-five were formalin fixed and paraffin embedded while 19 were frozen. Finally, the lung cancer data was composed of 85 normal tissue samples and 120 tumor samples, created from two batches of processing; this was the only dataset that was microRNA based. All 206 were used in the batch removal effort, but only a subset was used for the differential expression analysis. To determine the impact of batch removal, principal variance component analysis [23] was used to determine the amount of variability due to batch effect.

The analysis of the head and neck data, the melanoma data, and the lunch cancer data indicated that the batch effect and the interaction between batch and group effects accounted for 51.4%,

41.1%, and 26.8% of the overall variation of the data; conversely, the main group effect is 2.2%, 2.1%, and 9.3% of the variation. For the lung data, after the batch removal methods were employed, the variation due to batch effects was reduced to less than 2%; both variations of ComBat removed it completely. The variation to group effect was increased from 2.2% to 3.2% for mean-centering, 15.3% for the parametric ComBat, 14.6% for nonparametric ComBat, and 4.4% for SVA. Ratio-based methods were not used, as the second batch lacked a reference group. For the melanoma data, the mean-centering reduced the batch effect (and interaction term) to 1.2%; the other methods were generally less effective and either increased the interaction variation or left much of the batch effect present. For the lung cancer data, both versions of ComBat greatly increased the variability due to interaction, which offset their ability to reduce the batch effect. Mean-centering and SVA were both effective for this dataset. The ratio-methods were ineffective on all three datasets.

A second study [6] looked at impact on batch effect reduction in microRNAseq data. This study had liver samples from 24 patients; the samples were then divided into four groups. These were normal (six samples), steatosis (eight samples), steatohepatitis (seven samples), and cirrhosis (three samples). A library was constructed on the total RNA and microRNASeq was performed twice on the same library, using the same machine, but with the processing of the second batch occurring 10 days later. There were significant differences in the read counts and read alignments between pairs in batches A and B; ideally, the results between pairs should be perfectly matched. Hence, the goal was to test if batch effect removal would improve the matches. The study examined several different strategies including quantile normalization, conditional quantile normalization, and median-centering. To determine agreement, the study performed cluster analysis, to measure the distance between two samples. Subtyping accuracy was calculated as the number of correct pair agreements divided by the total number of pairs, which was 24. Before utilizing batch effect removal, the subtype accuracy was 8.3%. Quantile normalization had no impact on the task; the subtype accuracy remained at 8.3%. Conditional quantile normalization improved the accuracy to 29%. Interestingly, median-centering had the best impact, resulting in a subtype accuracy of 54.2%.

In [24], the impact on differential expression analysis of median quantization, quantile normalization, and cyclic loess normalization was investigated, along with other methods. In addition, the effect of combining ComBat with normalization was also explored; the study did not indicate whether the parametric or nonparametric version was utilized. The microRNA expression data was composed of 96 serous ovarian cancer cells and 96 endometrioid endometrial cancer cells. The results indicated that, without normalization, the true positive rate, false positive rate, and false discovery rate were

53%, 55%, and 90%. When median normalization was applied, rates of 85%, 11%, and 54% were achieved and when quantile normalization was utilized, rates of 93%, 12%, and 54% were obtained. Cyclic loess had rates of 96%, 12%, and 54%. When ComBat was utilized on the non-normalized data, the true positive rate, false positive rate, and false discovery rate were 66%, 1%, and 16%. When ComBat was applied first, followed by median normalization, the rates achieved were 84%, 4%, and 32%. When ComBat was applied first, followed by quantile normalized, the rates became 93%, 9%, and 48%; when cyclic loess was applied after ComBat, the rates were 91%, 7%, and 42%. It was concluded that the choice of normalization methods largely depended on the tradeoff desired between the true positive rate and false positive rate.

Another study [11] compared the effectiveness of three normalization techniques: Median normalization (of the global median variation), quantile normalization, and cyclic loess when applied to a single-color microRNA microarray dataset. To determine if the methods created a bias within the data, MA plots and loess curves were calculated on the adjusted data; the quantile normalization removed the most bias, whereas the other methods were not as effective. Similarly, when examining the removal of error variance, quantile normalization was again deemed the best at removing variance with respect to expression values. Quantile normalization also reduced the overall mean-squared error with respect to expression values.

3 Discussion

As can be seen in the previous section, there is still debate about which batch effect removal method results in the best performance, this is partly due to the fact that each study mentioned above, as well as other in the literature, are all dealing with different types of data, different types of problems, and different formulations for determining success. Moreover, in [9], it was determined that the use of study group or other forms of outcomes, when used as a covariate in removing batch effects, could lead to misleading results. Hence, the best advice in selecting and using batch removal techniques is two-fold. First, it would be advisable to test and evaluate multiple batch effect removal methods for a problem to ascertain the "best" for a given problem. Second, it is important to understand the potential biases that may be introduced by the removal; blind use of the procedures may result in unreliable outcomes. This, along with the fact that batch effects removal techniques are not sufficient for many problems, indicates that there are multiple opportunities to create better generic and problem-specific removal methods.

References

1. Aggarwal CC (2015) Data mining: the textbook. Springer, New York. doi:10.1007/978-3-319-14142-8
2. Munson MA (2012) A study on the importance of and time spent on different modeling steps. ACM SIGKDD Explor Newsl 13:65–71. doi:10.1145/2207243.2207253
3. Adriaans P, Zantinge D (1996) Data mining. Addison-Wesley, Reading, MA
4. Duhamel A, Nuttens MC, Devos P et al (2003) A preprocessing method for improving data mining techniques. Application to a large medical diabetes database. Stud Heal Technol Inf 95:269–274
5. Jiawei H, Kamber M, Han J, Pei J (2012) Data mining: concepts and techniques. Morgan Kaufmann Publishers, Walthham, MA. doi: 10.1016/B978-0-12-381479-1.00001-0
6. Guo Y, Zhao S, Su P-F et al (2014) Statistical strategies for microRNAseq batch effect reduction. Transl Cancer Res 3:260–265
7. Ding F (2013) A comparative study of different strategies of batch effect removal in microarray data: a case study of three datasets. Master thesis, University of Pittsburgh
8. Vaisipour S (2014) Detecting, correcting, and preventing the batch effects in multi-site data, with a focus on gene expression microarrays. Doctoral thesis, University of Alberta
9. Nygaard V, Rødland EA, Hovig E (2016) Methods that remove batch effects while retaining group differences may lead to exaggerated confidence in downstream analyses. Biostatistics 17:29–39
10. Li C, Wong WH (2001) Model-based analysis of oligonucleotide arrays: expression index computation and outlier detection. Proc Natl Acad Sci U S A 98:31–36
11. Rao Y, Lee Y, Jarjoura D et al (2008) A comparison of normalization techniques for microRNA microarray data. Stat Appl Genet Mol Biol 7:Article22
12. Park T, Tsui SK-W, Chen L, et al (2010) 2010 {IEEE} International conference on bioinformatics and biomedicine, {BIBM} 2010, Hong Kong, China, Dec 18–21, 2010, Proceedings
13. Bolstad BM, Irizarry RA, Astrand M, Speed TP (2003) A comparison of normalization methods for high density oligonucleotide array data based on variance and bias. Bioinformatics 19:185–193. doi:10.1093/bioinformatics/19.2.185
14. Hu J, He X (2007) Enhanced quantile normalization of microarray data to reduce loss of information in gene expression profiles. Biometrics 63:50–59
15. Wu Z, Aryee MJ (2010) Subset quantile normalization using negative control features. J Comput Biol 17:1385–1395
16. Hansen KD, Irizarry RA, Wu Z (2012) Removing technical variability in RNA-seq data using conditional quantile normalization. Biostatistics 13:204–216
17. Leek JT, Storey JD (2007) Capturing heterogeneity in gene expression studies by surrogate variable analysis. PLoS Genet 3:1724–1735
18. Buja A, Eyuboglu N (1992) Remarks on parallel analysis. Multivariate Behav Res 27: 509–540
19. Storey JD, Tibshirani R (2003) Statistical significance for genomewide studies. Proc Natl Acad Sci U S A 100:9440–9445
20. Johnson WE, Li C, Rabinovic A (2007) Adjusting batch effects in microarray expression data using empirical Bayes methods. Biostatistics 8:118–127. doi:10.1093/biostatistics/kxj037
21. Dudoit S, Yang YH, Callow MJ, Speed TP (2002) Statistical methods for identifying differentially expressed genes in replicated cDNA microarray experiments. Stat Sin 12: 111–139
22. Cleveland WS, Devlin SJ (1988) Locally weighted regression: an approach to regression analysis by local fitting. J Am Stat Assoc 83:596
23. Scherer A (2009) Batch effects and noise in microarray experiments: sources and solutions. Wiley Blackwell, Oxford
24. Qin LX, Zhou Q (2014) MicroRNA array normalization: an evaluation using a randomized dataset as the benchmark. PLoS One 9:e98879

Chapter 15

Logical Reasoning (Inferencing) on MicroRNA Data

Jingsong Wang

Abstract

Logical reasoning played an important role in artificial intelligence. Applying logical reasoning on microRNA data brings intelligence into data analysis. Here, we provide basic introduction about logic (especially propositional logic) and automated reasoning based on knowledge described in the form of logic rules. We also introduce tools that could be used for building automated reasoning systems with microRNA data.

Key words Logical reasoning, Propositional logic, Inference rule

1 Introduction of Knowledge-Based Systems and Inference

Logics are formal languages that focus on knowledge representation and inference. They investigate fundamental problems such as truth and axiomatizable theories. In computer science, logics have been used for solving many problems, such as program verification, automated theory proving, and logic programming. Logics have played an important role especially in the area of artificial intelligence to build expert systems, where people use logics as a tool to describe their knowledge and understanding of the world, and use logical reasoning to draw new conclusions.

McCarthy's proposal [1] defines a system with two components: "a knowledge base, which encodes what we know about the world, and a reasoner (inference engine), which acts on the knowledge base to answer queries of interest...This aspect of the proposal became the basis for a class of reasoning systems known as knowledge-based or model-based systems, which have dominated the area of automated reasoning since then" [2]. Systems built in such a way separate our knowledge description from the actual reasoning process. Due to the express power of logics, especially first-order logic (FOL), logic rules are widely used to build the knowledge base. Meanwhile, logical deduction is used as the reasoning engine.

Jingshan Huang et al. (eds.), *Bioinformatics in MicroRNA Research*, Methods in Molecular Biology, vol. 1617, DOI 10.1007/978-1-4939-7046-9_15, © Springer Science+Business Media LLC 2017

Computer science studies the problem of automated reasoning, i.e., it focuses on how to make reasoning programmable. Logic provides us with formal languages with which we can describe our knowledge and define the reasoning process formally. Such a kind of languages makes automated reasoning possible through the use of computers.

A reasoning algorithm, or an inference algorithm, is a procedure for deriving a sentence from the knowledge base (*KB*). The basic problem of inference can be expressed in the following way:

- We have a *KB* (which consists of a set of sentences).
- We have a query *Q* (which is a sentence).
- We want to determine whether KB entails *Q*, denoted by *KB* |= *Q*.[1]

Note that an inference algorithm is sound if it derives only sentences that are entailed by the knowledge base, and an inference algorithm is complete if it can derive any sentence that is entailed by the knowledge base.

An inference engine is normally a software program that implements some inference algorithms. Thus, it can be used to automatically generate new facts or answer queries from a given knowledge base.

By definition, *KB* |= *Q* means every model of *KB* will be a model of *Q*. So a naive approach for inference is to do model checking, i.e., we iterate all the possible settings of the symbols. This approach is sound and complete. However, it is 2^n complexity. In practice, we mostly resort to other approaches, such as resolution and chaining (which includes forward chaining and backward chaining[2]). We will introduce these approaches in the following sections, using the language of propositional logic.

2 Propositional Logic and Inference

We give basic introduction of propositional logic in this section and also briefly cover concepts of first-order logic. A logic needs to provide its definition of syntax (how legal sentences are defined), semantics (what does a sentence mean), and inference procedure (what sentence can we conclude based on existing knowledge). So the introduction comes with a set of definitions first, which are the building blocks for propositional logic. We borrow most definitions from [3] and follow its way of naming.

[1] Informally speaking, we want to prove *Q* based on *KB*.

[2] Here we focus on logic deduction, even though there are also other approaches regarding the inference process, such as abduction and induction.

2.1 Propositional Logic

Propositional logic studies propositions and relationships among them. These propositions are the simplest atomic sentences. For example, below are a set of atomic sentences:

Biologists study living organisms.

Bacteria are single-celled organisms.

DNA is a molecule.

Atomic sentences such as above normally could have a value, which we called *truth value*, indicating the relation of corresponding proposition to truth. The truth value can be either *true* or *false* in classical logic.[3] The subjective of propositional logic is to formally define truth values of more complex propositions based on the truth value of atomic propositions that compose them.

Definition 1
Syntax:

An atomic formula has the form Ai, where $i \geq 1$. Then we can define formulas:

1. *Atomic formulas are formulas.*
2. *If A is a formula, then $\neg A$ is a formula.*
3. *If both A and B are formulas, then both $A \wedge B$ and $A \vee B$ are formulas.*

Definition 2
Semantics:

We use set $\{0, 1\}$ to represent truth values. Function $\upsilon: \Psi \rightarrow \{0, 1\}$, where Ψ is any subset of the atomic formulas, is called an assignment. For a function $\upsilon': \Psi' \rightarrow \{0, 1\}$, where Ψ' is the set of formulas that are composed only by atomic formulas from Ψ, i.e., $\Psi \subseteq \Psi'$, then we can define:

1. *For atomic formula $A_i \in \Psi$, $\upsilon'(A_i) = \upsilon(A_i)$.*
2. *$\upsilon'(\neg A) = 1$, when $\upsilon'(A) = 0$. Otherwise, $\upsilon'(\neg A) = 0$.*
3. *$\upsilon'(A \wedge B) = 1$, when $\upsilon'(A) = 1$ and $\upsilon'(B) = 1$. Otherwise, $\upsilon'(A \wedge B) = 0$.*
4. *$\upsilon'(A \vee B) = 1$, when $\upsilon'(A) = 1$ or $\upsilon'(B) = 1$. Otherwise, $\upsilon'(A \vee B) = 0$.*

From the above definitions, we can see that the truth value of a formula can be determined given an assignment over atomic formulas occurring in it.

[3] Multi-valued logics (such as fuzzy logic) allow for more than two truth values, which can be interpreted as degrees of truth. This however is not the topic of this chapter. Here, we only use *true* or *false* for truth value.

Definition 3

Suitable Assignment:

If an assignment $\upsilon: \Psi \rightarrow \{0, 1\}$ *is defined over all atomic formulas contained by a formula A,* i.e., Ψ = *{atomic formulas of A}, then* υ *is suitable for A.*

Definition 4

Model:

If an assignment υ *is suitable for a formula A and* $\upsilon(A) = 1$, *then* υ *is a model of A, denoted by* $\upsilon / = A$.

Definition 5

Satisfiable and Unsatisfiable:

If a formula A has at least one model, then it is satisfiable. Otherwise, formula A is unsatisfiable.

Based on the above definitions, we can see that we can test all possible assignments over atomic formulas occurring in a formula to determine whether it is satisfiable. This is called the truth table method. Even though this approach is sound and complete, and it is programmable, it does not have good performance, which is exponential regarding the number of atomic formulas. For a formula containing *n* atomic formulas, we will have to evaluate 2^n assignments. The satisfiability problem (SAT) is actually NP-complete. Thus, in practice, we often resort to other more efficient approaches.

Definition 6

Consequence (Entailment):

For a set of formulas $\Delta = \{F_1, ..., F_n\}$ $(n \geq 1)$ *and a formula A, in case that, given any assignment* υ *that is suitable for each of A,* F_1, ..., *and* F_n, *if* υ *is a model of formula* $F_1 \wedge F_2 \wedge ... \wedge F_n$, *then it is also a model of A, we say that A is a logical consequence (entailment) of* Δ. *We can denote this by* $\Delta \models A$.

It is easy to prove that if *A* is a consequence of Δ, then formula $F_1 \wedge F_2 \wedge ... \wedge F_n \wedge \neg A$ is unsatisfiable. Actually, we can even prove that the reverse is also true. This relationship between logical consequence and satisfiability is described in the following theorem:

Theorem 7

For a set of formulas $\Delta = \{F_1, ..., F_n\}$ $(n \geq 1)$ *and a formula A,* $\Delta \models A$ *if and only if* $F_1 \wedge F_2 \wedge ... \wedge F_n \wedge \neg A$ *is unsatisfiable.*

Theorem 7 is important in logical proof methods because it allows us to reduce the problem of determining logical consequence to checking satisfiability.

Above are basic definitions and theorems that are foundations of propositional logic. For more complete information, please *see* [3].

2.2 Inference Rules

Inference rules in logic are patterns that we can use to apply on existing sentences to derive new conclusions. The patterns can be expressed in a form like

$$\frac{P_1, P_2, \ldots, P_n}{C}$$

where P_n is premise and C is conclusion.

Figure 1 shows a list of major rules for inference that were summarized in [4]. With these rules, we can draw logically sound conclusions given a knowledge base that consists of a set of sentences. With inference rules, an inference engine (a software program) can automate the process of adding new facts into the knowledge base through pattern searching and matching.

Rule	Name
$\frac{A \rightarrow B, A}{B}$	Modus Ponens
$\frac{A \rightarrow B, \neg B}{\neg A}$	Modus Tollens
$\frac{A \vee B, \neg A}{B}$	Disjunctive Syllogism
$\frac{A \rightarrow B, B \rightarrow C}{A \rightarrow C}$	Hypothetical Syllogism
$\frac{A \wedge B}{A}$	Simplification
$\frac{A}{A \vee B}$	Addition
$\frac{A, B}{A \wedge B}$	Conjunction
$\frac{A \vee B, \neg A \vee C}{B \vee C}$	Resolution

Fig. 1 Inference Rules

We will start to introduce resolution first, which is a sound and complete proof strategy. We will also introduce the chaining-based approaches, whose inference procedure however is not complete, or is complete only for a *KB* that is in some restricted forms, such as Horn form (a conjunction of Horn clauses, which will be defined in the next section). The chaining inference approaches based on inference rules with the use of modus ponens can be categorized into two sets: forward chaining and backward chaining, which will be explained separately. More detailed introduction about chaining can be found in [5].

Note that all these inference approaches work with both propositional logic and first-order logic. However, we only describe the propositional logic version for ease of understanding and discussion.

2.2.1 Resolution

Resolution is a powerful inference rule for propositional logic (also for first-order logic). Basically, there is only a single rule that can be repeatedly used. However with the help of resolution, we are able to build an inference engine that is sound and complete.

Resolution was invented by Robinson [6]. The goal of resolution is to prove unsatisfiability of a formula. Note that many problems can be reduced to unsatisfiability problem.

In order to apply resolution, we require that the set of formulas are in conjunctive normal form (CNF) defined below. Note that we can always convert a formula into its CNF.

Definition 8
Conjunctive Normal Form:

If a formula is in a form of a conjunction of disjunctions of literals, we say that the formula is in conjunctive normal form. Note that a literal is either an atomic formula, or negation of an atomic formula. The set of literals appearing in a disjunction is called a clause. Thus a formula in CNF can be represented as a set of clauses.

Note that a clause that contains at most one positive literal is called *Horn clause*, and a formula in CNF whose clauses are all Horn clauses is a *Horn formula*.

Horn clauses can be written in a form of implication, where the premise is the conjunction of a set of positive literals and the conclusion can be a positive literal. Also note that a Horn clause with exactly one positive literal is called *definite clause*. A definite clause consisting of one literal, which is positive, is a *fact*. Horn clauses are widely used in inference as deciding entailment with Horn clauses can be done in time linear in the size of *KB*.

Definition 9
Resolvent:

If C_1 *and* C_2 *are clauses that contain literals* L_1 *and* L_2 *separately,* i.e., $L_1 \in C_1$ *and* $L_2 \in C_2$, *where* L_1 *and* L_2 *are complementary literals, then* $(C_1 - \{L_1\}) \cup (C_2 - \{L_2\})$ *is a clause that is called resolvent of* C_1 *and* C_2. *Note that atomic formula and its negation make a pair of complementary literals.*

Note that any resolvent of C_1 and C_2 (of Definition 9) is a consequence of $\{C_1, C_2\}$. Also a resolvent can be an empty clause. This happens when both L_1 and L_2 are the only literals of C_1 and C_2 separately (Remember that L_1 and L_2 are complementary literals). We denote the empty clause by $\square$. Note that empty clause is unsatisfiable, and a set of clauses that contain empty clause is unsatisfiable.

Also, if we use R to represent one of such resolvents, and then for a formula A in CNF that is represented by a set of clauses, denoted by $\mathbb{C}$, where $C_1 \in \mathbb{C}$ and $C_2 \in \mathbb{C}$, and a formula B that is represented by the set of clauses $\mathbb{C} \cup \{R\}$, then we can prove that A and B are equivalent, i.e., any assignment that is suitable for A and B, it evaluates A and B the same truth value. The detailed proof can be found in [3].

So we can extend a set of clauses $\mathbb{C}$ by adding a resolvent of any two clauses from $\mathbb{C}$ to form a new set $\mathbb{C}'$. We can repeat the same step on the new set $\mathbb{C}'$. If we keep repeating such a process, it can be proved that, after a finite step, we will get a stable set of clauses that will not change, i.e., we cannot produce new resolvent from the set. We denote such a final set as $\mathbb{C}^*$.

Theorem 10

A set of clauses $\mathbb{C}$ *is unsatisfiable if and only if* $\square \in \mathbb{C}^*$.

We skip the proof for Theorem 10. Please check [3] for a detailed proof.

Based on Theorem 10, we can determine a set of clauses $\mathbb{C}$ is unsatisfiable once we find an empty clause from $\mathbb{C}^*$. The process of finding empty clause is called *derivation*, with which we can prove unsatisfiability of the original set of clauses.

Therefore, given a knowledge base KB and a query Q, with resolution we can use proof by refutation to prove $KB \models Q$. The basic process is shown in Fig. 2 (Algorithm 1). Note that resolution is sound and complete for proof by refutation.

2.2.2 Forward Chaining

Forward chaining approach is data driven. We start from facts, and use available facts to match premises of available rules to derive new facts. The new facts will be added to KB for inference until the query is found, which is normally represented by a conjunction of goals.

The basic idea of forward chaining can be described in the following steps:

Step 1: Create a fact base that is initialized with available facts in the KB.

Step 2: Fire all rules whose premises are satisfied by facts from current fact base.

Step 3: Add all the conclusions to the fact base.

Step 4: Stop if all goals are in the fact base or no new facts are added to the fact base. Otherwise, we repeat step 2.

Algorithm 1 Propositional Resolution

```
function RESOLUTION(KB, Q)                          ▷ Q is the query
    clause set 𝒞 ← CNF representation of KB and ¬Q
    resolvent set Θ ← {};
    while true do
        n ← |Θ|;
        for each clause C_i ∈ 𝒞 do
            for each clause C_j ∈ 𝒞 do
                R ← resolvent of C_i, C_j;
                if R exists then
                    if □ ∈ R then
                        return true;
                    else
                        Θ ← Θ ∪ R;
                    end if
                end if
            end for
        end for
        n′ ← |Θ|;
        if n = n′ then
            return false;
        end if
        𝒞 ← 𝒞 ∪ Θ;
    end while
end function
```

Fig. 2 Algorithm 1: Propositional Resolution

Figure 3 (Algorithm 2) shows the basic procedure of forward chaining in a form of function.

We can see that forward chaining is an approach that we tend to generate everything based on existing facts. It may not be efficient in some cases as we might generate much more irrelevant conclusions before all goals are included.

There are some algorithms proposed to address the efficiency problem, such as Rete [7], developed by Charles Forgy.

2.2.3 Backward Chaining

Backward chaining approach is goal driven. Unlike forward chaining, which starts from facts, backward chaining starts from the query, which is normally represented by a conjunction of goals. We try to prove all premises of rules that conclude the query.

The basic idea of backward chaining can be described in the following steps:

Step 1: Create a fact base that is initialized with available facts in the *KB*.

Step 2: Create a hypothesis set that is initialized with goals.

Step 3: If the hypothesis set is not empty, choose one goal from it to validate.

Algorithm 2 Forward Chaining

```
function FC(KB, Q)                                        ▷ Q is the query
    fact base set Ω ← facts in KB;
    rule base set Γ ← rules in KB;
    goal set Θ ← goals from Q;
    while not Θ ⊆ Ω do
        n ← |Ω|;
        for each rule R ∈ Γ, which concludes C do
            premise set Φ ← premises of R;
            if Φ ⊆ Ω then
                Ω ← Ω ∪ {C};
            end if
        end for
        n′ ← |Ω|;
        if n = n′ then
            return false;
        end if
    end while
    return true;
end function
```

Fig. 3 Algorithm 2: Forward Chaining

- If the goal is in fact base, then we eliminate it from the hypothesis set.
- Otherwise, we find a rule that concludes the goal. We add all premises of the rule that are not in fact base into the hypothesis set.

Step 4: Stop if hypothesis set is empty. Otherwise, we repeat step 3.

Figure 4 (Algorithm 3) shows the basic procedure of backward chaining in a form of function.

2.3 First-Order Logic and Reasoning Under Uncertainty

Propositional logic alone is not expressive enough for practical knowledge representation and reasoning. On the one hand, for many real-world problems, we need to represent more general objects and properties, and the functions and relationship among objects. In addition, even the rules of inference need to be more general. Therefore, we need more expressive and powerful languages. On the other hand, the knowledge we have in the real world always comes with uncertainty. For example, we are not sure, or not accurately certain about the data quality, or the rules we can use are not 100% appropriate. Thus, we have to handle the problem of reasoning under uncertainty.

2.3.1 First-Order Logic

First-order logic (or predicate logic) extends and generalizes propositional logic by introducing new concepts such as constants, variables, functions, predicates, and quantifiers. These new concepts make building more complex sentences possible.

Algorithm 3 Backward Chaining

```
function BC(KB, Q)                                   ▷ Q is the query
    fact base Ω ← facts in KB;
    rule base Γ ← rules in KB;
    hypothesis set Θ ← goals from Q;
    while Θ ≠ ∅ do
        n ← |Θ|;
        pick a G ∈ Θ;
        if G ∈ Ω then
            Θ ← Θ − {G};
        else
            if exist a rule R ∈ Γ that concludes G then
                for each premise P of R do
                    Θ ← Θ ∪ {P};
                end for
            end if
        end if
        n′ ← |Θ|;
        if n = n′ then
            return false;
        end if
    end while
    return true;
end function
```

Fig. 4 Algorithm 3: Backward Chaining

For example, below are examples of knowledge that we want to describe, which, however, could not be represented by propositional logic:

There are some organisms that are single-celled.

All organisms have RNA.

Using first-order logic, we can describe the above sentences in the following form:

$\exists x(\mathit{Organism}(x) \wedge \mathit{SingleCelled}(x))$

$\forall x(\mathit{Organism}(x) \rightarrow \mathit{Has}(\mathit{RNA}))$

In the above examples, we have used the existential quantifier ("$\exists$") and universal quantifier ("$\forall$"). We have also used variable ("x"), constant ("*RNA*"), and predicate ("*Organism*," "*SingleCelled*," and "*Has*"). Here "x" and "*RNA*" are terms. "$\mathit{Organism}(x)$," "$\mathit{SingleCelled}(x)$," and "$\mathit{Has}(\mathit{RNA})$" are formulas, which are actually atomic formulas. "$\exists x(\mathit{Organism}(x) \wedge \mathit{SingleCelled}(x))$" and "$\forall x(\mathit{Organism}(x) \rightarrow \mathit{Has}(\mathit{RNA}))$" are also formulas, which have "x" as *bound* variable and no *free* variables. Thus they are called *closed* formulas.

Compared with propositional logic, first-order logic brings many new features to logic language family, and thus has highly increased the expressive power to help people handle real-world problems. However, the better express power also means more complex procedure when doing reasoning.

For example, even though resolution still works with first-order logic, a few extra steps that we do not need to consider with propositional logic are now necessary. One problem is that we need to extend propositional resolution to handle variables and quantifiers. Therefore, given a formula, we need first to standardize variables so that one variable will be quantified only once in the formula. Then, we need to eliminate existential quantifier and universal quantifier sequentially. This process is called *Skolemization*, which will convert a first-order formula while maintaining its satisfiability. After that, we can work on transforming the formula into its CNF form.

For the first-order logic version of resolution, each resolution step comes with a substitution of variables, which will make two clauses resolvable. Such a substitution is called *unifier*. There might be multiple unifiers for a set of unifiable literals. However, we will only look for the *most general unifier* (MGU) that makes the least substitutions needed. The way of producing MGU is a very important process during FOL resolution. The original algorithm was introduced by Robinson [6, 8] and people have been working on finding more efficient algorithms as its pattern matching nature is important also for many other applications. The unification is also useful when doing *answer extraction*. However, for the problem of answer extraction, we do not have to terminate until empty clause is found.

2.3.2 Reasoning Under Uncertainty

Another problem in the real world we have to handle is reasoning under uncertainty. For example, in many cases, the knowledge we have may look like the following sentence:

DNA is almost the same for cells of the same organism.

Describing such knowledge requires more powerful languages that traditional first-order logic cannot fit, as it only handles true and false values, which are not always applicable for modern expert systems. Besides knowledge representation, we also need to be able to do reasoning with such a kind of languages.

There have been many works targeting such a problem from difference perspectives. From logic perspective, there have been fuzzy logic and multivalued logic. From the reasoning approach perspective, there has been work of combining first-order logic with probabilistic models, such as Bayesian networks. More discussions about uncertainty handling can be found in [9].

3 MicroRNA Data and Reasoning Tools

It has been found that microRNA (miRNA) plays important roles in both living organism development and genetic diseases. To discover functions of miRNA, researchers have been focusing on identifying miRNAs and their target genes as well as relationships between them at the post-transcriptional level of the gene regulatory network [10]. Many public databases have been used to help researchers to validate or build models to predict the most effectively targeted messenger RNA (mRNA). These databases include PubMed, miRDB, TargetScan, miRanda, and so on. However, as a fact that different research communities may have been using different methodologies and describing experiments in different formats, common features from different sources may be presented in totally different ways. Complexities from data create difficulties for researchers and make miRNA knowledge discovery a time-consuming and error-prone task.

Ontology has been used in bioinformatics to annotate database records and support data consistency. Researchers have been motivated to develop open ontologies that use Web Ontology Language (OWL), a semantic web language, to standardize representations of samples, assays, and data analysis methods [11], including domain-specific ontologies, such as the miRNA domain-specific application ontology [12].

The formal basis of OWL is description logic (DL), a decidable fragment of first-order logic. Description logic [13, 14] is a logic language family that can formally represent the terminological knowledge of an application domain in a structured way. It defines *concepts*, *roles*, and *individuals* and thus makes knowledge easy to read and understand, while, unlike FOL, having effective procedures for deciding the inference problems. Informally speaking, we can map DL terms into corresponding FOL ones. For example, individual names correspond to constants of FOL, while concept names and role names correspond to unary predicates and binary predicates of FOL separately. Thus, all the DL reasoning problems can be translated to equivalent reasoning problems of FOL.

There have been various tools that can be used to build knowledge base for knowledge representation and knowledge-based reasoning. One of the most widely used programming languages in the logic programming paradigm is Prolog [15]. Prolog is based on first-order logic over Horn clauses, and its inference uses first-order resolution (SLD-resolution [16]) and backward chaining. The frequently used rule engine for Java platform is Drool [17], which is based on forward and backward chaining methods. Jess [18] is also used to build expert systems based on rules, which supports declarative approach. Jess supports forward and backward chaining and working memory queries. Both Drool and Jess's inference engines use Rete pattern matching algorithm [7] to optimize inference speed.

Regarding building more robust inference engines that support semantic-based reasoning, besides general-purpose logical reasoning, ontology languages (especially description logic languages) are commonly used to specify rules in knowledge base.

Apache Jena [19], an open-source semantic web framework for Java, provides rich APIs to interact with RDF and OWL languages. We can use Protégé [20], an open-source ontology editor, to load, edit, and save OWL and RDF ontologies. Its ontology visualization allows researchers to navigate ontology relationships in an interactive and powerful way.

References

1. McCarthy J (1960) Programs with common sense. RLE and MIT Computation Center, pp 300–307
2. Darwiche A (2009) Modeling and reasoning with Bayesian networks. Cambridge University Press, Cambridge
3. Schöning U (2001) Logic for computer scientists. Birkhäuser Boston, c/o Springer-Verlag New York, Inc., New York, NY
4. Rosen KH, Krithivasan K (1995) Discrete mathematics and its applications, vol 6. McGraw-Hill, New York, NY
5. Russell SJ, Norvig P, Canny JF, Malik JM, Edwards DD (2003) Artificial intelligence: a modern approach, vol 2. Prentice Hall, Upper Saddle River
6. Robinson JA (1965) A machine-oriented logic based on the resolution principle. JACM 12(1):23–41
7. Forgy CL (1982) Rete: a fast algorithm for the many pattern/many object pattern match problem. Artif Intell 19:17–37. doi:10.1016/0004-3702(82)90020-0
8. Robinson JA (1971) Computational logic: the unification computation. In: Meltzer B, Michie D (eds) Machine intelligence, vol 6. Edinburgh University Press, Edinburgh, Scotland, pp 63–72
9. Wang J, Byrnes J, Valtorta M, Huhns M (2012) On the combination of logical and probabilistic models for information analysis. Appl Intell 36(2):472
10. Tran DH, Satou K, Ho TB (2008) Finding microRNA regulatory modules in human genome using rule induction. BMC Bioinformatics 9(12):1
11. Bandrowski A, Brinkman R, Brochhausen M, Brush MH, Bug B, Chibucos MC et al (2016) The ontology for biomedical investigations. PLoS One 11(4):e0154556
12. Huang J, Gutierrez F, Strachan HJ, Dou D, Huang W, Smith B, Blake AJ, Eilbeck K, Natale DA, Lin Y, Wu B, de Silva N, Wang X, Liu Z, Borchert GM, Tan M, Ruttenberg A (2016) OmniSearch: a semantic search system based on the Ontology for MIcroRNA Target (OMIT) for microRNA-target gene interaction data. J Biomed Semantics 7:25
13. Baader F, Sattler U (2001) An overview of tableau algorithms for description logics. Stud Logica 69(1):5–40
14. Calvanese D, De Giacomo G, Lenzerini M, Nardi D (2001) Reasoning in expressive description logics. In: Robinson A, Voronkov A (eds) Handbook of automated reasoning, vol 2. Elsevier Science, Amsterdam, pp 1581–1634
15. Roussel F (1975) Prolog: Manuel de reference et d'Utilisation. Groupe d'Intelligence Artificielle, Marseille-Luminy
16. Kowalski R, Kuehner D (1971) Linear resolution with selection function. Artif Intell 2(3–4):227–260
17. Browne P (2009) JBoss Drools business rules. Packt Publishing Ltd., Birmingham, UK
18. Jess, the Rule Engine for the Java Platform (Sept 2009) by Sandia National Laboratories. http://www.jessrules.com/jess
19. Apache Jena, A free and open source Java framework for building Semantic Web and Linked Data applications. https://jena.apache.org
20. Musen MA (2015) The Protégé project: a look back and a look forward. AI Matters 1(4):4–12. doi:10.1145/2757001.2757003, http://protege.stanford.edu

Chapter 16

Machine Learning Techniques in Exploring MicroRNA Gene Discovery, Targets, and Functions

Sumi Singh, Ryan G. Benton, Anurag Singh, and Anshuman Singh

Abstract

In recent years, the role of miRNAs in post-transcriptional gene regulation has provided new insights into the understanding of several types of cancers and neurological disorders. Although miRNA research has gathered great momentum since its discovery, traditional biological methods for finding miRNA genes and targets continue to remain a huge challenge due to the laborious tasks and extensive time involved. Fortunately, advances in computational methods have yielded considerable improvements in miRNA studies. This literature review briefly discusses recent machine learning-based techniques applied in the discovery of miRNAs, prediction of miRNA targets, and inference of miRNA functions. We also discuss the limitations of how these approaches have been elucidated in previous studies.

Key words MicroRNA, mRNA, Target prediction, Machine learning, Data mining, miRNA target prediction, miRNA gene identification, miRNA regulatory network modules, MRMs, Functional miRNA-mRNA regulatory modules, MRMs, miRNA functional annotation

1 Introduction

miRNAs are short RNA molecules of around 22 nucleotides that are found in plants, animals, and some DNA viruses. miRNAs are identified within noncoding regions of genes, within introns of protein-coding regions, and within intergenic regions. They are known to have been highly conserved across evolution. miRNAs bind to a specific mRNA region post transcription. By targeting the specific mRNA regions, miRNAs can repress mRNA expression by either degrading or inhibiting translation.

1.1 miRNA Biogenesis and Pairing between miRNA-Target mRNA

Biogenesis of miRNAs begins in the nucleus with the transcription of the miRNA gene by RNA Polymerase II. The long primary miRNA transcripts (pri-miRNAs) produced exhibit a characteristic folding pattern that forms hairpin structures. Subsequently, pri-miRNAs undergo a cleavage process by a nuclear microprocessor complex, consisting of Drosha, an RNase III enzyme, and a protein called

Jingshan Huang et al. (eds.), *Bioinformatics in MicroRNA Research*, Methods in Molecular Biology, vol. 1617, DOI 10.1007/978-1-4939-7046-9_16,

DGCR8 (DiGeorge critical region 8). The resultant hairpin precursor miRNA (pre-miRNA) is then exported to the cytoplasm where it is further acted upon by another RNase III enzyme called Dicer; a double-stranded, mature miRNAs of about 22 base pairs (*bp*) is formed. In order for mature miRNAs to function, the double helix needs to bind to a ribonucleoprotein called the RNA-induced silencing complex (RISC), which allows the helix to unwind to unveil the single-stranded, functioning miRNA [1]. In animals, it is known that the 5′ end of miRNA pairs with the 3'UTR of target mRNAs. However, the pairing can either follow a perfect complementarity base pairing pattern between target mRNA to the 5′ end of miRNAs at second to seventh nucleotides of miRNA, which is called the "seed" region. It may also follow an imperfect complementarity base pairing pattern, creating a partial sequence complementation [2].

In the last few decades, significant developments have been made in the discovery of miRNAs, the identification of their targets, and the inferencing of their functions. This includes the ascertainment of several physical and functional characteristics of miRNA that are indicative of the miRNA functions and targets; these characteristics include information such as folding patterns, thermodynamic properties, and sequence conservation. With the advancement in computational learning techniques, these characteristics can be used to develop models to identify novel miRNA genes and their targets and to predict their functions. The following sections will provide an overview of machine learning methods that have been utilized in the literature with respect to miRNA genes identification (discovery), targets, and functions.

2 Machine Learning and miRNA Genes Identification

Over the years, large numbers of miRNAs have been identified for a number of species. According to a recent release, the miRBase [3], the collective database of miRNAs, has exceeded approximately 35,000 mature miRNAs in around 223 species [3]. The identification of miRNA genes, however, is not a straightforward task. Several methods, using a variety of approaches, have been meticulously strategized. One complication is that the miRNA genes are often expressed independently, although some studies show clusters of two to seven genes co-expressing [4].

The first miRNA in *C. elegans* was discovered using classic forward genetics, based on sequence conservation. It involved identifying sequences conserved between closely related species, validating pre-miRNA features, and ruling out hairpins that did not fall within the conservation pattern. Despite development of high-throughput sequencing techniques, computational tools have become imperative in complementing experimental validation in miRNA discovery [2].

Computational methods predominantly utilize miRNA characteristics such as phylogenetic sequence conservation, secondary structure information like hairpin structure and minimal folding free energy [5]. Both **MiRscan**, **miRSeeker**, and **Srnaloop** [6] identify conserved hairpin sequences similar to known miRNAs. While **miRseeker**, in addition, matches specific miRNA patterns like diverged loop sequence, **Srnaloop** uses shorter base pair lengths of 140–300. However, a major drawback with conservation-based approaches is the failure to detect non-conserved miRNAs and species-specific mRNAs.

Unlike biological and conservation-based computational methods, machine-learning models are not entirely dependent on sequence conservation patterns. These methods can utilize other miRNA sequence and structural characteristics like folding energy, to state one. The most popular machine learning-based approach for identifying miRNA genes is classification [5], for which there are a number of potential approaches and methods.

The following sections detail some of the popular classification techniques used in miRNA genes identification; Table 1 summarizes the methods discussed.

2.1 Support Vector Machine (SVM)

SVM is a well-known classifier that has shown to be efficient in dealing with classification problems. The **Triplet-SVM** method [7] makes use of triple elements to decode local contiguous structure-sequence properties of miRNAs. A triple element refers to a set of features that indicates the pairing state of every three adjacent nucleotides, which, ideally, will allow true miRNAs that are separated from false hairpins. This method is known to be accurate in animals though its performance in other species is comparatively lower [8]. **miR-abela** [9] predicts mammalian miRNAs, largely, those clustered around known miRNAs with high specificity based on 40 pre-miRNAs characteristics including stem length, folding free energy, and hairpin loop length. However, its low sensitivity can pose a limitation [8]. **RNAmicro** [10] is based on RNA structure prediction and sequence analysis and uses tools such as **RNAz** [11]. **RNAz** identifies candidates in accordance with sequence conservation, structural properties, and thermodynamic stability. **RNAz** is known for its high sensitivity, although it is not free of false positives [12]. **miPred** [13] emerged as a successful SVM classifier with high performance. It included 29 features of miRNAs including hairpin folding, dinucleotide frequencies, and thermodynamics. Its dependence on intrinsic properties instead of the common conservation patterns led to its notable accuracy and sensitivity. **microPred** [14] extends **miPred** by adding 19 more features; the inclusion resulted in higher sensitivity and specificity. In addition, there have been efforts to address the common class imbalance problems [15]; however, this is yet not a solved issue.

Table 1
Methods for miRNA gene identification

Name	Number of samples	Species	Features	Performance
miRNA gene prediction				
Triplet-SVM (SVM)		Human, extended to 11 species	Paired or unpaired nucleotide	Accuracy - 90%
miR-abela (SVM)	+ve - 178 −ve - 5395	Human, Rat, Mouse	40 features like FFE, length of stem, length of HpL	Sensi - 71%, Spec - 91%
miPred (SVM)	Tr → 200 (+ve), 400 (−ve); Te → 123 (+ve), 246 (−ve); Va → 1918 nonhuman	Train and Test → Human Va → Non-human	Global and Intrinsic HpL	Train Acc - 93.5%, Test Acc - 93.5%, Test Se - 84.5%, Test Sl - 97.97%
microPred (SVM-RBF)	Train → 695 +ve, 8494 −ve Va → 6095 non-human +139 virus	Human, Virus, Non-human	29 of miPred + 19 more MFE, TD	Avg.Va Acc - 93% for non-human +viral
RNAmicro (SVM)	+ve 147, −ve 383	Mammals, Non-mammals	Alignment, TD, StrF	Avg Se = 87%, Avg Sp = 99%
ProMiR (HMM)	−ve → 1000 random human genes, +ve unspecified	Human	Pairwise sequence classified as match, mismatch, delete, insertion	
HHMMir (HMM)		Human, applicable to other species	SS, FE	Se - 84%, Sp - 88%
MiRRim (HMM)		Human	Evolutionary, SS	Se - 70%, Sp - 90%
BayesMirFind (Naive Bayes)	+ve 117 miRNAs −ve 300 random	*C. elegans*	miRNA SeqF and SS	150 −ve Se - 83%, Sp - 96%. 300 −ve Se - 43% , Sp - 99%
miR-KDE	+ve 1983 from 40 species, −ve 3988 pseudo hairpins.	Human and non-human	29 features, four stem-loop features	Avg. Se = 93%, Avg. Sp = 94%, Avg. Acc = 93%

Note: *Train* training Set, *Test* test set, *Va* validation, *Se* sensitivity, *Sp* specificity, *Acc* accuracy, *Sl* selectivity, *Avg* average, *FPR* false positive rate, *FE* free energy, *MFE* minimum free energy, *FFE* folding free energy, *HpL* hairpin loop, *TD* thermodynamic, *SS* secondary structure, *GO* gene ontology, *SeqF* sequence based features, *StrF* structure based features, *Norm* normalized, *bp* base pair

2.2 Hidden Markov Model (HMM)

Hidden Markov Models [15], which are based on probability distribution, have been applied in some miRNA genes identification methods like in **ProMiR** [16]. **ProMir** is based on a probabilistic co-learning method using structure and sequence properties of human pre-miRNAs. **MiRRim** [17] is a sequence and structure-based HMM algorithm that is found to perform efficiently in detecting candidates clustered with known miRNAs. **HHMMiR** [18] implements a Hierarchical Hidden Markov Model (HHMM) in which minimum free energy is used to get secondary structures through RNAFold which is then classified. This method is known for its high sensitivity and specificity and for defining functional roles of the miRNAs [8].

2.3 Naive Bayes Classifier

BayesMirFind [19] is a classic example of a Naive Bayes Classifier which is based on independence in prediction factors, that is, the presence of a particular feature in a class is independent of or unrelated to that of any other feature. It performs classification based on structure and sequence information from several species. Despite having a low number of false positives in the tests conducted by [19], its overall performance level was lower when compared to other classification methods. Other machine learning-based methods for identifying miRNA include **miR-KDE**. **miR-KDE** [20] is based on a relaxed variable kernel density estimator (RVKDE). This method has proven to be efficient in finding miRNAs from species largely distant from humans.

3 Machine Learning in Predicting miRNA Targets

The techniques discussed in the previous section were concerned with identifying miRNA genes. In this section, we will discuss how to identify miRNA targets. To begin with, the complexities involved with the partial sequence complementation and the lack of well-defined 3'UTR boundaries, in addition to the small size of miRNAs, pose constant challenges in target prediction. Adding to the complexity is the fact that a single miRNA can bind to several target sites on the mRNA; moreover, a single mRNA transcript can contain target sites for several miRNAs. One solution to this problem, as described by Kleftogiannis et al. [15], is to *predict miRNA targets based on a filtering approach*. The filtering approach is to create a pool of possible targets by sifting sequences based on their thermodynamics characteristics and complementarily; these pools are called seed pools. The **Stark** method [21] uses **HMMer** [22], a tool that searches for complementary sequences and creates a database of 3'UTRs that are further filtered by conservation and thermodynamics properties. **miRanda** [23] first identifies binding sequences with added emphasis on seed complementarity. The sequences are then filtered based on free energy and conservation.

TargetScan [24] is based on exact base pairing to the seed region in miRNA, followed by filtering by estimating the thermodynamic free energy of the pairing; however, it does not function well when the targets are loosely conserved [25]. A 38-nucleotide window is used in the **DIANA-microT** method [26, 27], which scans for binding sites and predicting conserved targets based on thermodynamic stability. **PicTar** [28] is based on an algorithm that works by aligning 3'URTs and then filtering based upon their thermodynamic stability [27].

Despite new developments in computational algorithms, filtering approaches fail in predicting targets that are not conserved; they also have issues with mismatch seeds. Furthermore, although the interpretability is high with the filtering approaches, their overall prediction performance remains low. To resolve this, many researchers have begun exploring the use of machine learning methods.

3.1 Machine Learning Approaches

Recent developments in machine learning techniques for predicting miRNA targets include support vector machines, statistical methods, including Bayesian classifiers, along with non-statistical, such as artificial neural networks and support vector machines. In addition, methods that combing multiple machine learning methods or methods that combine filtering with machine learning have also been proposed. A brief overview of these approaches will be presented in the next two sections; Table 2 provides a compact summarization of the approaches.

3.1.1 Statistical Methods

MicroTar [29] picks sequences of miRNA and its potential mRNA targets, predicts their hybridization energy and minimum free energy to identify seed sites, and finally uses a statistical analysis to predict targets. This method successfully predicts non-conserved targets though the prediction performance is only moderate. **MirZ** [30] is a web server of functional target miRNAs predicted using a novel Bayesian model in which phylogenetic distribution of target sequences is studied for individual miRNAs. Apart from good predicting performance, this method is known for retrieving functional interactions between miRNAs and their targets. **GenMIR++** [31] is another Bayesian model that uses Gene Ontology annotations to predict mRNA targets.

3.1.2 Non-Statistical Methods

MTar [32] is an Artificial Neural Network verifier that locates miRNA targets based on 16 parameters including position, thermodynamics, and structure. Although this method is found to be comprehensive, the optimization of parameters remains a difficulty. **miTarget** [33] avoids the parameter optimization problem by using an SVM classifier in their **miTarget. miTarget** uses 41 positional, thermodynamic, and structural features; it also exploits Gene Ontology as part of the process for target prediction. A major problem in this method is the lack of a standardization of negative

Table 2
Methods for Predicting miRNA Targets

Name	Number of samples	Species	Features	Performance
miRNA target prediction				
MicroTar (Statistical)	129 total predictable sites	*C. elegans*, Drosophila, mouse	Unbound MFE, constrained fold duplex free energy.	
MirZ (Bayesian)	297 for building miRNA profile	Humans, Drosophila, Mouse, C. elegans	SeqF	
GenMIR++ (Bayesian)	104 human miRNAs	Human	GO	FPR = 3.5%
MTar (ANN)	+ve - 150 positives −ve - 200 negative	Human	16 features like position, TD, StrF	
miTarget (SVM-RBF)	+ve - 152 positives, −ve - 246 negatives	Various organisms	41 different features like StrF, TD and Position	Maximum ROC 88.7%
targetMiner (SVM-RBF)	Train → 289 (+ve), Test → 187 (+ve), Test → 59 (−ve), Tissue specific → 37 (+ve) Tissue specific → 145 (−ve)	Primarily human	90 target features	For all 90 features: Se - 69%, Sp - 67.8% For 30 selected feature: Se - 76.5%, Sp - 66.1%
multiMiTar (SVM + AMOSA)	Train → 289 (+ve), Test → 187 (+ve), Test → 59 (−ve), Tissue specific → 37 (+ve) Tissue specific → 145 (−ve)	Primarily human	39 target features selected using multi-objective optimization	Se = 90%, Sp = 70%
Yan et al. (SVM + ADABoost)	48 +ve, 16 −ve		12 sets of features for each target region with four different regions	Maximum Acc. Reported 82.95%

Note: ***Train*** training set, *Test* test set, *Va* validation, *Se* sensitivity, *Sp* specificity, *Acc* accuracy, *Sl* selectivity, *Avg* average, *FPR* false positive rate, *FE* free energy, *MFE* minimum free energy, *FFE* folding free energy, *HpL* hairpin loop , *TD* thermodynamic, *SS* secondary structure, *GO* gene ontology, *SeqF* sequence based features, *StrF* structure based features, *Norm* normalized, *bp* base pair samples. With the development of the SVM classifier, **TargetMiner** [34], several of previous limitations were addressed. For instance, negative samples were methodologically identified, resolving the lack of negative samples encountered by **miTarget**. A richer set of features were also selected, in this case, set of 90 target features. Using a radial basis function (RBF) as the kernel, which mirrors **miTarget**, TargetMiner achieves a high predictive performance. However, a drawback found with this method is the interpretability of the classification model. **MultiMiTar** [35] methodology also addresses the drawback with the negative sampling set by incorporating high-quality negative samples and biologically relevant target sites. This is achieved by integrating a SVM classifier with Archived Multi-objective Simulated Annealing (AMOSA) technique. The limitation posed by this method is the small size of sample sets; the generalizability of the resulting models is difficult to establish.

3.1.3 Ensemble and Hybrid Methods

A study [36] tested several machine learning methods and concluded that the SVM classifier is the most efficient in miRNA target prediction. As a result, using SVM classifier as the base, an ensemble classifier was developed with the help of a meta-algorithm Adaboost [37, 38]; the ensemble integrates ten SVM classifiers. In addition, the ensemble method also incorporates feature selection to select and utilize only those features that are highly informative. **TargetSpy** [39] is another ensemble method designed to remove the need for seed matching and conservation properties. Using 43 features, TargetSpy uses MultiBoost [40], which uses decision stumps [41] as the base learner; the performance of the model was equivalent with a number of state-of-the-art methods. In addition to methods that used the same underlying base classification technique, models that use a combination of two or more miRNA target predicting methods have been tested. For instance, **NBmiRTar** [42] utilizes a Bayesian algorithm and a filtering method based on miRanda score [43] while **DIANA-microT-ANN** [42] does the filtering of potential targets and then applies an Artificial Neural Network classifier to predict final targets.

4 Machine Learning in Inferring miRNA Functions

By this point, we have provided overviews of machine-learning techniques to identify miRNA genes and targets. However, one last problem needs to be addressed, which is how to predict their function. Functional knowledge can provide insights into the biology of miRNA-regulated diseases. However, not all miRNAs being discovered carry defined functions in the regulation of gene expression. Hence, it is imperative to identify miRNAs with functional roles and also infer their specific functions in the gene regulatory network [44]. Liu et al. (2014) [2] categorize the functional analysis of miRNAs into functional annotation and regulatory module. Regulatory modules can be subdivided into miRNA regulatory network modules (MRMs) or functional miRNA-mRNA regulatory modules (FMRMs), where FMRMs are a network of miRNAs and their target mRNAs. A graphical representation of the inference process can be seen in Fig. 1.

4.1 miRNA Functional Annotation

Functional annotation of miRNA is based on the assumption that miRNAs and their targets carry closely related functions. Therefore, by studying the functions of target genes from reliable sources such as DAVID [45] and WebGestalt [46], functions of related miRNAs can be annotated [2]. For example, **MAGIA** [47] and Functional Assignment of miRNAS via Enrichment (**FAME**) [48] use statistical methods to infer miRNA functions. On the other hand, **miRDB** [49] uses a wiki editing interface that permits the public to directly update miRNA functional annotations. Regardless of the approach, the major limitation of miRNA functional annotation methods is their sole dependence on target prediction. These annotation methods typically fail to predict the functions of miRNAs that bind to targets mRNAs outside the 3'UTR. Thus, methods that infer miRNA functions beyond target base pairing became inevitable.

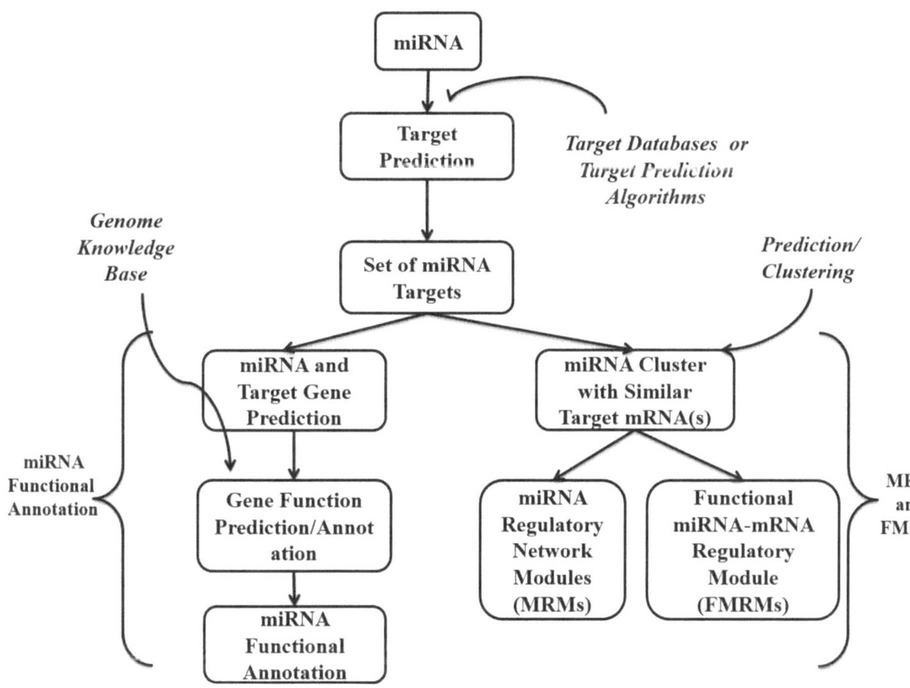

Fig. 1 miRNA functional inference process

4.2 Predicting miRNA Regulatory Module (MRM) Using Machine Learning Techniques

Further studies showed that miRNA functions can be inferred by integrating information from target prediction sources with expression profiles of miRNAs and mRNAs obtained by microarray or NGS techniques (referred to as predicting MRMs). The principle of miRNAs negatively regulating their target mRNAs is commonly used in predicting MRMs. For instance, **Huang et al.** (2007) [31] construct a Bayesian network that represents the relationship between miRNA and mRNA and then applies the miRNA-mRNA downregulation principle at the expression level. This method can detect potential miRNAs and mRNAs that are co-functional. A probabilistic method proposed by **Joung et al.** (2007) [50] integrates information from two sources, namely, the expression profiles of groups of miRNA-mRNAs, which have similar biological functions, and the miRNA target prediction. While the method is effective, it does require the setting of several parameters, which is a nontrivial task.

One potential issue with the above methods is they utilize at most two sources of data; arguably, it would be better to incorporate three or more sources. One example of incorporating more than two sources can be found in the study conducted by **Zhang et al.** (2011) [51]. In their study, they integrate three different sources using a multiplicative updating algorithm that integrates data from three sources: (a) target predictions, (b) expression profiles of miRNAs and their targets, and (c) the gene-gene interaction network and effectively identified miRNA-gene regulatory modules. Another method that incorporates multiple sources is reported by **Tran et al.** (2008) [52]. Their method is a rule-based method, which seeks to find interactions between the human cancer miRNAs and mRNAs. The rule is based upon decision tree, association rule mining, and separate-and-conquer methods; the results indicate that the MMRs discovered have high confidence.

Methods of predicting MRMs could only identify co-expressing miRNA-mRNA groups. However, their roles in specific biological conditions or diseases were not addressed. In order to further probe into the functional roles of MRMs, understanding their biological implications is important.

4.3 Machine Learning for Inferring FMRMs

The third category of inferring functions of miRNAs is by integrating information from target prediction sources with biological knowledge of miRNAs, related to a specific disease or condition (inferring FMRMs). Several algorithms have been proposed to aid in the discovery of FMRMs; several of the algorithms for discovering MRMs and FMRMS are summarized in Table 3. For instance, a learning structure based on Bayesian network called Splitting and Averaging of Bayesian networks (SA-BNs) is proposed by **Liu et al.** (2009) [53, 54]. This method integrates target predictions and expression profiles of miRNAs and mRNAs. The SA-BN is then applied on the miRNA samples to characterize their FMRMs. **Nunez-Iglesias et al.** (2010) [55] use a permutation method to

Table 3
Methods for Inferring FMRMs

Name	Number of samples	Species	Features	Performance
miRNA function prediction—MRM				
Tran et al. (Rule Based)	121human miRNA, 801 mRNA	Human	miRNAs	Confidence > 0.75 Coverage > 3
Joung et al. (Probabilistic learning)	99 human miRNA, 2012 mRNA	Human	Parametric adjusted population size, minimum subset size	Maximum reported fitness score = 0.75
Zhang et al. (Multiplicative Updating Algorithm)	559 miRNAs, 12,456 genes	Human		
Houng et al. (Bayesian)	104 human miRNAs	Human	GO	FPR- 3.5%
miRNA function prediction—FMRM				
Lui et al. (2010) (Probabilistic Graphical Model)	1112 probe of miRNA, 19,223 probes of mRNA	Mouse		Minimum coverage of 22% on validation sets.

Train training set, *Test* test set, *Va* validation, *Se* sensitivity, *Sp* specificity, *ACC* accuracy, *Sl* selectivity, *Avg* average, *FPR* false positive rate, *FE* free energy, *MFE* minimum free energy, *FFE* folding free energy, *HpL* hairpin loop, *TD* thermodynamic, *SS* secondary structure, *GO* gene ontology, *SeqF* sequence based features, *StrF* structure based features, *Norm* normalized, *bp* base pair

determine the correlation between expression levels of miRNAs and mRNAs of test and control samples. Statistical techniques then identify the FMRMs from the miRNA-mRNA pairs. **Liu et al.** (2010) [56] frame a probabilistic method for FMRM discovery which integrates expression profiles of miRNAs and mRNAs with or without using target prediction information. In this graphical model, FMRMs are defined as latent variables that control the miRNA and mRNA expression values that are again linked wide to biological functions.

5 Discussion

miRNAs, since their discovery in the early 1990s, have been of interest to several research groups across the world. There has been an exponential development in the computational methods applied to the identification of miRNA genes, their targets and regulatory mechanisms. Machine learning algorithms have overcome not only the difficulties of experimental procedures involved in miRNA discovery and target predictions but also the limitation of conservation-based computational approaches. Among such methods developed recently, SVM classifiers have shown to be efficient in the identification of novel miRNA genes in spite of a few drawbacks such as low sensitivity and occurrence of false positives. Also, SVM classifiers were found to be the most efficient of the miRNA target prediction methods [36]. Inferring miRNA functions as well has gained rapid attention with the discovery of a large number of miRNA genes and targets.

The fact that a single miRNA can have multiple targets and multiple regulatory pathways creates huge potential in improvements in miRNA studies. Therefore, future developments in machine learning methods to identify miRNA genes to predict their targets and to infer their functions are expected to continue to be dynamic.

References

1. Winter J, Jung S, Keller S et al (2009) Many roads to maturity: microRNA biogenesis pathways and their regulation. Nat Cell Biol 11:228–234. doi:10.1038/ncb0309-228
2. Liu B, Li J, Cairns MJ (2014) Identifying miRNAs, targets and functions. Brief Bioinform 15:1–19. doi:10.1093/bib/bbs075
3. Kozomara A, Griffiths-Jones S (2014) MiRBase: annotating high confidence microRNAs using deep sequencing data. Nucleic Acids Res 42:68–73. doi:10.1093/nar/gkt1181
4. Mendes ND, Freitas AT, Sagot MF (2009) Survey and summary: current tools for the identification of miRNA genes and their targets. Nucleic Acids Res 37:2419–2433. doi:10.1093/nar/gkp145
5. Li L, Xu J, Yang D et al (2010) Computational approaches for microRNA studies: a review. Mamm Genome 21:1–12. doi:10.1007/s00335-009-9241-2
6. Berezikov E, Cuppen E, Plasterk RH (2006) Approaches to microRNA discovery. Nat Genet 38(Suppl):S2–S7. doi:10.1038/ng1794
7. Xue C, Li F, He T et al (2005) Classification of real and pseudo microRNA precursors using local structure-sequence features and support vector machine. BMC Bioinformatics 6:310
8. Gomes CPC, Cho JH, Hood L et al (2013) A review of computational tools in microRNA discovery. Front Genet 4:1–9. doi:10.3389/fgene.2013.00081
9. Sewer A, Paul N, Landgraf P et al (2005) Identification of clustered microRNAs using an ab initio prediction method. BMC Bioinformatics 6:267
10. Hertel J, Stadler PF (2006) Hairpins in a Haystack: recognizing microRNA precursors in comparative genomics data. Bioinformatics 22:197–202. doi:10.1093/bioinformatics/btl257
11. Washietl S, Hofacker IL, Stadler PF (2005) From the cover: fast and reliable prediction of noncoding RNAs. Proc Natl Acad Sci 102:2454–2459. doi:10.1073/pnas.0409169102
12. Lindow M, Gorodkin J (2007) Principles and limitations of computational microRNA gene and target finding. DNA Cell Biol 26:339–351. doi:10.1089/dna.2006.0551
13. Ng KLS, Mishra SK (2007) De novo SVM classification of precursor microRNAs from genomic pseudo hairpins using global and intrinsic folding measures. Bioinformatics 23:1321–1330. doi:10.1093/bioinformatics/btm026
14. Batuwita R, Palade V (2009) microPred: effective classification of pre-miRNAs for human miRNA gene prediction. Bioinformatics 25:989–995. doi:10.1093/bioinformatics/btp107
15. Kleftogiannis D, Korfiati A, Theofilatos K et al (2013) Where we stand, where we are moving: surveying computational techniques for identifying miRNA genes and uncovering their regulatory role. J Biomed Inform 46:563–573. doi:10.1016/j.jbi.2013.02.002
16. Nam JW, Shin KR, Han J et al (2005) Human microRNA prediction through a probabilistic co-learning model of sequence and

structure. Nucleic Acids Res 33:3570–3581. doi:10.1093/nar/gki668
17. Terai G, Komori T, Asai K, Kin T (2007) miRRim: a novel system to find conserved miRNAs with high sensitivity and specificity. RNA 13:2081–2090
18. Kadri S, Hinman V, Benos PV (2009) HHMMiR: efficient de novo prediction of microRNAs using hierarchical hidden Markov models. BMC Bioinformatics 10:S35
19. Yousef M, Nebozhyn M, Shatkay H et al (2006) Combining multi-species genomic data for microRNA identification using a Naïve Bayes classifier. Bioinformatics 22:1325–1334. doi:10.1093/bioinformatics/btl094
20. Chang DT-H, Wang C-C, Chen J-W (2008) Using a kernel density estimation based classifier to predict species-specific microRNA precursors. BMC Bioinformatics 9(Suppl 12):S2. doi:10.1186/1471-2105-9-S12-S2
21. Stark A, Brennecke J, Russell RB, Cohen SM (2003) Identification of Drosophila microRNA targets. PLoS Biol 1(3):E60
22. Eddy SR (1996) Hidden Markov models. Curr Opin Struct Biol 6:361–365. S0959-440X(96)80056-X [pii]
23. Enright AJ, John B, Gaul U et al (2003) MicroRNA targets in Drosophila. Genome Biol 5:R1
24. Lewis BP, Shih IH, Jones-Rhoades MW et al (2003) Prediction of mammalian microrna targets. Cell 115:787–798
25. Min H, Yoon S (2010) Got target? Computational methods for microRNA target prediction and their extension. Exp Mol Med 42:233–244. doi:10.3858/emm.2010.42.4.032
26. Kiriakidou M, Nelson PT, Kouranov A et al (2004) A combined computational-experimental approach predicts human microRNA targets. Genes Dev 18:1165–1178
27. Maziere P, Enright AJ (2007) Prediction of microRNA targets. Drug Discov Today 12:452–458. doi:10.1016/j.drudis.2007.04.002
28. Krek A, Grün D, Poy MN et al (2005) Combinatorial microRNA target predictions. Nat Genet 37:495–500
29. Thadani R, Tammi MT (2006) MicroTar: predicting microRNA targets from RNA duplexes. BMC Bioinformatics 7(Suppl 5):S20. doi:10.1186/1471-2105-7-S5-S20
30. Hausser J, Berninger P, Rodak C et al (2009) MirZ: an integrated microRNA expression atlas and target prediction resource. Nucleic Acids Res 37:266–272. doi:10.1093/nar/gkp412
31. Huang JC, Babak T, Corson TW et al (2007) Using expression profiling data to identify human microRNA targets. Nat Methods 4:1045–1049. doi:10.1038/nmeth1130
32. Chandra V, Girijadevi R, Nair AS et al (2010) MTar: a computational microRNA target prediction architecture for human transcriptome. BMC Bioinformatics 11(Suppl 1):S2. doi:10.1186/1471-2105-11-S1-S2
33. Kim S-K, Nam J-W, Rhee J-K et al (2006) miTarget: microRNA target gene prediction using a support vector machine. BMC Bioinformatics 7:411. doi:10.1186/1471-2105-7-411
34. Bandyopadhyay S, Mitra R (2009) TargetMiner: MicroRNA target prediction with systematic identification of tissue-specific negative examples. Bioinformatics 25:2625–2631. doi:10.1093/bioinformatics/btp503
35. Mitra R, Bandyopadhyay S (2011) MultiMiTar: a novel multi objective optimization based miRNA-target prediction method. PLoS One 6(9):e24583. doi:10.1371/journal.pone.0024583
36. Yan X, Chao T, Tu K et al (2007) Improving the prediction of human microRNA target genes by using ensemble algorithm. FEBS Lett 581:1587–1593. doi:10.1016/j.febslet.2007.03.022
37. Schapire RE (2013) Explaining AdaBoost. In: Empirical inference: Festschrift honor Vladimir N. Vapnik. Springer, Berlin, Heidelberg, pp 37–52
38. Freund Y, Schapire RE (1997) A decision-theoretic generalization of on-line learning and an application to boosting. J Compu Syst Sci 55:119–139. doi:10.1006/jcss.1997.1504
39. Sturm M, Hackenberg M, Langenberger D, Frishman D (2010) TargetSpy: a supervised machine learning approach for microRNA target prediction. BMC Bioinformatics 11:292. doi:10.1186/1471-2105-11-292
40. Webb GI (2000) MultiBoosting: a technique for combining boosting and wagging. Mach Learn 40:159–196
41. Iba W, Langley P (1992) Induction of one-level decision trees. ML92 proceeding of the ninth int conf mach learn aberdeen, Scotland, 1–3 July 1992, pp 233–240
42. Reczko M, Maragkakis M, Alexiou P et al (2012) Accurate microRNA target prediction using detailed binding site accessibility and machine learning on proteomics data. Front Genet 2:1–13. doi:10.3389/fgene.2011.00103
43. Yousef M, Jung S, Kossenkov AV et al (2007) Naive Bayes for microRNA target predictions—machine learning for microRNA targets.

Bioinformatics 23:2987–2992. doi:10.1093/bioinformatics/btm484

44. Wong N, Wang X (2015) miRDB: an online resource for microRNA target prediction and functional annotations. Nucleic Acids Res 43:D146–D152. doi:10.1093/nar/gku1104
45. Huang DW, Lempicki RA, Sherman BT (2009) Systematic and integrative analysis of large gene lists using DAVID bioinformatics resources. Nat Protoc 4:44–57
46. Wang J, Duncan D, Shi Z, Zhang B (2013) WEB-based GEne SeT AnaLysis toolkit (WebGestalt): update 2013. Nucleic Acids Res 41(Web Server issue):W77–W83
47. Sales G, Coppe A, Bisognin A et al (2010) Magia, a web-based tool for miRNA and genes integrated analysis. Nucleic Acids Res 38(Web Server issue):W352–W359
48. Ulitsky I, Laurent LC, Shamir R (2010) Towards computational prediction of microRNA function and activity. Nucleic Acids Res 38:e160–e160. doi:10.1093/nar/gkq570
49. Wang X (2008) miRDB: a microRNA target prediction and functional annotation database with a wiki interface. RNA 14:1012–1017. doi:10.1261/rna.965408.was
50. Joung JG, Hwang KB, Nam JW et al (2007) Discovery of microRNA-mRNA modules via population-based probabilistic learning. Bioinformatics 23:1141–1147. doi:10.1093/bioinformatics/btm045
51. Zhang S, Li Q, Liu J, Zhou XJ (2011) A novel computational framework for simultaneous integration of multiple types of genomic data to identify microrna-gene regulatory modules. Bioinformatics 27(13):i401–i409. doi:10.1093/bioinformatics/btr206
52. Tran D, Satou K, Ho T et al (2008) Finding microRNA regulatory modules in human genome using rule induction. BMC Bioinformatics 9:S5. doi:10.1186/1471-2105-9-S12-S5
53. Liu B, Li J, Tsykin A (2009) Discovery of functional miRNA-mRNA regulatory modules with computational methods. J Biomed Inform 42:685–691. doi:10.1016/j.jbi.2009.01.005
54. Liu B, Li J, Tsykin A et al (2009) Exploring complex miRNA-mRNA interactions with Bayesian networks by splitting-averaging strategy. BMC Bioinformatics 10:408. doi:10.1186/1471-2105-10-408
55. Nunez-Iglesias J, Liu CC, Morgan TE et al (2010) Joint genome-wide profiling of miRNA and mRNA expression in Alzheimer's disease cortex reveals altered miRNA regulation. PLoS One 5(2):e8898. doi:10.1371/journal.pone.0008898
56. Liu B, Liu L, Tsykin A et al (2010) Identifying functional miRNA-mRNA regulatory modules with correspondence latent dirichlet allocation. Bioinformatics 26:3105–3111. doi:10.1093/bioinformatics/btq576

Chapter 17

Involvement of MicroRNAs in Diabetes and Its Complications

Bin Wu and Daniel Miller

Abstract

Diabetes is a severe condition worldwide. It is characterized by chronic hyperglycemia and is caused by defects in insulin production, secretion, and action. Both genetic and environmental factors contribute to the development of type 1 and type 2 diabetes. The pathogenesis of diabetes is complex and the underlying molecular mechanisms are only partially understood. MicroRNAs (miRNAs) play a fundamental role in diabetes and its complications. This chapter focuses on the dysregulation of miRNAs involved in the regulation of pancreatic islet insulin production and secretion as well as action and signaling in peripheral tissues. The roles of miRNAs in the development of diabetic complications are also discussed. Modulating miRNA expression, by either upregulation or inhibition, holds a promise as a strategy for treating this metabolic disease.

Key words MicroRNA, Diabetes, Insulin, Insulin resistance, Glucose homeostasis, Diabetic complications

1 Introduction

Diabetes mellitus is a metabolic disorder characterized by chronic hyperglycemia and the late development of micro- and macrovascular complications, including diabetic nephropathy, cardiomyopathy, neuropathy, and retinopathy [1]. It is garnering attention as a public health concern and, due to its prevalence, a significant economic burden. According to a World Health Organization (WHO) report, there were 171 million cases of diabetes worldwide in the 2000 and it was estimated that the number of cases will rise to 366 million by 2030 [2]. Mokdad et al. estimated that costs incurred in the treatment of myocardial infarction, stroke, end-stage renal disease, retinopathy, and foot ulcers secondary to diabetes account for almost 14 percent of health care expenditures in the United States [3].

Clinical diabetes is divided into two classifications: type 1 diabetes (T1D) and type 2 diabetes (T2D). T1D is generally the result of autoimmune pancreatic β-cell destruction that causes an absolute insulin deficiency. T2D is caused by insulin resistance (impaired

Jingshan Huang et al. (eds.), *Bioinformatics in MicroRNA Research*, Methods in Molecular Biology, vol. 1617,
DOI 10.1007/978-1-4939-7046-9_17, © Springer Science+Business Media LLC 2017

insulin action) leading to a relative insulin deficiency [4]. Insulin deficiency plays a major role in the development of diabetic hyperglycemia and metabolic disorders such as dyslipidemia. Hyperglycemia and dyslipidemia, in turn, play important roles in diabetes-related complications [5]. It is well established that genetic factors are closely associated with the development of both T1D and T2D. Kolfschoten et al. reported on the potential usage of microRNA for treating this genetic disorder [6]. MicroRNA are small, single-stranded, noncoding RNAs that repress the expression of targeted mRNAs. They perform alongside transcription factors in a complementary role to regulate gene expression. MiRNAs function by partially binding to sequences in the 3′-untranslated region (3′-UTR) of target, interfering with the translation but not disrupting the mRNA. In the human genome, approximately 30% of all protein-coding genes are regulated by miRNA which indicates that they play a substantial role in the control of biological functions [7]. MiRNAs may play an active role in regulating glucose hemostasis via modulating insulin-producing β-cell function and insulin signaling in the peripheral tissues such as liver, muscle, and adipose tissue [8]. This chapter will describe the potential roles that microRNA play in the pathogenesis of diabetes and its secondary complications, their possible diagnostic relevance, and possible therapeutic applications.

2 MiRNAs and Insulin Secretion, Pancreatic β Cell Development

Proper insulin secretion from pancreatic β-cells with normal function in peripheral tissues is crucial for glucose homeostasis. The expression of MiRNAs is highly tissue-specific with multi-faceted effects. It was determined that there are several MiRNAs selectively expressed in insulin-producing β-cells. In murine insulinoma the pancreatic β-cell line (MIN6 cells), mir-375, was identified as the most abundant, evolutionarily conserved, islet-specific miRNA [9]. The miR-375 gene is located in an intergenic region between the bA2-crystallin (*cryba2*) and coiled-coil domain-containing protein 108 (*Ccdc108*). The pri-miR-375 gene is controlled at the transcriptional level in the pancreas [10]. MiR-375 is expressed in islet β-cells and non-β-cells where it influences glucose homeostasis by inhibiting insulin secretion as well as pancreatic α- and β-cell mass [11, 12]. This was corroborated by Poy et al. who noted that insulin secretion was increased when they used antogomirs to suppress miR-375 expression [9]. The regulatory mechanism by which miR-375 regulates insulin secretion is not well understood, but Kolfschoten et al. posited that downregulation of myotrophin (*Mtpn*) by miR-375 was the method of action as reduction of myotrophin expression by RNA interference produced similar effects [6]. MiR-375 also enhances β-cell lipoapoptosis by downregulating *Mtpn* expressions in NIT-1 cells, a pancreatic β-cell line established from spontaneous β-cell adenoma developing mice [13]. El Ouaamari et al. found that miR-375 may regulate the expression of 3^1-phosphoinositide-dependent protein kinase-1 (PDK1), a link in the PI3 kinase signaling pathway and regulator of β-cell functions [14]. The reduced expression of PDK1 mediated by miR-375 causes a decrease in insulin secretion stimulated by glucose, as well as a decreased insulin DNA synthesis [14]. In agreeance with this finding, both Guay et al. and Poy et al. noted hyperglycemia in miR-375 knockout [8, 12]. A role in pancreatic islet development was also suggested by major defects caused by targeted inhibition of miR-375 in zebrafish [15].

Besides miR-375, the expression of 107 other miRNAs have been identified during murine pancreas development [16] including four miRNAs specific to islets (miR-7, miR-9, miR-375, and miR-376) prevalent during human pancreas islet development [11]. MiR-124a2, miR-195, miR-15a, miR-15b, and miR-16 inhibited the expression of transcription factors also playing a role in pancreatic development [17, 18]. MiR-124a is also prevalent in the pancreatic β-cells [19, 20]. β-cell line MIN6 upexpression of miR-124a suppressed Rab GTPase family 27A (Rab27A) as well as Noc2 expression and enhanced SNAP25, Rab3A, and Synapsin-1A production [21]. Rab27A is a target of miR-124a and other regulatory effects are perpetrated through indirect means [21]. Alterations to Rab27A levels have been associated with increased basal insulin secretion and reduced insulin secretion in the presence of glucose stimulation [21]. Overexpression of miR-124 also repressed Mtpn production inhibiting insulin secretion via the same mechanism as mir-375 [22]. Baroukh et al. also demonstrated that miR-124a targets both forkhead box protein A2 (FoxA2) and cAMP-responsive element binding protein (Creb), transcription factors involved in β-cell differentiation, glucose metabolism, and insulin secretion [17]. Overexpression of miR-124a in insulin-secreting cell lines (MIN6 and INS-1) increased basal-free intracellular Ca^{2+} and caused defects in glucose-stimulated Ca^{2+} response [17].

It was reported that miR-9 may affect insulin secretion both in vitro [23] and in vivo [24]. Plaisance et al. showed in cell line INS-1E that elevation of miR-9 suppresses the expression of the one cut homeobox 2 (Onecut-2) which downregulates granuphilin/Slp4 [23]. Silencing Onecut-2 decreased glucose and potassium induced insulin exocytosis by increasing granuphilin expression [23]. Ramachandran et al. showed that miR-9 affects SIRT1 (silent mating type information regulation 2 homolog 1) expression in insulin-secreting cells during glucose-induced insulin secretion [24]. These results suggest that β-cells insulin secretory capacity is influenced by miR-9. MiR-96 has also been shown to enhance Granuphilin expression, thereby indirectly controlling insulin. Noc2, a Rab effector protein involved in secretion, was also shown to be downregulated by miR-96 [21].

MiR-195, miR-15a, miR-15b, and miR-16 inhibit the expression of important transcription factors during pancreatic development [18]. Downregulation of mir-15a in MIN6 cells was observed during prolonged exposure to high glucose levels [25]. Sun et al. found that changes in mir-15a expression were positively correlated with insulin biosynthesis in MIN6 cells and that uncoupling protein-2 (UCP-2) served as the intermediary in the regulation [25]. MiR-15a was shown to be significantly underexpressed in the plasma of T2DM patients, suggesting an association between miR-15a and β-cell dysregulation in T2DM [25].

Roggli et al. examined miRNA involvement in proinflammatory cytokine-mediated β-cell cytotoxicity. They reported reduced insulin secretion and sensitization to cytokine-triggered cell death in MIN6 cells and human pancreatic islets after prolonged exposure to proinflammatory cytokines interleukin-1 β (IL-1b) and tumor necrosis factor alpha (TNF-α) [26]. They observed significant upregulation of miR-21, miR-34a, and miR-146 after exposure to the cytokines. They also observed increased expression of miR-34a and miR-146a during the onset of prediabetic insulitis in the islets of nonobese diabetic mice [26]. Lovis et al. observed the same result in MIN6 cells and pancreatic islets isolated from diabetic *db/db* mice after prolonged exposure to saturated fatty acids [27], which is associated upregulation of miR-34a and enhanced activation of p53 which resulted in an increase in cellular apoptosis and impaired glucose-induced insulin secretion. They also observed that enhanced expression of miR-34a in MIN6 cells suppressed vesicle-associated membrane protein 2 (VAMP2) [27]. Lovis et al. also found miR-34a was upregulated during adipogenesis and its expression levels were positively correlated with the body mass index (BMI) [28]. Taken together, these results indicate that miR-34a and miR-146 might be a mediator linking cytoplasmic inflammation and islet β-cell dysfunction.

3 MiRNAs and Insulin Action on Peripheral Tissue

3.1 MiRNAs Regulating Insulin Action in Muscle

Besides its involvement in islet β-cell insulin production, miRNAs also influence insulin action in peripheral tissue. Insulin resistance (IR) or insulin sensitivity is termed to reflect the hypoglycemic ability of insulin on peripheral tissues such as muscle, liver, and adipose tissue. Skeletal muscle contributes to approximately 75% of total body glucose consumption [29]. The roles of miRNAs in muscle metabolism were explored with both diabetic animal models and human patients. The expression profiles of miRNAs in skeletal muscle after a 3 h euglycemic-hyperinsulinemic clamp showed decreased levels of miR-1, miR-133a, miR-206, and miR-29a/c [30]. Expression of miR-29a and miR-29b was upregulated in skeletal muscles of Goto–Kakizaki (GK) rat, which is used as a model of nonobese T2D [31]. Insulin-mediated downexpression of miR-1 and miR-133a was found to involve transcription factors such as sterol regulatory element binding protein-1c (SREBP-1c) and myocyte enhancer factor 2C (MEF-2C) [30]. In addition, T2D patients were found to exhibit reduced skeletal muscle miR-133a expression, which was associated with higher fasting glucose levels [32]. Yu et al. investigated the role of miR-1 and miR-133 in glucose homeostasis using cardiomyocytes and found that glucose exposure increased miR-1 expression levels which suppressed insulin-like growth factor-1 (IGF-1) [33]. IGF-1 and IGF-1 receptor were validated targets of miR-1 [34] and both IGF-1 and IGF-receptor were found to be important determinants of insulin sensitivity in muscle [35]. Horie et al. demonstrated that increased levels of MiR-133a/b lead to a decreased expression of Kruppel-like transcription factor 15 (KLF15), a known regulator of insulin-regulated glucose transporter 4 (GLUT4), which resulted in decreased insulin-stimulated glucose uptake [36]. These findings suggest that dysregulation of miR-1 and miR-133 may contribute to insulin resistance in muscle [36].

MiR-24 and miR-144 also have reported involvement in muscle insulin sensitivity. The plasma of diabetic patients and the skeletal muscle tissue of both GK and Wistar rats exhibited decreased levels of miR-24 [37]. MiRNA profile comparisons between GK rats and Wistar rats showed miR-24 and miR-126 to be underexpressed in the muscle of GK rats [38]. Huang et al. demonstrated that p38 mitogen-activated protein kinase (MAPK) is a target of miR-24 in humans and mice [39]. Since p38 MAPK increases insulin-responsive GLUT4 translocation to the plasma membrane [40], miR-24 may regulate glucose hemostasis via p38 MAPK pathway in muscle. Upregulation of miR-144 was also found in insulin-responsive skeletal muscle of diabetic animals. Moreover, insulin resistance was also found to be promoted by inhibiting the expression of insulin receptor substrate-1 (IRS-1) which plays a vital role in the insulin-signaling cascade and IRS-1 is a direct target of miR-144 [41].

3.2 MiRNAs Regulate Lipid Metabolism and Insulin Action in Adipose Tissue

Over-production of adipokines, free fatty acids, and inflammatory mediators in adipose tissue are key contributing factors in systemic insulin resistance [42]. Ectopic accumulation of specific lipid metabolites (diacylglycerols or ceramides) outside of adipose tissue may be a common pathway leading to impaired insulin signaling [42]. There is emerging evidence indicating that miRNAs are involved in lipid metabolism and adipogenesis. Regulation of the biosynthesis of cholesterol, fatty acids, and phospholipids is regulated by transcription factors such as Sterol Regulatory Element-Binding Proteins (SREBPs), Carbohydrate

Response Element-Binding Protein (ChREBP), CCAAT-Enhancer-Binding Protein (C/EBP), Forkhead box protein O1 (FoxO1) to maintain proper homeostasis [43]. Sacco and Adeli found that miR-33, miR-122, miR-370, and miR-378 are regulators of lipid metabolism [44]. Human SREBP-encoding genes were also recently found to host highly conserved miRNAs, including miR-33a and -b on chromosomes 22 and 17, respectively [45]. MiR-33a functions in concert with the SREBP-2 cholesterogenic transcription factor to boost intracellular cholesterol levels [45, 46]. MiR-33a and -b were found to downregulate the expression of ATP-binding cassette transporter (subfamily A, member 1) ABCA1. ABCA1 promotes the transformation of free cholesterol from within the cell to ApoA1 which is involved in the creation of high-density lipoproteins (HDL) [46, 47]. In murine models, suppression or knockout ablation of miR-33a caused increased hepatic and macrophage ABCA1 expression as well as circulating HDL levels [47]. In addition to SREBP, it was shown that miR-33a and miR-33b regulate fatty acid β-oxidation, the process by which fatty acids are converted to Acetyl-CoA used in the citric acid cycle and ATP/energy generation, through the control of several intermediary proteins [46]. Manipulation of miR-33a in islets produced negative correlation between changes in ABCA1 expression and glucose-stimulated insulin secretion and positive correlation with changes in cholesterol levels [48]. These results indicate a complex network of regulatory functions between SREBPs and their intronic miRNA that regulates cholesterol and lipid homeostasis as well as islet β-cell function.

Fat cell development (adipogenesis) and differentiation are major contributing factors to obesity and T2D [49]. MiR-143 has been shown to regulate adipocyte differentiation and its expression is upregulated during adipogenesis [50]. Experiments by Esau et al. also suggest that miR-143 has a similar involvement pattern in adipocyte differentiation and that extracellular signal-regulated kinase 5 (ERK5) is the relevant target [51]. A total of 65 miRNAs, including miR-143, were detected by Kajimoto et al. during pre-adipocyte differentiation, and the expression of 21 of those miRNAs was up- or downregulated [52]. In Drosophila, Xu et al. found that miR-14 regulated triacylglycerol levels [53] and Teleman and Cohen observed reduced insulin sensitivity in miR-278 mutants [54], but so far no homologues have been uncovered in mammals.

4 MiRNAs and Diabetic Complications

4.1 MiRNAs and Diabetic Nephropathy

Diabetic nephropathy (DN) is one of the important microvascular complications of diabetes. DN is the leading cause of end-stage renal disease (ESRD) in the United States. It is characterized histologically by glomerular basement membrane thickening, mesangial expansion, podocyte effacement, and glomerular sclerosis [55]. The miRNA expression profile of renal biopsies from patients with DN indicated that miR-192 expression was related to DN-associated chronic kidney failure (eGFR <15 ml/min/1.73 m^2 at time of biopsy) [56]. Reduced expression of miR-192 was noted in patients with tubulointerstitial fibrosis and low estimated GFR. In vitro, treatment of proximal tubular epithelial cells with transforming growth factor β (TGF-β) decreased miR-192 expression [56]. Kato et al. noted that TGF-β, smad-interacting protein 1 (SIP1), δ-crystallin enhancer binding protein (δEF1), collagen type I alpha 2 (Col1a2), and miR-192 form a regulatory loop controlling kidney function [57]. TGF-β upregulates miR-192 and miR-192 downregulates SIP1 via translational repression. SIP1 and δEF1 both work to suppress the E-box elements located on the Col1a2 promoter, so increased expression of miR-192 results in an increase of Col1a2. They also noted enhanced expression of TGF-β and miR-192 in glomeruli isolated from streptozotocin(STZ)-induced and diabetic db/db mice when compared to non-diabetic controls [57]. Putta et al. demonstrated that TGF-β, fibronectin, and collagen gene expression were inhibited and Zeb1/2 expression was enhanced in STZ-induced diabetic mice following antagomiR-induced silencing of miR-192 in vivo which resulted in remission of DN [58]. MiR-192 was observed to be elevated in animal models of renal fibrosis. In vitro, overexpression of Smad7 in tubular epithelial cells countered the miR-192-enhancing effects of TGF-β and knockdown of Smad7 enhanced miR-192 expression [59]. Smad3 was found to bind to the miR-192 promoter region whereby it mediated TGF-β-induced expression [59]. These results show that miR-192 plays a role in DN pathogenesis.

Du et al. noted that miR-29a expression was depressed in human proximal tubular epithelial cells cultured with high levels of glucose and TGF-β. The reduced levels of miR-29a present in diabetes may promote excessive collagen deposition, suggesting a role in the development of DN [60]. In cultured glomerular mesangial cells, Wang et al. found that miR-377 targets serine/threonine-protein kinase PAK1 and leads to reduced expression of superoxide dismutase (SOD) thereby promoting fibronectin production [61]. As increased levels of fibronectin may contribute to glomerular basement membrane thickening and mesangial expansion, miR-377-mediated reductions in SOD expression may contribute to DN pathogenesis [62].

4.2 MiRNAs and Diabetic Cardiac Complications

Diabetic cardiomyopathy is another severe complication resulting from both micro- and macro-vascular damage. Pathologic changes of diabetic cardiomyopathy may include fibrosis, capillary basement membrane thickening, periodic acid-Schiff (PAS)-positive material infiltration into the interstitium, and microaneurysm formation [63].

MiR-133 was the first miRNA shown to be dysregulated in diabetic hearts [64]. Clinical manifestations associated with the dysregulation of miR-133 include long QT syndrome (LQTS) [65] and cardiac hypertrophy [66]. LQTS is a disorder of the heart's conduction system which can create a predisposition for secondary ventricular arrhythmias which can result in syncope, cardiac arrest, and sudden death [67, 68]. Paulussen et al. identified studies linking the creation of the potassium channel involved in rapid delayed rectifier K^+ current (I_{Kr}) responsible for controlling repolarization to human ether-a-go-go-related gene (hERG) [69]. MiR-133 repression of hERG expression has been noted in arsenic-induced cardiac remodeling [70], but research into this relationship in a diabetic context has been largely based on findings retracted in 2011 [71, 72]. In the hearts of diabetic rabbits, serum response factor (SRF) was shown to upregulate miR-133, which was present at high levels [65]. Therefore, it is likely (pending confirmation in a diabetic context) that overexpression of SRF leads to mir-133-mediated suppression of hERG which depresses I_{Kr}, consequently prolonging the QT interval that is clinically associated with LQTS.

MiR-133 is also involved in the pathogenesis of cardiac hypertrophy [66]. Cardiac hypertrophy is a thickening of the myocardium that can decrease the volume of the heart chambers, and as a stress response to hypertension, heart valve stenosis, and aberrant conduction [66]. In vitro experiments showed a negative correlation between miR-133 expression and the presentation of cardiac hypertrophy [61]. Marked hypertrophy was noted in mice after the administration of miR-133 blocking oligonucleotides [66].

The involvement of miRNAs in the regulation of diabetic cardiomyopathy was investigated in vitro and in vivo by Shen et al. By examining the cardiac tissue of STZ-induced mice with diabetic cardiomyopathy, they identified 10 miRNAs (miR-195, miR-199a-3p, miR-700, miR-142-3p, miR-24, miR-21, miR-221,miR-499-3p, miR-208a, and miR-705) to be overexpressed and 6 miRNAs (miR-29, miR-1, miR-373, miR-143, miR-20a, and miR-220b) underexpressed when compared to their control [73]. They identified overexpression of miR-373 was associated with a concurrent reduction of MEF2C, which they concluded MEF2C was its target gene, in neonatal rat cardiomyocytes. They also noted that the p38 MAP kinase inhibitor SB203580 reduced the expression of miR-373 [73]. Lu et al. used a microarray-based approach to identify the role played by miR-223 in the diabetic heart [74]. They assessed ventricular biopsies from routine cardiac patients which revealed an increased expression of miR-223 in patients with T2D when compared to non-T2D patients. They also infected cultured neonatal rat ventricular myocytes (NRVM) with adenoviral expression vectors for miR-223 (Ad-miR-223) and noted that increased glucose uptake may have been due to the targeting of GLUT4 [74].

5 MiRNA as Potential Biomarkers in Diabetes

Diabetes is generally not detectable until well into the disease's progression. There has been some success with using miRNAs as biomarkers present in blood for detection of some diseases [6]. Chen et al. attempted to compare serum miRNA expression between T2DM patients and controls and found that the serum profile of diabetic patients contained three miRNAs which were not found in other disorders [75]. This study did not disclose the identities of the miRNAs that were differentially expressed. Zampetaki et al. also investigated the miRNA profiles of diabetic patients and found 13 miRNAs (miR-24, miR-21, miR-20b, miR-15a, miR-126, miR-191, miR-197, miR-223, miR-320, miR-486, miR-150, miR-29b, and miR-28-3p) to be differentially expressed in diabetic subjects [37]. They also identified miR-126 as a prospective predictor for DM with associated secondary peripheral artery disease. Fichtlscherer et al. performed a study in a cohort of patients with coronary artery disease (CAD) and noted that miR-17 and miR-145 expressions were generally suppressed, but that miR-145 was further decreased in patients with diabetes [76]. Wang et al. identified a five-miRNA panel (miR-661, miR-571, miR-770-5p, miR-892b, and miR-1303) were differentially expressed in T2DM patients [77]. Chen et al. expanded their search for markers into other tissues and fluids, in which they identified differential expression profiles including increased expression of miR-146a and miR-126 in plasma [78]. Finally, Pescador et al. found a three-miRNA panel (miR-15b, miR-138, and miR-376a) that they found to be significant for predicting diabetes and obesity [79]. These studies indicate that there is a substantial amount of ongoing research to find biomarkers for diabetes, not only as an independent disease, but in a variety of comorbid situations.

6 MiRNAs as Potential Therapeutic Targets

As the dysregulation of miRNA is implicated in the pathology of diabetes and its complications, alteration of miRNA expression is being investigated as a possible therapeutic vector. There are several techniques used to suppress miRNA expression and effect. Antisense nucleic acid derivatives bind to the targeted miRNA, thereby preventing it from interacting with its targets. Hutvágner et al. demonstrated the use of 2′-*O*-methyl oligonucleotides to silence let-7 expression in *C. elegans* larvae [80]. Stoffel et al. showed that derivatives of these oligonucleotides, termed antagomirs, are effective in mammalian systems by targeting miR-122 in mice [81]. Lanford et al. used locked nucleic acid (LNA)

Table 1
MiRNAs involving in diabetes and associated complications

MiRNAs	Tissue	Target gene	Function	Reference
miR-375	Pancreatic β-cell	Mtpn, t-SNAREs yeast homolog1A, p38 MAPK, MXI-1, PI3-K, PDK1	Suppressed glucose-induced insulin secretion	[9–15]
miR-124	Pancreatic β-cell	FoxA2, Creb, Mtpn, Rab27A, Noc2	Suppressed glucose metabolism and insulin secretion	[19–22, 84]
miR-124a	Pancreatic β-cell	Kir-6.2, FoxA2	Decreased glucose-stimulated Insulin secretion	[17]
miR-9	Pancreatic β-cell	Onecut-2, Sirt1	Suppressed insulin secretion	[23, 24]
miR-96	Pancreatic β-cell	Noc2	Increased granuphilin/Slp4 decreased Noc2	[21]
miR-15a/b	Pancreatic β-cell, adipose tissue, muscle	Uncoupling protein-2, DLK1	Increased insulin biosynthesis, increased oxygen consumption, reduced ATP generation	[25]
miR-21	Pancreatic β-cell	PTEN, PI3-K, AKT	Regulated pancreatic development	[26]
miR-34a	Pancreatic β-cell	VAMP2, SNARE	Reduced insulin secretion	[26, 27]
miR-146	Pancreatic β-cell, retina	NF-kB	Inhibition of NF-kB activation	[26, 27]
miR-1	skeletal muscles	IGF-1, IGF-1R, HERG, KCNJ2, GJA1, Bcl2, Irx5, Dll-1, Cdk9, Pim-1, Hsp60	Developed insulin resistance	[30, 31]
miR-133a/b	skeletal muscles	KLF15	Reduced insulin-stimulated glucose uptake, impaired glucose homeostasis	[36]
miR-24	skeletal muscles	p38 MAPK	Increases insulin-responsive GLUT4 translocation	[39, 40]
miR-144	skeletal muscles	IRS-1	Downregulation of IRS-1, cause IR	[41]

miR-33a/b	Islet	ABCA1, IRS-2	Inhibited fatty acid oxidation decreased glucose-stimulated insulin secretion, increased cholesterol levels	[47, 48]
miR-143	Adipose tissue	ERK5, ORP8, MAPK7	Elevated body weight and mesenteric fat weight, impair insulin-stimulated AKT activation and glucose homeostasis	[50–52]
miR-14, miR-278	Adipose tissue	–	Regulate adipocyte droplet size and triacylglycerol levels in insects	[53]
miR-192	Renal tissue	TGF-β, SIP1, δEF1 Col1a2,	Control of kidney function	[55–59]
miR-29a	Renal tissue	Collagen IV	Promote excess collagen deposition	[60]
miR-377	tubular epithelial cells	PAK1, SOD	Development of renal fibrosis	[61]
miR-133	heart	HERG, SRF	Long QT syndrome, cardiac hypertrophy	[66–70]
miR-373	cardiomyocytes	MEF2C, p38 MAPK	Reduced cell size	[73]
miR-223	ventricular myocytes	GLUT4	Glucose metabolism	[74]
miR-192	kidney	LNA-anti-miR-192	Improvement of renal fibrosis	[58]

antimiRs to decrease the levels of miR-122 in primates with chronic hepatitis C virus to upregulate a set of miRNA predicted to reduce the effects of the infection [82]. In a diabetic context, Frost et al. demonstrated that an antimiR-induced knockdown of let-7 can enhance insulin sensitivity in hepatic and muscle tissues [83]. Putta et al. showed that LNA-modified inhibitor of miR-192 (LNA-anti-miR-192) reduced miR-192 levels in STZ-induced mouse models of diabetic nephropathy which improved proteinuria and renal fibrosis symptoms [58]. The diabetic- and diabetic complication-related miRNAs as well as their roles in regulating glucose metabolism are summarized in Table 1. These efforts show that specific alteration of miRNA expression is possible and potentially of therapeutic benefit in the context of diabetes.

7 Perspectives and Conclusions

This chapter has highlighted some of the roles played by miRNA in the pathology of diabetes and its associated complications. Its involvement is part of a complex network of regulatory interactions involving tissues from many distinct areas of the body, including those of the pancreas, heart, skeletal muscles, and kidneys. Further research should continue to establish the regulatory changes involved in this disease as well as to establish effective and efficient methods for clinical diagnosis and treatment. Effort should be invested in refining the miRNA profiles that have been discovered for potential application in screening tests. Similarly, further exploration of miRNA manipulation should be pursued to develop practical treatments. Better knowledge of the effects of miRNA will allow us to increase quality of life not only for individuals with diabetes, but for patients with other diseases with significant genetic involvement.

References

1. Inzucchi SE, Sherwin RS (2011) Type 1 diabetes mellitus, Cecil Med. 24th Ed Phila. Pa Saunders Elsevier
2. Shaw JE, Sicree RA, Zimmet PZ (2010) Global estimates of the prevalence of diabetes for 2010 and 2030. Diabetes Res Clin Pract 87(1):4–14
3. Mokdad AH et al (Jan. 2003) Prevalence of obesity, diabetes, and obesity-related health risk factors, 2001. JAMA 289(1):76–79
4. Cecil RLF, Goldman L, Schafer AI (2012) Goldman's cecil medicine, expert consult premium edition—enhanced online features and print, single volume, 24: Goldman's cecil medicine. Elsevier Health Sciences, Amsterdam
5. Dokken BB (2008) The pathophysiology of cardiovascular disease and diabetes: beyond blood pressure and lipids. Diabetes Spectr 21(3):160–165
6. Kolfschoten IGM, Roggli E, Nesca V, Regazzi R (2009) Role and therapeutic potential of microRNAs in diabetes. Diabetes Obes Metab 11:118–129
7. John B, Sander C, Marks DS (2006) Prediction of human microRNA targets. Methods Mol Biol 342:101–113. Clifton, NJ
8. Guay C, Roggli E, Nesca V, Jacovetti C, Regazzi R (2011) Diabetes mellitus, a microRNA-related disease? Transl Res 157(4):253–264

9. Poy MN et al (2004) A pancreatic islet-specific microRNA regulates insulin secretion. Nature 432(7014):226–230
10. Avnit-Sagi T, Kantorovich L, Kredo-Russo S, Hornstein E, Walker MD (2009) The promoter of the pri-miR-375 gene directs expression selectively to the endocrine pancreas. PLoS One 4(4):e5033
11. Joglekar MV, Joglekar VM, Hardikar AA (2009) Expression of islet-specific microRNAs during human pancreatic development. Gene Expr Patterns 9(2):109–113
12. Poy MN et al (2009) miR-375 maintains normal pancreatic alpha- and beta-cell mass. Proc Natl Acad Sci U S A 106(14):5813–5818
13. Li Y et al (2010) miR-375 enhances palmitate-induced lipoapoptosis in insulin-secreting NIT-1 cells by repressing myotrophin (V1) protein expression. Int J Clin Exp Pathol 3(3):254–264
14. El Ouaamari A, Baroukh N, Martens GA, Lebrun P, Pipeleers D, van Obberghen E (2008) miR-375 targets 3′-phosphoinositide-dependent protein kinase-1 and regulates glucose-induced biological responses in pancreatic beta-cells. Diabetes 57(10):2708–2717
15. Kloosterman WP, Lagendijk AK, Ketting RF, Moulton JD, Plasterk RHA (2007) Targeted inhibition of miRNA maturation with morpholinos reveals a role for miR-375 in pancreatic islet development. PLoS Biol 5(8):e203
16. Lynn FC, Skewes-Cox P, Kosaka Y, McManus MT, Harfe BD, German MS (2007) MicroRNA expression is required for pancreatic islet cell genesis in the mouse. Diabetes 56(12):2938–2945
17. Baroukh N et al (2007) MicroRNA-124a regulates Foxa2 expression and intracellular signaling in pancreatic beta-cell lines. J Biol Chem 282(27):19575–19588
18. Joglekar MV, Parekh VS, Mehta S, Bhonde RR, Hardikar AA (2007) MicroRNA profiling of developing and regenerating pancreas reveal post-transcriptional regulation of neurogenin3. Dev Biol 311(2):603–612
19. Krichevsky AM, Sonntag K-C, Isacson O, Kosik KS (2006) Specific microRNAs modulate embryonic stem cell-derived neurogenesis. Stem Cells 24(4):857–864
20. Conaco C, Otto S, Han J-J, Mandel G (2006) Reciprocal actions of REST and a microRNA promote neuronal identity. Proc Natl Acad Sci U S A 103(7):2422–2427
21. Lovis P, Gattesco S, Regazzi R (2008) Regulation of the expression of components of the exocytotic machinery of insulin-secreting cells by microRNAs. Biol Chem 389(3):305–312
22. Cuellar TL, McManus MT (2005) MicroRNAs and endocrine biology. J Endocrinol 187(3):327–332
23. Plaisance V, Abderrahmani A, Perret-Menoud V, Jacquemin P, Lemaigre F, Regazzi R (2006) MicroRNA-9 controls the expression of granuphilin/Slp4 and the secretory response of insulin-producing cells. J Biol Chem 281(37):26932–26942
24. Ramachandran D, Roy U, Garg S, Ghosh S, Pathak S, Kolthur-Seetharam U (2011) Sirt1 and mir-9 expression is regulated during glucose-stimulated insulin secretion in pancreatic β-islets. FEBS J 278(7):1167–1174
25. Sun L-L, Jiang B-G, Li W-T, Zou J-J, Shi Y-Q, Liu Z-M (2011) MicroRNA-15a positively regulates insulin synthesis by inhibiting uncoupling protein-2 expression. Diabetes Res Clin Pract 91(1):94–100
26. Roggli E et al (2010) Involvement of microRNAs in the cytotoxic effects exerted by proinflammatory cytokines on pancreatic beta-cells. Diabetes 59(4):978–986
27. Lovis P et al (2008) Alterations in microRNA expression contribute to fatty acid-induced pancreatic beta-cell dysfunction. Diabetes 57(10):2728–2736
28. Ortega FJ et al (2010) MiRNA expression profile of human subcutaneous adipose and during adipocyte differentiation. PloS ONE 5(2):e9022
29. Stump CS, Henriksen EJ, Wei Y, Sowers JR (2006) The metabolic syndrome: role of skeletal muscle metabolism. Ann Med 38(6):389–402
30. Granjon A et al (2009) The microRNA signature in response to insulin reveals its implication in the transcriptional action of insulin in human skeletal muscle and the role of a sterol regulatory element-binding protein-1c/myocyte enhancer factor 2C pathway. Diabetes 58(11):2555–2564
31. He A, Zhu L, Gupta N, Chang Y, Fang F (2007) Overexpression of micro ribonucleic acid 29, highly up-regulated in diabetic rats, leads to insulin resistance in 3T3-L1 adipocytes. Mol Endocrinol 21(11):2785–2794
32. Gallagher IJ et al (2010) Integration of microRNA changes in vivo identifies novel molecular features of muscle insulin resistance in type 2 diabetes. Genome Med 2(2):9
33. Yu X-Y et al (2008) Glucose induces apoptosis of cardiomyocytes via microRNA-1 and IGF-1. Biochem Biophys Res Commun 376(3):548–552
34. Elia L et al (Dec. 2009) Reciprocal regulation of microRNA-1 and insulin-like growth factor-1

signal transduction cascade in cardiac and skeletal muscle in physiological and pathological conditions. Circulation 120(23):2377–2385
35. Sandhu MS, Heald AH, Gibson JM, Cruickshank JK, Dunger DB, Wareham NJ (2002) Circulating concentrations of insulin-like growth factor-I and development of glucose intolerance: a prospective observational study. Lancet 359(9319):1740–1745. Lond Engl
36. Horie T et al (2009) MicroRNA-133 regulates the expression of GLUT4 by targeting KLF15 and is involved in metabolic control in cardiac myocytes. Biochem Biophys Res Commun 389(2):315–320
37. Zampetaki A et al (2010) Plasma microRNA profiling reveals loss of endothelial miR-126 and other microRNAs in type 2 diabetes. Circ Res 107(6):810–817
38. Huang B et al (2009) MicroRNA expression profiling in diabetic GK rat model. Acta Biochim Biophys Sin 41(6):472–477
39. Kiriakidou M et al (2004) A combined computational-experimental approach predicts human microRNA targets. Genes Dev 18(10):1165–1178
40. Niu W et al (2003) Maturation of the regulation of GLUT4 activity by p38 MAPK during L6 cell myogenesis. J Biol Chem 278(20):17953–17962
41. Karolina DS et al (2011) MicroRNA 144 impairs insulin signaling by inhibiting the expression of insulin receptor substrate 1 in type 2 diabetes mellitus. PloS One 6(8):e22839
42. Samuel VT, Shulman GI (2012) Mechanisms for insulin resistance: common threads and missing links. Cell 148(5):852–871
43. Raghow R, Yellaturu C, Deng X, Park EA, Elam MB (2008) SREBPs: the crossroads of physiological and pathological lipid homeostasis. Trends Endocrinol Metab 19(2):65–73
44. Sacco J, Adeli K (2012) MicroRNAs: emerging roles in lipid and lipoprotein metabolism. Curr Opin Lipidol 23(3):220–225
45. Rayner KJ et al (2010) MiR-33 contributes to the regulation of cholesterol homeostasis. Science 328(5985):1570–1573
46. Gerin I et al (2010) Expression of miR-33 from an SREBP2 intron inhibits cholesterol export and fatty acid oxidation. J Biol Chem 285(44):33652–33661
47. Horie T et al (2010) MicroRNA-33 encoded by an intron of sterol regulatory element-binding protein 2 (Srebp2) regulates HDL in vivo. Proc Natl Acad Sci U S A 107(40):17321–17326
48. Wijesekara N et al (2012) miR-33a modulates ABCA1 expression, cholesterol accumulation, and insulin secretion in pancreatic islets. Diabetes 61(3):653–658
49. Kahn SE, Hull RL, Utzschneider KM (2006) Mechanisms linking obesity to insulin resistance and type 2 diabetes. Nature 444(7121):840–846
50. Xie H, Lim B, Lodish HF (May 2009) MicroRNAs induced during adipogenesis that accelerate fat cell development are downregulated in obesity. Diabetes 58(5):1050–1057
51. Esau C et al (2004) MicroRNA-143 regulates adipocyte differentiation. J Biol Chem 279(50):52361–52365
52. Kajimoto K, Naraba H, Iwai N (2006) MicroRNA and 3T3-L1 pre-adipocyte differentiation. RNA 12(9):1626–1632. N. Y. N
53. Xu P, Vernooy SY, Guo M, Hay BA (2003) The drosophila microRNA Mir-14 suppresses cell death and is required for normal fat metabolism. Curr Biol 13(9):790–795
54. Teleman AA, Cohen SM (2006) Drosophila lacking microRNA miR-278 are defective in energy homeostasis. Genes Dev 20(4):417–422
55. Adler S (2004) Diabetic nephropathy: linking histology, cell biology, and genetics. Kidney Int 66(5):2095–2106
56. Krupa A, Jenkins R, Luo DD, Lewis A, Phillips A, Fraser D (2010) Loss of MicroRNA-192 promotes fibrogenesis in diabetic nephropathy. J Am Soc Nephrol 21(3):438–447
57. Kato M et al (2007) MicroRNA-192 in diabetic kidney glomeruli and its function in TGF-β-induced collagen expression via inhibition of E-box repressors. Proc Natl Acad Sci U S A 104(9):3432–3437
58. Putta S, Lanting L, Sun G, Lawson G, Kato M, Natarajan R (2012) Inhibiting microRNA-192 ameliorates renal fibrosis in diabetic nephropathy. J Am Soc Nephrol 23(3):458–469
59. Chung ACK, Huang XR, Meng X, Lan HY (2010) miR-192 mediates TGF-beta/Smad3-driven renal fibrosis. J Am Soc Nephrol 21(8):1317–1325
60. Du B et al (2010) High glucose down-regulates miR-29a to increase collagen IV production in HK-2 cells. FEBS Lett 584(4):811–816
61. Wang Q et al (2008) MicroRNA-377 is up-regulated and can lead to increased fibronectin production in diabetic nephropathy. FASEB J 22(12):4126–4135. Off Publ Fed Am Soc Exp Biol
62. Schena FP, Gesualdo L (2005) Pathogenetic mechanisms of diabetic nephropathy. J Am Soc Nephrol 16(3 suppl 1):S30–S33
63. van Hoeven KH, Factor SM (1990) A comparison of the pathological spectrum of hypertensive, diabetic, and hypertensive-diabetic heart disease. Circulation 82(3):848–855
64. Tang X, Tang G, Özcan S (2008) Role of MicroRNAs in diabetes. Biochim Biophys Acta 1779(11):697–701

65. Zhang Y et al (2007) Ionic mechanisms underlying abnormal QT prolongation and the associated arrhythmias in diabetic rabbits: a role of rapid delayed rectifier K+ current. Cell Physiol Biochem 19(5–6):225–238. Int J Exp Cell Physiol Biochem Pharmacol
66. Carè A et al (2007) MicroRNA-133 controls cardiac hypertrophy. Nat Med 13(5):613–618
67. Collins KK, Van Hare GF (2006) Advances in congenital long QT syndrome. Curr Opin Pediatr 18(5):497–502
68. Mizusawa Y, Horie M, Wilde AAM (2014) Genetic and clinical advances in congenital long QT syndrome. Circ J 78(12):2827–2833
69. Paulussen A et al (2000) Analysis of the human KCNH2(HERG) gene: identification and characterization of a novel mutation Y667X associated with long QT syndrome and a non-pathological 9 bp insertion. Hum Mutat 15(5):483
70. Shan H et al (2013) Upregulation of microRNA-1 and microRNA-133 contributes to arsenic-induced cardiac electrical remodeling. Int J Cardiol 167(6):2798–2805
71. Xiao J et al (2007) MicroRNA miR-133 represses HERG K+ channel expression contributing to QT prolongation in diabetic hearts. J Biol Chem 282(17):12363–12367
72. Xiao J et al (2011) MicroRNA miR-133 represses HERG K+ channel expression contributing to QT prolongation in diabetic hearts. J Biol Chem 286(32):28656–28656
73. Shen E, Diao X, Wang X, Chen R, Hu B (2011) MicroRNAs involved in the mitogen-activated protein kinase cascades pathway during glucose-induced cardiomyocyte hypertrophy. Am J Pathol 179(2):639–650
74. Lu H, Buchan RJ, Cook SA (2010) MicroRNA-223 regulates Glut4 expression and cardiomyocyte glucose metabolism. Cardiovasc Res 86(3):410–420
75. Chen X et al (2008) Characterization of microRNAs in serum: a novel class of biomarkers for diagnosis of cancer and other diseases. Cell Res 18(10):997–1006
76. Fichtlscherer S et al (2010) Circulating microRNAs in patients with coronary artery disease. Circ Res 107(5):677–684
77. Wang C et al (2016) Increased serum microRNAs are closely associated with the presence of microvascular complications in type 2 diabetes mellitus. Sci Rep 6:20032
78. Chien H-Y et al (2015) Circulating microRNA as a diagnostic marker in populations with type 2 diabetes mellitus and diabetic complications. J Chin Med Assoc 78(4):204–211
79. Pescador N, Pérez-Barba M, Ibarra JM, Corbatón A, Martínez-Larrad MT, Serrano-Ríos M (2013) Serum circulating microRNA profiling for identification of potential type 2 diabetes and obesity biomarkers. PloS One 8(10):e77251
80. Hutvágner G, Simard MJ, Mello CC, Zamore PD (2004) Sequence-specific inhibition of small RNA function. PLoS Biol 2(4):E98
81. Krützfeldt J et al (2005) Silencing of microRNAs in vivo with ‘antagomirs’. Nature 438(7068):685–689
82. Lanford RE et al (2010) Therapeutic silencing of microRNA-122 in primates with chronic hepatitis C virus infection. Science 327(5962):198–201
83. Frost RJA, Olson EN (2011) Control of glucose homeostasis and insulin sensitivity by the let-7 family of microRNAs. Proc Natl Acad Sci U S A 108(52):21075–21080
84. Merrins MJ, Stuenkel EL (2008) Kinetics of Rab27a-dependent actions on vesicle docking and priming in pancreatic beta-cells. J Physiol 586(22):5367–5381

Chapter 18

MicroRNA Regulatory Networks as Biomarkers in Obesity: The Emerging Role

Lihua Zhang, Daniel Miller, Qiuping Yang, and Bin Wu

Abstract

Even though it is a pandemic health problem worldwide, the pathogenesis of obesity is poorly understood. Recently, emerging studies verified that microRNAs (miRNAs) are involved in complicated metabolic processes including adipocyte differentiation, fat cell formation (adipogenesis), obesity-related insulin resistance and inflammation. Many regulatory networks have been identified in murine adipose tissue, but those in human adipose tissue are not as well known. In addition, miRNAs have been detected in circulation, and thus may be usable as diagnostic indicators. MiRNAs may play an important part in regulating metabolic functions in adipose tissues and, by extension, obesity and its associated disorders. Consequently, they may be potential candidates for therapeutic targets and biomarkers.

Key words Obesity, Adipogenesis, Regulatory networks, Insulin resistance, Biomarkers, miRNAs

1 Introduction

Obesity (body mass index, BMI $\geq$30 kg/m^2) and obesity-related disease have reached pandemic proportion in developing and developed countries and now pose a tremendous threat to global public health. Not only obesity, but also overweight (BMI 25–30 kg/m^2), is highly associated with some chronic non-communicable diseases (NCDs), increases the likelihood of diabetes, hypertension, cardiovascular disease, stroke, and certain types of cancer, which has become a problem of epidemic scale [1]. According to the World Health Organization (WHO) 2014 Global Status Report of NCDs, the incidence of obesity has nearly doubled between 1980 and 2014 with estimates for 2014 of 11% of adult males and 15% of adult females [2]. Obesity has detrimental effects on public health, leading to decreased life expectancies and increased health care costs which make it a significant public health challenge [3], but it can be controlled by programs promoting physical activity and a healthy diet [1]. Therapeutic targets may be an option to supplement the

Jingshan Huang et al. (eds.), *Bioinformatics in MicroRNA Research*, Methods in Molecular Biology, vol. 1617,
DOI 10.1007/978-1-4939-7046-9_18,

behavioral programs, but development of such will require better understanding of the underlying mechanisms involved in adipose tissue dysfunction and obesity pathology.

MicroRNAs are a class of short, single-stranded, noncoding RNAs of approximately 20–23 nucleotides which are involved in the regulation of many biological processes [4].They influence biological and molecular processes in different tissues and cells, including adipose tissue and adipocytes [5, 6]. The negatively regulated genes are inhibited by specific, partial, or complete binding of sites complementary to the miRNA seed sequence (2–8 bp) in the 3′-Un-translated Regions (UTR) of mRNA. This action either blocks the translation or targets the transcript for destabilization or degradation which diminishes the protein output [7]. The nature of these binding attributes means that miRNA can regulate multiple genes and act across an entire genome. MiRNAs regulate complicated metabolic processes including adipocyte differentiation, adipogenesis, obesity-related insulin resistance (IR), and inflammation. Adipocyte MiRNAs have been observed in general circulation, and thus may provide a readily accessible means of detecting disturbed adipose tissue function [8]. As regulators of function in adipose tissues, miRNA may be viable targets for therapeutic interventions. Identification of the targets and the development of effective therapies should be the subject of further research.

The remainder of this chapter is organized as follows: Subheading 1 briefly summarizes state-of-the-art research in biogenesis and molecular functions of miRNAs in adipocyte development and adipogenesis; Subheading 2 introduces miRNAs and obesity-related insulin resistance; Subheading 3 describes greater details of miRNAs and obesity; and finally, Subheading 4 concludes that miRNAs can potentially act as early biomarkers for obesity-related disorders.

2 Biogenesis and Molecular Function of MiRNAs in Adipocyte Development and Adipogenesis

MiRNAs can promote or preclude adipocyte differentiation by regulating signal pathways associated with adipogenesis, suppressing transcription factors, or inhibiting the clonal expansion stage of mitosis [1]. Several miRNAs have been verified by different studies that play pivotal roles in the regulation of adipocyte differentiation, development, and adipogenesis (Table 1).

2.1 MicroRNAs in Adipocyte Differentiation and Development

The adipocyte differentiation has two primary phases: determination and terminal differentiation [9]. The first step involves embryonic stem cells (ESCs) or multipotent mesenchymal stem cells (MSCs) that are subjected to 3-isobutyl-1-methylxanthine, insulin dexamethasone, and bone morphogenetic proteins (BMPs)

Table 1
MicroRNAs associated with adipogenesis and adipocyte function

miRNAs	Experiment Model	Target gene	Function	Ref.	Target
miR-519d	Adipose tissue, preadipocyte	PPARa	Lipid accumulation (up)	[11]	Transcription factors
miR-138	MSC	EID-1	Anti-adipogenic (down)	[12]	Transcription factors
let-7	3T3-L1	HMGA2	Anti-adipogenesic (down)	[13]	Mitotic clonal expansion
miR-17-92	3T3-L1	RB2/P130	Pro-adipogenic (up)	[14]	Mitotic clonal expansion
miR-30a/d	Adipose tissue cell	RUNX2	Pro-adipogenic (up)	[15]	–
miR-375	3T3-L1	Erk1/2	Pro-adipogenic (up)	[16]	MAPK signaling pathway
miR-27a/27b	3T3-L1, MSC,OP9	PPARγ	Anti-adipogenic (down)	[17–19]	Transcription factors
miR-21	hASC	TGFBR2	Pro-adipogenic (up)	[20]	TGF signaling pathway
miR-31, -326	MSC	C/EBPα	Anti-adipogenic (down)	[21]	Transcription factors
miR-155	Macrophage	C/EBPβ	Anti-adipogenic (down)	[12]	Transcription factors
miR-143	3T3-L1,adipose tissue	Erk5	Pro-adipogenic (up)	[22, 38]	MAPK signaling pathway
miR-103,-107	3T3-L1	Acetyl CoA	Anti-adipogenesic (down)	[23, 24]	–
miR-8	MSC	TCF	Pro-adipogenic (up)	[25]	Wnt/b-catenin signaling pathway
miR-210	3T3-L1	TCF7L2	Pro-adipogenic (up)	[26]	Wnt/b-catenin signaling pathway
miR-146b	3T3-L1	SIRT1	Pro-adipogenic (up)	[27]	
miR-130	Adipose tissue	PPARγ	Anti-adipogenic (down)	[28]	
miR-30c	Adipose tissue cell	PAI-1, ALK2	Pro-adipogenic (up)	[29, 30]	–
miR-204/211	C3H10T1/2, BMSC	RUNX2	Pro-adipogenic (up)	[31]	–
miR-448	3T3-L1	KLF5	Pro-adipogenic (up)	[18]	
miR-145	DFAT cell	IRS1	Anti-adipogenic (down)	[32]	

(continued)

Table 1 (continued)

miRNAs	Experiment Model	Target gene	Function	Ref.	Target
miR-224	3T3-L1	EGR2	Anti-adipogenic (down)	[33]	
miR-14	Drosophila	P38 MAPK	Anti-adipogenic (down)	[34]	MAPK signaling pathway
miR-278	Drosophila	–	Regulators of adipose tissue	[35]	

Note: *PPARγ* peroxisome proliferator-activated receptor-γ, *3T3-L1* murine preadipocyte cell line, *OP9 cells* murine bone marrow stromal cell lines, *C/EBP* CCAAT-enhancer-binding protein, *ESCs* embryonic stem cells, *MSCs* multipotent mesenchymal stem cells, *Erk* extracellular regulated MAP kinase, *EID-1* EP300 interacting inhibitor of differentiation 1, *hASCs* human adipose tissue-derived mesenchymal stem cells, *HMGA2* high mobility group AT-hook 2, *DFAT* dedifferentiated fat cells, *KLF5* kruppel-like factor 5, *RUNX2* runt-related transcription factor 2, *SIRT1* sirtuin1, *MAPK* mitogen-activated protein kinases, *TGFβR2* transforming growth factor beta receptor II, *TCF7L2* transcription factor 7-like 2, *EGR2* early growth response, *PAI-1* phosphoribosylanthranilate isomerase, *ALK2* aurora-like kinase2

that cause the adipocyte precursor cells differentiate into preadipocytes. The second stage is the differentiation of preadipocytes into mature adipocytes, during which cells express many adipocyte-specific traits including increased glucose uptake and fat accumulation. It has been demonstrated that miRNAs can be responsible for regulating the adipogenic lineage commitment in pluripotent stem cells and mature fat cells, by controlling the expression of mature adipocyte markers, such as fatty acid binding protein 4 (FABP4) and insulin-sensitive glucose transporter-4 (GLUT4) [9].

According to research outcome from a preponderance of evidence, it was established that miRNAs were indispensable for terminal adipocyte differentiation and function, and it revealed that miRNAs play a vital role in adipogenesis in vitro [10]. Homozygous ablation of Dicer obviously destroyed adipogenesis and downregulated several adipocyte markers such as FAs (fatty acids), Peroxisome Proliferator-Activated Receptor-γ (PPARγ), FABP4, and GLUT4 before induction in preadipocytes.

Martinelli et al. [11] noted that MiR-519d suppressed the PPARa protein translation and enhanced lipid accumulation during preadipocyte differentiation, involved in adipocyte development. They also found that the amount of suppression was directly related to the levels of miR-519d.

A pertinent study by Yang et al. [12] showed that miR-138 partially targets EP300 interacting inhibitor of differentiation 1 (EID-1), which is an inhibitor of cell differentiation.

A well-known miRNA, let-7, when overexpressed inhibits 3T3-L1 differentiation during the clonal expansion stage of mitosis and, when upregulated later in the differentiation process, represses high mobility group AT-hook 2 (HMGA2), a structure altering transcription factor for chromatin [13].

Wang et al. found that upregulation of miR-17-92 during the clonal expansion stage accelerates adipocyte differentiation and, when transfected into 3T3L1 cells, can accelerate differentiation and increased triglyceride accumulation [14]. They determined via luciferase reporter assay that RB2/P130, a cell cycle repressor, was a target of miR-17-92.

In adipose tissue-derived stem cells, the miR-30 family (miR-30a/d/c) was found to play a role in promoting adipocyte differentiation [15].

Ling et al. [16] demonstrated that miR-375 promotes 3T3-L1 adipocyte differentiation by influencing the ERK1/2 pathway. This study verified that miR-375 expression increased in 3T3-L1 cells after differentiation was induced in preadipocytes and that the overexpression of miR-375 accelerates the process. MiR-375 levels were found to have a negative correlation with phosphorylation levels of Erk1/2 which was mediated by the extracellular mitogen-activated protein kinases (MAPK) signaling pathway.

2.2 MicroRNAs and Adipogenesis

It has been demonstrated that miR-27a and miR-27b are anti-adipogenic and have been shown to directly target PPARγ and CCAAT-enhancer-binding protein (C/EBP) [17–19]. Both miRNAs are downregulated upon hormonal induction of adipogenesis in vitro. Murine adipose tissue exhibited higher levels of MiR-27a in the stromal vascular fraction than in mature adipocytes [18]. Transfection of miRNAs in 3T3-L1 (murine preadipocyte cell line) or OP9 cells (Murine bone marrow stromal cell lines) inhibited adipocyte formation by blocking the expression of adipogenic markers after the same adipogenic stimulant treatment as 3T3-L1 cells. Therefore, the miR-27 gene family (miR-27a, miR-27b) is a significant negative regulator of adipogenesis and potential anti-adipogenic target [17–19].

Overexpression miR-138 can downregulate hormonal induction of adipogenesis in hASCs, reduced lipid droplet accumulation, and inhibited the expression of adipogenic transcription factors C/EBPα and PPARγ2 (one of PPARγ isoforms found in humans and mice) [12].

MiR-21 expression was found to be temporarily elevated after adipogenesis was induced in human adipose tissue-derived MSCs (hASCs) [20]. TGF-β signaling pathway inhibition by miR-21-induced repression of transforming growth factor beta receptor II (TGFβR2) was found to promote adipogenesis.

It has been demonstrated that expression of miR-31 and miR-326 was underexpressed during the adipogenesis process of hASCs by assessment via microarray with Quantitative real-time polymerase chain reaction (QRT-PCR) verification, and that it directly targets C/EBPα [21]. In the context of macrophage studies, miR-155 inhibits C/EBPβ, a transcription factor involved early in adipogenesis [12]. According to the data from 3T3-L1 cells, miR-143 targets Erk5 (extracellular regulated MAP kinase) and accelerates adipogenesis, presumably that prevents the phosphorylation and inactivation of C/EBPβ [22].

Recently, a computational study estimated that miR-103 and -107 human miRNA paralogs provide a regulatory mechanism for several metabolic pathways, including Acetyl CoA and lipid metabolism, in vertebrates [23]. Another study showed that miR-103 exhibits a nine-fold upregulation in early 3T3-L1 adipogenesis and experimentally confirmed as pro-adipogenic [24], but the possible role of miR-103 in adipogenesis still needs to be experimentally validated.

The genetic researchers revealed that miR-8 is a conserved negative regulator of Wnt signaling in mammalian ST2 cells by repressing TCF protein levels. It can directly target the mRNAs encoding two pathway elements, the *wntless* and CG32767 genes in Drosophila [25].

MiR-210 was demonstrated to target the TCF7L2 via a luciferase reporter assay, which can activate Wnt signaling in association with β-catenin. In addition, overexpression of miR-210 can accentuate an adipogenic phenotype hypertrophy and lipid droplet formation in 3T3-L1cells [26].

MiR-146b expression increases in 3T3-L1 cells during adipogenesis. Overexpression of miR-146b subsequently decreased sirtuin1 (SIRT1) mRNA both in the adipose tissues of diet-induced and genetically obese mice [27].

Another miRNA, miR-130, impaired adipogenesis by potently repressing and targeting to PPARγmRNA coding and 3′ UTR, and decreasing PPARγ. These perturbations have been linked to human obesity. It has been estimated that, compared with nonobese women, obese women had underexpression of PPARγ mRNA and overexpression of miR-130 in adipose tissues [28].

It has been demonstrated that overexpression of miR-30a and miR-30d promotes adipogenesis, and miR-30a/d positively modulated runt-related transcription factor 2 (RUNX2) [15, 29]. Promotion of adipogenesis in hASCs was effected by the targeting of two genes: PAI-1 (phosphoribosylanthranilate isomerase) and aurora-like kinase 2 (ALK2) [29, 30]. It was reported that miR-204 and its homologue miR-211can be upregulated in the adipocyte differentiation from human bone marrow stem cells. Overexpression of miR-204 promoted adipogenesis to directly targeting RUNX2 [31]. MiR-448 has been proposed to negatively regulate adipogenesis by activating serotonin (5-HT) receptors 5-HT2AR and 5-HT2CR, and suppressing Kruppel-like factor 5 (KLF5) [18]. KLF5 is a transcription factor that, when induced by C/EBPβ and C/EBPδ, promotes adipogenesis by contributing to the induction of PPARγ.

According to cell differentiation data, miR-145 is significantly upregulated in porcine dedifferentiated fat (DFAT) cells.

Adipogenesis was suppressed in subjects with high levels of miR-145 by targeting IRS1 and decreasing triglyceride accumulation [32].

Peng et al. [33] found that miR-224 impairs adipocyte early differentiation and regulates fatty acid metabolism. They found that this action was mediated by early growth response (EGR2) and that overexpression of miR-224 hampered adipocyte differentiation.

MiR-14 can repress lipid metabolism by modulating the p38 MAPK signaling pathway in Drosophila [34]. MiR-278 regulates energy homeostasis and insulin sensitivity, which has also been characterized in Drosophila microRNA samples.

MiR-278 targets the expanded transcript, and miR-278-deficient knockout flies display a large reduction in total body triglyceride content and fat body mass. Intriguingly, miR-278 mutants were insulin-resistant and had higher levels of insulin and circulating sugar mobilized from adipose tissue stores [35]. Although miR-278 has been identified in Drosophila as crucial regulators of adipose tissue, their mammalian homologues need further investigation.

Finally, Fig. 1 summarizes the regulation of adipogenesis of miRNAs in different stages mammalian adipogenesis. MiRNAs can perform as pro-adipogenic factors or anti-adipogenic factors in the adipogenesis process [36].

3 MicroRNAs: Emerging Role in Obesity

Recently, several miRNAs have been identified by different studies that could be used as feasible therapeutic targets for obesity and its consequent pathologies. These emerging roles of miRNAs in obesity are summarized in Table 2 and will be discussed in the following sections.

Notably, miR-122 displayed target and downregulated hepatic lipogenic genes and was implicated in cholesterol biosynthesis by the analysis of the functional annotation. Anti-sense oligonucleotide inhibition of miR-122 and silencing miRNA expression in antagomir-122-treated obese mice decreased plasma cholesterol levels in vivo by targeting hepatic lipogenic genes. The study [37] showed that antagomirs can silence specific miRNAs in vivo, and thus may be a tool for therapeutic applications. miR-122 target genes were specifically predicted that affect cholesterol biosynthesis genes and plasma cholesterol reduced.

A study involving leptin-deficient ob/ob and diet-induced obesity (DIO) mouse models demonstrated that miRNAs associated with adipogenesis were markedly and conversely profiled dysregulation of 3T3-L1 in preadipocytes and adipocytes [24]. Similar miRNAs were discriminately modulated between in vitro

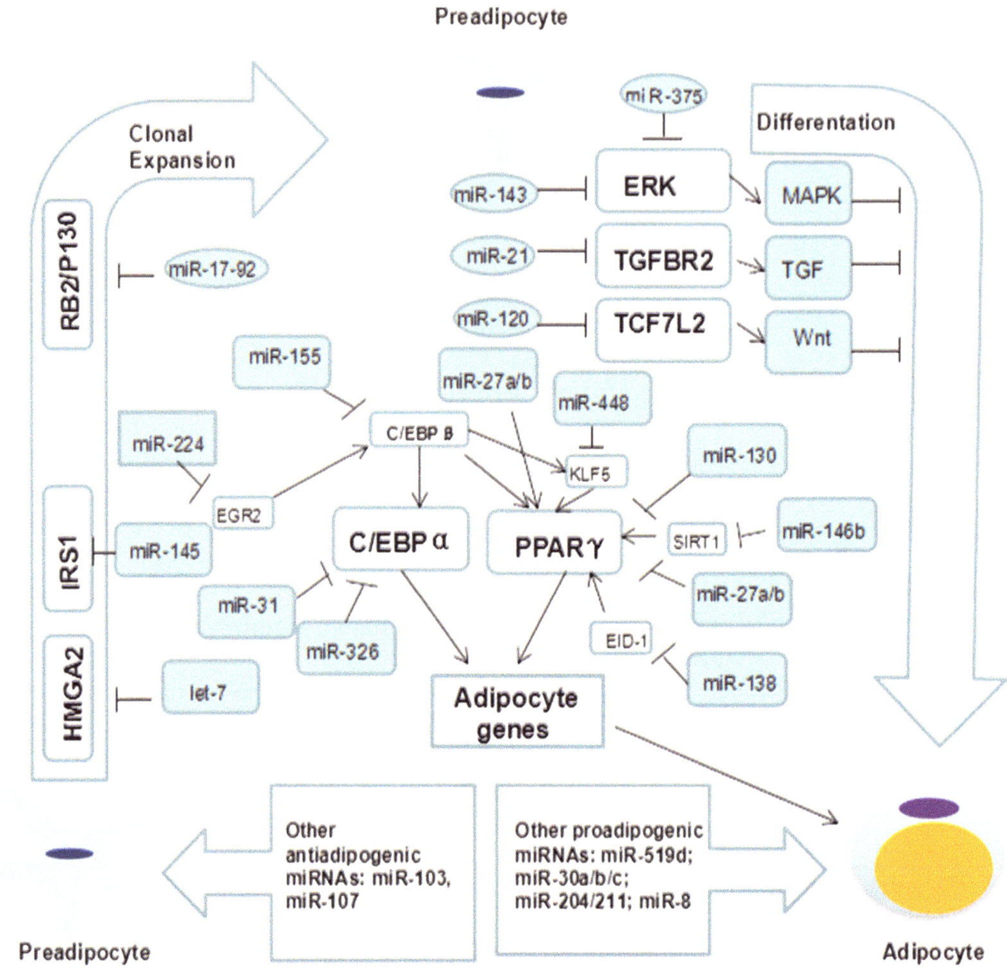

Fig. 1 Mammalian miRNAs regulate target genes during adipogenesis. Part of figure refers to the paper of Peng et al. [36]. The miRNAs in *rectangular blue boxes* have an anti-adipogenic role, obstructing adipogenesis by repressing their targets. MiRNAs in *oval blue boxes* are pro-adipogenic, promoting adipocyte differentiation

and in vivo during adipogenesis. MiR-422b, miR-148a, miR-103, miR-107, miR-30c, miR-30a-5p, and miR-143 were overexpressed during 3T3-L1 differentiation but generally underexpressed in cells isolated from ob/ob mice. The downregulation was speculated to be due to an inflammatory pathway response. The same study verified that the expression of miR-221 and 222 was decreased during adipogenesis and upregulated in obesity mouse models [24].

Another study focused on miR-143 expression in visceral adipose tissue isolated from obese mice, in which increased expression was noted. MiR-143 is implicated in alterations to PPARγ and aP2 expression [38].

MiR-335 was found to be upregulated in adipose tissue of three murine models of obesity, including leptin-deficient ob/ob mice, leptin-receptor-deficient db/db mice, and KKAy44 mice, and it may play a role in adipose hyperplasia [39].

Table 2
Relevant microRNAs involved in obesity

miRNAs	Biological system	Target gene	Function/dysfunction	Ref.
miR-222,-221	3T3-L1 Preadipocytes and adipocytes from leptin-deficient ob/ob and diet-induced obesity mouse models	–	Inverse expression patterns: decrease in adipogenesis and upregulated in obesity mouse models	[24]
miR-30c,-30a-5p,-148a,-103,-107, -422b, -143		PPARγ and aP2	Inverse expression patterns: upregulated in adipogenesis during 3T3-L1 differentiation, but downregulated in cells isolated from both mouse models of obesity	[24, 38]
miR-122	Liver in human	Hepatic lipogenic genes	Downregulated in fatty liver disease.; Involved in cholesterol biosynthesis	[37]
miR-335	Adipose tissue in mice	–	Upregulated in adipose tissue	[39]
miR-17-5p,-132, -99a,-325,-134,-181a,-145,-197	Adipose in human	–	Correlation between the expression of miRNAs and adipose tissue morphology and key metabolic indexes related to obesity and glucose metabolism	[40]
miR-519d	Adipose in human	PPARα	Overexpression disrupts fatty acid metabolism; Promotes cellular hypertrophy	[11, 39]
miR-205,-151,-34a,-133a,-329,-201,-330,-17-3p,-298,-328, -3805p	Liver in human	–	Deregulated in response to obesity	[41]

Note: *PPARγ* peroxisome proliferator-activated receptor-γ, *3T3-L1* murine preadipocyte cell line

A study demonstrated that miRNA isolated from multiple fat deposits taken from overweight and obese individuals, 16 miRNAs out of 106 miRNAs expressed had an expression pattern dependent on the adipose tissue. A significant correlation was identified between the expression of miRNA-17-5p, miRNA-132, miRNA-99a, miRNA-134, miRNA-181a, miRNA-145, miRNA-197, adipose tissue morphology, and key metabolic indexes related to obesity and glucose metabolism. The indexes investigated were visceral fat area, HbA1c, fasting plasma glucose (FPG), and leptin, adiponectin, interleukin-6 (IL-6) concentration. Negative correlations between miR-99a, miR-325, and IL-6 concentrations as well as between miR-181a and adiponectin level were determined [40].

A study of microarrayexpression profile analysis in subcutaneous adipose tissue (SAT) shows that out of 42 differently expressed microRNAs, overexpression of miR-519d was confirmed by QRT-PCR to accompany decreased protein levels of PPARAα (a predicted miR-519d target) in severely obese subjects. These studies also showed that miR-519d repressed translation of the PPARA protein which leads to increased lipid accumulation during preadipocyte differentiation [11].

It was found that miR-34a and miR-205 expressions were significantly increased in the obese murine liver, but expressions of miR-151, miR-133a, miR-329, miR-201, miR-330, miR-17-3p, miR-298, miR-328, and miR-380-5p were decreased [41].

Through microinjection technology in mice, the results indicate that a diet high in fat and sugar may induce trait inheritance via RNA signaling [42]. MiR-19b was used to induce metabolic alterations, such as obesity, to produce a diet-induced phenotype in the resulting progeny.

Based on these data, miRNA expression profiles are sensitive to obesity and miRNA are involved in the regulation of key proteins involved in adipogenesis and lipid homeostasis. Investigation into similar changes in miRNA biogenesis, transcription, and degradation may be warranted to determine their roles in dysregulation. Such investigation should uncover potential therapeutic targets that may be effective in combating obesity.

4 MicroRNAs and Obesity-Related Insulin Resistance

The inverse regulatory pattern for many miRNAs has significant implications for adipose tissue dysfunction in obese mice and humans during adipogenesis and obesity, and the interaction link between miRNAs and insulin resistance of obesity was summarized in Table 3 as the following section.

The study found that both miR-221 and the RNA-binding protein polypyrimidine tract-binding protein (PTB) bind Adiponectin receptor 1 (AdipoR1) 3′UTR inhibiting its production during muscle differentiation and in obesity. AdipoR1

Table 3
MicroRNAs involved in insulin resistance

miRNAs	Experiment model	Target gene	Ref.
miR-143	3T3-L1 ,adipocytes	–	[25]
miR-221	HepG2	ADIPOR1	[43]
miR-221	Primary human adipocytes	ADIPOR1, ETS1	[44]
miR-93	Human subcutaneous adipose tissue,3T3-L1	GLUT4	[45]
miR-130a-3p	Primary hepatocytes, mouse model ,HepG2	GRB10	[46]
miR-190b	Huh7	IGF1	[47]
miR-802	Hepa1-6, mouse model	Hnf1b	[48]
miR-122	HepG2	PTP1B	[49]
miR-181a	HepG2, primary hepatocytes	Sirt1	[50]
miR-99a	HepG2, HL77002	mTOR	[51]
miR-320	3T3-L1 adipocyte	PI3-K-AKT	[52]
miR-103,-107	Adipocytes in obese mice	caveolin-1	[53]
miR-29a/b/c	3T3-L1 adipocytes	–	[54]
miR-33a/b	Hepatic cell lines	IRS2	[55]
miR-126	SK-Hep1 hepatocytes	IRS-1	[57]
miR-24	Rats' skeletal muscle	p38 MAPK	[58]

Note: *ADIPOR1* diponectin receptor 1, *ETS1* v-ets Erythroblastosis virus E26 oncogene homologue 1, *GRB10* the growth factor receptor-bound protein 10, *IGF-1* insulin like growth factor, *HNF1B* hepatocyte nuclear factor 1beta, *PTP1B* protein tyrosine phosphatase 1B, *HNF4a* hepatocyte nuclear factor 4a, *JNK1* c-Jun N-terminal kinase1, *SIRT1* sirtuin 1, *PKM2* pyruvate kinase M2, *PI3-K* phosphatidylinositol 3-kinase, *IRS2* insulin receptor substrate 2, *ABCA1* adenosine triphosphate-binding cassette transporter A1, *SREBPs* sterol regulatory element-binding proteins, GLUT4 glucose transporter-4, mitogen-activated protein kinases (MAPK), *mTOR* mechanistic target of rapamycin

mediates adiponectin's pleiotropic effects and is involved in control of insulin resistance as well as being a receptor for adiponectin [43].

Meerson et al. [44] conducted a population study validated using QRT-PCR, immunoblots, and luciferase assays. They noted that miR-221 was overexpressed in obese patients and found that it affected fat metabolism downstream of leptin and tumor necrosis factor α (TNF-α). They observed that miR-221 directly targets and downregulates adiponectin receptor 1 (ADIPOR1) and Erythroblastosis virus E26 oncogene homologue 1 (ETS1). ETS1 associated with insulin resistance in primary human adipocytes plays a role in metabolic homeostasis.

Overexpression of miR-93 was seen in patients with insulin resistance. Further analysis validated that GLUT4 was a target of miR-93 which may explain its contribution to insulin resistance [45].

Xiao et al. [46] reported in mouse models that miR-130a-3p targets growth factor receptor-bound protein 10 (GRB10) in hepatic cells. GRB10 regulates the tyrosine kinase signaling cascade. They found that overexpression of miR-130a-3p in mice improved glucose clearance, but subsequent overexpression of GRB10 contributed to insulin resistance.

MiR-190b regulates cellular differentiation, proliferation, and the suppression of apoptosis. It takes part in controlling glucose homeostasis and enhances insulin sensitivity in hepatocellular carcinoma samples by targeting insulin-like growth factor (IGF-1). Therefore, changes in miR-190b expression may serve as a diagnostic marker hepatocellular dysfunction induced insulin resistance [47].

Kornfeld et al. [48] observed glucose intolerance and insulin resistance in obese mouse models coincident with overexpression of miR-802 and that liver function improved when miR-802 levels were reduced in obese patients. They also found that miR-802 suppresses the hepatocyte nuclear factor 1beta (Hnf1b) gene, and validated the finding by QRT-PCR and luciferase assays in vitro and in vivo. It provided strong evidence that therapeutic adjustment of miR-802 may reverse insulin resistance.

Yang et al. [49] found that miR-122 was underexpressed in mice fed a high fat diet. They found that it regulates the Protein tyrosine phosphatase 1B (PTP1B) expression by binding to its 3′-UTR and is associated with insulin resistance in liver cells. C-Jun N-terminal kinase 1 (JNK1) suppresses the expression of hepatocyte nuclear factor 4a (HNF4a) which promotes the expression of miR-122. JNK1 may provide a target for insulin resistance treatment by this regulatory path.

Zhou et al. [50] found that miR-181a targets sirtuin 1 (SIRT1) in liver cells. They found that overexpression of miR-181a resulted in leading to insulin resistance and suppression of the same improved insulin sensitivity.

Li et al. [51] found that hepatic cell lines treated with insulin can induce miR-99a expression and negatively regulate the mechanistic target of rapamycin (mTOR) and thereby modulate Pyruvate kinase M2 (PKM2) and glucose metabolism. Ling et al. [52] examined miRNA expression profile differences between insulin-sensitive and insulin-resistant 3T30L1 adipocytes. Out of the 79 dysregulated miRNAs, miR-320 expression was noted to show a 50-fold increase in insulin-resistant (IR) adipocytes. They established through bioinformatic techniques that miR-320 targeted the p85 subunit of phosphatidylinositol 3-kinase (PI3-K). In addition, they transfected adipocytes with antisense oligonucleotides against miR-320 (anti-miR-320 oligo) and noted an improvement in insulin sensitivity in previously resistant adipocytes. Enhancement of p85 expression, phosphorylation of Akt, and the protein expression of the glucose transporter GLUT-4, as well as insulin-stimulated glucose uptake was demonstrated and attributed to the improvement of IR in the same study. They concluded that the alleviation of insulin resistance in adipocytes may be associated with insulin–PI3-K signaling pathways.

It was demonstrated that the expression of miR-103 and miR-107 was upregulated in adipocytes of obese mice. Silencing of miR-103/107 can improve glucose homeostasis and insulin sensitivity and directly upregulate target gene- caveolin-1, a critical regulator of the insulin receptor. This was concomitant with stabilization of the insulin receptor, increased insulin signaling, and insulin-stimulated glucose uptake which decreased adipocyte size. These findings demonstrate that miR-103/107 may be a new target for the potential treatment for obesity [53].

Xie et al. [24] profiled the expression of more than 370 miRNAs during adipogenesis of preadipocyte 3T3-L1 cells and adipocytes from leptin-deficient ob/ob and diet-induced obese mice by using miRNA microarrays. Changes in key miRNAs were validated by RT-PCR. They found miR-103 and miR-143 to be overexpressed during adipogenesis and underexpressed in obese adipocyte samples.

He et al. found [54] three members of the miR-29 family, miR-29a, miR-29b, and miR-29c, demonstrated increased expression in the muscle, fat, and liver of diabetic rats. They used an adenovirus to induce overexpression of miR-29a/b/c in 3T3-L1 adipocytes which resulted in insulin resistance. They showed that miR-29 does not target Akt directly and proposed other unknown intermediaries to be involved in the signaling pathway.

MiR-33a/b embedded within introns of the sterol regulatory element-binding proteins (SREBPs) genes target the adenosine triphosphate-binding cassette transporter A1 (ABCA1) for post-transcriptional repression. ABCA1 was an important regulator of high-density lipoprotein (HDL) synthesis and reverse cholesterol transport [55].

Dávalos et al. [56] found that miR-33a and miR-33b were involved in regulating cholesterol homeostasis. They found that both were in the regulatory pathways of a number of enzymes involved in the process including carnitine *O*-octaniltransferase, carnitine palmitoyltransferase 1A, hydroxyacyl-CoA-dehydrogenase, Sirtuin 6 (SIRT6), AMP kinase subunit-α, and insulin receptor substrate 2 (IRS2). They observed that IRS2 was involved in the liver insulin-signaling pathway. They found an inverse response in fatty acid oxidation and insulin signaling to modulation of mir-33a and -b. They concluded that miR-33a and -b may be useful therapeutic targets.

Ryu et al. [57] confirmed that miR-126 directly targeted to IRS-1 3′UTR using reporter gene assay. They also demonstrated that miR-126 was actively involved in the development of insulin resistance induced by mitochondrial dysfunction via a reduction in the expression of IRS-1 protein.

It was found that miR-24 showed the most prominent expression difference in all miRNAs. P38 MAPK, which is a direct target of miR-24, also showed subsequent change. All the data showed that miR-24 might be associated with diabetes and insulin resistant through downregulation of p38 MAPK [58].

5 MicroRNAs as Early and Potential Biomarkers in Obesity and Related Metabolic and Cardiovascular Diseases

The worldwide increase in the incidence of obesity has implications for public healthcare. It is a major risk factor for type 2 diabetes and other metabolic diseases, cardiovascular disease, and a general increase in population mortality [1]. It is, however, difficult to evaluate every obese patient with different risks for developing future metabolic and cardiovascular complications. Therefore, biomarkers for early identification and verification of obese patients, especially those with high risk of diverse complications, are urgently needed.

MicroRNAs, as highly conserved noncoding RNA molecules, express with the characteristic of tissue and cell specific manner, and exert post-transcriptional effects on gene expression. They play important roles in many biological and pathological processes including diabetes, obesity, and metabolic disease [6]. They can also be released into the peripheral circulation where they remain stable and can be easily detected [5]. Thus, it is expected that miRNA found in tissue, plasma, or serum could be used for personalized putative diagnosis and early screening contributing to more timely and targeted treatment (Table 4).

Compared with healthy control subjects, the expression of let-7e and miR-296-5p was significantly elevated in plasma of obese patients with hypertension [59]. In addition, the expression of miR-1, miR-133, and miR-499-5p (cardiac-specific miRNAs) was found to be consistently increased in the plasma of patients and mice models with acute myocardial infarction (AMI) within hours after the onset. These miRNAs represent novel biomarkers of cardiac damage and obese-related cardiovascular diseases [60, 61].

Wang et al. [62] found that miR-208a was detected in all patients with AMI within 4 h of the onset of symptoms, but it remained undetectable in plasma of non-AMI patients. They reported that niR-208a was detected in 100% AMI patients within 4 h of the onset of symptoms and remained detectable in 90.9% AMI patients thereafter. They proposed that it could be used as a biomarker for detecting myocardial injury. Corsten et al. [63] found that miR-208b and miR-499 were highly elevated in the plasma from acute myocardial infarction patients.

Table 4
MicroRNAs as candidate biomarkers in obesity, obesity-related metabolic, and cardiovascular diseases in the circulation

miRNAs	Species	Biological system	Expression	Obesity and related diseases	Ref.
let-7e, miR-296-5p	Human	Plasma	Elevated	HT vs. control	[59]
miR-1,-133a/b,-495b	Human/mice	Plasma	Elevated	STEMI vs. control	[60, 61]
miR-208a	Human	Plasma	Elevated	STEMI vs. non-AMI vs. control	[62]
miR-208b,-499	Human	Plasma	Elevated	AMI vs. control	[63]
miR-17/92,-126,-155	Human	Plasma	Decreased	CAD vs. control	[64]
miR-181a/b/c	Human	Monocyte	Decreased	Obese and non-obese patients	[65]
miR-146a	Human/in vitro	PBMCs	Elevated	ACS vs. stable CAD	[66]
miR-146b-5p	Human	Monocytes	Decreased	Obesity vs. control	[67]

Note: *PBMCs* peripheral blood mononuclear cells, *HT* hypertension, *STEMI* acute ST-segment elevation MI, *ACS* acute coronary syndrome, *CAD* coronary artery disease

Notably, compared with healthy controls, circulating expression levels of miR-126, miR-17, miR-92a, and the inflammation-associated miR-155 were greatly decreased in patients with coronary artery disease (CAD), which were validated in a second cohort of patients with documented CAD and controls. This research showed that circulating levels of four vascular and inflammation-associated miRNAs were significantly downregulated in patients with CAD [64].

Coming from a cohort study sampling morbidly obese, high-risk obese, and nonobese patients, the expression of miR-181a was also found downregulated in monocytes of obese patients. Even after adjustment for traditional confounding risk factors, the expression of miR-181a was associated both with a higher number of metabolic syndrome components and with CAD [65]. Indeed, compared with patients of stable CAD, miR-146a was significantly increased in patients with ACS in human PBMCs. It was confirmed in vitro that overexpression of miR-146a in PBMCs significantly upregulated the function of type 1 helper T cells and induced protein expression of NF-kB p65, TNF-α, and mast cell proteinase-1 (MCP1) [66].

Hulsmans et al. [67] found that MiR-146b-5p inhibits NFkB-mediated inflammation by targeted repression of interleukin-1 receptor-associated kinase (IRAK) 1 and TNF receptor-associated factor-6 (TRAF6). They also reported that in morbidly obese patients miR-146b-5p expression was significantly decreased in blood monocytes. They noted that while the anti-inflammatory action of adiponectin was reduced, but not its insulin signaling potential. After using an antisense inhibitor to silence miR-146b-5p, the result was increased expression of IRAK1 and TRAF6, which can lead to more NF-kB p65 DNA binding activity and TNF-α.

The miRNA presented here are aberrantly expressed in the peripheral circulation. Easy access to samples and the ease of detection make them potential candidates for use as biomarkers for obesity-related diseases.

6 Conclusions

MicroRNA are involved with the regulation of many biological processes, including proliferation, differentiation, apoptosis, and metabolic functions in adipose tissues. Obesity causes changes to these processes that are ultimately reflected in the miRNA expression profiles of the affected tissues which are detectable both in tissue itself and possibly in the peripheral circulation. Use of these differential profiles could be useful to the medical community for early detection and diagnosis of obesity as well as associated diseases and conditions which could aid in improving the level of care and quality of life as well as help combat this prevalent metabolic disorder.

References

1. Haslam DW, James WP (2005) Obesity. Lancet 366(9492):1197–1209. doi:10.1016/s0140-6736(05)67483-1
2. World Health Organization (2014) Global status report on noncommunicable diseases 2014: attaining the nine global noncommunicable diseases targets; a shared responsibility. World Health Organization, Geneva
3. Heneghan HM, Miller N, Kerin MJ (2010) Role of microRNAs in obesity and the metabolic syndrome. Obes Rev 11(5):354–361. doi:10.1111/j.1467-789X.2009.00659.x
4. Zamore PD, Haley B (2005) Ribo-gnome: the big world of small RNAs. Science 309(5740):1519–1524. doi:10.1126/science.1111444
5. Bartel DP (2004) MicroRNAs: genomics, biogenesis, mechanism, and function. Cell 116(2):281–297
6. Lagos-Quintana M, Rauhut R, Lendeckel W, Tuschl T (2001) Identification of novel genes coding for small expressed RNAs. Science 294(5543):853–858. doi:10.1126/science.1064921

7. Bartel DP (2009) MicroRNAs: target recognition and regulatory functions. Cell 136(2):215–233. doi:10.1016/j.cell.2009.01.002
8. Hulsmans M, Holvoet P (2013) MicroRNAs as early biomarkers in obesity and related metabolic and cardiovascular diseases. Curr Pharm Des 19(32):5704–5717
9. Rosen ED, MacDougald OA (2006) Adipocyte differentiation from the inside out. Nat Rev Mol Cell Biol 7(12):885–896. doi:10.1038/nrm2066
10. Mudhasani R, Imbalzano AN, Jones SN (2010) An essential role for Dicer in adipocyte differentiation. J Cell Biochem 110(4):812–816. doi:10.1002/jcb.22625.
11. Martinelli R, Nardelli C, Pilone V, Buonomo T, Liguori R, Castano I, Buono P, Masone S, Persico G, Forestieri P, Pastore L, Sacchetti L (2010) miR-519d overexpression is associated with human obesity. Obesity (Silver Spring) 18(11):2170–2176. doi:10.1038/oby.2009.474
12. Liu S, Yang Y, Wu J (2011) TNFalpha-induced up-regulation of miR-155 inhibits adipogenesis by down-regulating early adipogenic transcription factors. Biochem Biophys Res Commun 414(3):618–624. doi:10.1016/j.bbrc.2011.09.131.
13. Sun T, Fu M, Bookout AL, Kliewer SA, Mangelsdorf DJ (2009) MicroRNA let-7 regulates 3T3-L1 adipogenesis. Mol Endocrinol 23(6):925–931. doi:10.1210/me.2008-0298
14. Wang Q, Li YC, Wang J, Kong J, Qi Y, Quigg RJ, Li X (2008) miR-17-92 cluster accelerates adipocyte differentiation by negatively regulating tumor-suppressor Rb2/p130. Proc Natl Acad Sci U S A 105(8):2889–2894. doi:10.1073/pnas.0800178105
15. Zaragosi LE, Wdziekonski B, Brigand KL, Villageois P, Mari B, Waldmann R, Dani C, Barbry P (2011) Small RNA sequencing reveals miR-642a-3p as a novel adipocyte-specific microRNA and miR-30 as a key regulator of human adipogenesis. Genome Biol 12(7):R64. doi:10.1186/gb-2011-12-7-r64
16. Ling HY, Wen GB, Feng SD, Tuo QH, Ou HS, Yao CH, Zhu BY, Gao ZP, Zhang L, Liao DF (2011) MicroRNA-375 promotes 3T3-L1 adipocyte differentiation through modulation of extracellular signal-regulated kinase signalling. Clin Exp Pharmacol Physiol 38(4):239–246. doi:10.1111/j.1440–1681.2011.05493.x.
17. Lin Q, Gao Z, Alarcon RM, Ye J, Yun Z (2009) A role of miR-27 in the regulation of adipogenesis. FEBS J 276(8):2348–2358
18. Kinoshita M, Ono K, Horie T, Nagao K, Nishi H, Kuwabara Y, Takanabe-Mori R, Hasegawa K, Kita T, Kimura T (2010) Regulation of adipocyte differentiation by activation of serotonin (5-HT) receptors 5-HT2AR and 5-HT2CR and involvement of microRNA-448-mediated repression of KLF5. Mol Endocrinol 24(10):1978–1987. doi:10.1210/me.2010-0054
19. Karbiener M, Fischer C, Nowitsch S, Opriessnig P, Papak C, Ailhaud G, Dani C, Amri EZ, Scheideler M (2009) microRNA miR-27b impairs human adipocyte differentiation and targets PPARgamma. Biochem Biophys Res Commun 390(2):247–251. doi:10.1016/j.bbrc.2009.09.098
20. Kim YJ, Hwang SJ, Bae YC, Jung JS (2009) MiR-21 regulates adipogenic differentiation through the modulation of TGF-beta signaling in mesenchymal stem cells derived from human adipose tissue. Stem Cells 27(12):3093–3102. doi:10.1002/stem.235
21. Tang YF, Zhang Y, Li XY, Li C, Tian W, Liu L (2009) Expression of miR-31, miR-125b-5p, and miR-326 in the adipogenic differentiation process of adipose-derived stem cells. OMICS 13(4):331–336. doi:10.1089/omi.2009.0017
22. Esau C, Kang X, Peralta E, Hanson E, Marcusson EG, Ravichandran LV, Sun Y, Koo S, Perera RJ, Jain R, Dean NM, Freier SM, Bennett CF, Lollo B, Griffey R (2004) MicroRNA-143 regulates adipocyte differentiation. J Biol Chem 279(50):52361–52365. doi:10.1074/jbc.C400438200
23. Wilfred BR, Wang WX, Nelson PT (2007) Energizing miRNA research: a review of the role of miRNAs in lipid metabolism, with a prediction that miR-103/107 regulates human metabolic pathways. Mol Genet Metab 91(3):209–217. doi:10.1016/j.ymgme.2007.03.011
24. Xie H, Lim B, Lodish HF (2009) MicroRNAs induced during adipogenesis that accelerate fat cell development are downregulated in obesity. Diabetes 58(5):1050–1057. doi:10.2337/db08-1299
25. Kennell JA, Gerin I, MacDougald OA, Cadigan KM (2008) The microRNA miR-8 is a conserved negative regulator of Wnt signaling. Proc Natl Acad Sci U S A 105(40):15417–15422. doi:10.1073/pnas.0807763105
26. Qin L, Chen Y, Niu Y, Chen W, Wang Q, Xiao S, Li A, Xie Y, Li J, Zhao X, He Z, Mo D (2010) A deep investigation into the adipogenesis mechanism: profile of microRNAs regulating adipogenesis by modulating the canonical Wnt/beta-catenin signaling pathway. BMC Genomics 11:320. doi:10.1186/1471-2164-11-320
27. Ahn J, Lee H, Jung CH, Jeon TI, Ha TY (2013) MicroRNA-146b promotes adipogenesis by suppressing the SIRT1-FOXO1 cas-

cade. EMBO Mol Med 5(10):1602–1612. doi:10.1002/emmm.201302647.
28. Lee EK, Lee MJ, Abdelmohsen K, Kim W, Kim MM, Srikantan S, Martindale JL, Hutchison ER, Kim HH, Marasa BS, Selimyan R, Egan JM, Smith SR, Fried SK, Gorospe M (2011) miR-130 suppresses adipogenesis by inhibiting peroxisome proliferator-activated receptor gamma expression. Mol Cell Biol 31(4):626–638. doi:10.1128/mcb.00894-10
29. Enomoto H, Furuichi T, Zanma A, Yamana K, Yoshida C, Sumitani S, Yamamoto H, Enomoto-Iwamoto M, Iwamoto M, Komori T (2004) Runx2 deficiency in chondrocytes causes adipogenic changes in vitro. J Cell Sci 117(Pt 3):417–425. doi:10.1242/jcs.00866
30. Karbiener M, Neuhold C, Opriessnig P, Prokesch A, Bogner-Strauss JG, Scheideler M (2011) MicroRNA-30c promotes human adipocyte differentiation and co-represses PAI-1 and ALK2. RNA Biol 8(5):850–860. doi:10.4161/rna.8.5.16153
31. Huang J, Zhao L, Xing L, Chen D (2010) MicroRNA-204 regulates Runx2 protein expression and mesenchymal progenitor cell differentiation. Stem Cells 28(2):357–364. doi:10.1002/stem.288
32. Guo Y, Chen Y, Zhang Y, Zhang Y, Chen L, Mo D (2012) Up-regulated miR-145 expression inhibits porcine preadipocytes differentiation by targeting IRS1. Int J Biol Sci 8(10):1408–1417. doi:10.7150/ijbs.4597
33. Peng Y, Xiang H, Chen C, Zheng R, Chai J, Peng J, Jiang S (2013) MiR-224 impairs adipocyte early differentiation and regulates fatty acid metabolism. Int J Biochem Cell Biol 45(8):1585–1593. doi:10.1016/j.biocel.2013.04.029.
34. Xu P, Vernooy SY, Guo M, Hay BA (2003) The drosophila microRNA Mir-14 suppresses cell death and is required for normal fat metabolism. Curr Biol 13(9):790–795
35. Teleman AA, Maitra S, Cohen SM (2006) Drosophila lacking microRNA miR-278 are defective in energy homeostasis. Genes Dev 20(4):417–422. doi:10.1101/gad.374406
36. Peng Y, Yu S, Li H, Xiang H, Peng J, Jiang S (2014) MicroRNAs: emerging roles in adipogenesis and obesity. Cell Signal 26(9):1888–1896. doi:10.1016/j.cellsig.2014.05.006.
37. Krutzfeldt J, Rajewsky N, Braich R, Rajeev KG, Tuschl T, Manoharan M, Stoffel M (2005) Silencing of microRNAs in vivo with 'antagomirs'. Nature 438(7068):685–689. doi:10.1038/nature04303
38. Takanabe R, Ono K, Abe Y, Takaya T, Horie T, Wada H, Kita T, Satoh N, Shimatsu A, Hasegawa K (2008) Up-regulated expression of microRNA-143 in association with obesity in adipose tissue of mice fed high-fat diet. Biochem Biophys Res Commun 376(4):728–732. doi:10.1016/j.bbrc.2008.09.050
39. Nakanishi N, Nakagawa Y, Tokushige N, Aoki N, Matsuzaka T, Ishii K, Yahagi N, Kobayashi K, Yatoh S, Takahashi A, Suzuki H, Urayama O, Yamada N, Shimano H (2009) The up-regulation of microRNA-335 is associated with lipid metabolism in liver and white adipose tissue of genetically obese mice. Biochem Biophys Res Commun 385(4):492–496. doi:10.1016/j.bbrc.2009.05.058
40. Kloting N, Berthold S, Kovacs P, Schon MR, Fasshauer M, Ruschke K, Stumvoll M, Bluher M (2009) MicroRNA expression in human omental and subcutaneous adipose tissue. PLoS One 4(3):e4699. doi:10.1371/journal.pone.0004699
41. Zhao E, Keller MP, Rabaglia ME, Oler AT, Stapleton DS, Schueler KL, Neto EC, Moon JY, Wang P, Wang IM, Lum PY, Ivanovska I, Cleary M, Greenawalt D, Tsang J, Choi YJ, Kleinhanz R, Shang J, Zhou YP, Howard AD, Zhang BB, Kendziorski C, Thornberry NA, Yandell BS, Schadt EE, Attie AD (2009) Obesity and genetics regulate microRNAs in islets, liver, and adipose of diabetic mice. Mamm Genome 20(8):476–485. doi:10.1007/s00335-009-9217-2
42. Grandjean V, Fourre S, De Abreu DA, Derieppe MA, Remy JJ, Rassoulzadegan M (2015) RNA-mediated paternal heredity of diet-induced obesity and metabolic disorders. Sci Rep 5:18193. doi:10.1038/srep18193
43. Lustig Y, Barhod E, Ashwal-Fluss R, Gordin R, Shomron N, Baruch-Umansky K, Hemi R, Karasik A, Kanety H (2014) RNA-binding protein PTB and microRNA-221 coregulate AdipoR1 translation and adiponectin signaling. Diabetes 63(2):433–445. doi:10.2337/db13-1032
44. Meerson A, Traurig M, Ossowski V, Fleming JM, Mullins M, Baier LJ (2013) Human adipose microRNA-221 is upregulated in obesity and affects fat metabolism downstream of leptin and TNF-alpha. Diabetologia 56(9):1971–1979. doi:10.1007/s00125-013-2950-9
45. Chen YH, Heneidi S, Lee JM, Layman LC, Stepp DW, Gamboa GM, Chen BS, Chazenbalk G, Azziz R (2013) miRNA-93 inhibits GLUT4 and is overexpressed in adipose tissue of polycystic ovary syndrome patients and women with insulin resistance. Diabetes 62(7):2278–2286. doi:10.2337/db12-0963
46. Xiao F, Yu J, Liu B, Guo Y, Li K, Deng J, Zhang J, Wang C, Chen S, Du Y, Lu Y, Xiao Y,

Zhang Z, Guo F (2014) A novel function of microRNA 130a-3p in hepatic insulin sensitivity and liver steatosis. Diabetes 63(8):2631–2642. doi:10.2337/db13-1689.

47. Hung TM, Ho CM, Liu YC, Lee JL, Liao YR, Wu YM, Ho MC, Chen CH, Lai HS, Lee PH (2014) Up-regulation of microRNA-190b plays a role for decreased IGF-1 that induces insulin resistance in human hepatocellular carcinoma. PLoS One 9(2):e89446. doi:10.1371/journal.pone.0089446
48. Kornfeld JW, Baitzel C, Konner AC, Nicholls HT, Vogt MC, Herrmanns K, Scheja L, Haumaitre C, Wolf AM, Knippschild U, Seibler J, Cereghini S, Heeren J, Stoffel M, Bruning JC (2013) Obesity-induced overexpression of miR-802 impairs glucose metabolism through silencing of Hnf1b. Nature 494(7435):111–115. doi:10.1038/nature11793
49. Yang YM, Seo SY, Kim TH, Kim SG (2012) Decrease of microRNA-122 causes hepatic insulin resistance by inducing protein tyrosine phosphatase 1B, which is reversed by licorice flavonoid. Hepatology 56(6):2209–2220. doi:10.1002/hep.25912.
50. Zhou B, Li C, Qi W, Zhang Y, Zhang F, Wu JX, Hu YN, Wu DM, Liu Y, Yan TT, Jing Q, Liu MF, Zhai QW (2012) Downregulation of miR-181a upregulates sirtuin-1 (SIRT1) and improves hepatic insulin sensitivity. Diabetologia 55(7):2032–2043. doi:10.1007/s00125-012-2539-8
51. Li W, Wang J, Chen QD, Qian X, Li Q, Yin Y, Shi ZM, Wang L, Lin J, Liu LZ, Jiang BH (2013) Insulin promotes glucose consumption via regulation of miR-99a/mTOR/PKM2 pathway. PLoS One 8(6):e64924. doi:10.1371/journal.pone.0064924
52. Ling HY, Ou HS, Feng SD, Zhang XY, Tuo QH, Chen LX, Zhu BY, Gao ZP, Tang CK, Yin WD, Zhang L, Liao DF (2009) CHANGES IN microRNA (miR) profile and effects of miR-320 in insulin-resistant 3T3-L1 adipocytes. Clin Exp Pharmacol Physiol 36(9):e32–e39. doi:10.1111/j.1440-1681.2009.05207.x
53. Trajkovski M, Hausser J, Soutschek J, Bhat B, Akin A, Zavolan M, Heim MH, Stoffel M (2011) MicroRNAs 103 and 107 regulate insulin sensitivity. Nature 474(7353):649–653. doi:10.1038/nature10112
54. He A, Zhu L, Gupta N, Chang Y, Fang F (2007) Overexpression of micro ribonucleic acid 29, highly up-regulated in diabetic rats, leads to insulin resistance in 3T3-L1 adipocytes. Mol Endocrinol 21(11):2785–2794. doi:10.1210/me.2007-0167
55. Najafi-Shoushtari SH, Kristo F, Li Y, Shioda T, Cohen DE, Gerszten RE, Naar AM (2010) MicroRNA-33 and the SREBP host genes cooperate to control cholesterol homeostasis. Science 328(5985):1566–1569. doi:10.1126/science.1189123
56. Davalos A, Goedeke L, Smibert P, Ramirez CM, Warrier NP, Andreo U, Cirera-Salinas D, Rayner K, Suresh U, Pastor-Pareja JC, Esplugues E, Fisher EA, Penalva LO, Moore KJ, Suarez Y, Lai EC, Fernandez-Hernando C (2011) miR-33a/b contribute to the regulation of fatty acid metabolism and insulin signaling. Proc Natl Acad Sci U S A 108(22):9232–9237. doi:10.1073/pnas.1102281108
57. Ryu HS, Park SY, Ma D, Zhang J, Lee W (2011) The induction of microRNA targeting IRS-1 is involved in the development of insulin resistance under conditions of mitochondrial dysfunction in hepatocytes. PLoS One 6(3):e17343. doi:10.1371/journal.pone.0017343
58. Huang B, Qin W, Zhao B, Shi Y, Yao C, Li J, Xiao H, Jin Y (2009) MicroRNA expression profiling in diabetic GK rat model. Acta Biochim Biophys Sin Shanghai 41(6):472–477
59. Li S, Zhu J, Zhang W, Chen Y, Zhang K, Popescu LM, Ma X, Lau WB, Rong R, Yu X, Wang B, Li Y, Xiao C, Zhang M, Wang S, Yu L, Chen AF, Yang X, Cai J (2011) Signature microRNA expression profile of essential hypertension and its novel link to human cytomegalovirus infection. Circulation 124(2):175–184. doi:10.1161/circulationaha.110.012237
60. D'Alessandra Y, Devanna P, Limana F, Straino S, Di Carlo A, Brambilla PG, Rubino M, Carena MC, Spazzafumo L, De Simone M, Micheli B, Biglioli P, Achilli F, Martelli F, Maggiolini S, Marenzi G, Pompilio G, Capogrossi MC (2010) Circulating microRNAs are new and sensitive biomarkers of myocardial infarction. Eur Heart J 31(22):2765–2773. doi:10.1093/eurheartj/ehq167
61. Kuwabara Y, Ono K, Horie T, Nishi H, Nagao K, Kinoshita M, Watanabe S, Baba O, Kojima Y, Shizuta S, Imai M, Tamura T, Kita T, Kimura T (2011) Increased microRNA-1 and microRNA-133a levels in serum of patients with cardiovascular disease indicate myocardial damage. Circ Cardiovasc Genet 4(4):446–454. doi:10.1161/circgenetics.110.958975
62. Wang GK, Zhu JQ, Zhang JT, Li Q, Li Y, He J, Qin YW, Jing Q (2010) Circulating microRNA: a novel potential biomarker for early diagnosis of acute myocardial infarction in humans. Eur Heart J 31(6):659–666. doi:10.1093/eurheartj/ehq013
63. Corsten MF, Dennert R, Jochems S, Kuznetsova T, Devaux Y, Hofstra L, Wagner DR, Staessen JA, Heymans S, Schroen B

(2010) Circulating MicroRNA-208b and microRNA-499 reflect myocardial damage in cardiovascular disease. Circ Cardiovasc Genet 3(6):499–506. doi:10.1161/circgenetics.110.957415

64. Fichtlscherer S, De Rosa S, Fox H, Schwietz T, Fischer A, Liebetrau C, Weber M, Hamm CW, Roxe T, Muller-Ardogan M, Bonauer A, Zeiher AM, Dimmeler S (2010) Circulating microRNAs in patients with coronary artery disease. Circ Res 107(5):677–684. doi:10.1161/CIRCRESAHA.109.215566

65. Hulsmans M, Sinnaeve P, Van der Schueren B, Mathieu C, Janssens S, Holvoet P (2012) Decreased miR-181a expression in monocytes of obese patients is associated with the occurrence of metabolic syndrome and coronary artery disease. J Clin Endocrinol Metab 97(7):E1213–E1218. doi:10.1210/jc.2012-1008

66. Guo M, Mao X, Ji Q, Lang M, Li S, Peng Y, Zhou W, Xiong B, Zeng Q (2010) miR-146a in PBMCs modulates Th1 function in patients with acute coronary syndrome. Immunol Cell Biol 88(5):555–564. doi:10.1038/icb.2010.16

67. Hulsmans M, Van Dooren E, Mathieu C, Holvoet P (2012) Decrease of miR-146b-5p in monocytes during obesity is associated with loss of the anti-inflammatory but not insulin signaling action of adiponectin. PLoS One 7(2):e32794. doi:10.1371/journal.pone.0032794

Chapter 19

Expression of MicroRNAs in Thyroid Carcinoma

Gaohong Zhu, Lijun Xie, and Daniel Miller

Abstract

MicroRNA (miRNA) are negative regulators of gene expression and subsequent protein production. This method of action translates into regulatory control over cellular processes, including development, signaling, metabolism, and apoptosis. A broad range of miRNA are shown to have abnormal expressions in thyroid cancers which could explain the pathology of tumor oncogenesis and disease progression. A review is conducted of the current research on miRNA dysregulation in thyroid cancers, including papillary thyroid carcinoma (PTC), follicular thyroid carcinoma (FTC), anaplastic thyroid cancer (ATC), and medullary thyroid carcinoma (MTC). Dysregulated miRNA and their associated regulatory pathways are identified and their oncogenic and pathological significance are discussed.

Key words Thyroid cancer, MicroRNA, Gene expression

1 Introduction

Follicular cell-derived carcinomas are divided by histological and clinical features. Histological classifications include well-differentiated thyroid carcinomas (WDTCs), poorly differentiated thyroid carcinomas (PDTCs), and undifferentiated thyroid carcinomas [1]. WDTCs are less aggressive cancers which include papillary thyroid carcinomas (PTCs) and follicular thyroid carcinomas (FTCs). PDTCs are moderately aggressive carcinomas. Anaplastic thyroid cancers (ATCs) are highly undifferentiated and extremely aggressive [2]. Clinical classifications include medullary thyroid carcinoma (MTC). MTC is a malignant tumor of the parafollicular cells (C-cells) constituting approximately 5% of thyroidal malignancies having both hereditary (25%) and sporadic (75%) oncogenic origins [3].

MicroRNA (miRNA) suppress protein-coding gene expression and may play significant roles in all cellular processes implicated in carcinogenesis, cell differentiation, and proliferation. MicroRNA expression is dysregulated in many human thyroid cancers, including PTCs, FTCs, ATCs, and MTCs. Studies have shown that many miRNA are upregulated in human thyroid carcinomas: miR-146,

Jingshan Huang et al. (eds.), *Bioinformatics in MicroRNA Research*, Methods in Molecular Biology, vol. 1617,
DOI 10.1007/978-1-4939-7046-9_19, © Springer Science+Business Media LLC 2017

miR-221, miR-222, miR-155, and miR-181a in human PTC [4, 5], miR-192, miR-197, miR-328 and miR-346 in FTC, and the MiR-17-92 cluster in ATC when compared with normal tissues and follicular carcinoma cell lines [6]. Among these dysregulated miRNAs, some were related to the thyroid tumor invasion and metastasis. Additionally, peripheral blood and serum miRNA expression in thyroid tumors have been studied recently and the somatic mutations have been related to deregulated miRNA expression in thyroid tumors. For example, miR-146b was overexpressed significantly in the BRAF-positive PTC and miR-146 was significantly overexpressed in RAS-positive PTCs [7, 8]. The expression profile of MTC was characterized by an overexpression miR-21, miR-127, miR-154, miR-224, miR-323, miR-370, miR-9*, miR-183, and miR-375 [9]. There is now a substantial amount of research concerning miRNA alterations occurring in thyroid tumors. This knowledge has enhanced our understanding of thyroid cancer and offered diagnostic and prognostic markers for thyroid tumors.

2 MicroRNAs and Thyroid Carcinoma

MicroRNA is a kind of noncoding small molecule RNA, which is composed of between 19 and 25 nucleotides [10]. It is believed that miRNA mediates mRNA degradation and inhibits translation. In mammals, the second through eighth nucleotides (the seed sequence) in microRNA are complementary to the 5′terminal and 3′UTR of the mRNA target gene and, by binding at these sites, regulate the target gene expression in the post-transcriptional phase. Dysregulation miRNA may be closely related to the pathogenesis and pathology of many diseases [11].

In recent years, the correlations between microRNA-mediated post-transcriptional gene silencing (PTGS) and tumor formation have become a hot topic. First, microRNA is involved in the processes of cell differentiation, division, proliferation, metabolism, and apoptosis. Second, more than half of microRNA were located in or near the tumor-related genomic regions and fragile sites, the amplification region, or the broken point region [12]. Third, microRNA expressed abnormally in a variety of tumor cells. Finally, mutations or polymorphisms in the microRNA precursor affected the processing of microRNA maturing and cancer susceptibility [13]. These all suggest that microRNA are closely related to tumorigenesis. The expression of some microRNA in tumor formation was downregulated and selective upregulation of these microRNAs could inhibit tumor occurrence [14]. Now many scholars believed that a variety of microRNA are related to the incidence of thyroid carcinoma and its development, metastasis, and prognosis and that altering the expression of these miRNA may be of therapeutic benefit.

Thyroid carcinoma is a malignant tumor that develops from the epithelial cells of the thyroid. It is the most common malignant tumor in the endocrine system and the rate of incidence has increased in recent years. Most thyroid carcinomas have their origins in the follicular epithelium. Over 90% of thyroid cancers are classified as differentiated thyroid carcinomas (DTC), which includes thyroid carcinoma papillary (PTC) and follicular thyroid carcinoma (FTC) [15]. In some studies of thyroid carcinomas, FTC and PTC were closely related to microRNA, which was a kind of "carcinogenic" and played a role in regulating transcription. These microRNAs primarily functioned as a regulator of proliferation and apoptosis. Recent studies reported that the expression of microRNA in thyroid carcinoma was disordered. Overexpression of microRNA in PTC or FTC and low expression in thyroid carcinoma played an important role in the development of thyroid carcinoma [16].

3 Expression of MicroRNAs in PTC

The analysis of miRNA in PTC is generally performed via miRNA chip analysis. Some miRNAs such as miR146b-5p, miR-221, miR-222, miR-210, miR-214, miR-1244, miR-134, miR-127-3p, miR-130b, miR-17, miR-199a-5p, miR-342, miR-768-3p, and miR-720 were upregulated in aggressive PTCs whereas some, including miR-1278, miR-16-1, miR-613, miR-1225-5p, miR-1268, miR-1826, miR-637, miR-1231, miR-1302, and miR-486-5p, were downregulated relative to nonaggressive PTC tissues [17]. Compared with normal thyroid tissues, some miRNAs, including miR-1, miR-191, miR-486, and miR-451, had reduced expression rates in PTC.

Labbaye et al. [18] reported MiR-146a as a regulator for CXCR4, which is a known fusion protein and chemokine receptor, and can act on stromal cell-derived factor-1 (SDF-1, CXCLI2). They identified a regulatory pathway where promyelocytic leukemia zinc-finger (PLZF) protein, a transcription factor, inhibited miR-146a production, which in turn suppressed CXCR4 translation. They found that CXCR4 was highly expressed in K562-PLZF cells and played a major role in the mechanism of primary tumor lymph node metastasis. Therefore, miR-146a downregulated in PTC cells played a key role in the process of tumor lymph node metastasis. However, Pallante et al. [19] found seven of eight specimens were detected with increased miR-221, miR-222, and miR-181b expression in thyroid needle biopsy. And the expression levels of miR-222 and miR-221 were not increased in thyroid adenoma and benign thyroid nodules. Thus, if miR-221 was detected in normal thyroid tissues, it suggested that the normal thyroid tissue might be cancerous [20]. MiR-222 could regulate the expression of cellular matrix metal protein I and superoxide dismutase 2, which might affect the migration and invasion of cancer cells. Visone et al. found that forced expression of miR-221 and miR-222 could reduce the levels of p27Kip1 protein in thyroid cancer cells, but the level of p27Kip1 mRNA was not significantly changed [4, 5]. Mutation of BRAF gene and RET/PTC gene rearrangement were common genetic changes in PTC. It was found that miR-146 was upregulated in the PTC-1 cell line, which might play a role in tumor formation and development, but miR-221, miR-222, and miR-181b expression did not increase significantly. It was also found miR-222 expression was downregulated in the BRAF mutant cell lines, but miR-146 and miR-221 were not significantly upregulated [21].

Chou et al. [5] found that the expressions of miR-146b, miR-222, and miR-221 were significantly higher in PTC and even more after metastasis. MiR-146b in PTC patients whose BRAF gene mutated was significantly higher than those in PTC patients whose BRAF gene was not mutated. It was found that miR-146, miR-222, and miR-221 were overexpressed in PTC tissues and thyroid cell lines and the expression of KIT protein was significantly decreased or not detected [22]. Maybe, miR-146, miR-222, and miR-221 combined to the key region of KIT 3′-UTR and appeared single-nucleotide polymorphism, leading to KIT transcription and protein level decrease. The upregulated expression of miR-146, miR-222, and miR-221 were identified as characteristics of human PTC. The expression level of miRNA in thyroid tissues could be used to differentiate the benign and malignant thyroid. It could be helpful for tumor classification and the identification of poorly differentiated tumors and tumor tissues.

RT-qPCR and Western blotting analysis of miRNA in PTC conducted by Lv et al. [23] found a significant negative correlation between miR-26a and CKS2 expression in human PTC cell lines TPC-1 and CGTH W3 as well as resected PTC specimens. Their analysis also showed that miR-26a suppresses CKS2 expression which inhibited growth. Peng et al. [24] suggested that miR-199b-5p may be helpful in evaluating PTC invasiveness and could be used as a reference for setting up a scientific treatment schedule. They found miR-1996b-5p was highly expressed among patients with extrathyroidal invasion and cervical lymph node metastasis and this showed statistical significance (p = 0.047, 0.01) in their research.

Hardin et al. [25] discovered through RT-qPCR, Western blotting, and siRNA experiments that cell proliferation and invasion increased when the expression of miR-146b-5p in papillary thyroid carcinoma cell line BCPAP was inhibited. They concluded that miR-146-5p played an important role in regulating PTC cell proliferation and invasion. A study conducted by Cantara et al. [26]

reported the search for miRNA in the blood of samples of each patient (12 PTCs and 12 NGs) in a Caucasian population. They found miR-190 was upregulated whereas miR-95, miR-579, and miR-29b were downregulated by RT-qPCR. The miRNAs identified in their study were different from those of a similar Chinese report and they posited that the differing genetic background of the patients may have been responsible. Igci et al. [27] found elevated levels of miR-30a-5p in serum as well as HC-PTC and non-HC-PTC fine needle aspiration biopsy (FNAB) samples by pre- and postoperative pathological diagnosis and RT-qPCR. They suggested that miR-30a-5p could be used as a biomarker for PTC.

3.1 The Relationship Between Genes and MicroRNAs in PTC

Thyroid carcinoma coincides with large numbers of genetic events. The occurrence of PTC was related to the oncogene fusion of chromosome recombination (RET/PTC1 and RET/PTC3) as well as RAS and BRAF gene mutation. These gene changes were related to the activation of MAPK signaling pathway. The activation of MAPK signaling pathway was closely related to the formation, growth, and metastasis of tumors [28]. Geraldo et al. [29] found miR-146b-5p was highly overexpressed in a case report of a young male patient with an aggressive, BRAF-T1799A-positive papillary thyroid carcinoma. They also found that activation of MAPK pathway in normal thyroid cells increased miR-146b-5p levels in vitro. It means that the overexpression of miR-146b-5p could be related to a thyroid-specific oncogenic activation, which may include the MAPK pathway. Yu et al. [30] found that serum levels of let-7e, miR-151-5p, and miR-222 were significantly overexpressed in PTC patients versus patients with benign nodules by RT-qPCR and microarrays and suggested their potential as tools for long-term observation.

Huang et al. [31] found that the mutation rate of BRAF(V600E) was 47.8% between 69 cases of PTC patients and normal thyroid tissues and that BRAF gene mutation caused the overexpression of miR-203 and miR-21. BRAF mutation and miR-21 overexpression were closely related to the invasion and metastasis of PTC as well as tumor recurrence. Another study group found BRAF(V600E) gene mutated in PTC and the expression of miRNA was disordered. The expression levels of miR-21 and miR-203 were closely related to BRAF mutation and the high expression of miR-21 was significantly associated with tumor lymph node metastasis. In addition, it was found that the expression level of miR-151-5p and miR-222 in tumor tissues and serum of PTC were closely related to tumor lymph node metastasis, tumor size, and clinical stage [32]. These miRNAs could be used as an index to judge treatment effectiveness.

Deng et al. [33] collected tumor specimens and tumor-adjacent tissues from 60 PTC patients and two human papillary thyroid carcinoma cell lines: TPC-1 and K1. They found miR-146b-5p induced epithelial-to-mesenchymal transition (EMT) and might promote PTC metastasis through the regulation of Wnt/β-catenin signaling by performing a computational search, luciferase assay, RT-qPCR, and Western blotting. The results suggested novel potential therapeutic targets for the treatment of PTC. Geraldo et al. [34] analyzed nonhuman thyroid models, cancer cell lines, tumor tissue with benign lesions, and FNAB samples by microarray and RT-qPCR and reported a number of results. Their findings suggested that miR-146b-5p, miR-221/222, miR-181a/b, and miR-155 could regulate ACVR1B, BMPR1A, and BMP8A, which are the members of the TGF-β pathway. They also found that SFRP1, an inhibitor of the TGF-β pathway, may be regulated by miR-146b-5p and miR-221. They suggested that GAS1, a Hedgehog pathway inhibitor, may be regulated by miR-34a-5p. Additionally, they found insulin receptor substrate-1 (IRS1) to be a target of miR-146b-5p and PRKCQ to be a target of both miR-224 and miR-31. Finally, CCND3 (cyclin D3) was found to be regulated by miR-138 in the PTC datasets. Lee et al. [35] also found the mean levels of miR-146b and miR-155 expression were higher in the PTC group than in the benign group in 89 patients by RT-qPCR and Western blotting. Yang et al. [17] found overexpression of miR-221/222 and miR-146b-5p suppressed the expression of TIMP3 and ZNFR3. They also found underexpression of miR-613 and miR-16 permitted upexpression of FN1 and ITGA2 in aggressive PTC.

Wang et al. [36] found that expression of miR-101 was downregulated in PTC tissues and cell lines. RT-qPCR and Western blotting revealed that it negatively regulated Rac1 gene expression in 16 paired PTC tissue specimens. Zhu et al. [37] found miR-182 suppressed the expression of CHL1, a promotor of cell proliferation and invasion, in both human cell lines and PTC tissues. They proposed this result demonstrates that miR-182 could be therapeutic target for treating PTC. Liu et al. [38] reported that miR-204-5p regulated IGFBP5 expression and potentially be used as a tumor suppressant for PTC. Li et al. [39] discovered that miR-29a was generally underexpressed in PTC tissues, and its levels were negatively correlated with tumor size, TNM stage, and lymph node metastasis. They found that AKT3 expression was suppressed by miR-29a, mitigating phosphatidylinositol 3-kinase (PI3K)/AKT pathway activation. Minna et al. [40] have demonstrated that miR-199a-3p was underexpressed in human PTC specimens and in PTC-derived cell lines by RT-qPCR and displayed tumor suppressor functions in PTC.

The miRNA expressions for PTC are summarized in Tables 1, 2, 3, and 4.

Table 1
MicroRNAs (upregulated) and clinical significance in PTC

Reference	Sample sources	Method	MicroRNA (up)	Potential target genes	Potential function	Clinical significance
[29]	thyroid tumor tissue, specimens paired with adjacent normal thyroid tissues	miRNA microarray, qRT-PCR	miR-146b-5p /miR-222-3p /miR-221-3p /miR-203 /miR-32-5p /miR199b-5p	KIT (EGFR)	As molecular markers of PTC diagnosis and prognosis	evaluating PTC invasiveness
[30]	adjacent normal thyroid tissues	RT-qPCR, Western blotting, siRNA experiments	miR-146b-5p	PRRX1	Cell proliferation and invasion increased	PTC cell proliferation and invasion
[32]	patients with sporadic PTC undergoing surgical resection	RT-qPCR, 3′UTR Luciferase reporter assays	miR-146b-5p	IRAK1-luc/TRAF6-luc/PTC1-luc	The Toll-like receptor and cytokine signaling pathway	evaluating PTC invasiveness
[37]	human PTC tissues, cell lines	RT-qPCR, Western blotting, siRNA experiments	miR-182	CHL1	Cell proliferation and invasion	A novel therapeutic strategy against PTC
[39]	PTC tissues	RT-qPCR, Western blotting, siRNA experiments	miR-29a	AKT3	PI3K/AKT pathway activation	Tumor size/TNM stage/lymph node metastasis
[18, 19]	thyroid needle biopsy, thyroid adenoma, benign thyroid nodules	microRNA chip analysis	miR-222/miR-221/ miR-181b	tumor necrosis factor (TNF)/THRB	Mitosis/cell cycle regulation/ apoptosis	PTC
[5]	Cell line TPC-1	microRNA chip analysis, Western blotting, RT-qPCR	miR-221/miR-222	p27Kipl/matrix meta protein I/superoxide dismutase 2	RET/PTC-RAS-BRAF signal pathway	The migration and invasion of cancer cells
[34]	nonhuman thyroid models, thyroid cancer cell lines, FNAB samples	Microarray, RT-qPCR, Next generation sequencing	miR-146b-5p/miR-221/ miR-34a-5p/miR-224/miR-31/ miR-146b-5p/miR-138	ACVR1B/BMPR1A/ BMP8A	Wnt/β-catenin signaling	extra-thyroidal invasion/ multicentricity/ higher TNM

Table 2
MicroRNA (upregulated) and Potential function in PTC

Reference	Sample sources	Method	MicroRNA (up)	Potential target genes	Potential function
[20]	PTC-1 cell line/ BRAF mutant cell lines	microRNA chip analysis	miR-146	c-myc	tumor formation and development
[21]	PTC with metastasis/PTC tissues/cell lines	microRNA chip analysis	miR-146b/ miR-222/ miR-221/ miR-181b	RET/TRK/B-raf/ras /Kit	cell differentiation and growth

Table 3
MicroRNA (upregulated) and Potential target genes in PTC

Reference	Sample sources	Method	MicroRNA (up)	Potential target genes
[22]	Specimens informalin fixed paraffin embedded/thyroid fine needle aspiration biopsy	microRNA chip analysis	miR-221/ miR-222/miR-146b	CK19, CITED1, galectin 3, deiodinase 1, thyroglobulin, pendrin
[33]	Tumor specimens/tumor adjacent tissues/PTC cell lines TPC-1/PTC cell lines K1	Computational search, luciferase assay, RT-qPCR, Western blotting	miR-146b-5p	β-catenin, Slug, N-cadherin, vimentin, EMT, ZNRF3

4 Expression of MicroRNAs in FTCs

FTC is a type of WDTC and is more aggressive than PTC and a number of research efforts have been made to identify miRNA dysregulation in the histotype. Recently, the abnormal regulation of FTC in miRNA was studied. Results of these studies indicate that miRNAs may become valuable markers to distinguish these tumors. The different miRNA expressions in FTCs are shown in Tables 5, 6, 7.

Weber et al. [6] found that miR-192, miR197, miR328, and miR346 in FTC are expressed highly by analyzing FTC and follicular adenoma. They found that overexpression of miR-346 or miR-197 could induce cell proliferation in vitro. FTC-133, K5 cell line, and papillary thyroid carcinoma cell line NPA87 were transfected with antisense oligo nucleotide of miR-197 and miR-346, and they found cell growth was inhibited in FTC-133 and K5 cell lines, but the cell growth in NPA87 cell line was not affected because of lacking miR197 and miR-346. They also found that overexpression of miR-346 and miR-197 could inhibit the expression of target genes in vivo and in vitro. They further confirmed the two target genes of miR197 (ACVR1 and TSPAN3) and the

Table 4
MicroRNA (downregulated) and clinical significance in PTC

Reference	Sample sources	Method	MicroRNA (down)	Potential target genes	Potential function	Clinical significance
[41]	PTC samples	microRNA chip analysis	miR-1, miR-191, miR-486, miR-451	CXCR4	A cascade pathway	Primary tumor lymph node metastasis
[23]	PTC specimens/normal thyroid tissues/PTC cell lines TPC-1/PTC cell lines CGTH W3	RT-qPCR/Western blotting	miR-26a	CyclinB1, cdk1, bcl-xl, AKT	Cellular proliferation	Lymph node metastasis
[36]	TPC -1/HTH83 cells/16 paired PTC tissue specimens with lymph node metastasis	RT-qPCR/Western blotting/migration and invasion assay	miR-101	Rac1	mediates cell migration and invasion	lymph node metastasis

Table 5
MicroRNA (upregulated) and clinical significance in FTC

Reference	Sample sources	Method	MicroRNA (up)	Potential target genes	Potential function	Clinical significance
[6]	FTC/follicular adenoma/FTC-133/NPA87	RT-qPCR/Western blotting	miR-192/miR-197/miR-328/miR-346	ACVR1/TSPAN3/ACVR1/EFEMP2	Cell proliferation	Transformation of benign to malignant tumors
[8]	Thyroid neoplastic samples/non-neoplastic samples/FNA samples	RT-qPCR	miR-187/miR-221/miR-222/miR-146b/miR-155/miR-22/miR-197	RET/PTC1/RET/PTC3/PAX8/PPARγ	MAPK pathway	Individual tumor types
[41]	Patients with a solitary or prominent scintigraphically cold thyroid nodule FA/FC	RT-qPCR/miRNA expression analyses	miR-221/miR-96/miR-182	VPS26A/ABCC1	Cell-growth	Tumor malignant
[42]	Patients with metastatic minimally invasive follicular thyroid carcinoma	Comprehensive quantitative analysis of miRNA expression/RT-qPCR	miR-10b/miR-92a/miR-221/miR-222/miR-222*/miR-375	CDKN1B/CDKN1C	cell growth/cell cycle progression	Thyroid carcinogenesis / tumorigenesis

Table 6
MicroRNA (upregulated) and clinical significance in FTC

Reference	Sample sources	Method	MicroRNA (up)	Potential target genes	Clinical significance
[43]	Patients undergoing thyroid resection/ primary cell lines	RT-qPCR	miR-371-3	C19MC	Distant metastasis
[44]	Cold thyroid nodule	RT-qPCR	miR-142–3p	RAP2A/S1PR1/ SMAD2/TGFBR1/ VEGFA	Tumor suppressive function

Table 7
MicroRNA (downregulated) and clinical significance in FTC

Reference	Sample sources	Method	MicroRNA (down)	Potential target genes	Clinical significance
[45]	Follicular adenoma/ follicular variant of PTC/cold thyroid nodule/ FA/FC	qRT-PCR, miRNA expression analyses	miR-199b-5-p, miR-144	VPS26A, ABCC1	Thyroid carcinogenesis, tumorigenesis
[46]	Human neoplastic thyroid tissues/ normal adjacent tissue/the contralateral normal thyroid lobe	qRT-PCR, Western blotting	miR-191	CDK6	Benign or malignant
[47]	Patients with a solitary	miRNA expression analyses	miR-106b	ETS, FN1, LIFR, PPARGC1A, PTPN4, RAP2A, S1PR1, SMAD2, TGFBR1, VEGFA	The development and progression of thyroid cancer

target gene of miR-346 (EFEMP2) by RT-PCR and Western blotting. They found that ACVR1, TSPAN3, and EFEMP2 expression were decreased in the presence of elevated expressions of miR-197 and miR-346 in FTC. The abnormal expression of the three target genes could promote the proliferation and invasion of thyroid cancer together. MiR-197 and miR-346 were associated with the occurrence of FTC. It shows that a small portion of miRNA expression in FTC might be involved in the development of benign and malignant tumors.

Nikiforova et al. [8] found the most upregulated miRNAs in FTC were miR-187, miR-224, miR-155, miR-222, and miR-221 and that there were no miRNA overexpressed in hyperplastic nodules. They also found that the expression of miRNA varied based on the degree of differentiation degree in the thyroid carcinoma tissues. MiR-187, miR-221, miR-222, and miR-181b showed at least threefold increase in expression in all kinds of cancer tissues, and the expression level was different in different tissues. Among them, the expression of miR-221 in FTC was at least 27.8-fold higher than that in PTC [43]. Colamaio et al. [46] collected human neoplastic thyroid tissues and either normal adjacent tissue or the contralateral normal thyroid lobe with follicular adenoma (n = 24), FTC (n = 24), PTC (n = 15), ATC (n = 8), and FVPTC (n = 6) and confirmed miR-191 downregulation played a role in follicular adenoma, FTC, and follicular variant of PTC by quantitative RT-PCR and Western blotting. They concluded that CDK6 was a target for miR-191. Takizawa [42] found the miR-221/222 cluster, miR-10b, and miR-92a were significantly upregulated in 34 patients with metastatic minimally invasive follicular thyroid carcinoma selected from 200 patients between 1991 and 2009 by comprehensive quantitative analysis of miRNA expression.

Rossing et al. [45] discovered many miRNAs were downregulated, especially miR-199b-5p and miR-144, which were essentially not expressed in FTC by RT-qPCR and miRNA and mRNA expression analyses. They also found that MiR-199b-5p reduced cell-growth and that almost 30% of the computational predicted targets were downregulated by pre-miR-199b in cultured thyroid cells and correspondingly upregulated in thyroid carcinoma lacking the miRNA. Carvalheira et al. [47] reported that the restoration of miR-106b expression in WRO and TPC1 thyroid carcinoma cell lines inhibited C1orf24 expression at both mRNA and protein levels by RT-qPCR and Western blotting. This indicated that the decreased miR-106b expression and increased C1orf24 expression might have a synergistic effect during the development and progression of thyroid cancer. Colamaio et al. [44] found that FTCs and FTC cell lines expressed tumor specific, shorter forms of ASH1L and MLL1 proteins. They found miR-142–3p modulated the levels of these tumor-associated forms and reactivated thyroid-specific Hox gene expression, likely contributed to its tumor suppressive function.

Finally, overexpression of miRNAs significantly affected migration. Wojtas et al. [48] presented data that suggested that miR-146b and miR-183 inhibit apoptosis and promote migration in FTS. Roncati et al. [49] found that pre-miR-146a was underexpressed in neoplastic tissues from 39 FTC cases and that the G allele was observed in neoplastic tissues. They concluded that the GG and GC alleles appear to be associated with an increased risk for FTC.

5 MiRNA Expression in Anaplastic Thyroid Cancers (ATCs)

Anaplastic thyroid cancer (ATC) is the most lethal histotype of thyroid cancer, responsible for more than one-third of thyroid cancer-related deaths. The most striking difference between ATCs and other thyroid carcinomas derived from follicular cells is that they displayed a significantly decreased expression of various miRNAs [16, 50] and increased expression of several miRNAs [8, 51]. The deregulation in miRNAs has been implicated in tumor genesis and cancer progression. Molecular interference to restore the expression of tumor suppressor miRNAs, or to blunt overexpressed oncogenic miRNAs, has therefore been suggested as a promising therapeutic approach to ameliorate the treatment of ATC.

5.1 Downregulated MiRNAs in ATC

Contrary to the expression in PTCs, miR-138 was found to be severely decreased in ATC samples and ATC-derived cell lines [52, 53]. MiR-125b, which we found to be downregulated, is reportedly upregulated in PTC compared with normal thyroid tissue, but is downregulated in ATC. Braun et al. [50] found that miR-30 and miR-200 were underexpressed in ATC and could serve as markers to distinguish ATC from PTC and FTC. The most significantly decreased miRNAs in expression were miR-30d, miR-125b, and miR-26a [51]. Zhang et al. [54] showed in vitro and in vivo that ATC cells could be sensitized to cisplatin by inhibiting beclin 1-mediated autophagy with a miR-30d mimic. These findings are summarized in Table 8.

5.1.1 Potential Target Genes and Function of Down-MiRNAs in ATC

Specific miRNAs are exclusively downregulated in ATC, which can acquire more aggressive tumor characteristics (i.e., enhanced cell invasion and migration). Besides an important transcriptional activator of miR-200 is p53, knockdown EGFR in ATC cells restores miR-200 expression and represses the expression of mesenchymal markers via EGF signaling pathway [59]. The miR-200 family is also an important regulator of the EMT process by regulating ZEB1 and ZEB2 protein levels. Downregulation of miR-200 in ATC would potentiate the TGF-mediated EMT switch and enhance aggressiveness. EZH2 is overexpressed in ATC, which enhances cell proliferation, migration, and invasion via repressing the expression of thyroid transcription factor PAX8 [60]. Another important cellular process is autophagy through targeting the key autophagy-promoting protein, Beclin1 (gene *BECN1*), which sensitizes cancer cells to cisplatin treatment by repressing Beclin1. A marked decrease in the expression of let-7 is observed in ATC [16, 50, 61]. let-7 enhances the expression of thyroid transcription factor-1 (TTF1/NKX2–1), a key factor in maintaining the expression of iodine metabolizing genes and thyroid differentiation which is usually lost in ATC. Loss of let-7 is associated with refractory response to chemotherapy and radiotherapy treatments (resulting in a poorer prognosis), and represses the EMT process in ATC [62, 63]. The miRNA gene targets and functions are summarized in Table 9.

Table 8
MiRNA expression in ATC

References	miRNA	Specimen type	Detection technique
Downregulated miRNA			
[19]	miR-30-d, miR-125b-1/2, miR-25, miR-30a-5p, miR-224, miR-92-2, miR-138-1, miR-26a, miR-125a/b	Tissue, cell	Microarray, northern blots, situ hybridization, qRT-PCR
[52]	miR-138	Tissue, cell lines	
[50]	miR-200a/b/c, miR-30a/b/c/d/e, miR-30a-3p, miR –141, miR -26a/b, miR-99a/b, miR-138, miR-19b, miR-29b/c, miR-125a/b, miR-130a, let-7a/c/d/f/g/I, miR-7, miR-331-3p	Tissue	RT-PCR
[51]	let-7c, miR-30d, 26a, miR-304-5p, miR-125d	Paraffin-embedded tissue	RT-PCR
Upregulated miRNA			
[19]	miR-222, miR-198, let-7f-1, let-7a-2	Tissue, cell	Microarray, qRT-PCR
[55–57]	miR-146b		
[19, 51]	miR-221, miR-30d	Paraffin-embedded tissue	Northern blots, Situhybridization, RT-PCR
[19, 51, 56]	miR-222		
[51]	miR-181b, miR–21		
[8]	miR-302c, miR-214, miR-205, miR-137, miR-187, miR-221, miR-155, miR-224, miR-222,	Tissue	RT-PCR, RT-qPCR
[8, 53]	miR-21, miR-146b, miR-221, miR-222		
[53, 58]	miR-106a/b, miR-19a/b, miR-17-5p, miR-92–1, miR-18a, miR-20a	ARO cells	Northern blot, microarrays
[53]	miR-17-3p, miR-17-5p, miR-92–1, miR-18a, miR-19a/b	ATC cell lines	Northern blot, microarrays
[58]	miR–20a	Tissue, cell lines	qRT-PCR

Table 9
MiRNA targets gene and function in ATC

miRNAs	Validated targets	Cellular processes	References
Downregulated miRNA			
miR-200 family	ZEB1, ZEB2, β-Catenin	EMT and proliferation	[22, 50]
miR-30 family	Beclin1, EZH2, VIM	Autophagy gene, condensation, and EMT	[54, 55, 64]
let-7 family	RAS HMGA2 LIN28	Proliferation, histone modification, stemness	[55]
miR-25	EZH2, BIM, KLF4	Chromatin condensation, apoptosis	[55, 65]
miR-125	MMP1, HMGA2, LIN28A	Invasion, histone modification	[19, 55, 66]
miR-138	hTERT	Metastatic, invasive phenotypes and stemness	[52]
miR-26a	Cyclins D2 and E2	Cell cycle arrest	[67]
miR-25, miR-30d	EZH2	Oncogenic activity	[55]
miR-30a	Beclin 1, lox	Proliferation, invasion, metastasis	[68, 69]
miR-4295	CDKN1A	Proliferation and invasion	[70]
Upregulated miRNA			
miR-221/−222	p27, RECK, PTEN	Cell cycle, growth, and invasion	[19, 56]
miR-17-92 cluster	p21, TIMP3, PTEN	Cell growth and invasion	[53, 56]
miR-146a/−146b	NFκB, THRB, SMAD4	Cell differentiation, proliferation, invasion	[55–57, 71]
miR-17 family	STAT3, MAPK14	Modulate epithelial	[72]
miR-20a	LIMK1	Proliferation, Invasion	[58]

5.1.2 Downregulated MiRNAs in ATC

Hebrant [73] reported that in 11 ATC samples p53 mutation was found in 4 (36.4%), BRAF mutation in 2 (18%), PIK3CA mutation in 1(10%). One sample showed both BRAF and p53 mutations (ATC1). They noted that ATC frequently exhibits genetic alteration of T1799A in the BRAF coding sequence and this alteration also frequently presents in PTC. They suggested that this finding indicates WDTCs could give rise to undifferentiated carcinomas [8]. They continued to examine the miRNA expression profiles of 11 ATC samples by microarrays and noted 17 downregulated and 1 upregulated miRNA. They suggested these dysregulations were responsibly for dysfunction in the EMT process and that the LOX gene is a key player in the transition. They also suggested that tumor-associated macrophages (TAM) amplified tumor aggression and showed that they constitute approximately 50% of the ATC tissue [73].

ATC has characteristics suggestive of a tumor enriched in cancer stem cells (CSC) originating from thyroid stem cells. Specific microRNA signatures have been identified in many CSCs that seem to play a role in the EMT [74, 75]. The enriched pathways are related to aggressive behaviors such as extra-cellular matrix (ECM) receptor interaction, focal adhesion (MAPK), and regulation of actin cytoskeleton (Cell Cycle) and cytokine receptors [34].

5.2 Upregulated MiRNAs in ATC

Common miRNAs such as miR-146, miR-221, miR-222, and the miR-17-92 cluster are upregulated in aggressive ATC. High levels of the miR-17-92 cluster are detected in ATC, associated with poor clinical-pathological features of cancer such as extrathyroidal invasion, short time recurrence, and distant metastases. ARO and FRO cells caused complete growth arrest via transfection with the miR-17-92 cluster inhibitors, which could be a novel target for ATC treatment [8, 53]. In fact, miR-221 and miR-222 are highly upregulated in PTCs but were not upregulated in ATC [34]. Only the miR-222 shows an increase in ATC, but at a lower proportion. This would apparently preclude the development of ATC from PTC through cancer progression. These findings are summarized in Table 8.

6 MiRNA Expression in MTC

A number of researchers have investigated miRNA expressions in MTC. Hudson et al. [76] identified overexpression of miR-375 and miR-10a and underexpression of miR-455 in 15 MTC samples. They noted that the expression of YAP1, a growth inhibitor, was mediated by miR-375 and they concluded that this regulatory pathway was important in MTC progression. Duan et al. [77] demonstrated that miR-129-5p was underexpressed in MTC samples and that it suppresses tumor growth and development by suppressing AKT. They propose that treatments that supplement miR-129-5p levels may be effective in the treatment of MTC. Abraham et al. [78] examined differential expression profiles in MTC of hereditary and sporadic origins in resected tissues. They found that the levels of miR-183 and miR-375 were higher in sporadic samples and were predictive of metastasis to the lateral lymph nodes. Finally, Mian et al. [9] examined the aberrant expression of nine miRNA. They noted marked overexpression of miR-21, miR-127, miR-154, miR-224, miR-323, miR-370, miR-9*, miR-183, and miR-375. They noted that miR-127 levels were lower in sporadic MTC samples with somatic RET mutations and that upexpression of miR-224 was noted in earlier stages of the disease, in cases without metastasis, and after treatment resulting in termination of the cancer. They concluded that of all the miRNA studied, miR-224 held the most promise as a prognostic biomarker.

7 Conclusion

This chapter has reviewed the variety of miRNA dysregulations presented in a number of thyroid cancers.

References

1. Kondo T, Ezzat S, Asa SL (2006) Pathogenetic mechanisms in thyroid follicular-cell neoplasia. Nat Rev Cancer 6:292–306
2. Yau T, Lo CY, Epstein RJ et al (2008) Treatment outcomes in anaplastic thyroid carcinoma: survival improvement in young patients with localized disease treated by combination of surgery and radiotherapy. Ann Surg Oncol 15:2500–2505. doi:10.1245/s10434-008-0005-0
3. Albores-Saavedra J, LiVolsi VA, Williams ED (1985) Medullary carcinoma. Semin Diagn Pathol 2:137–146
4. Visone R, Russo L, Pallante P et al (2007) MicroRNAs (miR)-221 and miR-222, both overexpressed in human thyroid papillary carcinomas, regulate p27Kip1 protein levels and cell cycle. Endocr Relat Cancer 14:791–798
5. Chou CK, Chen RF, Chou FF et al (2010) miR-146b is highly expressed in adult papillary thyroid carcinomas with high risk features including extrathyroidal invasion and the BRAF(V600E) mutation. Thyroid 20:489–494. doi:10.1089/thy.2009.0027
6. Weber F, Teresi RE, Broelsch CE et al (2006) A limited set of human MicroRNA is deregulated in follicular thyroid carcinoma. J Clin Endocrinol Metab 91:3584–3591. doi:10.1210/jc.2006-0693
7. Nikiforova MN, Nikiforov YE (2009) Molecular diagnostics and predictors in thyroid cancer. Thyroid 19:1351–1361. doi:10.1089/thy.2009.0240
8. Nikiforova MN, Tseng GC, Steward D et al (2008) MicroRNA expression profiling of thyroid tumors: biological significance and diagnostic utility. J Clin Endocrinol Metab 93:1600–1608. doi:10.1210/jc.2007-2696
9. Mian C, Pennelli G, Fassan M et al (2012) MicroRNA profiles in familial and sporadic medullary thyroid carcinoma: preliminary relationships with RET status and outcome. Thyroid 22:890–896. doi:10.1089/thy.2012.0045
10. Huang Y, Shen XJ, Zou Q, Zhao QL (2010) Biological functions of microRNAs. Bioorg Khim 36:747–752
11. Huang Y, Shen XJ, Zou Q et al (2011) Biological functions of microRNAs: a review. J Physiol Biochem 67:129–139. doi:10.1007/s13105-010-0050-6
12. Lee EJ, Gusev Y, Jiang J et al (2007) Expression profiling identifies microRNA signature in pancreatic cancer. Int J Cancer 120:1046–1054. doi:10.1002/ijc.22394
13. Fabbri M, Ivan M, Cimmino A et al (2007) Regulatory mechanisms of microRNAs involvement in cancer. Expert Opin Biol Ther 7:1009–1019. doi:10.1517/14712598.7.7.1009
14. van Kouwenhove M, Kedde M, Agami R (2011) MicroRNA regulation by RNA-binding proteins and its implications for cancer. Nat Rev Cancer 11:644–656. doi:10.1038/nrc3107
15. Gorgone S, Campenni A, Calbo E et al (2009) Differentiated thyroid cancers. G Chir 30:26–29
16. Menon MP, Khan A (2009) Micro-RNAs in thyroid neoplasms: molecular, diagnostic and therapeutic implications. J Clin Pathol 62:978–985. doi:10.1136/jcp.2008.063909
17. Yang Z, Yuan Z, Fan Y et al (2013) Integrated analyses of microRNA and mRNA expression profiles in aggressive papillary thyroid carcinoma. Mol Med Rep 8:1353–1358. doi:10.3892/mmr.2013.1699
18. Labbaye C, Spinello I, Quaranta MT et al (2008) A three-step pathway comprising PLZF/miR-146a/CXCR4 controls megakaryopoiesis. Nat Cell Biol 10:788–801. doi:10.1038/ncb1741
19. Visone R, Pallante P, Vecchione A et al (2007) Specific microRNAs are downregulated in human thyroid anaplastic carcinomas. Oncogene 26:7590–7595

20. Garofalo M, Quintavalle C, Di Leva G et al (2008) MicroRNA signatures of TRAIL resistance in human non-small cell lung cancer. Oncogene 27:3845–3855. doi:10.1038/onc.2008.6
21. Cerutti J, Trapasso F, Battaglia C et al (1996) Block of c-myc expression by antisense oligonucleotides inhibits proliferation of human thyroid carcinoma cell lines. Clin Cancer Res 2:119–126
22. Pallante P, Visone R, Ferracin M et al (2006) MicroRNA deregulation in human thyroid papillary carcinomas. Endocr Relat Cancer 13:497–508. doi:10.1677/erc.1.01209
23. Lv M, Zhang X, Li M et al (2013) miR-26a and its target CKS2 modulate cell growth and tumorigenesis of papillary thyroid carcinoma. PLoS One 8:e67591. doi:10.1371/journal.pone.0067591
24. Peng Y, Li C, Luo DC et al (2014) Expression profile and clinical significance of microRNAs in papillary thyroid carcinoma. Molecules 19:11586–11599. doi:10.3390/molecules190811586
25. Hardin H, Guo Z, Shan W et al (2014) The roles of the epithelial-mesenchymal transition marker PRRX1 and miR-146b-5p in papillary thyroid carcinoma progression. Am J Pathol 184:2342–2354. doi:10.1016/j.ajpath.2014.04.011
26. Cantara S, Pilli T, Sebastiani G et al (2014) Circulating miRNA95 and miRNA190 are sensitive markers for the differential diagnosis of thyroid nodules in a Caucasian population. J Clin Endocrinol Metab 99:4190–4198. doi:10.1210/jc.2014-1923
27. Igci YZ, Ozkaya M, Korkmaz H et al (2015) Expression levels of miR-30a-5p in papillary thyroid carcinoma: a comparison between serum and fine needle aspiration biopsy samples. Genet Test Mol Biomarkers 19:418–423
28. Voskas D, Ling LS, Woodgett JR (2014) Signals controlling un-differentiated states in embryonic stem and cancer cells: role of the phosphatidylinositol 3′ kinase pathway. J Cell Physiol 229:1312–1322. doi:10.1002/jcp.24603
29. Geraldo MV, Fuziwara CS, Friguglieti CU et al (2012) MicroRNAs miR-146-5p and let-7f as prognostic tools for aggressive papillary thyroid carcinoma: a case report. Arq Bras Endocrinol Metabol 56:552–557
30. Yu S, Liu Y, Wang J et al (2012) Circulating microRNA profiles as potential biomarkers for diagnosis of papillary thyroid carcinoma. J Clin Endocrinol Metab 97:2084–2092. doi:10.1210/jc.2011-3059
31. Huang Y, Liao D, Pan L et al (2013) Expressions of miRNAs in papillary thyroid carcinoma and their associations with the BRAFV600E mutation. Eur J Endocrinol 168:675–681. doi:10.1530/EJE-12-1029
32. Huang YH, Lin YH, Chi HC et al (2013) Thyroid hormone regulation of miR-21 enhances migration and invasion of hepatoma. Cancer Res 73:2505–2517. doi:10.1158/0008-5472.CAN-12-2218
33. Deng X, Wu B, Xiao K et al (2015) MiR-146b-5p promotes metastasis and induces epithelial-mesenchymal transition in thyroid cancer by targeting ZNRF3. Cell Physiol Biochem 35:71–82. doi:10.1159/000369676
34. Geraldo MV, Kimura ET (2015) Integrated analysis of thyroid cancer public datasets reveals role of post-transcriptional regulation on tumor progression by targeting of immune system mediators. PLoS One 10:e0141726. doi:10.1371/journal.pone.0141726
35. Lee YS, Lim YS, Lee JC et al (2015) Differential expression levels of plasma-derived miR-146b and miR-155 in papillary thyroid cancer. Oral Oncol 51:77–83. doi:10.1016/j.oraloncology.2014.10.006
36. Wang C, Lu S, Jiang J et al (2014) Hsa-microRNA-101 suppresses migration and invasion by targeting Rac1 in thyroid cancer cells. Oncol Lett 8:1815–1821. doi:10.3892/ol.2014.2361
37. Zhu H, Fang J, Zhang J et al (2014) miR-182 targets CHL1 and controls tumor growth and invasion in papillary thyroid carcinoma. Biochem Biophys Res Commun 450:857–862. doi:10.1016/j.bbrc.2014.06.073
38. Liu L, Wang J, Li X et al (2015) MiR-204-5p suppresses cell proliferation by inhibiting IGFBP5 in papillary thyroid carcinoma. Biochem Biophys Res Commun 457:621–626. doi:10.1016/j.bbrc.2015.01.037
39. Li R, Liu J, Li Q et al (2015) miR-29a suppresses growth and metastasis in papillary thyroid carcinoma by targeting AKT3. Tumour Biol 37:3987–3996. doi:10.1007/s13277-015-4165-9
40. Minna E, Romeo P, De Cecco L et al (2014) miR-199a-3p displays tumor suppressor functions in papillary thyroid carcinoma. Oncotarget 5:2513–2528. doi: 10.18632/oncotarget.1830
41. Pallante P, Visone R, Croce CM, Fusco A (2010) Deregulation of microRNA expression in follicular cell-derived human thyroid carcinomas. Endocr Relat Cancer 17:F91–F104. doi:10.1677/ERC-09-0217

42. Takizawa T (2013) The miR-221/222 cluster, miR-10b and miR-92a are highly upregulated in metastatic minimally invasive follicular thyroid carcinoma. Int J Oncol. doi:10.3892/ijo.2013.1879
43. Rippe V, Dittberner L, Lorenz VN et al (2010) The two stem cell microRNA gene clusters C19MC and miR-371-3 are activated by specific chromosomal rearrangements in a subgroup of thyroid adenomas. PLoS One 5:e9485. doi:10.1371/journal.pone.0009485
44. Colamaio M, Puca F, Ragozzino E et al (2015) miR-142-3p down-regulation contributes to thyroid follicular tumorigenesis by targeting ASH1L and MLL1. J Clin Endocrinol Metab 100:E59–E69. doi:10.1210/jc.2014-2280
45. Rossing M, Borup R, Henao R et al (2012) Down-regulation of microRNAs controlling tumourigenic factors in follicular thyroid carcinoma. J Mol Endocrinol 48:11–23. doi:10.1530/JME-11-0039
46. Colamaio M, Borbone E, Russo L et al (2011) miR-191 down-regulation plays a role in thyroid follicular tumors through CDK6 targeting. J Clin Endocrinol Metab 96:E1915–E1924. doi:10.1210/jc.2011-0408
47. Carvalheira G, Nozima BH, Cerutti JM (2015) microRNA-106b-mediated down-regulation of C1orf24 expression induces apoptosis and suppresses invasion of thyroid cancer. Oncotarget 6:28357–28370. doi: 10.18632/oncotarget.4947
48. Wojtas B, Ferraz C, Stokowy T et al (2014) Differential miRNA expression defines migration and reduced apoptosis in follicular thyroid carcinomas. Mol Cell Endocrinol 388:1–9. doi:10.1016/j.mce.2014.02.011
49. Roncati L, Pignatti E, Vighi E et al (2014) Pre-miR146a expression in follicular carcinomas of the thyroid. Pathologica 106:58–60
50. Braun J, Hoang-Vu C, Dralle H, Huttelmaier S (2010) Downregulation of microRNAs directs the EMT and invasive potential of anaplastic thyroid carcinomas. Oncogene 29:4237–4244. doi:10.1038/onc.2010.169
51. Schwertheim S, Sheu SY, Worm K et al (2009) Analysis of deregulated miRNAs is helpful to distinguish poorly differentiated thyroid carcinoma from papillary thyroid carcinoma. Horm Metab Res 41:475–481. doi:10.1055/s-0029-1215593
52. Mitomo S, Maesawa C, Ogasawara S et al (2008) Downregulation of miR-138 is associated with overexpression of human telomerase reverse transcriptase protein in human anaplastic thyroid carcinoma cell lines. Cancer Sci 99:280–286. doi:10.1111/j.1349-7006.2007.00666.x
53. Takakura S, Mitsutake N, Nakashima M et al (2008) Oncogenic role of miR-17-92 cluster in anaplastic thyroid cancer cells. Cancer Sci 99:1147–1154. doi:10.1111/j.1349-7006.2008.00800.x
54. Zhang Y, Yang WQ, Zhu H et al (2014) Regulation of autophagy by miR-30d impacts sensitivity of anaplastic thyroid carcinoma to cisplatin. Biochem Pharmacol 87:562–570. doi:10.1016/j.bcp.2013.12.004
55. Vergoulis T, Vlachos IS, Alexiou P et al (2012) TarBase 6.0: capturing the exponential growth of miRNA targets with experimental support. Nucleic Acids Res 40:D222–D229. doi:10.1093/nar/gkr1161
56. Bhaumik D, Scott GK, Schokrpur S et al (2008) Expression of microRNA-146 suppresses NF-kappaB activity with reduction of metastatic potential in breast cancer cells. Oncogene 27:5643–5647. doi:10.1038/onc.2008.171
57. Jazdzewski K, Boguslawska J, Jendrzejewski J et al (2011) Thyroid hormone receptor beta (THRB) is a major target gene for microRNAs deregulated in papillary thyroid carcinoma (PTC). J Clin Endocrinol Metab 96:E546–E553. doi:10.1210/jc.2010-1594
58. Xiong Y, Zhang L, Kebebew E (2014) MiR-20a is upregulated in anaplastic thyroid cancer and targets LIMK1. PLoS One 9:e96103. doi:10.1371/journal.pone.0096103
59. Zhang Z, Liu ZB, Ren WM et al (2012) The miR-200 family regulates the epithelial-mesenchymal transition induced by EGF/EGFR in anaplastic thyroid cancer cells. Int J Mol Med 30:856–862. doi:10.3892/ijmm.2012.1059
60. Borbone E, Troncone G, Ferraro A et al (2011) Enhancer of zeste homolog 2 overexpression has a role in the development of anaplastic thyroid carcinomas. J Clin Endocrinol Metab 96:1029–1038. doi:10.1210/jc.2010-1784
61. Schwertheim S, Worm K, Schmid KW, Sheu-Grabellus SY (2014) Valproic acid downregulates NF-kappaB p50 activity and IRAK-1 in a progressive thyroid carcinoma cell line. Horm Metab Res 46:181–186. doi:10.1055/s-0034-1367043
62. Takamizawa J, Konishi H, Yanagisawa K et al (2004) Reduced expression of the let-7 microRNAs in human lung cancers in association with shortened postoperative survival. Cancer Res 64:3753–3756. doi:10.1158/0008-5472.CAN-04-0637
63. Cui SY, Huang JY, Chen YT et al (2013) Let-7c governs the acquisition of chemo- or radioresistance and epithelial-to-mesenchymal transition phenotypes in docetaxel-resistant

lung adenocarcinoma. Mol Cancer Res 11:699–713. doi:10.1158/1541-7786.MCR-13-0019-T

64. Esposito F, Tornincasa M, Pallante P et al (2012) Down-regulation of the miR-25 and miR-30d contributes to the development of anaplastic thyroid carcinoma targeting the polycomb protein EZH2. J Clin Endocrinol Metab 97:E710–E718. doi:10.1210/jc.2011-3068
65. Fuziwara CS, Kimura ET (2014) MicroRNA deregulation in anaplastic thyroid cancer biology. Int J Endocrinol 2014:1–8. doi:10.1155/2014/743450
66. Wu D, Ding J, Wang L et al (2013) microRNA-125b inhibits cell migration and invasion by targeting matrix metallopeptidase 13 in bladder cancer. Oncol Lett 5:829–834. doi:10.3892/ol.2013.1123
67. Kota J, Chivukula RR, O'Donnell KA et al (2009) Therapeutic microRNA delivery suppresses tumorigenesis in a murine liver cancer model. Cell 137:1005–1017. doi:10.1016/j.cell.2009.04.021
68. Zhu H, Wu H, Liu X et al (2009) Regulation of autophagy by a beclin 1-targeted microRNA, miR-30a, in cancer cells. Autophagy 5:816–823
69. Boufraqech M, Nilubol N, Zhang L et al (2015) miR30a inhibits LOX expression and anaplastic thyroid cancer progression. Cancer Res 75:367–377. doi:10.1158/0008-5472.CAN-14-2304
70. Shao M, Geng Y, Lu P et al (2015) miR-4295 promotes cell proliferation and invasion in anaplastic thyroid carcinoma via CDKN1A. Biochem Biophys Res Commun 464:1309–1313. doi:10.1016/j.bbrc.2015.07.128
71. Geraldo MV, Yamashita AS, Kimura ET (2012) MicroRNA miR-146b-5p regulates signal transduction of TGF-β by repressing S...: Journal & E-Book List. Oncogene 31:1910–1922
72. Carraro G, El-Hashash A, Guidolin D et al (2009) miR-17 family of microRNAs controls FGF10-mediated embryonic lung epithelial branching morphogenesis through MAPK14 and STAT3 regulation of E-cadherin distribution. Dev Biol 333:238–250. doi:10.1016/j.ydbio.2009.06.020
73. Hebrant A, Floor S, Saiselet M et al (2014) miRNA expression in anaplastic thyroid carcinomas. PLoS One 9:e103871. doi:10.1371/journal.pone.0103871
74. Arancio W, Carina V, Pizzolanti G et al (2015) Anaplastic thyroid carcinoma: a ceRNA analysis pointed to a crosstalk between SOX2, TP53, and microRNA biogenesis. Int J Endocrinol 2015:439370. doi:10.1155/2015/439370
75. Yu Z, Pestell TG, Lisanti MP, Pestell RG (2012) Cancer stem cells. Int J Biochem Cell Biol 44:2144–2151. doi:10.1016/j.biocel.2012.08.022
76. Hudson J, Duncavage E, Tamburrino A et al (2013) Overexpression of miR-10a and miR-375 and downregulation of YAP1 in medullary thyroid carcinoma. Exp Mol Pathol 95:62–67. doi:10.1016/j.yexmp.2013.05.001
77. Duan L, Hao X, Liu Z et al (2014) MiR-129-5p is down-regulated and involved in the growth, apoptosis and migration of medullary thyroid carcinoma cells through targeting RET. FEBS Lett 588:1644–1651. doi:10.1016/j.febslet.2014.03.002
78. Abraham D, Jackson N, Gundara JS et al (2011) MicroRNA profiling of sporadic and hereditary medullary thyroid cancer identifies predictors of nodal metastasis, prognosis, and potential therapeutic targets. Clin Cancer Res 17:4772–4781. doi:10.1158/1078-0432.CCR-11-0242

Index

A

Acute coronary syndrome (ACS) 255
Acute kidney injury 62
Acute myocardial infarction (AMI) 61, 254
ACVR1 and TSPAN3 ....268, 270
ACVR1B 266, 267
Adenosine triphosphate-binding cassette transporter A1 (ABCA1) 230, 235, 251, 253
Adipocyte differentiation 230, 242–248
Adipogenesis 228–230, 242–250, 253
Adiponectin receptor 1 (ADIPOR1) 250, 251
AGO2 .... 3, 29, 44, 59
AGO-miRNA complexes 3
Alzheimer's disease 6, 7, 13, 61, 129
Amyotrophic lateral sclerosis (ALS) 61
Anaplastic thyroid cancers (ATCs) 261, 272–276
Animal models 45, 228, 231
Animal/xenografts models 62
AntagomiR 6, 231, 247
Antagomirs 6, 62, 99, 233, 247
Anti-miRNA oligonucleotides (AMOs) 62
Anti-miRs 62
Antisense 8–10, 13, 14, 47–49, 62, 233, 256, 268
Anti-sense oligonucleotides 13, 99, 252
ASE left (ASEL) 163
ASE right (ASER) 163
ASH1L and MLL1 proteins 272
ATAC-seq 165
Aurora-like kinase 2 (ALK2) 243, 244, 246

B

Bacterial noncoding RNAs
Batch effect 187–195
Beta-cell function 59
Bioinformatics 3, 16, 40, 78, 117, 123, 165, 174, 208, 252
Biomarkers 5, 11–13, 57, 233, 256, 265
Blood 5, 57–59, 61, 63, 233, 256, 262, 265
Bio-Ontology 83–90
BMP8A 266, 267
BMPR1A 266, 267
Bone morphogenetic proteins (BMPs) 242
BRAF(V600E) 265
Breast cancer 3–6, 11–13, 58, 127

C

Caenorhabditis elegans 2, 27, 34, 93, 96, 114, 135, 136, 153, 161–163, 212, 214, 217, 233
Cancers/tumors 3, 27, 44–45, 58, 126, 160, 179, 193, 220, 241, 261
Carbohydrate response element-binding protein (ChRE-BP) 229–230
Cardiac hypertrophy 129, 232, 235
Cardiovascular diseases (CVDs) 60, 61, 254–256
CCAAT-enhancer-binding protein (C/EBP) 230, 243–245
CCND3 (cyclin D3) 45, 266
ceRNAs 8, 15
ChIP-seq 33, 165
Chronic lymphocytic leukemia (CLL) 4, 5, 58
CircRNA 8, 15
Circulating microRNAs 58
cis-regulatory element (CRE) 160, 161, 166
c-Jun N-terminal kinase 1 (JNK1) 251, 252
Clustered regularly interspaced short palindromic repeats (CRISPRs) 48, 50–51
Cog-1 163
Coronary artery disease (CAD) 60, 233, 255
Crohn's disease 61
Cross-linking immunoprecipitation (CLIP) 47, 97, 101, 102, 116, 120
Crosslinking immunoprecipitation and sequencing of hybrids (CLASH) 102

D

Data mining 73, 116, 117, 187
Data representation 88
Deadenylation 3, 57, 159
Decay 10, 34, 123, 159
Dedifferentiated fat (DFAT) cells 244, 246
Degenerated *k*-mer 185
Destruction of host microRNAs by viruses 47
Diabetes 58–60, 63, 75, 179, 225–226, 234–235, 241, 254
Diabetes mellitus 60, 225
Diabetes-related complications 226
Diabetic cardiac complications 231–232
Diabetic cardiomyopathies 231, 232
Diabetic kidney disease 61, 62

Jingshan Huang et al. (eds.), *Bioinformatics in MicroRNA Research*, Methods in Molecular Biology, vol. 1617, DOI 10.1007/978-1-4939-7046-9, © Springer Science+Business Media LLC 2017

Diabetic macrovascular complications
Diabetic nephropathy (DN) 225, 230–231, 236
Diagnostics 57
Dicer................ 2, 7, 28–30, 32, 34, 44, 59, 99, 160, 212, 244
Diffuse large B cell lymphoma (DLBCL)..........................59
DiGeorge critical region 8 (DGCR8) 29, 59, 212
Dimension decreasing 179
DNase-seq..165
DROSHA..2, 28, 29, 34, 159, 211

E

Early growth response (EGR2)..............................244, 247
Ectopic pregnancy 58, 61
EFEMP2...270, 271
EGF signaling pathway..273
Embryonic stem cells (ESCs).................13, 15, 33, 242, 244
Enhancer 51, 124, 160–162, 164, 165, 231
EP300 interacting inhibitor of differentiation 1 (EID-1) 243, 244
Ether-a-go-go-related gene...232
Euglycemic-hyperinsulinemic clamp...............................228
Exosomes.. 2, 5, 13, 58
Exportin-5...28, 29, 59
Expression profile.................................58, 59, 61, 164, 176, 220, 221, 228, 231, 233, 250, 252, 256, 262, 275, 276
Extracellular regulated MAP kinase (Erk) 244, 246

F

Factor analysis 184, 185
Fatty acid binding protein 4 (FABP4).............................244
Feed-back loops..163
Feed-forward loops (FFLs) 125, 126, 163
FN1 and ITGA2 gene..266
Follicular thyroid carcinomas (FTCs) 261, 268–272
Fomivirsen...62
Free fatty acids..229
Functional annotations 117, 128, 219, 247
Functional miRNA-mRNA regulatory modules (FMRMs)...219

G

Gapped *k*-mer 182, 183, 185
Gene *BECN1* 273
Gene expression............................... 2, 3, 6, 9, 14, 35, 45, 48, 51, 52, 57, 60, 61, 78, 94, 98, 123, 124, 126, 127, 157, 159, 161, 163, 164, 179, 190–192, 218, 226, 231, 254, 261, 262, 266, 272
Gene identification..214
Gene regulation.................................99, 109, 110, 162–164
Gene regulatory network.................................. 13, 159, 162, 164–166, 208, 218
Gene targeting..34, 273
Genome-wide analysis.......................................93–103, 164
Glioblastoma 4, 58, 59
Glucose homeostasis.................226, 229, 234, 235, 252, 253
Glucose transporter-4 (GLUT4) 229, 251
Growth factor receptor-bound protein 10 (GRB10)........251

H

Hepatic diseases...62
Hepatitis C virus (HCV) 40, 44, 47, 60
Hepatocellular carcinoma (HCC) 33, 44, 58, 252
Hepatocyte nuclear factor 1beta (HNF1B).............251, 252
Hepatocyte nuclear factor 4a (HNF4a)...................251, 252
High mobility group AT-hook 2 (HMGA2)....... 5, 244, 275
High-density lipoproteins (HDL)...........................230, 253
High-dimension...179–185
High-throughput sequencing of RNA isolated by crosslinking immunoprecipitation (HITS-CLIP) 47, 101
Host gene regulation by viral microRNAs
Host microRNAs regulating viruses................ 39–46, 49, 50
Human adipose tissue-derived mesenchymal stem cells (hASCs)..244
Hypertension (HT)............................14, 232, 241, 254, 255

I

Illumina 170, 171, 173, 174
Immunoprecipitation..........................47, 100–103, 116, 120
Individual-nucleotide resolution CLIP (iCLIP) 102
Initiator (Inr) sequences 160
Insulin receptor substrate-1 (IRS1)................. 243, 247, 266
Insulin resistance (IR) 225, 228, 229, 234, 242, 250–254
Insulin secretion 226–228, 230, 234, 235
Insulin sensitivity......................228–230, 236, 247, 252, 253
Insulin-like growth factor-1 (IGF-1)..................... 229, 234, 251, 252
Insulin-sensitive glucose transporter-4 (GLUT4)............244
Ion Torrent 170, 171, 173, 174
Ipomersen..62

K

Kidney diseases..61
KIT 3′-UTR 264
Kmer..179–183
Kruppel-like 243
Kruppel-like factor 5 (KLF5).................................244, 246
Kruppel-like transcription factor 15 (KLF15)..........229, 234
K-tuple 179, 181–182
Kynamro..62

L

Let-7 .... 3–6, 15, 34, 59, 62, 161, 162, 233, 243, 244, 273, 275
Let-7 family 34, 59, 275
Leukemia..4, 5, 41, 58, 59

Lipid metabolism 60, 229–230, 246, 247
Long non-coding RNAs (lncRNAs) 1, 8–16, 27, 35, 51, 120
Long QT syndrome............235
Lsy-6 163
Lung adenocarcinoma 10, 58

M

Machine learning............94, 96–98, 111, 115–116, 124, 135, 136, 141, 149–151, 155, 211–222
Mechanistic target of rapamycin (mTOR)............4, 251, 252
Medullary thyroid carcinoma (MTC) 261, 262, 276–277
Messenger RNA (mRNA) 2, 3, 5, 7, 9, 10, 15, 27–29, 35, 46, 47, 57, 62, 93, 94, 96, 97, 100–102, 109, 125, 159, 174, 181, 208, 211, 226, 242, 246, 262, 264, 272, 276–277
Messenger RNA degradation............3, 10, 31, 102, 262
Methylation............9, 31, 32, 165, 193
Microarray............ 63, 78, 98, 99, 117, 139, 142, 169, 172, 175, 183, 185, 188, 192, 195, 220, 232, 245, 250, 253, 265–267, 274, 275
MicroRNA (miRNA) 1–16, 27–35, 39–46, 49, 50, 57–63, 102, 109–120, 123–130, 134–157, 159–166, 176, 185, 188, 192–195, 197–209, 222, 225–236, 241–256, 261–277
MicroRNA-122............34
MicroRNA degradation 32, 34–35, 47, 102
MicroRNA genomic loci............28, 160
MicroRNA processing............ 28, 34, 44, 262
MicroRNA response to viral infection 46
MicroRNA sequencing............176
MicroRNA tailing............32, 34
MicroRNA target databases............165
MicroRNA target prediction 96, 112, 120, 134, 135, 140, 142–144, 146–148, 150–152, 154, 156, 215–220, 222
MicroRNA transcription 2, 3, 5, 28, 29, 31–33, 35, 57, 123–125, 127, 159–163, 179, 211, 242, 243, 246, 250, 254, 262, 273
MicroRNA web resources 120
Microvesicles 2, 58
miR-1 .... 8, 60–62, 129, 228, 229, 232, 234, 254, 255, 263, 269
miR-8............243, 246
miR-9............6, 7, 164, 227, 234
miR-10b 59, 62, 270, 272
miR-14............ 230, 235, 247
miR-15a 4, 43, 59, 62, 227, 228, 233, 234
miR-16............4, 43, 58, 61, 62, 227, 228, 250, 263, 266
miR-17~92 cluster............ 4, 5, 7, 59
miR-17-3p 249, 250
miR-17-5p 7, 249, 250
miR-17-92............ 245, 275, 276
miR-17-92............262
miR-21 .... 2, 4, 5, 8, 45, 46, 59, 228, 230, 232–234, 245, 262, 265, 274, 276
miR-22 .... 45, 60, 61, 161, 211, 212, 230
miR-22* 61
miR-23a 60, 61
miR-24 ....60, 229, 232–234, 251, 254
miR-25 .... 59, 274, 275
miR-26a 60, 62, 264, 269, 273–275
miR-27 .... 35, 47, 164, 245
miR-27a 60, 61, 245
miR-27a/27b 243
miR-27b 245
miR-29 ....8, 59, 61, 232, 253
miR-29a 7, 60, 61, 228, 231, 235, 251, 253, 266, 267
miR-29b 7, 62, 228, 233, 253, 265, 274
miR-29c 253
miR-30 family 245
miR-30a-5p............59, 248, 249, 265, 274
miR-30c 119, 129, 248, 249
miR-31 .... 59, 245, 266, 267
miR-33a 62, 230, 235, 249, 251, 253
miR-33a/b 251, 253
miR-34 ....59, 162
miR-34a 4, 6, 60, 62, 228, 234, 249, 250
miR-92a 5, 42, 61, 255, 270, 272
miR-93 252
miR-96 .... 59, 227, 234
miR-99a 4, 249–252
miR-101 ....59, 61, 62, 129, 266, 269
miR-103 ....59, 246, 248, 249, 251, 253
miR-106a 61
miR-107 ....59, 61, 119, 227, 243, 246, 248, 249, 251, 253
miR-122............ 44, 60, 62, 230, 236, 247, 249, 251
miR-125a 59, 129
miR-125b 3, 43, 59, 273
miR-126 .... 59–61, 119, 229, 233, 251, 253, 255
miR-130 .... 243, 246, 251
miR-130a-3p............252
miR-132 .... 60, 249, 250
miR-133 .... 15, 35, 62, 129, 229, 232, 235, 254
miR-133a 228, 229, 234, 250, 255
miR-134 .... 62, 249, 250, 263
miR-138 .... 42, 233, 244, 245, 266, 267, 273–275
miR-141 .... 5, 15, 59
miR-143 .... 62, 230, 232, 235, 245, 248, 251, 253
miR-145 ....15, 33, 59, 62, 119, 233, 246, 249, 250
miR-146a 5, 7, 8, 61, 228, 233, 255, 263, 272, 275
miR-146b 7, 246, 255, 256, 262, 264–268, 270, 272, 274
miR-148a 60, 248
miR-150 .... 6, 43, 61, 233
miR-151 ....249, 250

miR-152 59
miR-155 .... 42–44, 46, 59, 61, 245, 255, 262, 266, 270, 271
miR-181a 60, 249, 250, 252, 255, 262, 266
miR-190b 252
miR-191 .... 61, 233, 263, 269, 271, 272
miR-192 .... 62, 231, 235, 236, 262, 268, 270
miR-194 62
miR-196a 62, 119
miR-197 .... 61, 119, 233, 249, 250, 262, 268, 270
miR-199 62
miR-199a-3p 60, 232, 266
miR-199a-5p 61, 119, 263
miR-200 family 273, 275
miR-200a 5, 59, 60
miR-200c 59, 61
miR-201 250
miR-203 .... 59, 119, 265, 267
miR-204 .... 119, 246
miR-205 .... 249, 250
miR-208a 61, 232, 254, 255
miR-210 .... 60, 62, 246, 263
miR-211 243
miR-221 .... 45, 59, 232, 248–251, 262–264, 266–268, 270, 271, 274–276
miR-223 .... 43, 45, 48, 61, 62, 232, 233, 235
miR-224 .... 247, 262, 266, 267, 271, 274, 276, 277
miR-278 .... 230, 235, 247
miR-298 .... 119, 249, 250
miR-320 .... 3, 233, 251, 252
miR-323-3p 61
miR-325 .... 249, 250
miR-326 .... 243, 245
miR-328 .... 61, 249, 250, 262, 270
miR-329 250
miR-330 .... 249, 250
miR-335 .... 59, 248, 249
miR-362-3p 61
miR-372 59
miR-373 .... 3, 59, 119, 232, 235
mir-375 .... 119, 226, 227, 234, 245, 262, 270, 276
miR-380-5p 249, 250
miR-448 .... 44, 246
miR-502 62
miR-519d 250
miR-520c 59
miR-532-3p 61
miR-802 .... 251, 252
miRBase 2, 27, 44, 109, 134, 139, 153, 165, 175, 212
miRNA* 2
miRNA-16-1 59
miRNA-122 .... 34, 233
miRNA-433 61
miRNA replacement 62
miRNA sponge 6, 99
Mitogen-activated protein kinase (MAPK) 229, 234, 235, 243–245, 251, 254, 265, 270, 276
Multipotent mesenchymal stem cells (MSCs) 242, 244, 245
MYC 5, 162

N

Network motifs 125–128, 162, 163
Neurodegenerative diseases 3, 6–7, 11, 13–14, 61, 63
Next-generation sequencing (NGS) 63, 78, 117, 120, 169–176, 220
Non-coding RNAs 1, 4, 27, 31, 35, 51, 226
Non-supervised method 183–185
Normalization 189–190, 192, 194, 195

O

Obesity 75, 230, 233, 249, 255, 256
Oncogenes 4, 5, 11, 15, 33, 44, 59, 62, 251, 265
Ontology 85, 86, 89, 208, 214, 216, 217, 221
Ovarian cancer 58, 194

P

p53 .... 12, 45, 162, 228, 273, 275
Pancreatic cancer 58, 59
Papillary thyroid carcinomas (PTCs) 58, 261–269, 271–273, 276
Parallel analysis of RNA ends (PARE) 102
Parkinson's disease 6, 13, 14, 61
PAX8 .... 270, 273
Peripheral blood mononuclear cells (PBMCs) 255
Peroxisome proliferator-activated receptor-γ (PPARγ) 45, 243–246, 248, 249, 270
Phosphatidylinositol 3-kinase (PI3-K) 234, 251, 252, 266, 267
Phosphoribosylanthranilate isomerase (PAI-1) 243, 244, 246
Photoactivatable-ribonucleoside-enhanced crosslinking and immunoprecipitation (PAR-CLIP) 101
PI3K/AKT pathway 251
Plasma 5, 57, 59, 62, 63, 228, 229, 233, 247, 250, 254, 255
Poorly differentiated thyroid carcinomas (PDTCs) 261
PRC2 .... 9, 11–13
Precursor miRNA (pre-miRNA) 2, 28, 30, 34, 99, 127, 212, 213, 215
Preinitiation complex (PIC) 160
Primary miRNA (pri-miRNA) 2, 28, 34, 159, 211
Principal component analysis (PCA) 184, 185
PRKCQ 266
Prognostics 58, 61, 262, 277
Promoter 3, 5, 9, 11, 33, 51, 124–125, 127, 129, 130, 162, 165, 231
Prostate cancer 12, 58, 59
Protein tyrosine phosphatase 1B (PTP1B) 251, 252
Pyruvate kinase M2 (PKM2) 251, 252

Q

Quantitative real-time polymerase chain reaction (QRT-PCR) 245, 250–252, 267, 271, 274

R

Regulation 5, 9–12, 14, 15, 27–32, 44, 47–49, 52, 58, 61, 93, 94, 98–100, 102, 110, 115, 117, 118, 123–130, 134, 163, 166, 179, 218, 220, 228, 232, 242, 246–248, 250, 254, 256, 266–268, 276
Regulatory interactions 125, 130
Regulatory network modules 219
Regulatory networks 13, 27, 28, 30, 46, 126, 127, 130, 163, 165, 256
Resources 83–86, 120, 180
Reverse transcription qualitative PCR (RT-qPCR) 169, 264–272
Rheumatoid arthritis 61
RNA editing 32, 34, 47, 118
RNA immunoprecipitation (RIP) 100–102
RNA-induced initiation of transcriptional silencing (RITS) 31–32
RNA-induced silencing complex (RISC) 2, 3, 6, 28–31, 51, 98, 102, 116, 117, 120, 212
RNA Pol II 160, 161
RNA Pol III 160
RNA-seq 47, 98, 100, 101, 165, 174
RS2 (insulin receptor substrate 2) 251

S

Saliva 57, 59, 63
Semantic web 78, 83–85, 87–90, 208, 209
Serum 5, 14, 52, 59, 60, 62, 63, 232, 233, 254, 262, 265
Serum response factor (SRF) 14, 232, 235
Single-nucleotide polymorphism (SNPs) 5, 32–34, 130, 170, 175, 264
Sirtuin1 (SIRT1) 244, 246
Sliced inverse regression (SIR) 183, 185
Smad-interacting protein 1 (SIP1) 231, 235
Small interfering RNAs (siRNAs) 13, 31–32, 51, 99
Small RNAs (sRNAs) 1, 35, 48, 49, 52, 125, 175
SOLiD 170, 171, 173, 174
Splicing 3, 9–11, 28, 118, 160
STEMI (acute ST-segment elevation MI) 255
Sterol regulatory element-binding proteins (SREBPs) 229, 230, 251, 253
Supervised method 183–184
Synergistic 124, 126, 129–130, 272

T

TARBP2 .... 30, 59
Target prediction 96, 97, 110–117, 120, 134, 135, 140, 142–144, 146–148, 150–152, 154, 156, 215–222
TargetScan 3, 95, 97, 112, 113, 119, 128, 136, 144, 155, 156, 208, 216
TF-miRNA network 128–129, 163
TGF-β pathway 266
Therapeutic approach 273
Therapeutics 12, 45, 52, 57, 77, 226, 233–236, 241, 242, 247, 250, 252, 253, 262, 266, 267, 273
Thyroid cancer 261–264, 271–277
TIMP3 and ZNFR3 gene 266
Tissue-specific 9, 58, 99, 217, 226
3T3-L1 cells 245, 246, 253
Transcription factor (TF) 6, 14, 33, 35, 124–130, 160–163, 165, 226–230, 242–246, 263, 273
Transcription factor 7-like 2 (TCF7L2) 244, 246
Transcriptional start sites (TSS) 124, 125, 160
Transcriptome 98–100, 165
Transforming growth factor-β (TGF-β) 45, 231, 235, 244, 245
Transforming growth factor beta receptor II (TGFβR2) 245
Translation 2, 3, 6, 10, 14, 27–31, 35, 44, 48, 49, 57, 99, 100, 125, 126, 211, 226, 242, 244, 250, 262, 263
Translational repression 27–30, 35, 49, 99, 117, 159, 231
Translation repression 57
Triacylglycerol 230, 235
TTF1/NKX2-1 273
Tumor suppressor 4–6, 11, 13, 15, 33, 44, 45, 59, 62, 266, 272, 273
Type 1 diabetes (T1D) 59, 60, 225, 226
Type 2 diabetes (T2D) 60, 75, 225, 226, 229, 230, 232, 254

U

Undifferentiated thyroid carcinomas (UDTCs) 261
Urine 5, 57–59, 63
Urothelial bladder cancer 59

V

v-ets Erythroblastosis virus E26 oncogene homologue 1 (ETS1) 251
Viral diseases 40–44
Viral infections 40, 44, 46, 60, 63
Viral microRNAs 39–52
Viral microRNAs cancer relevance 128
Viral noncoding RNA 35
Vitravene 62

W

Well-differentiated thyroid carcinomas (WDTCs) 261, 268, 275
Wnt/β-catenin 266, 267

Z

ZEB1 and ZEB2 protein 42, 231, 273

MIX
Papier aus verantwortungsvollen Quellen
Paper from responsible sources
FSC® C105338

If you have any concerns about our products,
you can contact us on
ProductSafety@springernature.com

In case Publisher is established outside the EU,
the EU authorized representative is:
Springer Nature Customer Service Center GmbH
Europaplatz 3, 69115 Heidelberg, Germany

Printed by Libri Plureos GmbH
in Hamburg, Germany